ADVANCES IN

EXPERIMENTAL
SOCIAL PSYCHOLOGY

VOLUME 12

CONTRIBUTORS TO VOLUME 12

Andrew Baum

J. W. Berry

Nancy Cantor

David P. Farrington

David L. Hamilton

Susan Kippax

Walter Mischel

John P. Murray

J. Philippe Rushton

Mark Snyder

Stuart Valins

ADVANCES IN

Experimental

Social Psychology

EDITED BY

Leonard Berkowitz

DEPARTMENT OF PSYCHOLOGY
UNIVERSITY OF WISCONSIN
MADISON, WISCONSIN

VOLUME 12

ACADEMIC PRESS
New York   San Francisco   London   1979
A Subsidiary of Harcourt Brace Jovanovich, Publishers

ACADEMIC PRESS, INC.
111 Fifth Avenue, New York, New York 10003

United Kingdom Edition published by
ACADEMIC PRESS, INC. (LONDON) LTD.
24/28 Oval Road, London NW1 7DX

LIBRARY OF CONGRESS CATALOG CARD NUMBER: 64–23452

ISBN 0–12–015212–6

PRINTED IN THE UNITED STATES OF AMERICA

79 80 81 82   9 8 7 6 5 4 3 2 1

CONTENTS

Contributors ix

PART I. STUDIES IN SOCIAL COGNITION

Prototypes in Person Perception

Nancy Cantor and Walter Mischel

I.	Orientation	4
II.	The Nature of Categories at Different Levels of Abstraction	13
III.	Determining Prototypicality	28
IV.	Structure in the Head or in the World?	43
	References	47

A Cognitive–Attributional Analysis of Stereotyping

David L. Hamilton

I.	Introduction	53
II.	Cognitive Biases *Resulting in* Stereotypic Conceptions	55
III.	Cognitive Biases *Resulting from* Stereotypic Conceptions . . .	64
IV.	Behavioral Consequences of Stereotypes	76
V.	Summary	79
	References	81

Self-Monitoring Processes

Mark Snyder

I.	Introduction	86
II.	The Identification of Self-Monitoring	89
III.	The Consequences of Self-Monitoring	93
IV.	The Processes of Self-Monitoring	100
V.	The Individual in Social Psychology	111
	References	124

PART II. SOCIAL INFLUENCES AND SOCIAL INTERACTION

Architectural Mediation of Residential Density and Control: Crowding and the Regulation of Social Contact

Andrew Baum and Stuart Valins

I.   Introduction 132
II. Density and the Arousal of Crowding Stress 139
III. Architectural Mediation of Residential Density 149
References 172

A Cultural Ecology of Social Behavior

J. W. Berry

I.   A Cross-Cultural Perspective 177
II. An Ecological–Cultural–Behavioral Model 179
III. Some Studies of Social Behavior 185
IV. Applications 200
V.   Conclusions 202
References 203

Experiments on Deviance with Special Reference to Dishonesty

David P. Farrington

I.   Deviance and Experimentation 208
II. Operationally Defining and Measuring Deviance in Experiments 214
III. Experiments on Dishonesty 230
IV. Conclusions 241
References 242

From the Early Window to the Late Night Show: International Trends in the Study of Television's Impact on Children and Adults

John P. Murray and Susan Kippax

I.   Introduction 254
II. Television's Culture Context 256
III. Television's Impact on Daily Life 260

IV.   Impact of Televised Violence   270
V.   Other Aspects of Television's Impact   288
VI.   Functions of Television   292
VII. Television and the "Real" World   298
VIII. Conclusions, Implications, and Research Priorities   301
      References   307

Effects of Prosocial Television and Film Material on the Behavior of Viewers

J. Philippe Rushton

I.   Introduction   322
II.   Theoretical Constructs for Understanding Television Effects   323
III. Television's Effect on Altruistic Behavior   328
IV.   Television's Effect on Friendliness   335
V.   Television's Effect on Behavior Involving Self-Control   339
VI.   Television's Effect on Diminishing Fears   342
VII. Conclusions   345
      References   346

SUBJECT INDEX   353
CONTENTS OF OTHER VOLUMES   356

CONTRIBUTORS

Numbers in parentheses indicate the pages in which the authors' contributions begin.

Andrew Baum, *Uniformed Services University, School of Medicine, Bethesda, Maryland 20014* (131)

J. W. Berry, *Psychology Department, Queen's University, Kingston, Ontario, Canada K7L 3N6* (177)

Nancy Cantor, *Department of Psychology, Princeton University, Princeton, New Jersey 08540* (3)

David P. Farrington, *Institute of Criminology, University of Cambridge, Cambridge, England* (207)

David L. Hamilton, *Department of Psychology, University of California, Santa Barbara, California 93106* (53)

Susan Kippax, *School of Behavioral Sciences, Macquarie University, North Ryde, New South Wales 2113, Australia* (253)

Walter Mischel, *Department of Psychology, Stanford University, Stanford, California 94305* (3)

John P. Murray, *School of Behavioral Sciences, Macquarie University, North Ryde, New South Wales 2113, Australia* (253)

J. Philippe Rushton, *Department of Psychology, University of Western Ontario, London, Ontario, Canada N6A 5C2* (321)

Mark Snyder, *Department of Psychology, University of Minnesota, Minneapolis, Minnesota 55455* (85)

Stuart Valins, *Department of Psychology, State University of New York at Stony Brook, Stony Brook, New York 11790* (131)

PART I
STUDIES IN SOCIAL
COGNITION

PROTOTYPES IN PERSON PERCEPTION[1]

Nancy Cantor

PRINCETON UNIVERSITY
PRINCETON, NEW JERSEY
and

Walter Mischel

STANFORD UNIVERSITY
PALO ALTO, CALIFORNIA

I. Orientation 4
  A. Purpose 4
  B. The Goals and Functions of Person Categorization 5
  C. Person Categories and Object Categories 8
  D. Empirical Implications of Fuzzy Categories 12
  E. Overview: The Study of Person Categorization 13
II. The Nature of Categories at Different Levels of Abstraction 13
  A. Taxonomies for Objects and for People 13
  B. An Exercise in the Construction of Person Taxonomies 15
  C. Gains and Losses at Different Levels 19
  D. Summary and Future Directions 25
III. Determining Prototypicality 28
  A. The Prototype Approach 29
  B. Prototypicality Rules: Full View 31
  C. Prototypicality Rules: Restricted View 36
  D. From Prototypes to Social Behavior 42
IV. Structure in the Head or in the World? 43
  A. The Object Domain 44
  B. The Person Domain 45
  References 47

[1]Preparation of this chapter and the research by the authors was supported in part by research grant MH-6830 to Walter Mischel from the National Institute of Health, United States Public Health Service. We would like to thank the following people for their helpful comments on earlier versions of this manuscript: Leonard Berkowitz, Eugene Borgida, John Darley, Phoebe Ellsworth, Rita French, Sam Glucksberg, Tory Higgins, Curt Hoffman, E. E. Jones, John Kihlstrom, Anne Locksley, Harriet Nerlove Mischel, Thane Pittman, Diane Ruble, Martin Seligman, Mark Snyder, and Shelley Taylor.

3

ADVANCES IN EXPERIMENTAL SOCIAL
PSYCHOLOGY, VOL. 12

I. Orientation

A. PURPOSE

Casual observation as well as voluminous empirical research attest to the pervasive human tendency to categorize not just objects but also people into groups, types, or other slots. As Rosch, Mervis, Gray, Johnson, and Boyes-Braem (1976) point out, "one of the most basic functions of all organisms is the cutting up of the environment into classifications by which nonidentical stimuli can be treated as equivalent" (p. 382). In order to reduce the complexity of the external stimulus world, the layperson may group both objects and people according to similarities in their essential features, label these natural categories, and communicate about the similarities and differences between these kinds or types of objects through this system of shared names or category labels.

A particularly prevalent natural classification scheme for grouping people is based on personality attributes inferred from everyday behavior and social interaction. Lay perceivers often seem to act like personologists in their search for dispositional explanations of other people's behaviors (cf. Jones, Kanouse, Kelley, Nisbett, Valins, & Weiner, 1972; Ross, 1977). Studies of children show a developmental progression from categorization schemes based on appearance and role status to categorizations based on internal motivations and dispositional attributes (Livesley & Bromley, 1973; Peevers & Secord, 1973; Ruble, Feldman, Higgins, & Karlovac, 1978). Rather than basing the categorization scheme for people on variations in the external stimulus environment (as a true "situationist" might), the adult lay perceiver seems to use the information contained in a situation in which a person is observed as a further guide toward the person's dispositions (e.g., Jeffery & Mischel, 1978; Jones & Davis, 1965; McArthur, 1972).

However, while inferred internal dispositions in the form of trait terms often play an important part in how we all categorize each other (e.g., Mischel, Jeffery, & Patterson, 1974), they are only one aspect of the everyday categorization of people into different kinds—different "natural kinds" (Quine, 1969). Studies of how people freely describe and "type" one another also suggest the extensive use of categories involving physical appearance, gender, race, social occupation and role constructs, behavioral scripts, and so on (Abelson, 1976; Bem, 1978; Cohen, 1977; Fiske & Cox, 1977; McGuire, McGuire, Child, & Fujioka, 1978). To cite a few such studies: Cohen (1977) has drawn extensively on the commonly held stereotype or "prototype" of the typical "librarian" and "waitress"; Sandra Bem (1978) has documented the cognitive biases associated with sex-role stereotypes; Schank and Abelson (1977) have initiated a large program of study on the major behavioral events and their associated scripts (e.g., restaurant script, birthday party scripts) into which common life events can be divided.

These studies, and many others like them, attest to the richness and pervasiveness of human categorization schemes based on a great variety of social, behavioral, and cultural categories. Thus, a comprehensive approach to the classification of people must take account of such common categories as social and occupational roles (a used-car salesman type) as well as more abstract constructs (an extravert type). Recognizing both their generality in person perception and their diverse specific content, we want to explore the basic nature and function of such person classification schemes. Specifically, in what ways are they fundamentally similar to—and different from—the classifications applied to objects? What are the rules that guide the categorization of people? What are the consequences—the potential gains and losses—of applying such categorizations to people for various purposes? These are the kinds of questions that have motivated our recent theorizing and program of research. This paper provides a brief glimpse of the various theoretical and empirical approaches we have taken to study person categories and categorization. Other recent reviews provide a comprehensive and representative survey of the literature on person perception and social cognition emerging from other laboratories (e.g., Hamilton, 1979; Hastie, in press; Nisbett & Ross, in press; Taylor & Crocker, in press).

B. THE GOALS AND FUNCTIONS OF PERSON CATEGORIZATION

In the course of their everyday social interactions, people presumably ask themselves many different questions about each other: "Do I like this person?" (the evaluative question); "What will he or she do next?" (the prediction question); "Why did he or she behave that way?" (the causality question). Each of these different forms of social judgment has stimulated its own literature in the study of person perception (e.g., Anderson, 1962; Zajonc, 1978, on the evaluative question; Jones *et al.*, 1972, on the causality question; Nisbett and Ross, in press, on the prediction question). The present article is concerned with yet another form of social judgment characterized by the "typing" question: "What kind of a person is he or she?" This social judgment is a fundamental one for personality psychology. However, as Jerome Bruner pointed out many years ago, categorization also may be central for social perception:

> What can be said about a theoretical model of perception that would be of relevance to the social psychologist? . . . The first, and perhaps most self-evident point upon reflection, is that perceiving or registering of an object or an event in the environment involves an act of categorization. We "place" things in categories. That is a "man" and he is "honest" . . . . Each of the words in quotation marks involves a sorting or placement of stimulus input on the basis of certain cues that we learn how to use. (Bruner, 1958, pp. 92-93)

Bruner defined one area of particular interest in the study of person categorization—the process by which certain categories come to be readily accessible for use in categorization. As he said, "The likelihood that a sensory input will be categorized in terms of a given category is not only a matter of fit between sensory input and category specifications. It depends also on the accessibility of a category'' (Bruner, 1957, p. 132). Interest in the issues of category accessibility has been renewed recently as cognitive–social psychologists attempt to understand the person categorization process (e.g., Higgins, Rholes, & Jones, 1977; Wyer & Srull, in press).

Bruner also considered the various functions that categorization serves in the perceptual process. Categorization seems to allow one to simplify and reduce an otherwise potentially overwhelming number of stimuli. It selectively focuses attention on certain aspects of particular stimuli, grouping these stimuli under a unifying category label and then allowing the perceiver to predict the specific features of any one of the category members on the basis of general expectations about the category.

Generalizing Bruner's points to the social domain, a categorization scheme allows one to structure and give coherence to one's general store of knowledge about people, providing expectations about typical behavior patterns and the range of likely variation between types of people and their characteristic behaviors. Every social experience helps to fill out one's knowledge of the likely behavior and attributes of different types of persons. The resulting expectations, in turn, affect one's impressions of individuals. Instead of needing a distinct category for every possible form of the "political animal," for example, one can code people and their behavior in terms of a few simple categories: the redneck bigot, the bleeding-heart liberal, the zealous revolutionary. The use of a few such simple cognitive categories about people in general reduces and simplifies what one needs to know and look for in particular people. Applying our categories about other people often allows us to feel an almost instant general understanding of someone we hardly know. After 5 min of Archie Bunker's televised tirades on the decay of the neighborhood, one may feel competent to predict simply on the basis of the belief that he is a "bigot," not only his other political views but even his taste in food, movies, and friends. Having typed a person as being more or less a particular sort, one is guided by general expectations about what that type of person is or is not likely to do and this reduces the range of actions expected from the person in particular situations, inducing a sometimes illusory sense of control over the course of social interactions. Categorizations simplify what would otherwise be overwhelming data and give us more economical and coherent knowledge of people.

However, a reliance on preconceived typologies to structure one's perceptions of people has its costs as well as its value, potentially encouraging attributions of the characteristics associated with a category to each member, even when those characteristics may not fit the individual. Such gratuitous attributions may constrain the subsequent behavior of the perceived as well as biasing the perceptions and actions of the perceiver. A focus on the gist and coherence underlying diverse behavior may undermine attention to the details and nuances of specific behavior. A tendency to exaggerate and overgeneralize the structure that actually exists in the individual's behavior may lead us to underestimate the incompleteness and flexibility in that structure. By searching for "good fits" to our general type categories, we may misjudge—and mistreat—people who poorly fit our preconceptions.

These expectations about the role of categories in social cognition have received considerable empirical support. Cognitive–social psychologists have recently begun to demonstrate a great deal about the consequences, for both social thought and social behavior, of labeling a particular target individual as a member of a social or dispositional category (see, for example, Carlston, 1977; Cohen, 1977; Higgins, in press; Rothbart, 1977; Snyder & Swann, 1978a; Snyder & Uranowitz, 1978; Taylor, Fiske, Etcoff, & Ruderman, 1978). When a target individual fits well in a particular category (or has been labeled as a member of that category), not only does memory for details of his/her behavior improve in general (e.g., Cantor & Mischel, in press), but attributes commonly associated with that category are ascribed more freely to that person in written impressions and/or in recall/recognition protocols (e.g., Cantor & Mischel, in press; Cohen, 1977; Hamilton, 1977; Kelley, 1950; Snyder & Uranowitz, 1978; Tsujimoto, 1978). Having been labeled with a category, the target person may come more and more to fit our image of the "ideal" category member. All of the knowledge associated with the category label may be applied to structuring and providing coherence to the particular knowledge associated with the target individual. In contrast, having typed someone as a particular kind of person, we may sometimes selectively emphasize behavior that seems inconsistent and incongruent with our original impression. Such a contrast phenomenon would result in an overrepresentation of category-inconsistent material in memory for the target person (e.g., Hastie, in press). Similar processes of assimilation and contrast also occur when we answer questions and introspect about our own traits and characteristic dispositions (e.g., Markus, 1977; Rogers, Kuiper, & Kirker, 1977). In either case, whether it be assimilation or contrast, information processing both about the self and about others is guided and determined, in part, by the particular category label that has been used to type the individual.

Once trait impressions are formed—and they may be formed very quickly—they may become tenacious, with perceivers biased to maintain consistency. For example, when perceivers who have formed a trait impression observe subsequent behaviors which are consistent with their initial impression of the stimulus person's dispositions, they attribute them to the stimulus person's "real self," whereas inconsistent subsequent behaviors are attributed to superficial and transient factors (e.g., Bell, Wicklund, Manko, & Larkin, 1976; Hayden & Mischel, 1976). The inconsistency at the behavioral level tends to be resolved by assuming "underlying consistency" at the trait level or by attributing inconsistent behaviors to transient environmental causes. These strategies help observers to maintain their impressions of trait consistency even in the face of observed behavioral inconsistency. "Surface" inconsistencies may be especially easy to resolve when behaviors are ambiguous (as they often are) and lend themselves easily to diverse interpretations. A random selection of such ambiguous behaviors might be seen as providing confirmatory evidence for the perceiver's preconceptions. Moreover, the labeling process constrains our behavior toward the (labeled) individual, and his/her behavior comes more and more to resemble our expectations for persons of that "type," confirming and adding fresh support for the original categorization (e.g., Rubovits & Maehr, 1973; Snyder & Swann, 1978a; Snyder, Tanke, Berscheid, 1977; Zanna & Pack, 1975).

C. PERSON CATEGORIES AND OBJECT CATEGORIES

The bulk of this research on social cognition has focused on the consequences of categorization or "stereotyping," with less attention given to the process that might underlie the formation of natural categories about people. We know a good deal about the end results of the categorization process but much less about its initial stages. What are the salient units of categorization? At what level of abstraction do we find and/or perceive coherent "person types"? What configurations of behavioral evidence are most likely to activate or prime a particular person category? These are the sorts of questions that have recently begun to receive more attention (cf. Higgins, in press) and that we have begun to pursue.

The cognitive literature on object perception has recently flourished (see Rosch, 1978; Tversky, 1977), providing many novel experimental and theoretical approaches to the same issues about the structure and nature of natural categories. While people certainly differ from objects as stimuli, the categorization rules and conceptual structures used in person and object perception may not be fundamentally different. Moreover, to the degree that differences do exist we can, presumably, gain finer insight into person categorization systems by comparing and contrasting them against this baseline of object categorization.

1. Fuzzy Categories for Common Objects

In our pursuit of the analogy between object perception and person perception, we begin by reviewing the nature of the basic natural categories used to divide and codify the object environment. What are the properties of these natural categories? Are they well structured, distinct categories with clearly defined properties and a finite list of members that fit the category membership rules? How do objects come to be classified in a particular object category? Do all the objects labeled with one category label share a small set of critical, defining properties?

Until recently, the study of natural classification systems has been guided by the classical, traditional view which asserts that category members all possess a small set of critical features: all Xs have features X_1 and X_2. This view in turn suggests an all-or-none criterion for category membership—an object either has all the defining features of a category or it does not, and membership depends on having all of these critical features. Strictly speaking, to be categorized as a square, rather than as a rectangle, a geometric object must have four equal sides joined at right angles. Even a slight deviation from these critical specifications will require that the object not be placed in the square category. Put more formally, the traditional view addresses itself to well-defined categories that have the following properties: (1) Membership is fully determined by possession of a small set of singly necessary and jointly sufficient features or attributes; (2) all members possess all of those critical features and are therefore equally qualified as members of the category; (3) there are distinct boundaries between categories and hence no ambiguous examples that fit in more than one category at the same level of abstraction in the taxonomy; and (4) the possession of certain critical features cannot ameliorate the absence of other critical features in the membership test—therefore, all critical features are equally important in determining categorization.

However, when one turns from the abstract world of logic and formal, artificial systems to common, everyday categories—to songbirds and bedroom furniture and extraverted people—those criteria cannot be met. As Wittgenstein (1953) first argued, the members of common, everyday categories do not all share all of a set of singly necessary and jointly sufficient features critical for category membership. When one examines a set of objects all labeled by one general term, one will find not a single set of features shared by all members of the category but a pattern of overlapping similarities, a *family resemblance structure*. In his words:

> We see a complicated network of similarities overlapping and criss-crossing; sometimes overall similarities, sometimes similarities of detail. I can think of no better expression to characterize these similarities than "family resemblances," for the various resemblances between the members of a family: build, features, color of eyes, gait, temperament, etc., overlap and criss cross in the same way. (Wittgenstein, 1953; 66, 67, © Basil Blackwell, Oxford)

Following Wittgenstein, many linguists, philosophers, and psychologists (cf. Labov, 1973; Lakoff, 1972; Lehrer, 1970; Rosch *et al.*, 1976; Smith, 1978; Tversky, 1977) have criticized the classical view that all category members possess all of the defining features of the category and thus are equally good category exemplars. In contrast, they suggest that natural semantic categories are "fuzzy sets" that violate the expectations of the classical all-or-none position (cf. Lakoff, 1972; Rosch, 1975; Wittgenstein, 1953; Zadeh, 1965). Recently

Rosch (1975) has suggested that categories are organized around prototypical or focal stimuli (the best examples of a concept), with less prototypical or good members forming a continuum away from the central prototypic exemplars. Data from Rosch and her colleagues (1976) as well as those from Smith and his co-workers (1974) suggest that people reliably rate members of a category as being better or worse exemplars of the category. Presumably all such members possess enough of whatever critical features exist to define category membership, yet they still differ in how well they fit the abstract concept represented by the category name. McCloskey and Glucksberg (1978) have also demonstrated the existence of fuzzy boundaries separating members from nonmembers in many common semantic categories. They find that subjects disagree and vary from session to session in decisions about whether particular items belong in particular categories (e.g., is a bookend a piece of furniture?).

The notion of a continuum of category membership is also directly represented in language by *linguistic hedges* of the sort emphasized by Lakoff (1972). For example, we might point to two extraverts and say : "Kathy is a real extravert;" "Jane is, in a manner of speaking, an extravert." Labov (1973) points out that dictionary definitions tend to make use of hedges, such as "cup is used chiefly to drink from." The use of such devices has prompted Lakoff (1972) and Zadeh (1965) to refer to natural concepts as "fuzzy sets" "ill-defined classes" without strict logical boundaries.

The "fuzzy sets" approach suggests that a categorization decision will be probabilistic in nature, with members of a category varying in degree of membership (prototypicality) and with many ambiguous borderline cases resulting in overlapping and fuzzy boundaries between categories. Such fuzzy sets are then best studied with respect to their central, clear exemplars (the prototypical members), rather than by concentrating energy on distinguishing between ambiguous, borderline cases. Finally, just as the categories themselves are fuzzy, the taxonomies that connect these categories are also often ill defined and fuzzy (cf. Kintsch, 1974; Lehrer, 1974).

2. Fuzzy Categories for Persons

The characterization of natural object categories as fuzzy sets or fuzzy categories is even more appropriate when applied to the person domain and to such everyday person categories as extraverts, party poopers, or public relations (PR) types. Clearly it would be difficult to find a set of necessary and sufficient features shared by all members of any particular person category that one would want to use as the definitive test of category membership.[2] For example, while

---

[2]This difficulty is reflected in the enduring problem of how to select appropriate criteria for validating personality constructs (e.g., Cronbach & Meehl, 1955).

most extraverts are talkative and sociable most of the time, some extraverts seem primarily dominating and active rather than warm and sociable or are sociable in some contexts and not in others. For a category such as extraverts, there exists a continuum of category membership—some people are better extraverts than are others—rather than a fixed set of tests which all extraverts pass equally well. Boundaries between the category of extraverts and other closely related categories are fuzzy. A particular person may be just as much an introvert as an extravert or just as often exhibit emotionally unstable behavior as extraverted behavior (does acting cheery and sociable at a funeral make one "strange" or an "extravert"?). Moreover, the nature of a person's behavior, and hence the attributes upon which category membership depend, are subject to contextual variation. Given that an individual's behavior varies across contexts and over time, category membership is unlikely to be a function of possession of all of a specific group of features but will depend on a configuration of critical "signs" which suggest that a fair portion of the person's behavior can be explained by using a particular category label. Such probabilistic decision making will result in fuzzy person categories whose members vary from the clear, good central cases to the unstable, ambiguous borderline cases.

What we have just said about person categories also applies to person taxonomies: The looseness of structure characteristic of natural object taxonomies (e.g., Kintsch, 1974; Lehrer, 1974) is certainly paralleled and probably intensified when one forms person category taxonomies. For example: (1) There are clearly multiple classification schemes that one could use to divide up the people one observes in any given environment. Not only are there multiple personality typologies used by personologists (cf. Mischel, 1976), but lay perceivers also draw on large numbers of social categories (e.g., gender, race, occupation) to form person taxonomies. (2) Second, even within any one particular person taxonomy, a specific subordinate person category, such as door-to-door salesman, could easily be seen as belonging to more than one higher, more inclusive category, such as PR type or comic joker type, within the same taxonomy. Therefore a particular lower level category in a person taxonomy does not necessarily belong to one and only one higher level, more inclusive category in that taxonomy. (3) Finally, the "disjointness" principle (which requires nonoverlapping sets) is clearly violated in most person taxonomies. One can easily imagine a PR type who is also a comic joker or a social activist who is also a religious devotee, or a hydrophobic who is also an acrophobic. Depending heavily on the context in which he/she is observed, a particular person may be cross-classified in more than one category at the same level of inclusiveness in a person taxonomy. Person taxonomies, like their natural object counterparts, are fuzzy. In both domains, the boundaries and class inclusion relations are characteristically vague and ill defined. A wheelchair is both a chair and a vehicle, depending on the context and purpose; and the boundaries between a shrub and a tree, or the colors gold and tangerine, are hardly rigid (Lehrer, 1974).

D. EMPIRICAL IMPLICATIONS OF FUZZY CATEGORIES

The realization that natural categories and taxonomies are often ill defined has led to the development of a research strategy in the object domain that focuses on those structural characteristics that seem to be true of, rather than violated by, common categorization systems. These efforts are reflected in two main focuses of research: (1) First, there has been renewed interest in studying the rules by which objects come to be categorized as members of particular categories. For instance, promising strides have been made in the concept acquisition literature as a result of the suggestion that category concepts may be learned by retaining information about particular known instances (or exemplars) of a category rather than through the abstraction of a set of general rules about the critical features shared by all category members (cf. Brooks, 1978; Medin & Schaffer, 1978; Walker, 1975). The characterization of natural categories as fuzzy sets and the recognition of a continuum of category membership has also led to the development of the prototype approach to concept acquisition and categorization (cf. Rosch, 1978; Smith, 1978). Like the exemplar position, the prototype approach emphasizes the probabilistic nature of category decisions, suggesting that novel instances are categorized by virtue of the degree to which they are "prototypical" of the category in question. Rosch and Mervis (1975), Tversky (1977), and others have presented extensive studies aimed at uncovering the configurations of attributes associated with prototypical category members, as well as the rules commonly used to judge prototypicality. These investigators have also shown that prototypical category members are easier to learn, to classify, to name, and to image than are nonprototypical exemplars of common categories (see Rosch, 1978)—it helps to be prototypical in the natural object domain. (2) Second, attention has been drawn recently to the varying levels of inclusiveness at which objects can be categorized. In particular, Rosch *et al.* (1976) have suggested that categories at moderate levels of inclusiveness in common object taxonomies may be most optimal for a variety of categorization tasks, and identify such "basic" categories according to the following criteria: Basic categories (such categories as chairs and cars) contain objects that can be richly described with respect to their characteristic features and physical shape, easily distinguished from objects in other closely related categories, and routinely interacted with via simple motor programs. The formation and use of categories at the (moderately inclusive) basic level of abstraction minimizes the cognitive effort associated with making too many fine discriminations at a more molecular level of abstraction (a level containing such categories as kitchen chairs or sports cars), while still allowing the perceiver to convey a rich set of information about the objects within a category, with a few simple category labels. Categorizations at a more abstract and inclusive level (a level containing such categories as furniture or vehicles) result in categories that contain such a mixture of different objects that it is difficult to describe the attributes of the typical category member. Rosch and her colleagues (1976) have demonstrated the existence of such a basic level in numerous natural object taxonomies showing the advantages for information processing of categorizing at this basic level of abstraction.

E. OVERVIEW: THE STUDY OF PERSON CATEGORIZATION

The post-Wittgenstein "revisionist" approach to the categorization of natural objects suggests several guidelines for study of the nature and function of person categories and classification systems: (1) We should look to see if categories at different levels of abstraction in a person taxonomy have distinct properties and vary systematically in the characteristics commonly associated with their members. Following the lead of Bruner's now old "new look" in perception (Bruner, 1958; Higgins et al., 1977; Taylor & Fiske, 1978; Wyer & Srull, in press), we need to examine different kinds of person categories to discover the most accessible, salient, and optimal categorizations for different purposes. (2) While the borders of person categories may be fuzzy, the central, clearest examples of each category may be quite distinct from those in other categories. Just as recent efforts in cognitive psychology have centered on studying the "clear" or prototypical examples of categories rather than the fuzzy, borderline ones, we need to identify the prototypical cases and the rules used to judge prototypicality in the categorization of people.

In the remainder of this paper we present some examples of common person taxonomies and examine: (1) the characteristics of person categories at different levels of inclusiveness or abstraction and (2) the rules used to identify prototypical exemplars of person categories. It is hoped that these efforts will simultaneously allow us to explore the similarities and differences between person and object perception and shed some light on the nature of different kinds of conceptual units commonly used to construe people's personalities and social behavior.

II. The Nature of Categories at Different Levels of Abstraction

A. TAXONOMIES FOR OBJECTS AND FOR PEOPLE

A taxonomy provides a system for dividing the perceived world (people, events, objects) into equivalence classes that vary in inclusiveness or category size. A particular object or person can be classified at varying levels of abstraction or inclusiveness. So, for example, one could group a set of people into a very abstract category, such as the set of emotionally unstable people; into one or more less inclusive categories, such as all neurotics versus criminal madmen; or into many very specific categories, such as hysterical neurotics, compulsive neurotics, stranglers, rapists, torturers, and so on. Person categories from different levels in a taxonomy may exhibit particular characteristics that make them especially suited for certain purposes. For example, specific "subordinate" level units for characterizing persons might be very useful for molecular behavioral analyses and predictions of a person's concrete behavior in a highly specified situation. By contrast the higher, more inclusive person categories might be better suited for abstracting rich configurations of attributes about people that would both capture the gist of a person's character and differentiate this person from other general types of people.

In the present research, we strove to find out what gains and what losses might be associated with dividing up the person environment into categories at each level of inclusiveness. To study this question, it is necessary to gather descriptions of members of various person categories and assess the richness, vividness, and distinctiveness of the images commonly associated with each category label. Does the label "emotionally unstable person" signify and convey as rich and vivid an image as does the less general label "hysterical neurotic"? Is the image of a typical rapist more detailed and concrete than that of a typical criminal madman? Learning about the uses and limits of person categories at different levels of abstraction may also help clarify the enduring and perplexing problem of selecting the most appropriate units for the study of social behavior. Like the "naive observer," the trained clinician and personality assessor must also evaluate the usefulness of particular social labels used in categorizing people.

We were guided in this work by the pioneering studies of common object taxonomies conducted by Rosch and her colleagues (1976). By simply asking subjects to describe the attributes (physical appearance, shape, function, movements) common to the objects subsumed under different category labels, Rosch *et al.* were able to show that certain levels of abstraction in a three-level taxonomy maximized such desirable qualities as the richness (number) of attributes commonly associated with most category members. Consider, for example, an object taxonomy in which furniture is the top or superordinate level, chairs are at the next or middle level, and types of chairs are at the lowest level (as illustrated in the right-hand portion of Fig. 1). While people list many attributes that are common to chairs (e.g., seat, sit on it, legs, arms, etc.) there are few, if any, attributes that are true of pieces of furniture in general. Further, cutting the object environment into even more fine-grained categories, such as kitchen chair, living room chair, dining room chair, results in rich categories (i.e., many common attributes) but not very distinctive categories. For instance, the kitchen chair and the dining room chair have many characteristic attributes, but so many of

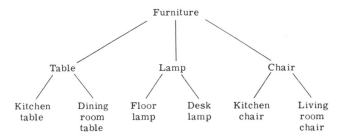

Fig. 1.   An example of a common object taxonomy.

them are shared by members of both categories that the objects in each category are not very distinctive or differentiated. Rosch and her colleagues concluded that the optimal level of abstraction in the three-level object taxonomies was the middle level; at that level, broad, inclusive, but still rich categories are formed. These basic level categories are inclusive enough to cover many different kinds of objects within one category but detailed and vivid enough to allow one to describe in great detail the typical appearance, shape, and function of a typical category member. Further, these categories are not as finely tuned as the subordinate level ones, so that objects labeled by different category names are really different—the members of one basic level category (e.g., chairs) do not share many features in common with the members of a different category in the same taxonomy (e.g., tables). In contrast, the members of one particular subordinate category (e.g., kitchen chairs) are often almost indistinguishable from the members of another subordinate category (e.g., dining room chairs) in the same taxonomy. As a result, the richness and detail gained by making such specific, finely tuned categorizations is at the expense of category distinctiveness or differentiation. This is not the case at the basic level—where the categories are both rich in attributes and well differentiated one from another. Categorizing at this level of abstraction maximizes both parsimony—a few broad categories are formed—and richness—there are many features common to members of each particular category—making for an ideal communicative and cognitive system.

B.   AN EXERCISE IN THE CONSTRUCTION OF PERSON TAXONOMIES

As a preliminary step in our study of the characteristics of categories at different levels of inclusiveness in the person domain, we needed to find taxonomies of commonly used person categories for which agreement exists about the hierarchical relations between categories. We emphasize that our aim was not to find "the" primary, best, and/or most frequently used ones in naturalistic person perception. As George Kelly (1955) has long insisted, the same people and the same human attributes are open to alternative constructions.

Therefore, the present taxonomies (illustrated in Fig. 2) are intended merely as one example of a person categorization system. Indeed the multiplicity of personality typologies (cf. Mischel, 1976)—from authoritarians to xenophobes—should be a warning to those of us studying natural categories about people that the likely sets of common category systems will be large. Moreover, at least in the person domain, it seems likely that what is the middle level and what is superordinate and subordinate is not immutable: That is, level may depend on the context, the purpose, and the frame of reference one adopts. Alternative taxonomies, in which the same category has either a higher or a lower position relative to other categories in the hierarchy, always seem possible but the inclusiveness (breadth) of the category remains stable.

In constructing these taxonomies, we strove to include categories that are frequently used by "naive observers" and that vary in inclusiveness or level of abstraction. At the most abstract "superordinate" level we began with four categories—the extraverted person, the cultured person, the person committed to a belief or cause, and the emotionally unstable person—that emerge repeatedly as general factors in peer-rating studies of personality (e.g., Norman, 1963). The

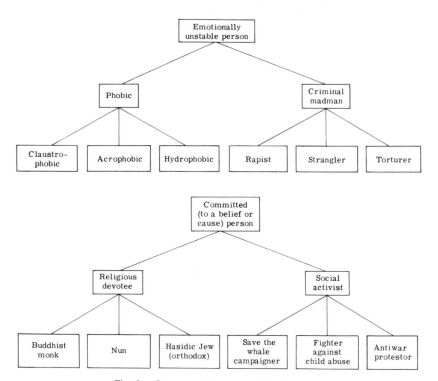

Fig. 2.   Some tentative taxonomies of persons.

"middle" and "subordinate" levels were constructed to contain less inclusive, more specific person categories, such as social activist and antiwar protestor, respectively. We included a variety of such categories about types of people in order to try to sample from the large array of possible person categories used in everyday conversation and in social psychological studies of stereotyping and categorization (cf. Cohen, 1977; Hamilton, 1979; Schank & Abelson, 1977). The categories used here (summarized in Fig. 2) included categorizations based on social and occupational roles (e.g., door-to-door salesman), personal attributes (e.g., comic joker), and psychiatric disorders (e.g., hydrophobic).

We used a card-sorting task to assess the consensual agreement for the "hierarchical" relations within each of the four taxonomies. For that purpose, each of five judges sorted the 32 middle and lower level categories into piles under the four superordinate categories. First, they placed all those items under a given superordinate label that were "members" of the class of people represented by the superordinate category label. So, for example, according to our expectations, gourmet and donator to art museums (subordinate-level categories) and man of the world and patron of the arts (middle-level categories) should all

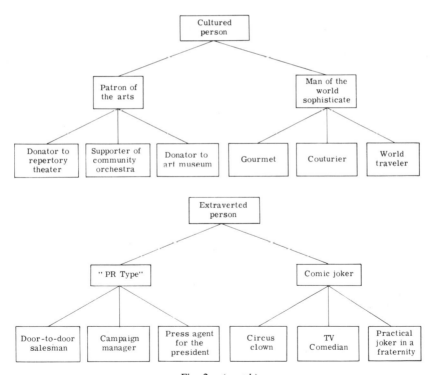

Fig. 2.   (*contd.*)

have been sorted under the superordinate label "cultured person." After they had sorted the cards into four large piles (under our initial four superordinate constructs), the judges further subdivided each pile into as many smaller, less inclusive categories as they felt existed in each large pile. For instance, again according to our expectations, the judges should have now separated patron of the arts from man of the world (forming two middle-level categories) and placed the subordinate category of donator to the art museum under the patron category and gourmet under the man of the world category. In this manner the judges would have created a cultured person hierarchy (taxonomy) with categories at three levels of inclusiveness.

The data from these card sorts were then submitted to a hierarchical clustering analysis to see whether the judges' (sorting) hierarchies agreed or matched our prior expectations. The average co-occurrence frequencies for each of the 276 pairs of the 24 subordinate-level category names (averaged across the five judges) were analyzed using the Hiclus method (Johnson, 1967). The procedure used in this analysis constructs a "*hierarchical* system of cluster representations, ranging from one in which each of the objects is represented as a single cluster to one in which all objects are grouped together as a single cluster" (Hiclus Manual, S. C. I. P., 1976, p. 1). For example, starting from the bottom, the three kinds of phobics would be clustered together in a phobics cluster if they frequently co-occurred in the judges' card sorts. Then, at a later stage in the analysis, that cluster would be joined with the cluster of criminal madmen to form the larger emotionally unstable cluster. This analysis allowed us to check whether our expectations about the particular hierarchical structure of these taxonomies were matched in the card sorts of our judges. To make assertions about categories at different levels in these taxonomies, it was critical to have agreement about these levels.

The clustering solution (using the compactness–diameter method) obtained for the data from our card-sorting procedure is illustrated in Fig. 3. The hierarchical clustering solution, based on the average sort of our five judges, provided strong validation for our intuitions about the structure of these person taxonomies. The expected subordinate person types did indeed cluster appropriately within each of the four main taxonomies. For example, the three religious person types and the three social activist person types all cluster together to form one large cluster, while the three phobics and the three criminal madmen also cluster together to form a separate superordinate cluster. The clustering analysis also supported our expectations that there would be two major subdivisions (subclusters) within each of the four superordinate categories. For example, at the lowest level in the emotionally unstable tree, the three phobics did form one cluster and the three criminal madmen another separate cluster, while at a higher point in the tree these two middle-level clusters were united to form a six-person cluster representing the superordinate category of emotionally unstable types. The clustering solution was taken as support for our intuitions

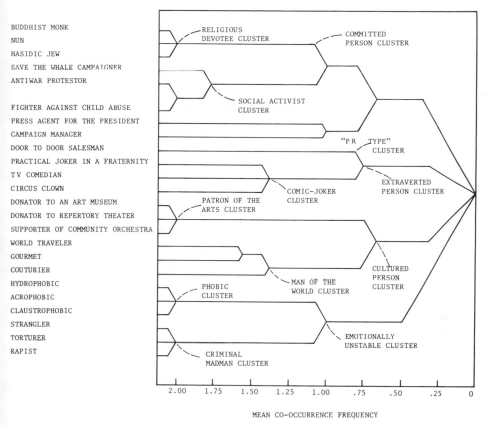

BUDDHIST MONK
NUN
HASIDIC JEW
SAVE THE WHALE CAMPAIGNER
ANTIWAR PROTESTOR

FIGHTER AGAINST CHILD ABUSE
PRESS AGENT FOR THE PRESIDENT
CAMPAIGN MANAGER
DOOR TO DOOR SALESMAN
PRACTICAL JOKER IN A FRATERNITY
T V COMEDIAN
CIRCUS CLOWN
DONATOR TO AN ART MUSEUM
DONATOR TO REPERTORY THEATER
SUPPORTER OF COMMUNITY ORCHESTRA
WORLD TRAVELER
GOURMET
COUTURIER
HYDROPHOBIC
ACROPHOBIC
CLAUSTROPHOBIC
STRANGLER
TORTURER
RAPIST

RELIGIOUS DEVOTEE CLUSTER
COMMITTED PERSON CLUSTER
SOCIAL ACTIVIST CLUSTER
"P R TYPE" CLUSTER
EXTRAVERTED PERSON CLUSTER
COMIC-JOKER CLUSTER
PATRON OF THE ARTS CLUSTER
CULTURED PERSON CLUSTER
MAN OF THE WORLD CLUSTER
PHOBIC CLUSTER
EMOTIONALLY UNSTABLE CLUSTER
CRIMINAL MADMAN CLUSTER

2.00   1.75   1.50   1.25   1.00   .75   .50   .25   0

MEAN CO-OCCURRENCE FREQUENCY

Fig. 3.   Hierarchical clustering solution for card-sorting data of person category labels.

that these four taxonomies were reasonably good examples of a person classification system.[3]

C.   GAINS AND LOSSES AT DIFFERENT LEVELS

Our taxonomies illustrate the obvious fact that people can be sorted into many different kinds of categories or units that vary in inclusiveness or abstractness. Such units may vary from narrow, specific, and concrete subordinate categories

[3]Three of the four hierarchies—the emotionally unstable, cultured, and committed ones—each have the expected two middle-level clusters in the tree structures. The only exception to this pattern is in the extraverted hierarchy, in which the expected "PR type" cluster containing the campaign manager, press agent, and door-to-door salesman did not emerge in the card-sorting data. Contrary to our expectations, the press agent and the campaign manager were classified in the committed hierarchy instead of being placed in the extravert cluster. As a result of this classification, the
(continued p. 20)

(e.g., strangler, door-to-door salesman, practical joker) to broad, general, and abstract superordinate ones (e.g., emotionally unstable persons, extraverts). Our taxonomies include a wide variety of different person categories, from those based on cultural and social roles to those based on personal dispositions, such that the main common denominator is the variation in inclusiveness across the different levels in the taxonomy. Having validated the perceived hierarchical structure of these taxonomies, we now could ask questions about the structure of person categories at these different levels of inclusiveness. Are the images commonly associated with middle-level categories such as "PR type" and comic joker type richer in number of attributes and more vivid than those used to describe members of superordinate categories, such as extraverts and cultured persons? Do people associate a richer set of attributes with members of subordinate categories such as practical joker, than with members of more abstract categories, such as comic joker types? These were the sorts of questions that motivated the research to be reported next.

Adapting to the person domain the procedure used by Rosch et al. (1976) to search for basic level categories in the object domain, we gave a group of 90 Stanford University undergraduates 2½ min. to list the attributes that they believed to be characteristic of and common to the members of the category of persons labeled by each name in our person taxonomies. Each subject listed attributes for (four) categories at one level of abstraction in the taxonomies. For example, one subject listed attributes common to extraverts, cultured persons, emotionally unstable persons, and committed persons (superordinate categories), while another subject generated attribute lists for "PR types," patrons of the arts, social activists, and phobics (middle-level categories). Ten subjects altogether gave attributes for any particular category. The attribute lists for each of the 36 categories were then scored for consensus. For each category, a list of attributes was obtained which contained only those attributes that at least two subjects had listed for the category. As a final refining stage, four judges indicated the percentage of members of each category for which each attribute would be true. So, for example, a judge might decide that 60% of all cultured people would be rich, while 90% of all patrons of the arts would be rich, as would be 95% of donators to art museums.

Final lists of the attributes rated as common to at least 50% of the members of each person category were then compiled. These lists included only those attrib-

---

expected three-member "PR type" cluster was not observed in the extravert hierarchy. While the clustering solution generally fit precisely with our expectations, the deviation in the extravert hierarchy was clear. We, therefore, replaced press agent to the president with press agent to a movie star and campaign manager with Madison Avenue advertising man, and in a new sorting of these cards (by another naive judge), the extraverted hierarchy now took on the expected form. The only other change that we made in later studies with these hierarchies was to replace couturier with wine connoisseur in the cultured person hierarchy.

utes for each particular category that received a mean weight of at least 50%
across the four judges' ratings.[4] We chose this 50% inclusion criterion in order to
obtain a list of attributes that were believed to be common to a core majority of
the members of each category, without requiring that all or almost all members
possess each attribute. This 50% inclusion criterion, used in all of the following
analyses, excludes purely idiosyncratic images that are not central to the category, without at the same time forcing the principles of a well-defined category
structure on inherently "fuzzy" categories.

1. Richness

First we examined the relative richness—the number of attributes judged to
be true of at least 50% of the members of a category—at each level in our
taxonomies. The richer the category the more one knows and can predict about a
person who is in it.

Figure 4 shows the relative richness of the categories at each level of abstraction in our four person taxonomies and in Rosch's *et al.* (1976) object taxonomies. The results reveal a pattern of gains in the number of shared attributes from
the superordinate to middle level to subordinate level, for person categories, that
is quite similar to the pattern obtained by Rosch *et al.* (1976) for such natural
object taxonomies as birds and furniture. Note that the middle and lowest level
categories maximize the richness (number) of attributes associated with the category for persons as well as for objects.[5]

2. Differentiation

Categorics also differ in the degree to which attributes that are common to
many members of a particular category are also common to the members of other
closely neighboring categories in the same taxonomy. The more such overlap
occurs, the less "differentiated" or distinct the categories at a particular level of
abstraction in a. given taxonomy are from each other. In turn, the less differentiated the categories are from each other, the less well they will serve in

---

[4]We also tabulated these lists, including only those attributes given at least a 50% weight by (any)
three of the four judges. These final lists did not differ in any significant way from those tabulated
using the mean weight given by all four judges as the cutoff criterion.

[5]If these taxonomies conformed to strict taxonomic structure, then all attributes rated as characteristic of a superordinate category should also be rated as characteristic of all of the other lower level
categories in that particular taxonomy. Our taxonomies did not conform to this criterion. On the
average, 78% of the attributes rated as characteristic of a particular superordinate category were also
rated as characteristic of both middle-level categories subsumed under that superordinate one. This
rather high level of "nesting" diminished greatly (to an average of 51%) when the percentage of
attributes that were rated as characteristic of all of the middle- and subordinate-level categories under
the superordinate one was tabulated. The cultured person taxonomy conformed least to this "full-
nesting" property. Similar failures to conform to nesting properties have been noted by Lehrer (1974)
in her studies of common object taxonomies.

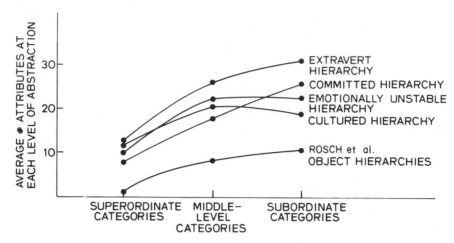

Fig. 4.   Richness of categories at different levels of abstraction in person and object hierarchies.

contrasting differences between people in the one category and those in another
category in the same taxonomy.

We computed the overlap of attributes across categories by comparing the
attribute lists for a particular category with the lists obtained for its close
neighboring categories at the same level of abstraction. For example, the overlap
in the attributes was computed between (1) the four superordinate categories
(cultured, extravert, unstable, committed), (2) the two middle-level categories in
each taxonomy (e.g., religious devotee and social activist), and then (3) each set
of three closely related subordinate categories in each taxonomy (e.g., antiwar
protestor, save the whale campaigner, fighter against child abuse). [The final
overlap score for the subordinate categories in each taxonomy was computed by
averaging the overlap scores from the two sets of (three) subordinate categories.
For example, the overlap score for the three social activists was averaged with
the overlap score for the three religious devotees to get the final subordinate-level
score for the committed taxonomy.]

The data summarized in Table I show that, as expected, categorizations at the
superordinate level result in the most well-differentiated, nonoverlapping
categories: There were no attributes that were shared by all four superordinate
categories. The average number of attributes shared by any pair of the four
superordinate categories was .67. By contrast, the subordinate categories were
the least distinctive (i.e., they shared the greatest number of features across
categories at the same level of inclusiveness in a given taxonomy), and they were
considerably less distinctive than the middle-level categories. In the process of
making finely tuned, specific subordinate categorizations, one sorts into different
categories people who actually have quite a bit in common, such that members of

TABLE I

DIFFERENTIATION: AVERAGE NUMBER OF SHARED ATTRIBUTES ACROSS CATEGORIES AT THE SAME
LEVEL OF ABSTRACTION[a]

Hierarchy	Level of abstraction		
	Superordinate[b]	Middle	Subordinate
Cultured	0	9	10.5
Extraverted	0	8	23
Committed	0	4	15.5
Emotionally unstable	0	2	20

[a]Fewer shared attributes indicate greater differentiation among categories.

[b]There was no attribute shared by all four superordinate categories. The average number of attributes shared by any pair of superordinate categories was .67.

one category may even share as many attributes with members of a different category from the same taxonomy and level of inclusiveness as they do with those in their own category. For example, when the middle-level category of criminal madmen is split into two subordinate categories, such as rapist and strangler, the same attributes used to characterize the members of one subordinate category, say the strangler, may equally well serve to describe the members of the other subordinate category—the rapist. As a result of this "overlap" across categories, the categories are no longer very distinctive—it becomes difficult to find distinguishing or special attributes that serve to differentiate the members of the one category from those in the other category. Since one of the purposes of categorization is to highlight and contrast the differences between one "kind" (category) of person and another, the large amount of overlap at the subordinate level makes this level less than ideal. However, it is only necessary to move one level up in our hierarchies—to the middle level—to find categories that are both rich and distinctive. There are many attributes that characterize a religious devotee, and these attributes are not completely identical to those associated with the contrasting middle-level category of social activists. This greater degree of category differentiation seems, from our data, to be characteristic of the more inclusive middle-level categorizations.

3. Vividness and Concreteness

What is the nature of the additional attributes gained as one moves down the taxonomy from superordinate to middle-level to subordinate categories? To answer this question we did a content analysis of the attribute lists, categorizing attributes as to whether they concerned: (1) physical appearance or possessions, (2) socioeconomic status (e.g., rich, high class), (3) traits, (4) behavioral attributes (e.g., goes to theater, smiles) of the persons in the category. Table II

TABLE II

AVERAGE NUMBER OF ATTRIBUTES OF DIFFERENT TYPES FOR CATEGORIES AT DIFFERENT LEVELS IN THE TAXONOMIES

Attribute type	Level in taxonomy		
	Superordinate	Middle	Subordinate
Physical appearance or possessions	.50	1.50	2.33
Socioeconomic status	.25	.38	.54
Trait dispositions	8.75	15.75	17.21
Behaviors	1.50	3.88	4.75

presents the average number of each of these types of attributes associated with categories at the three levels of abstraction. Note that the total number of attributes of each type increases from the superordinate to the middle and subordinate levels of abstraction. While physical appearance attributes are rarely present at the superordinate level, at least one or two physical attributes on the average are gained as one moves from highly inclusive superordinate person categories to the more concrete middle- and lowest level person categories. Indeed, while it is difficult to imagine a physical appearance that is shared by most members of a superordinate person category—for example, a visual image of the typical committed person—it is not difficult to form an image of a religious devotee, a social activist, or a Buddhist monk, or an antiwar protestor.

We also conducted a separate study to test directly the notion that more finely tuned, subordinate-level categorizations maximize vividness and concreteness in the images commonly associated with different types of persons. For this purpose, we asked 30 subjects to describe their visual images of person types from the three different levels in our four taxonomies. Ten subjects described their images of person types from the superordinates; 10 others described their images of the middle-level person types; and still another 10 subjects described their images of subordinate person types. These lists of imageable characteristics were then coded for consensus (agreement by at least two of the 10 subjects) and the richness (number) of attributes associated with categories at each level of abstraction was tabulated. As expected, the number of concrete, visible details common to two or more of the 10 subjects' images of different person types increased from the broader superordinate-level ($\bar{x} = 10.25$) categories to the middle-level ($\bar{x} = 14.75$) categories to the more finely tuned subordinate-level ones ($\bar{x} = 16.25$). The lower (and middle) level categories seem to maximize the vividness and concreteness of the person images commonly associated with members of the category. So, for example, a door-to-door salesman was described as male, wearing a cheap leisure suit (polyester wardrobe), chubby, with a grin on his "all-American face," short, neatly trimmed hair, talking fast and constantly, carrying a leather bag, and so on. Likewise, consider the donator to the repertory theater, commonly pictured as a middle-aged or elderly female, heavy set (plump), well-dressed in a mink coat or designer clothes, good jewelry, and a nice, smiling face. The richness of the images associated with these subordinate-level categorizations make them ideal for certain purposes, such as picking someone out of a crowd on the basis of only a category label. Just as the less inclusive object categories that Rosch *et al.* (1976) studied had more common shape attributes than the abstract superordinate categories, so too do subordinate- and middle-level person categories (e.g., door-to-door salesman and "PR type") elicit richer, more vivid images than do the more abstract, inclusive superordinate ones (e.g., extraverts).

D. SUMMARY AND FUTURE DIRECTIONS

We are becoming increasingly convinced of the usefulness of applying to the domain of people the methods and insights provided by the "revisionist" approach to the study of object categorization. Our pursuit of the analogy between the categorizations of common everyday objects—pants and chairs and cars—and that of people—extraverts and madmen and activists—so far has yielded considerable convergence. The consensually rated attribute lists associated with person types at the middle level in these taxonomies were richer, in our data, than those judged to be true of members of the superordinate categories and there was less overlap between the attribute lists for neighboring categories at this level of abstraction than at the more finely tuned and detailed level of subordinate categorizations. The subordinate categories maximized richness and imageability, but at the cost of overlap (differentiation), such that categories at this level would be less than ideal for highlighting the differences between the types of persons in neighboring categories.

The kinds of person categories illustrated by the middle level in our taxonomies appear to have much utility, maximizing the intersection of richness, differentiation, and vividness, while reducing the cognitive load entailed in distinguishing too many categories (such as occurs at the subordinate level). Categorization at this level of inclusiveness, with these kinds of categories, in naturalistic person perception may allow one to use just a few basic categories to capture the gist of another person's character in a rich and vivid way, while still allowing one to contrast that person with other broadly discriminable types. This middle-level unit may be optimal to describe what a person is like in general, to distinguish how two people differ from each other, and bring to bear one's conceptual knowledge about person types in general in order to flesh out the description of a particular person. In contrast, to predict what specific molecular behaviors a person will engage in when observed under particular, well-defined circumstances, the more finely tuned, specific, narrow categories of the subordinate level may be more useful. Moreover, to reduce the whole person domain to two or three major categories or dimensions, as in a grand theory of personality (cf. Jung, 1923; Eysenck, 1967), one may want to use the highest, most inclusive or superordinate level. While consistent, coherent descriptions, capturing the gist of another's behavior, are achieved by moving to more abstract levels of person categorization, more vivid, salient person images require less inclusive slots.

The attribute listing technique used by Rosch and her colleagues (1976) to study natural object taxonomies, and illustrated here for a small sample of person taxonomies, seems to be a relatively simple one. Yet analysis of the results of such studies can provide insight into the relative richness, vividness, and distinctiveness of the prototype images commonly associated with members of different categories. This technique seems ideally suited not just for categorizing tables and sports cars and birds but for all sorts of categories commonly used in the social domain. How rich, one might ask, is the list of attributes commonly associated with the prototype of a "female" or of a "German"? Can one gain any richness, vividness, or differentiation from communicating and categorizing with less inclusive units such as "housewife" and "Nazi"? Are there richer behavioral scripts (cf. Schank & Abelson, 1977) associated with birthday parties than with parties, or with parties as compared to social events? Can clinicians describe a typical schizophrenic more easily and fully than they can a typical person with a functional psychosis? Application of the present techniques and analyses to the domain of social, ethnic, and cultural categories, as well as in the study of situation categories, seems warranted given the widespread current interest in the cognitive determinants of stereotyping (cf. Hamilton, 1979) and in the "automatic" scripts and causal schemata that may guide behavior in social situations (cf. Abelson, 1976; Langer, 1978; Nisbett & Wilson, 1977). Similarly, studies of the relative gains and losses associated with different assessment or diagnostic categories might be timely and useful for clinical practitioners and personnel assessors.

As one example of the potential directions for such work, we have started to explore the utility for behavioral predictions of making social categorizations at varying levels of inclusiveness. Again, we want to see whether certain levels of abstraction in social categorization allow particularly rich behavioral predictions on the basis of information about category membership. For this purpose, we asked 30 people to describe the interactions they would expect to have if they were going to interact with a particular person in a particular situation. Different subjects were asked to make predictions with regard to members of particular subordinate, middle-level, and superordinate categories selected from the four person taxonomies. For instance, one subject described the likely behaviors of an "extravert in a social situation," another wrote about a "comic joker in a social situation," and still a third subject predicted the interactions that he/she would have with a "practical joker in a social situation." Our subjects provided detailed descriptions of the likely behavior of members of different person categories. Here, for example, is one description of an interaction with a "PR type in a social situation":

> This interaction would probably involve a "big sell." Not necessarily of the product but of something, anything. The man would have a booming voice and no one in the room would be able to get a word in edgewise. I would not like this person and would shy away from his presence. This man would be a conservative politician type . . . .
>
> (Subject No. 29, Cantor, Mischel, & Hood, 1979).

Simply on the basis of a category label the observer is willing to predict (whether accurately or not) details of the interaction that include behavioral responses as well as his/her evaluative reaction to the event. The "PR type" is predicted to be male, rather overwhelming, and consequently quite unpleasant. In real life, such expectations would constrain and shape the course that any actual interaction with such a person would take (e.g., Rubovits & Maehr, 1973; Snyder & Swann, 1978a; Zanna & Pack, 1975).

These data will be analyzed with the techniques described earlier in this chapter, testing for the relative gains and losses in the richness of detail associated with the predictions about person types from categories at different levels of inclusiveness. In particular, we will look at the data from the subordinate- and middle-level categorizations, comparing the relative merits of making fine-grained categorizations (at the subordinate level) with those of using fewer, more inclusive categories from the more abstract middle level. Perhaps the more inclusive categorizations will prove sufficient, enabling detailed, rich predictions to be made on the basis of just a few "basic" categories.

The eventual goal of the present line of research is to apply the insights gained from these attribute listing studies to develop techniques that allow us to match the unique properties of categories (at particular levels of abstraction) to the specific demands of a particular categorization task. For instance, our preliminary work suggests that behavior analysts would want to use molecular, fine-tuned categories in their assessments, while clinicians might prefer categorizing at a more inclusive level when writing case reports that aim to compare and contrast major types of patients in a clinical population. Moreover, turning from the trained to the "naive" observer, it would be particularly interesting to see whether there exists a general intuitive grasp of the "optimal" level of categorization for each component social judgment task. For example, do people naturally prefer to work at a subordinate level of categorization when their ultimate task requires information of a visual nature (e.g., picking someone out from a crowd of people)? Or is there one preferred level of categorization that is most accessible and therefore used more quickly to name and categorize persons and/or situations? Investigation of such issues can potentially provide us with a fuller picture of the relative merits of, as well as the natural proclivities for, categorizing the social world in different ways, with different size categories, and for different purposes. A few studies have begun to explore the types of categorization lay perceivers prefer for particular purposes and tasks (e.g., Jeffery & Mischel, 1978; Mischel, Jeffery, & Patterson, 1974), but much further work is needed to test directly the applications of the present techniques and analyses to the everyday categorization of people both by the layperson and by the professional assessor.

III.　Determining Prototypicality

　　Decisions about the right category for everyday objects are usually fairly automatic, with little doubt about what things are chairs rather than tables, or tables rather than desks, or beds rather than couches. Sometimes, however, the boundaries become fuzzy even in the world of simple physical objects, and there may be a thin distinction between the stool that looks like a table or between the couch and the bed that it resembles. Analogous decisions obviously become much more difficult in the domain of semantic categories about the attributes of people. For example, a Michigan professor submitted the following description of a desired lovemate to the *New York Review of Books* classified section:

> Michigan Prof., British, unattached, nonmacho; vacationing summer England, etc., welcomes small, merry, intelligent, (comely?) *She*—sharing expenses, adventures, tent, bread and cheese, laughter—whatever. Anywhere, but Midwest/Ontario likeliest, for prior encounter, joint flight. NYR, Box 15311. (Reprinted with permission from the *New York Review of Books,* © 1978 Nyrev, Inc., March 23, 1978.)

How do we decide that someone is a perfect example of the class of intelligent persons? What is the configuration of features that indicates membership in the class of "comely women"? Even in the popular press, there is awareness that such decisions are complex. The *San Francisco Chronicle* under the headline "Are You an Introvert or Extrovert?" warned:

> We all know—or think we know—which of our friends and acquaintances are extroverts and we may even feel that we have a pretty good idea where on the sliding scale we ourselves lie. Actually, categorization is not that easy. While there is a very good chance that the back-slapping salesman is in fact a high-level extrovert and the mild-mannered clerk a clear-cut introvert, *superficial appearances can be very misleading."* (*San Francisco Chronicle,* April 24, 1978, p. 16, © Chronicle Publishing Co., 1978)

　　The problem raised here is a central one in the study of categorization: Faced with the task of labeling or typing a new person or object, how does one decide whether a particular stimulus fits a particular category? At least three different approaches (the "classical" view, the "prototype" view, and the "exemplar" view) have been taken to answer this question. The "classical" position (cf. Vygotsky, 1965) suggests that the perceiver checks a short list of necessary and sufficient conditions for category membership and decides that a particular target stimulus fits in the category if and only if it possesses all of these "critical" features. As noted earlier, such a conception does not seem to fit the fuzzy nature of person categories. A potentially more useful approach has been emphasized recently in the concept acquisition literature under the rubric of "exemplar" models of categorization (cf. Brooks, 1978; Medin & Schaffer, 1978; Walker, 1975). According to the exemplar position, new instances are categorized on the basis of their similarity to old, known instances of the category. Thus a particular person may be labeled a "redneck bigot" because he has much in common with (is similar to) other known bigots, such as George Wallace. Promising strides already have been made in applying such models to the person domain (cf. Ebbesen & Allen, in press).

The remaining major approach to the categorization of objects is the "prototype" position. This position has a great deal in common with the exemplar approach because new instances are placed in particular categories on the basis of the degree to which they possess the common characteristics of the category. However, it differs from the exemplar position in that new instances may be compared to an abstract image or set of features (prototype) representing the category, as well as, or instead of, to particular known instances. At present it is difficult to predict how important this difference will turn out to be (cf. Ebbesen & Allen, in press) and we will restrict our attention here to applications of the prototype position to the person domain.

A. THE PROTOTYPE APPROACH

In the prototype view, categories at the same level in a taxonomy are considered to be essentially continuous—without clear-cut boundaries—and the clarity or separateness of categories is achieved by "conceiving of each category in terms of its *clear cases* rather than its boundaries" (Rosch, 1978, p. 36). Such a view deemphasizes the search for necessary and sufficient critical features and emphasizes instead a continuum of prototypicality ("goodness of membership") where degree of prototypicality is operationally defined by people's judgments of how well various objects fit with their image of the meaning implied by a category label.

1. Measuring Family Resemblance

In the analysis and measurement of such judgments, impressive progress has been made in the object domain. Eleanor Rosch and her colleagues (Rosch & Mervis, 1975) have adopted Wittgenstein's notions about family resemblances and applied them to specifying the prototypicality of a category member with respect to its category. They have developed a *family resemblance score* which can easily be computed for members of a wide range of common object categories, such as furniture, cars, or canaries. Basically, the family resemblance principle suggests that the most prototypic members of a category are those members who share many features in common with other members of their own category and few features in common with members of other closely related categories. To obtain the family resemblance score for a particular object with respect to a particular category, one computes a weighted sum, based on the number of features that an object shares with members of its own category minus the number of features it has that overlap with members of other closely related categories. The closely related "contrast" categories are not opposing categories, such as extraverts and introverts but are other very similar categories into which the object might very well be placed (e.g., extraverts and good samaritans, chairs and stools). The features, in this sum, are given differential weights according to the number of other members of the category that possess the particular feature in question. Rosch and Mervis (1975) demonstrated that prototypicality in the domain of common objects was reliably rated by naive observers. Further, their family resemblance measure correlated quite substantially (average correlation of .87) with these prototypicality ratings.

2. Person Prototypicality Judgments

Earlier we noted that in the natural classification of objects as well as persons the categories generally are fuzzy, with no obvious necessary and sufficient criterial properties so that the boundaries between closely related categories are ill defined. The intuitive classifiers of both objects and persons have fairly rich sets of features associated with particular categories; both people and objects vary in the degree to which they exemplify or fit those categories. Considerable theorizing and data suggest that the categorization of an object or a person requires an estimate of the degree of association with one category and distinctiveness from other related categories (e.g., Rosch, 1978; Tversky, 1977). In the person domain, we probably infer and abstract coherent configurations of signs as a basis for assigning a person to a particular type category (see Asch, 1946, for an early discussion of person configurations). So, for example, when one identifies a child as high in "ego strength," no one sign or even two or three signs must necessarily be repeated continuously by the child to enable such classification—it is the global configuration, not the molecular consistencies in behavior, that leads one to assign a person to a type category. It is probably the degree of "family resemblance," not the continuous surpassing of a few critical properties tests, that determines category membership in everyday person perception.

The degree to which configurational factors can be expected to influence prototypicality judgments about a person probably depends on the amount of information about that person available to the perceiver. For example, when one knows a person well, the surface inconsistencies in behavior across situations are probably less influential. Thus when one introspects about the character of a good friend or even about oneself, one tends to abstract the common elements from the massive store of specific behaviors (cf. Jones & Davis, 1965; Kelley, 1972). Having seen a friend behave in a variety of situations over a long span of time, one tries to ignore the surface inconsistencies and seeks the core consistencies. Despite the friend's occasional lapses into passivity, one might describe him or her as a "real mover," always on the go and willing to take a chance at any new adventure. Occasional lapses might even make his or her "basic" energetic temperament seem more salient and believable.

In contrast, when one makes a prototypicality judgment on the basis of only limited, casual observation or interaction with the target person, then attention may be more focused on a search for particular, highly central category attributes. Under such limited or "restricted view" conditions, the prototypicality estimate may be more sensitive to such situational variables as the variety of different contexts in which a given highly central category attribute is consistently exhibited, as well as the degree to which the person exhibits such attributes in unusual, "nonnormative" contexts (cf. Jones & Davis, 1965). Under conditions of limited observation, Kelley's (1972) discounting principle may come into effect, leading perceivers to be more vigilant in monitoring the specific circumstances in which the crucial behaviors are and are not exhibited.

Recognizing the potential differences in the factors influencing prototypicality judgments under "full" and "restricted" viewing conditions, we (Cantor, 1978; Cantor & Mischel, 1979) have directed our research efforts into both of these areas. The present discussion of prototypicality in the person domain begins with a summary of how prototypicality is judged under conditions of relatively rich and extensive exposure to a target individual, i.e., under full view conditions in which the observer has ample information about the judged person.

B. PROTOTYPICALITY RULES: FULL VIEW

In her dissertation, Cantor (1978) attempted to identify rules that people may use to make judgments of the degree of membership or prototypicality with respect to common person categories under "full view" conditions. A review of cognitive models of prototypes for categories of concrete objects and geometric forms (e.g., Reed, 1972; Rosch & Mervis, 1975; Tversky, 1977) and of empirical studies of personality configurations (e.g., Block, 1971; Jackson, 1972) indicates that the following three factors may influence prototypicality judgments in the person domain.

1. Breadth: The Number of Category-Consistent Attributes

In making judgments of prototypicality with respect to a particular type category, people may evaluate the "goodness of the configuration" of information about another person in terms of the breadth (number) of attributes possessed by that person and associated with that particular type category. The greater the breadth (number) of relevant attributes the better the total configuration and the more prototypical is the person with respect to that category.

This expectation emphasizes the number of different but related attributes observed in a person, not the consistency with which the person exhibits one crucial attribute of a type category. The ''good'' extravert may be outgoing in one place, energetic in another, and dominating in another, rather than always sociable (the cardinal extraverted trait) all the time that he/she is observed. Thus we expect that rather than insisting that the person constantly exhibit a specific defining attribute, the perceiver will evaluate the whole configuration of related attributes.

The expectation that people emphasize breadth and judge the goodness of the configuration when assessing someone's prototypicality is consonant with a growing trend in personality research to search for general coherence in the total pattern of a person's behavior rather than for cross-situational consistency in specific behaviors (cf. Block, 1977; Magnusson & Endler, 1977; Pervin, 1977). Rather than focus on the generality across situations of molecular behavior, personality theorists now seem to be trying to identify and differentiate people according to more general patterns of behaviors which endure over time, with various different behaviors emerging as a function of the particular context (e.g., Block, 1971). This configurational approach enables one to characterize personality at a rather molar (type) level, while still allowing for the interaction of person and situation variables in determining the behavior of a given individual at a particular time and in a particular situation. The raters in Block's (1971, 1977) studies, for example, distilled and selected information about personality from a variety of observations of the person over time (e.g., a nursery school teacher observes a child for a 5-month period) and structured this information into coherent dispositional attributions that attempted to capture the gist of what the person ''is like'' in general without emphasizing the molecular variations in behavior. Most importantly, this molar level of characterization is reliable across independent observers and reveals some general continuities in the pattern of an individual's attributes over time.

2. Dominance: The Number of Category-Consistent Attributes Relative to the Total

The degree to which the category-consistent attributes stand out or dominate in a configuration should also influence perceived prototypicality. Therefore, we assume that perceived prototypicality increases with increases in the ratio of the category-consistent attributes displayed relative to the total set of attributes displayed by the individual. Prototypicality will increase as the category-consistent attributes assume a position of ''figure'' against the ''background'' of the total configuration. This expectation suggests that the lay perceiver, like the trait theorist, looks for evidence that the particular disposition under consideration is central to and dominant in the target person's total personality. The analogous notion of separating the "central" or "source" traits from the more superficial characteristics of a person has been expressed often in personality psychology (e.g., Allport, 1937; Cattell, 1965).

3. Differentiation from Contrasting or Incompatible Categories

When people make judgments of prototypicality with respect to a particular person type, we expect that they: (1) consider particular attributes that are, to varying degrees, incompatible with this type and (2) negatively weight such attributes in judgments of prototypicality according to the degree of incompatibility with the type. Recent attempts in personality psychology to capture the natural oppositions between types of personalities (e.g., extraverts and introverts) have resulted in quasi-typologies, such as Eysenck's extraversion-introversion typology, which combine the dimensional emphasis on opposites and the typological emphasis on distinct personality types. Kelly (1963) also emphasizes the notion of contrasting thought categories in his personal constructs theory. For example, he postulates that "a person's construction system is composed of a finite number of dichotomous constructs" (p. 59). Structural analyses of ratings of perceived similarity or likelihood of co-occurrence traits also rely on a dimensional (rather than a typological) bipolar approach to capture the "natural" oppositions that emerge in person perception (cf. Rosenberg & Sedlak, 1972). There is clearly a need in any model of personality or of person perception to include attention to people's tendencies to perceive themselves and others in terms of psychologically opposing forces, incompatible types, or bipolar dimensions of behavior. Each type seems to have not only its own special related features but also its own particular set of incompatible behaviors and traits. Therefore, we suggest that people pay attention not only to the degree to which a person's attributes fit a particular type, but also to the degree to which they are incompatible with a particular type.

4. The Prototypical Extravert

The foregoing analysis has suggested that given extensive data about a person, prototypicality ratings should be a function of at least three factors: (1) the breadth (number) of category-consistent attributes possessed by the person, (2) the degree to which these attributes dominate or stand out in the total configuration, and (3) the number of attributes possessed by the person that are incompatible or inconsistent with the category in question. To see whether these factors were indeed associated with prototypicality in the person domain, Cantor (1978) asked subjects to describe, as fully as possible, the attributes of people whom they knew well and considered to be good, moderate, and poor examples of an extravert. This approach is similar to the one used by Rosch and Mervis (1975) to test the family resemblance measure in the object domain. In the present study, independent ratings of the prototypicality of each person (description) were correlated with various scores computed directly from these descriptions to test for the degree of association between the breadth, consistency, and dominance factors and perceived prototypicality. (This procedure also has been used with a second person category, bright–intelligent persons.)

Briefly, in the extravert study, each of 11 subjects provided full descriptions of the personalities of three friends: (1) a good example of an extravert, (2) a moderately good example of an extravert, and (3) a poor example of an extravert. (Subjects were asked to include in their descriptions any and all attributes characteristic of the target person, not simply those attributes related to extraversion.) Then another group of six naive judges read all 33 person descriptions and rated each description on an 11-point scale for degree of prototypicality with respect to extraversion. (The descriptions had been retyped, all identifying labels were removed, and they were presented in a different random order to each judge.)

As expected, prototypicality was reliably rated by naive perceivers, and readily recognizable factors were associated with the prototypical exemplar of the person category. The reliability of the mean of the six judges, computed by the procedure described by Winer (1971), was quite substantial (.87). Naive judges seemed to share perceptions about the placement of persons on a continuum of prototypicality. Further, relatively simple scores could be computed directly from each person description and correlated quite highly with the independent ratings of perceived prototypicality. Two scores in particular, reflecting the factors outlined earlier, were highly associated with perceived prototypicality. Perceived prototypicality was highly correlated (.79) with a *breadth-differentiation* score (computed by subtracting the number of introverted attributes from the number of extraverted ones listed in each person description). Similarly, the prototypicality ratings were substantially correlated (.79) with a *ratio-dominance* score (computed by taking the ratio of the number of extraverted attributes relative to the total number of attributes listed about each person). Combining these two scores into one score (the number of extraverted attributes minus the number of introverted ones, divided by the total number of attributes) produced a correlation of .85 with perceived prototypicality.

In sum, configurations of features that characterize a prototypical extravert from the present sample seemed to be exemplified by richness and breadth of association with the category, differentiation from a contrasting or opposing category, and dominance or salience of attributes associated with the category (relative to the total set of descriptive attributes). The prototypicality of configurations that varied on these dimensions was readily and reliably rated by the naive judges. Moreover, rules of judgment based on the above three factors did quite well in accounting for differences in perceived (rated) prototypicality with respect to the extravert category.

We expect that the rules for categorizing people—the rules used to distinguish extraverts from introverts, for example—share much with the rules that underlie the categorization of common objects—the rules used to distinguish cars from trucks. It seems reasonable that an efficient cognitive and linguistic system would evolve with fundamental similarities between objects and people. Empirically, we have found many similarities in the ways that prototypicality judgments are made about extraverts or bright–intelligent people and about objects, such as chairs or cars. In both domains prototypicality judgments show high interjudge reliability and relatively direct and simple rules can predict these judgments successfully. Judgments of prototypicality in both domains seem be highly associated with breadth of category-consistent attributes and differentiation from a contrasting category (e.g., Cantor, 1978; Rosch & Mervis, 1975; Tversky, 1977). Also, in both the domains of people and objects, common features seem to contribute more heavily to judgments of similarity and prototypicality than do distinctive or incompatible features (see, for example, Cantor, 1978; Tversky, 1977). Indeed, rules that predict prototypicality ratings solely on the basis of the number of category-consistent attributes possessed by the object or person do quite well in both domains. In the present study, for example, the correlation between the number of extraverted attributes and rated prototypicality with respect to extraversion was only somewhat (though significantly) lower than the association between prototypicality and the breadth-differentiation–ratio score ($r = .64$ vs. $r = .85$). Similarly, studies in which subjects are asked to test theories about other people on the basis of knowledge of their past behavior (e.g., Is Jane suitable for a job as a real-estate salesperson?) show that subjects consider evidence of possession of theory-confirming, consistent facts more relevant to testing the theory than evidence of possession of attributes that conflict with the theory, i.e., category-inconsistent facts (e.g., Snyder & Cantor, in press; Snyder & Swann, 1978b; Taylor, Crocker, & D'Agostino, 1978). Since "theory testing," as it is studied in these cases, is quite similar to judgments of prototypicality or categorization, these data may also be interpreted as further evidence of convergence across domains (cf. Snyder & Swann, 1978b; Wason & Johnson-Laird, 1972), and as further support for Tversky's (1977) claim that common attributes will be given more weight than distinctive ones in judgments of prototypicality.

So far we have only investigated prototypicality judgments in a small sample of person categories (e.g., extraverts, bright people, good Samaritans). We expect that further work with a more extensive sample of categories will show that the rules for making prototypicality judgments are not completely equivalent in the social and nonsocial domains and there are some signs of divergence even in our own small sample of studies. For instance, Cantor (1978) found that the most frequently used contrast category for the person category of extraverts was the polar-opposite introvert category. The contrast categories typically used in studies of object categorization are not opposing ones but closely neighboring categories from the same taxonomy (e.g., chair and stool). Another distinguishing factor associated with prototypicality judgments in the person domain is the relative dominance of the person's category-consistent attributes in his/her total personality. Although Tversky (1977) has also emphasized the importance of perceptual salience in object categorizations, this factor has not received much attention in that domain. Moreover, continuing work in the domain of person categories is likely to show that the more subtle person variables, such as facial expression, tone of voice, gestures, and so on, also influence person prototypicality judgments, leading to more divergence between these domains.

Potential divergence also arises from the multiplicity of alternative categorizations available for people compared to simple objects (cf. Cantor, 1977; Taylor, personal communication, 1978). People, even more than objects, seem to vary along numerous dimensions, each of which may be useful in suggesting relevant categorizations. So for example, Walter Cronkite is a friendly, grandfather type to his TV audience, a superbly successful anchorman for CBS network, and perhaps, a romantic lover to his wife. The category or label most appropriate to a particular target, at any given moment, may depend on the context of observation, the purpose or special interests of the observer (cf. Jeffery & Mischel, 1978), the recent exposure of the observer to particular categorizations (cf. Higgins, Rholes, & Jones, 1977), the specifics of the situation in which the target person is observed (cf. Price, 1974), and the particular set of other comparison persons in the environment at the time of categorization (cf. Taylor *et al.*, 1978). Context, the conjunction of all of these factors, may serve to limit the frame of reference in person categorizations by making salient particular categories into which the target person may best fit at the moment. While similar issues about the contextual determinants of category accessibility have also recently entered the literature on object perception and categorization (cf. Barsalou, 1978; Medin & Schaffer, 1978; Tversky, 1977) they may well be less central for things than for people.

C. PROTOTYPICALITY RULES: RESTRICTED VIEW

One often labels and describes another person on the basis of only partial, fragmented data obtained from very limited observation. Under these restricted view conditions, additional factors may influence prototypicality. We hypothesized that under these conditions prototypicality would be increased when the target individual exhibited the most central (highly associated) category attribute(s) consistently and intensely across many situations, and particularly in situations where such behavior is not routinely observed (i.e., nonnormative situations). When very little information is available about a person and a prototypicality judgment is required, it seems reasonable for the observer to concentrate on verifying that the person really belongs in the category at all—i.e., that he/she exhibits the most central (trait) attributes of the category. For example, under restricted view conditions, the prototypical extravert may be the one who seems to be consistently and naturally outgoing. (When more extensive observations are available, as when one describes a friend, then less central attributes, such as adventurous, active, dominating, and so on, become more influential in this prototypicality decision, as we saw in the preceding section.) To verify that the central attributes are present, the naive observer, like the trained personologist, may look at the temporal and cross-situational stability of these attributes to assess whether they are consistently and repeatedly exhibited in many situations (see, for example, Kelley's consistency principle: Kelley, 1967, 1972). Further, the observer may be particularly impressed when the target person exhibits these central category attributes in nonnormative situations where such behavior is neither required nor routinely observed (see, for examples, Kelley's consensus principle: Kelley, 1967; and Jones and Davis' correspondant inference theory: Jones & Davis, 1965; Jones et al., 1961). Thus the "pushy type" who maneuvers to the front of the line in a bank seems particularly self-important and aggressive by contrast to all the patient people quietly waiting their turns.

To test these hypotheses, Cantor and Mischel (1979) asked subjects to make forced-choice decisions, choosing the more prototypical extravert from among six different pairs of characters. These characters varied in the number of episodes in which they were portrayed as exhibiting outgoing behaviors (central to the extravert category) as opposed to less central category attributes (e.g., active, adventurous). The relative centrality of different attributes for the perception of extraversion was independently established in earlier work (e.g., Cantor & Mischel, 1977). In the present study, subjects uniformly chose the characters who exhibited outgoing behaviors in one episode and active and adventurous behaviors in the other two episodes. Completely parallel results were obtained from subjects who had to select the more prototypical bright–intelligent type under directly comparable conditions in which the central category attribute was intelligent (and the less central attributes were imaginative and skillful).

These results suggest that central category attributes become the focus of attention in prototypicality judgments made on the basis of scant evidence. The observer chooses, as the most prototypical extravert, the character who exhibited in all situations behaviors that are outgoing rather than the character who was outgoing in one situation, adventurous in another, and active in a third. This focus on highly central attributes seems similar to the "critical features" tests proposed by theorists such as Bruner and his colleagues (1966) and Vygotsky (1965). To be a prototypical extravert, it is critical that one frequently and consistently exhibit outgoing behaviors—the behaviors that are seen as most central to extraversion. However, a focus on the central trait attributes does not imply that all category members must exhibit the same exact pattern of behavior in the same contexts—they should simply exhibit as much behavior as possible that is closely related to the central trait attribute.

In her dissertation, Cantor (1978) also used a forced-choice paradigm, similar to the one described above, to investigate the influence of situational factors on prototypicality judgments under restricted view. In her study, characters were always observed in three episodes, but these episodes took place in different situations. The normative or nonnormative nature of the situations was varied systematically. (Recall that "normative" refers to the degree to which behavior relevant to the category is expected and typical in the particular context.) So, for example, one extravert might be seen acting outgoing at a party, a rally, and a carnival (all normative situations for outgoing behavior), while another performed the same behaviors but at a bus stop, post office, and library (i.e., all nonnormative situations for outgoing behavior). Similar comparisons were made between bright–intelligent characters who exhibited their intelligent behaviors either in normative (e.g., a laboratory) or nonnormative (e.g., a bar) situations.

Characters from both the extravert and bright categories also varied systematically with respect to the consistency of their behaviors—highly consistent characters were always outgoing or intelligent, while inconsistent characters were sometimes outgoing and sometimes shy or sometimes intelligent and other times unintelligent. The research thus examined the effects on prototypicality judgments of two variables—the normativeness of the situation for the behavior and the consistency of the behavior—that have been extensively studied in the domain of judgments of causality (for just two selected examples see: Jones, Davis & Gergen, 1961; McArthur, 1972).

Items 1–4 in Table III present selected examples of the different character types used in Cantor's (1978) forced-choice study, as well as a summary of the prototypicality preferences exhibited by subjects when asked to make choices between these different characters. The results revealed an interaction between consistency and situational normativeness. Under these restricted viewing conditions, the character who was consistently outgoing (or intelligent) in three different situations was perceived as more prototypical if the behaviors were nonnormative (i.e., unlikely), rather than normative, for those particular situations. So, the extravert who was consistently outgoing at a party, a rally, and a carnival was perceived as less prototypical than the one who was observed performing the same general behaviors but at a bus stop, library, and post office.

However, under certain circumstances this effect was reversed. In the same forced-choice procedure, subjects sometimes chose the characters who exhibited their behaviors in places where such behavior was routine over those who acted outgoing or intelligent in nonnormative situations. Specifically, when the charac-

TABLE III

PERCEIVED PROTOTYPICALITY FOR DIFFERENT CHARACTER TYPES

Sample character type[a]	Prototypicality choice
1. Cross-situationally consistent in normative situations (e.g., outgoing at party, rally, carnival)	The character who was cross-situationally consistent in three nonnormative situations was chosen as more prototypical than the one who was cross-situationally consistent in three normative situations (character type 2 > character type 1)[b]
2. Cross-situationally consistent in nonnormative situations (e.g., outgoing at library, bus stop, post office)	
3. Cross-situationally inconsistent in normative situations (e.g., intelligent at laboratory, planetarium and unintelligent at class)	The character who was inconsistent in three normative situations was chosen as more prototypical than the one who was inconsistent in three nonnormative situations (character type 3 > character type 4)[c]
4. Cross-situationally inconsistent in nonnormative situations (e.g., intelligent at bar, carnival and unintelligent at stadium)	
5. Extremely outgoing in three normative situations and minimally outgoing in three nonnormative situations	The character who was extremely outgoing in the normative situations was rated as more prototypically extraverted than the one who was extremely outgoing in the three nonnormative situations (character type 5 > character type 6)[b]
6. Extremely outgoing in three nonnormative situations and minimally outgoing in three normative situations	

[a] These characters were described by extensive (three-page) character profiles containing detailed information about their behavior and the contexts in which they were observed.

[b] These comparisons were statistically significant at the .01 level.

[c] These comparisons were statistically significant at the .05 level.

ters were not consistent in their outgoing (or intelligent) behaviors across all three episodes, then the observed choice preferences changed in favor of characters who were seen in places where people routinely acted outgoing (or intelligent). For example, the bright–intelligent character who was seen acting intelligently in two episodes and unintelligently in one episode was perceived as more prototypical if the episodes took place at a library, planetarium, and laboratory than at a bar, stadium, and carnival. Subjects in the other (high-consistency) condition of the same study had made the opposite prototypicality choice. In other words, the types of contexts that increased perceived prototypicality depended on the consistency of the character's behavior over time.

The forced-choice study showed that a consistently outgoing (or a consistently intelligent, bright type) was perceived as more prototypical when he/she was seen in nonnormative (as compared with normative) contexts but this pattern was reversed when the character was inconsistent. How can we explain this interaction? We hypothesized that prototypicality judgments based on observations of a person's behavior in nonnormative situations would be influenced by inferences about the person's likely behavior in normative situations (Cantor, 1978). So, for example, when rating the prototypicality of an extravert, the observer estimates the degree to which this person will be extremely outgoing in social situations (i.e., in situations in which a "true" extravert is expected to be outgoing).

Presumably observers infer that a character who shows consistently prototypical behavior where it is not normative (e.g., outgoing at library, bus stop, post office) will be even more prototypical in situations in which such behavior is normative (e.g., outgoing at party, rally, carnival). That is, one is likely to make a very strong inference that a character who is prototypical even when such behavior is not normative is apt to be even more prototypical in situations in which the behavior is routine. Indeed, in a second study, Cantor (1978) found that subjects were quite willing to infer that a particular person would be extremely outgoing (or intelligent) in situations that were normative for such behavior on the basis of observations of that person's outgoing (or intelligent) behavior in nonnormative situations. In other words, the rough estimate of the likelihood of intensely outgoing (or intelligent) behavior in normative situations may be greater for the character who was observed to be consistently outgoing (or intelligent) in the nonnormative situations because the observer makes a very strong inference about his/her likely behavior in the normative situations (cf. Jones & Davis, 1965).

However, consider the character who was inconsistent in his/her behavior in the nonnormative situations—sometimes acting outgoing but sometimes acting shy. An observer would be much less likely to infer that this character would be very outgoing in normative situations because this character has not created a clear impression of "outgoingness" in the nonnormative situation. If judgment of prototypicality requires choosing the character who is the most likely to be outgoing in normative situations, the observer would be safer, in this comparison, choosing the inconsistent character who was seen in the normative (as compared with the nonnormative) contexts. At least that character has been observed acting outgoing on some occasions in the normative situations.

The present analysis helps to explain the interaction between the consistency and normativeness factors found in the forced-choice study (Cantor, 1978). It also suggests that observers would not choose as more prototypical the character who was consistently outgoing (or intelligent) in nonnormative (as compared with normative) contexts if evidence were presented that such a character was not very outgoing or intelligent in normative situations. In other words, according to this analysis, the pattern of choice preferences previously noted depends on the subject's ability to infer that the character seen in nonnormative situations would also be very outgoing or intelligent in normative contexts. What happens when subjects are told that the character who was extremely and consistently outgoing in the three nonnormative situations, was not very outgoing when observed in the three normative situations? Under these conditions, subjects should no longer prefer the character who was very outgoing in the nonnormative situations because they cannot make the inference that he/she would also be very outgoing in the normative situations (since evidence to the contrary has now been presented). This study was conducted (Cantor, 1978) and it was found (as summarized in items 5 and 6 of Table III) that the prototypicality ratings did reverse, now in favor of the character who was at least very outgoing in the expected, normative situations.

In that study, all characters were observed in the three normative and in the three nonnormative situations. One character was extremely outgoing (six behaviors on a checklist) in the normative situations and minimally outgoing (one behavior on the checklist) in the nonnormative ones. Another character exhibited the reverse pattern of behaviors in situations—being extremely outgoing in the nonnormative situations and minimally outgoing in the normative ones. The character who was extremely outgoing in the three situations where such behavior was nonnormative (e.g., post office, library, bus stop) and only minimally outgoing in the three situations where such behavior was normative (e.g., party, rally, carnival) was rated as relatively unprototypical (mean rating of 5.48 on a 12-point scale). However, the character who performed many outgoing acts in the normative situations and few such acts in the nonnormative situations was rated as relatively prototypical (mean rating of 7.15 on a 12-point scale). Thus when it was clear that the character who was very outgoing in the nonnormative situations was not equally so in the normative ones, then he/she was perceived as a less prototypical extravert. This change in perceived prototypicality presumably occurred because the automatic assumption that someone who is very outgoing in the nonnormative situations will be even more outgoing in normative ones was contradicted by the additional evidence about the character's actual behavior in the normative situations. The observer's expectation that category-consistent behavior would also be exhibited intensely in the normative situations was changed, as reflected in the final prototypicality judgment.

In sum, perceived prototypicality (under restricted view conditions) appears to be a function of the degree of intensity and consistency with which the central trait attributes of a category can be expected to be exhibited by the target person in normative situations. (The details of an inference model incorporating these assumptions are given in Cantor, 1978.) The overall patterns of data also indicate that subjects were sensitive to the particular configuration of behaviors in situations associated with the target individual. Perceived prototypicality was not exclusively a function either of the target person's behavior or of the situations in which the behavior was observed: It depended on an interaction between the behaviors and the situations. Consistent behaviors were judged more prototypical when they occurred in nonnormative situations; inconsistent behaviors were seen as more prototypical when they occurred in normative situations. Our naive observers thus attended to the particular interaction patterns of each person's behavior within particular situations, presumably displaying intuitively the awareness of interactionism that is becoming increasingly recognized by professional personologists (Magnusson & Endler, 1977).

Note that naive observers are not always as sensitive as our subjects were to the context in which behavior occurs (e.g., Taylor & Crocker, 1978) and often ignore consensus information (e.g., McArthur, 1972; Nisbett & Borgida, 1975; Nisbett & Ross, in press). These divergent findings suggest that similar input variables may have different effects depending on the nature of the social judgment (e.g., predictions, attributions of causality, prototypicality judgments). Further, we suspect that information about behavioral norms that is directly embedded in descriptions of a single person in a variety of situations (as in our work) may be more compelling than statistical base-rate information. Such information may avoid the oft-mentioned problem of the dull, pallid quality of statistical information (cf. Nisbett & Borgida, 1975), but obviously much further work will be needed to specify just how particular input variables influence different kinds of social judgments (cf. Ruble & Feldman, 1976; Zuckerman, 1978).

D. FROM PROTOTYPES TO SOCIAL BEHAVIOR

The degree to which a person is a prototypical category member influences the ease (but not necessarily the accuracy) with which information about that person can be recalled, recognized and categorized (e.g., Cantor & Mischel, in press; Markus, 1977; Rogers, Rogers, & Kuiper, 1978; Tsujimoto, 1978). When a person is a prototypical category exemplar, then this association with the category can function as an organizational theme to structure the encoding of new information about the person, to provide expectations about his/her future behavior or actions, and to aid in the retrieval of his/her past behaviors. It is precisely when a person appears to be prototypical of a category that all of the social knowledge associated with that category can be brought to bear when asking: ''What is this person really like?''

Knowledge about person prototypes not only makes information processing easier, it also helps the perceiver to plan behavior in social interactions. For instance, people can readily imagine the prototypic person for a variety of situations (Snyder & Cantor, 1979) and such images can include valuable information about the most appropriate behavior for that situation. Several strategies can be used to apply prototype information for structuring one's behavior. In the ''prototype-situation'' strategy, the actor focuses on the demands of the situation, imagining a prototype of the ideal person for that situation and using that prototype image to guide his/her own choice of behavior (Snyder & Cantor, 1979). In the ''other-directed'' strategy, the actor plans his/her own behavior according to the expected characteristics of the other people in the social environment. (For an example of this strategy see Snyder & Swann, 1978a.) In the "self-directed" strategy, the actor focuses on his/her own characteristics and plans his/her behavior to be consistent with these characteristics. (For examples of the self-focused strategy see Markus, 1977; Rogers, Kuiper & Kirker, 1977; Snyder & Cantor, 1979.) Individual differences in the use of these cognitive strategies, as well as further explorations of the strategies themselves, merit further attention.

The conception of person categories as fuzzy sets, the application of the family resemblance idea, and the view that person categories are organized around prototypical examples, as discussed throughout this paper, seem to have clear implications for personality theory as well as for the study of how people understand each other. Guided by traditional trait theories, most research on consistency in personality in the past has searched for distinct person categories with clearly defined properties. The expectation of nomothetic trait psychology was that all members of a category would display all the critical features across a wide variety of contexts—an expectation that generally proved to be empirically dubious (e.g., Mischel, 1968; Peterson, 1968; Vernon, 1964). Liberalizing the conception of person categories in the directions suggested for natural object categories by Wittgenstein, Rosch, and others seems appropriate on both theoretical and empirical grounds. It is hoped that this will facilitate a more idiographic and configurational search for subtypes of people who display patterns of coherence under particular sets of conditions—a direction already evident in recent research (e.g., Bem & Allen, 1974; Bem & Funder, 1978; Magnusson & Endler, 1977; Mischel, 1973). Such a liberalization should also facilitate a search for the patterns of coherence under particular sets of conditions that perceivers identify and use to guide their judgments and to construct their understanding of people and themselves. Although personologists have urged the field to move in this direction for many years, such advice has proved hard to follow, perhaps in part because the fuzziness of person categories had not been articulated as explicitly as it can be in the light of the post-Wittgenstein analyses in the object domain. It is hoped that future work will give increasingly deep attention to the processes through which people categorize themselves and each other, to the rules they use in making such categorizations for various purposes, and to the reciprocal interactions between their person categories and their social behavior.

IV. Structure in the Head or in the World?

Throughout this paper we have discussed the cognitive units that people may use to categorize each other but have avoided the question of the links between those structures in perceivers and the actual characteristics of the perceived. Few topics in psychology have generated more heat than the thorny but enduring issue of the locus of perceived stimulus structure: Do the attributes which are associated in the head of the perceiver with one type of object or person actually reside in the particular stimulus object or person?

A. THE OBJECT DOMAIN

In the object domain Eleanor Rosch and her colleagues have recently opened a new line of debate on this old issue by once again challenging the view that the stimulus environment is an unstructured mass of information which must be tamed and differentiated by the linguistically alert child. The traditional view suggests that ''the physical and social environment of a young child is perceived as a continuum. It does not contain any intrinsically separate 'things.' The child, in due course, is taught to impose upon this environment a kind of discriminating grid which serves to distinguish the world as being composed of a large number of separate things, each labeled with a name'' (Leach, 1964, p. 34). The Rosch *et al.* position suggests instead that:

> The world does contain ''intrinsically separate things.'' The world is structured because real-world attributes do not occur independently of each other. Creatures with feathers are more likely also to have wings than creatures with fur, and objects with the visual appearance of chairs are more likely to have functional sit-on-ableness than objects with the appearance of cats. That is, combinations of attributes of real objects do not occur uniformly. Some pairs, triples, or ntuples are quite probable, appearing in combination sometimes with one, sometimes another attribute; others are rare; others logically cannot or empirically do not occur. (Rosch *et al.,* 1976, p. 383)

Rosch *et al.* provide a sensible compromise on this issue of whether the structure exists in the head of the perceiver or in the external world. They suggest that basic object groupings result from ''an interaction between the potential structure provided by the world and the particular emphasis and state of knowledge of the people who are categorizing'' (Rosch *et al.,* 1976, p. 430). There is structure in the environment in that ''the perceived world is not an unstructured total set of equiprobable co-occurring attributes'' (Rosch *et al.,* 1976, p. 428). There is structure in perceivers in that: (1) They are aware of and able to perceive complex attributes and sets of attributes; (2) they may be ignorant of or ignore certain attributes and attribute co-occurrences; and (3) they ''may know of the attributes and their correlational structure but exaggerate that structure, turning partial into complete correlations (as when attributes true only of many members of a category are thought of as true of all members)'' (Rosch *et al.,* 1976, 430). The structure of objects does not exist all in the world or all in the head. Rather, there is an interaction process by which the perceiver's tendencies to build coherent, well-structured classes of objects interacts with the already existing partial structure of the external object world. A related interactionist view was recently developed by Neisser (1976).

B. THE PERSON DOMAIN

Is what Rosch *et al.* have argued for objects also true for people? A long line of research in implicit personality theory and person perception (cf. D'Andrade, 1970; Hastorf, Schneider, & Polefka, 1970; Schneider, 1973) affirms the existence of shared meaning systems for structuring the world of people into bundles based on attributes that are likely to co-occur; it is clear that people can go from behavioral signs to agreed-upon dispositional attributions which in turn can form the basis for grouping people into different kinds of personalities. Moreover, judges may show high reliability in the behavior they expect and predict for different types (e.g., Reed & Jackson, 1975). For example, Block (1977) found high agreement between nursery school teachers' independent ratings of the dispositional characteristics of children (based on the California Q-sort items) as abstracted over time from a large repertoire of behavioral observations. The lay perceiver has a well-structured system of expectations about what behavioral signs go with what abstract dispositional qualities and about what abstract qualities, in turn, tend to cluster and co-occur in different kinds of people. Traits and types do seem to exist in the head of the perceiver.

Are these perceptions based on the actual qualities of the perceived people? While there is a lack of support for broadly based cross-situational consistencies in specific social behaviors (cf. Mischel, 1968), there is also growing support for more general patterns of consistency and coherence over time (cf. Block, 1971), across some situations in some people (cf. Bem & Allen, 1974), and in behavior as it is shaped and constrained by both the physical and the social environment (cf. Harré & Secord, 1973; Snyder & Swann, 1978a). Even at the molecular level of specific behavior-in-situation observations, there is at the least the statistically significant .30 level of consistency (Mischel, 1968), providing a basis for abstracting some significant coherence from people's behavioral repertoires. We suggest, that this level of structure may not be fundamentally dissimilar to the partial structure posited to exist by Rosch *et al.* (1976) in the world of common concrete objects. For example, there probably is a tendency for sociable behavior to co-occur with talkative and active behavior in certain types of persons (e.g., extraverts), just as sweet songs, feathers, and wings tend to co-occur in certain kinds of common objects (e.g., canaries).

Structure exists neither "all in the head" of the perceiver (cf. Shweder, 1975) nor "all in the person" perceived (cf., Epstein, 1977); it is instead a function of an interaction between the beliefs of observers and the characteristics of the observed, in the person domain as well as in the common object domain:

> ... even as simple an act as recognizing the letter "A" involves an active cognitive construction (not a mere reading of what is "really there"). Then surely the far more complicated perception of personal consistency in ourselves and others also requires an active imposition of order—a jump beyond the information given to construct the essential underlying gist of meaning from the host of behavioral fragments we observe. Human information processing—whether in the recognition of a best friends' enduring "warmth" or of the word "warmth" on the printed page—involves continuous interactions between what is "out there" in the world of "stimuli" and what is "in here" in the head of the perceiver.
>
> Consequently it may not be possible to assign the residence of dispositions exclusively either to the actor or to the perceiver; we may have to settle for a continuous interaction between observed and observer, for a reality that is constructed and cognitively created but not fictitious. In such a construction process, semantic networks are likely to figure heavily (e.g., D'Andrade, 1970, 1973; Shweder, 1975), and "prototypes" or "schemata" may be generated that permit a wide range of distortions and transformations in specific instances and still yield consistent agreement among observers about the underlying gist. (Mischel, 1977, p. 334)

Our own data on the effects of prototypicality on free recall and impression formation also provide support for an interactionist view of the determinants of person memory and person impressions (Cantor & Mischel, in press). In that study we tested the hypothesis that it is easier to process information about characters who fit well with and are, therefore, prototypical of shared beliefs about various personality types. Character prototypicality was manipulated in a free-recall and personality impression paradigm through variations in the consistency of a character's identification with preexisting beliefs about two personality-type categories—extraversion and introversion. Subjects also were given information about each character that varied in degree of abstraction from traits to concrete behavior. As predicted, both the amount and the nature of the information correctly recalled were significantly affected by the consistency of the character's identification with extraversion or with introversion. Character consistency also significantly affected the amount of material written in the personality impressions and the tendency to qualify the generality of the impressions. It is noteworthy that our subjects were clearly sensitive to variations in the internal consistency of the character descriptions. They were able to perceive the existing structure in those descriptions and to modulate their use of preexisting information in the face of inconsistency or "poor structure" in the data about the character. However, when confronted with "good structure" in the character description of the pure extravert and introvert, they presumably relied more on the information in their cognitive structures, in their "heads," to elaborate on these personality descriptions. In this sense, information is the head of the perceiver and in the world of the perceived interacted in the course of person perception. Thus, perceivers expect that certain behaviors go together, to some extent these co-occurrences do occur more often than by chance; in the search for the "gist" of another person's qualities, perceivers can discount molecular inconsistencies and exaggerate observed consistencies to build meaningful coherences. Rather than argue about the existence or reality of such coherences we need to continue to clarify with increasing depth their nature, organization, and functions.

REFERENCES

Abelson, R. P. Script processing in attitude formation and decision-making. In J. S. Carrol & J. W. Payne (Eds.), *Cognition and social behavior*. Hillsdale, N.J.: Erlbaum, 1976.

Allport, G. W. *Personality: A psychological interpretation*. New York: Holt, Rinehart & Winston, 1937.

Anderson, N. H. Application of an additive model to impression formation. *Science*, 1962, **138**, 817-818.

Asch, S. E. Forming impressions of personality. *Journal of Abnormal and Social Psychology*, 1946, **41**, 258-290.

Barsalou, L. *Context dependent categorization*. Unpublished manuscript, Stanford University, 1978.

Bell, L. G., Wicklund, R. A., Manko, G., & Larkin, C. When unexpected behavior is attributed to the environment. *Journal of Research in Personality*, 1976, **10**, 316-327.

Bem, D. J., & Allen, A. On predicting some of the people some of the time: The search for cross-situational consistencies in behavior. *Psychological Review*, 1974, **81**, 506-520.

Bem, D. J., & Funder, D. C. Predicting more of the people more of the time: Assessing the personality of situations. *Psychological Review*, 1978, **85**, 485-502.

Bem, S. L. Cognitive processes mediating sex typing and androgyny. Invited address at the meetings of the Western Psychological Association, San Francisco, April 1978.

Block, J. *Lives through time*. Berkeley, Calif.: Bancroft, 1971.

Block, J. Advancing the psychology of personality: Paradigmatic shift or improving the quality of research. In D. Magnusson & N. S. Endler (Eds.), *Personality at the crossroads: Current issues in interactional psychology*. Hillsdale, N.J.: Erlbaum, 1977.

Brooks, L. Nonanalytic concept formation and memory for instances. In E. Rosch & B. B. Lloyd (Eds.), *Cognition and categorization*. Hillsdale, NJ.: Erlbaum, 1978.

Bruner, J. S. On perceptual readiness. *Psychological Review*, 1957, **64**, 123-152.

Bruner, J. S. Social psychology and perception. In E. E. Maccoby, T. M. Newcomb, & E. L. Hartley (Eds.), *Readings in social psychology*. New York: Holt, Rinehart & Winston, 1958.

Bruner, J. S., Olver, R. P., & Greenfield, P. M. *Studies in cognitive growth*. New York: Wiley, 1966.

Cantor, N. *Prototypicality and personality*. Unpublished manuscript, Stanford University, 1977.

Cantor, N. *Prototypicality and personality judgments*. Unpublished doctoral dissertation, Stanford Universtiy, 1978.

Cantor, N., & Mischel, W. Traits as prototypes: Effects on recognition memory. *Journal of Personality and Social Psychology*, 1977, **35**, 38-48.

Cantor, N., & Mischel, W. Prototypicality and personality: Effects on free recall and personality impressions. *Journal of Research in Personality*, 1979, in press.

Cantor, N., & Mischel, W. *The effects of attribute centrality on perceived prototypicality*. Manuscript in preparation, Princeton University and Stanford University, 1979.

Cantor, N., Mischel, W., & Hood, S. Q. *Behavioral predictions for exemplars of different person type categories*. Manuscript in preparation, Princeton University and Stanford University, 1979.

Carlston, D. E. *The recall and use of observed behaviors and inferred traits in social inference processes.* Unpublished doctoral dissertation, University of Illinois, 1977.

Cattell, R. B. *The scientific analysis of personality.* Baltimore: Penguin, 1965.

Cohen, C. *Cognitive basis of stereotyping.* Paper presented at the meetings of the American Psychological Association, San Francisco, August 1977.

Cronbach, L. J., & Meehl, P. E. Construct validity in psychological tests. *Psychological Bulletin,* 1955, **52,** 281–302.

D'Andrade, R. *Cognitive structures and judgments.* Paper presented for T.O.B.R.E. research workshop on cognitive organization and psychological processes. Huntington Beach, Calif., August 1970.

D'Andrade, R. C. *Memory and assessment of behavior.* Unpublished manuscript, University of California at San Diego, Department of Anthropology, 1973.

Ebbesen, E. B., & Allen, R. B. Cognitive processes in implicit personality trait inferences. *Journal of Personality and Social Psychology,* in press.

Epstein, S. Traits are alive and well. In D. Magnusson & N. S. Endler (Eds.), *Personality at the crossroads: Current issues in interactional psychology.* Hillsdale, N.J.: Erlbaum, 1977.

Eysenck, H. J. *The biological basis of personality.* Springfield, Ill.: Thomas, 1967.

Fiske, S., & Cox, M. *Describing others: There's more to person perception than trait lists.* Paper presented at the meetings of the American Psychological Association, San Francisco, August 1977.

Hamilton, D. L. *Illusory correlation as a basis for social stereotypes.* Paper presented at the meetings of the American Psychological Association, San Francisco, August 1977.

Hamilton, D. A cognitive-attributional analysis of stereotyping. In L. Berkowitz (Ed.), *Advances in experimental social psychology* (Vol. 12). New York: Academic Press, 1979.

Harré, H., & Secord, P. *The explanation of social behavior.* Totowa, N.J.: Littlefield, 1973.

Hastie, R. Memory for information that is congruent or incongruent with a conceptual schema. In E. T. Higgins, C. P. Herman, & M. P. Zanna (Eds.), *Social cognition: The Ontario Symposium on personality and social psychology.* Hillsdale, N.J.: Erlbaum, in press.

Hastorf, A., Schneider, D., & Polefka, J. *Person perception.* Menlo Park, Calif.: Addison-Wesley, 1970.

Hayden, T., & Mischel, W. Maintaining trait consistency in the resolution of behavioral inconsistency: The wolf in sheep's clothing? *Journal of Personality,* 1976, **44,** 109–132.

Higgins, E. T. The communication game. In E. T. Higgins, C. P. Herman, & M. P. Zanna (Eds.), *Social cognition: The Ontario Symposium on personality and social psychology.* Hillsdale, N.J.: Erlbaum, in press.

Higgins, E. T., C. P. Herman, & M. P. Zanna (Eds.), *Social cognition: The Ontario Symposium on personality and social psychology.* Hillsdale, N.J.: Erlbaum, in press.

Higgins, E. T., Rholes, C. R., & Jones, C. R. Category assessibility and impression formation. *Journal of Experimental Social Psychology,* 1977, **13,** 141–154.

Jackson, D. N. A model for inferential accuracy. *Canadian Psychologist,* 1972, **13,** 185–194.

Jeffery, K. M., & Mischel, W. *Effects of purpose on the organization and recall of information in person perception.* Unpublished manuscript, Stanford University, 1978.

Johnson, S. Hierarchical clustering schemes. *Psychometrika,* 1967, **32,** 241–253.

Jones, E. E., & Davis, K. E. From actors to dispositions: The attribution process in person perception. In L. Berkowitz (Ed.), *Advances in experimental social psychology* (Vol. 2). New York: Academic Press, 1965.

Jones. E. E., Davis, K. E., & Gergen, K. J. Role playing variations and their informational values for person perception. *Journal of Abnormal and Social Psychology,* 1961, **63,** 302–310.

Jones, E. E., Kanouse, D. G., Kelley, H. H., Nisbett, R. E., Valins, S., & Weiner, B. (Eds.),

Attribution: Perceiving the causes of behavior. Morristown, N.J.: General Learning Press, 1972.

Jung, C. G. *Psychological types.* London: Routledge & Kegan Paul, 1923.

Kelley, H. H. The warm-cold variable in first impressions of persons. *Journal of Personality,* 1950, **18,** 431–439.

Kelley, H. H. Attribution theory and social psychology. In D. Levine (Ed.), *Nebraska Symposium on Motivation* (Vol. 15). Lincoln: University of Nebraska Press, 1967.

Kelley, H. H. Attribution in social interaction. In E. Jones, D. Kanouse, H. Kelley, R. Nisbett, S. Valins, & B. Weiner (Eds.), *Attribution: Perceiving the causes of behavior.* Morristown, N.J.: General Learning Press, 1972.

Kelly, G. A. *The psychology of personal constructs* (Vols. 1 & 2). New York: Norton, 1955.

Kelly, G. A. *A theory of personality: The psychology of personal constructs.* New York: Norton, 1963.

Kintsch, W. *The representation of meaning in memory.* Hillsdale, N.J.: Erlbaum, 1974.

Labov, W. The boundaries of words and their meanings. In C. J. Baily & R. Shuy (Eds.), *New ways of analyzing variations in English.* Washington, D.C.: Georgetown University Press, 1973.

Lakoff, G. Hedges: A study in meaning criteria and the logic of fuzzy concepts. *Papers from the 8th Regional Meeting, Chicago Linguistics Society.* Chicago: University of Chicago Linguistics Department, 1972.

Langer, E. J. Rethinking the role of thought in social interaction. In J. H. Harvey, W. J. Ickes, & R. F. Kidd (Eds.), *New directions in attribution research* (Vol. 2). Potomac, Md.: Erlbaum, 1978.

Leach, E. Anthropological aspects of language: Animal categories and verbal abuse. In E. E. Lenneberg (Ed.), *New directions in the study of language.* Cambridge: MIT Press, 1964.

Lehrer, A. Indeterminacy in semantic description. *Glassa,* 1970, **4,** 87–109.

Lehrer, A. *Semantic fields and lexical structure.* Amsterdam: North-Holland Publishing, 1974.

Livesley, W. J., & Bromley, D. B. *Person perception in childhood and adolescence.* New York: Wiley, 1973.

Magnusson, D., & Endler, N. S. Interactional psychology: Present status and future prospects. In D. Magnusson & N. S. Endler (Eds.), *Personality at the crossroads: Current issues in interactional psychology.* Hillsdale, N.J.: Erlbaum, 1977.

Markus, H. Self-schemata and processing information about the self. *Journal of Personality and Social Psychology,* 1977, **35,** 63–78.

McArthur, L. A. The how and what of why: Some determinants and consequences of casual attribution. *Journal of Personality and Social Psychology,* 1972, **22,** 171–193.

McCloskey, M. E., & Glucksberg, S. Natural categories: Well-defined or fuzzy sets? *Memory and Cognition,* 1978, **614,** 462–472.

McGuire, W. J., McGuire, C. V., Child, P., & Fujioka, T. Salience of ethnicity in the spontaneous self-concept as a function of one's ethnic distinctiveness in the social environment. *Journal of Personality and Social Psychology,* 1978, **36,** 511–520.

Medin, D. L., & Schaffer, M. M. Context theory of classification learning, *Psychological Review,* 1978, **85,** 207–238.

Mischel, W. *Personality and assessment.* New York: Wiley, 1968.

Mischel, W. Toward a cognitive social learning reconceptualization of personality. *Psychological Review,* 1973, **80,** 252–283.

Mischel, W. *Introduction to personality* (2nd ed.). New York: Holt, Rinehart, & Winston, 1976.

Mischel, W. The interaction of person and situation. In D. Magnusson & N. S. Endler (Eds.), *Personality at the crossroads: Current issues in interactional psychology.* Hillsdale, N.J.: Erlbaum, 1977.

Mischel, W., Jeffery, K. M., & Patterson, C. J. The layman's use of trait and behavioral information to predict behavior. *Journal of Research in Personality,* 1974, **8,** 231–242.

Neisser, U. *Cognition and reality: Principles and implications of cognitive psychology.* San Francisco: Freeman, 1976.

Nisbett, R. E., & Borgida, E. Attribution and the psychology of prediction. *Journal of Personality and Social Psychology,* 1975, **32,** 932–943.

Nisbett, R. E., & Ross, L. D. *Human inference: Strategies and shortcomings of informal judgment.* Century Series in Psychology. Englewood Cliffs, N.J.: Prentice-Hall, in press.

Nisbett, R. E., & Wilson, T. D. Telling more than we can know: Verbal reports on mental processes. *Psychological Review,* 1977, **84,** 231–259.

Norman, W. T. Toward an adequate taxonomy of personality attributes: Replicated factor structure in peer nomination personality ratings. *Journal of Abnormal and Social Psychology,* 1963, **66,** 574–583.

Peevers, B., & Secord, P. Developmental changes in attributions of descriptive concepts to persons. *Journal of Personality and Social Psychology,* 1973, **27,** 120–128.

Pervin, L. A. The representative design of person-situation research. In D. Magnusson & N. S. Endler (Eds.), *Personality at the crossroads: Current issues in interactional psychology.* Hillsdale, N.J.: Erlbaum, 1977.

Peterson, D. R. *The clinical study of social behavior.* New York: Appleton, 1968.

Price, R. H. The taxonomic classification of behaviors and situations and the problem of behavior-environment congruence. *Human Relations,* 1974, **27,** 567–585.

Quine, W. V. *Ontological relativity and other essays.* New York: Columbia University Press, 1969.

Reed, P. L., & Jackson, D. N. Clinical judgment of psychopathology: A model for inferential accuracy. *Journal of Abnormal Psychology,* 1975, **84,** 475–482.

Reed, S. K. Pattern recognition and categorization. *Cognitive Psychology,* 1972, **3,** 382–407.

Rogers, T. B., Kuiper, N. A., & Kirker, W. S. Self-reference and the encoding of personal information. *Journal of Personality and Social Psychology,* 1977, **35,** 677–688.

Rogers, T. B., Rogers, P. J., & Kuiper, N. A. *The self as a cognitive prototype.* Unpublished manuscript, University of Calgary, 1978.

Rosch, E. Cognitive reference points. *Cognitive Psychology,* 1975, **1,** 532–547.

Rosch, E. Principles of categorization. In E. Rosch & B. B. Lloyd (Eds.), *Cognition and categorization.* Hillsdale, N.J.: Erlbaum, 1978.

Rosch, E., & Mervis, C. Family resemblances: Studies in the internal structure of categories. *Cognitive Psychology,* 1975, **7,** 573–605.

Rosch, E., Mervis, C., Gray, W., Johnson, D., & Boyes-Braem, P. Basic objects in natural categories. *Cognitive Psychology,* 1976, **8,** 382–439.

Rosenberg, S., & Sedlak, A. Structural representations of perceived personality trait relationships. In A. K. Romney, R. Shepard, & S. B. Nerlove (Eds.), *Multidimensional scaling* (Vol. 2). New York: Seminar Press, 1972.

Ross, L. The intuitive psychologist and his shortcomings: Distortions in the attribution process. In L. Berkowitz (Ed.), *Advances in experimental social psychology* (Vol. 10). New York: Academic Press, 1977.

Rothbart, M. *Judgmental heuristics in stereotype formation and maintenance.* Paper presented at the meetings of the American Psychological Association, San Francisco, August 1977.

Ruble, D. N., & Feldman, N. S. Order of consensus, distinctiveness, and consistency information, and causal attributions. *Journal of Personality and Social Psychology,* 1976, **34,** 930–937.

Ruble, D. N., Feldman, N. S., Higgins, E. T., & Karlovac, M. *Locus of causality and the use of information in the development of causal attributions.* Unpublished manuscript, Princeton University, 1978.

Rubovits, P. C., & Maehr, M. L. Pygmalion black and white. *Journal of Personality and Social Psychology*, 1973, **25**, 210-218.

Schank, R., & Abelson, R. *Scripts, plans, goals, and understanding.* Hillsdale, N.J.: Erlbaum, 1977.

Schneider, D. J. Implicit personality theory: A review. *Psychological Bulletin*, 1973, **79**, 294-309.

SCIP (Campus Computing Stanford University), *How to use Hiclus*, Stanford University, Stanford, Calif., 1976.

Shweder, R. A. How relevant is an individual difference theory of personality? *Journal of Personality*, 1975, **43**, 455-485.

Smith, E. E. Theories of semantic memory. In W. K. Estes (Ed.), *Handbook of learning and cognitive processes* (Vol. 5). Hillsdale, N.J.: Erlbaum, 1978.

Smith, E. E., Shoben, E. J., & Rips, L. J. Structure and process in semantic memory: A featural model for semantic decisions, *Psychological Review*, 1974, **81**, 214-241.

Snyder, M., & Cantor, N. Testing hypotheses about other people: The use of historical knowledge. *Journal of Experimental Social Psychology*, 1979, in press.

Snyder, M., & Cantor, N. *Thinking about ourselves and others: Cognitive processes in self-monitoring.* Unpublished manuscript, University of Minnesota and Princeton University, 1979.

Snyder, M., & Swann, W. Behavioral confirmation in social interaction: From social perception to social reality. *Journal of Experimental Social Psychology*, 1978, **14**, 148-162. (a)

Snyder, M., & Swann, W. Hypothesis-testing processes in social interation. *Journal of Personality and Social Psychology*, 1978, **36**, 1202-1212. (b)

Snyder, M., & Uranowitz, S. Reconstructing the past: Some cognitive consequences of person perception. *Journal of Personality and Social Psychology*, 1978, **36**, 941-950.

Snyder, M., Tanke, E. D., & Berscheid, E. Social perception and interpersonal behavior: On the self-fulfilling nature of social stereotypes. *Journal of Personality and Social Psychology*, 1977, **35**, 656-666.

Taylor, S. E., & Crocker, J. Schematic bases of social information processing. In E. T. Higgins, C. P. Herman, & M. P. Zanna (Eds.), *Social cognition: The Ontario Symposium on personality and social psychology.* Hillsdale, N.J.: Erlbaum, in press.

Taylor, S. E., Crocker, J., & D'Agostino, J. Schematic bases of social problem-solving. *Personality and Social Psychology Bulletin*, 1978, **4**, 447-451.

Taylor, S. E., & Fiske, S. T. Salience, attention, and attribution: Top of the head phenomena. In L. Berkowitz (Ed.), *Advances in experimental social psychology* (Vol. 1). New York: Academic Press, 1978.

Taylor, S. E., Fiske, S. T., Etcoff, N. L., & Ruderman, A. J. Categorical and contextual bases of person memory and stereotyping. *Journal of Personality and Social Psychology*, 1978, **36**, 778-793.

Tsujimoto, R. N. Memory bias toward normative and novel trait prototypes. *Journal of Personality and Social Psychology*, 1978, **36**, 1391-1401.

Tversky, A. Features of similarity. *Psychological Review*, 1977, **84**, 327-352.

Vernon, P. E. *Personality assessment: A critical survey.* New York: Wiley, 1964.

Vygotsky, L. S. *Thought and language.* Cambridge Mass.: MIT Press, 1965.

Walker, J. H. Real-world variability, reasonableness judgments, and memory representations for concepts. *Journal of Verbal Learning and Verbal Behavior*, 1975, **14**, 241-252.

Wason, P. C., & Johnson-Laird, P. N. *Psychology of reasoning: Structure and content.* Cambridge, Mass.: Harvard University Press, 1972.

Winer, B. J. *Statistical principles in experimental design.* New York: McGraw-Hill, 1971.

Wittgenstein, L. *Philosophical investigations.* New York: Macmillan, 1953.

Wyer, R. S., & Srull, T. K. Category accessibility: Some theoretical and empirical issues concerning the processing of social stimulus information. In E. T. Higgins, C. P. Herman, & M. P. Zanna (Eds.), *Social cognition: The Ontario Symposium on personality and social psychology,* Hillsdale, N.J.: Erlbaum, in press.

Zadeh, L. A. Fuzzy sets. *Information and control,* 1965, **8,** 338–353.

Zajonc, R. B. *Exposure effect and its antecedents.* Paper presented at the 86th annual meeting of the American Psychological Association, Toronto, August, 1978.

Zanna, M. P., & Pack, S. J. On the self-fulfilling nature of apparent sex differences in behavior. *Journal of Experimental Social Psychology,* 1975, **11,** 583–591.

Zuckerman, M. Use of consensus information in prediction of behavior. *Journal of Experimental Social Psychology,* 1978, **14,** 163–171.

A COGNITIVE–ATTRIBUTIONAL ANALYSIS OF STEREOTYPING[1]

David L. Hamilton

UNIVERSITY OF CALIFORNIA
SANTA BARBARA, CALIFORNIA

I. Introduction 53
II. Cognitive Biases *Resulting In* Stereotypic Conceptions 55
   A. Consequences of the Categorization Process............................. 55
   B. The Power of Stimulus Salience 59
   C. Conclusion... 64
III. Cognitive Biases *Resulting From* Stereotypic Conceptions 64
   A. Influence of Stereotypes on Causal Attributions 65
   B. Influence of Stereotypes on Processing Information about Persons.............. 68
   C. Influence of Stereotypes on Processing Information about Groups 72
   D. Conclusion... 75
IV. Behavioral Consequences of Stereotypes...................................... 76
V. Summary 79
   References 81

I. Introduction

Attribution theory is concerned with the cognitive processes involved in how perceivers generate causal explanations for behavior. For the last decade it has been the primary area of research activity within the broader domain of person perception. More recently, it has been a major contributing factor to the currently developing interest in "social cognition," the direct and explicit study of the cognitive processes involved in social psychological phenomena, such as person perception. In this paper I attempt to bring this literature to bear on a topic in person perception which has considerable social significance, namely, stereotyp-

[1]Preparation of this chapter was supported in part by NIMH Grant 29418 and was completed while the author was a visiting Research Associate at Harvard University. The author expresses his appreciation to Shelley Taylor and Mark Zanna for their comments on an earlier version of the manuscript.

ing. I attempt to show that an analysis of this topic from an attributional and social cognition perspective can greatly facilitate our understanding of the processes involved in stereotyping.

Since the early writing of Heider on attribution processes a major distinction has been drawn between internal attributions, or explanations of behavior in terms of the actor's dispositions, abilities, and motivational states, and external attributions, which explain behavior in terms of the situational forces influencing the actor. This distinction has played a central role in a number of theoretical accounts regarding attribution processes (e.g., Jones & Davis, 1965; Jones & Nisbett, 1972; Kelley, 1967; Weiner, Frieze, Kukla, Reed, Rest, & Rosenbaum, 1972). One of Heider's early insights was that perceivers appeared to be more heavily influenced, in making their attributions, by the behavior they observed an actor perform than by the situational and interpersonal constraints under which the behavior was performed. This tendency, which Heider referred to as "behavior engulfing the field" (Heider, 1958), results in the overattribution of behavior to internal, dispositional causes, even when quite reasonable explanations in terms of situational factors are readily available. Empirical support for this phenomenon has been obtained in a number of studies (e.g., Jones & Harris, 1967). Thus perceivers seem prone to making internal attributions.

At present we do not have a thorough knowledge of the conditions under which perceivers make internal as opposed to external attributions, although research testing the propositions of correspondent inference theory (Jones & Davis, 1965; Jones & McGillis, 1976) and actor/observer differences (e.g., Jones & Nisbett, 1972) has provided some understanding of this issue. For example, internal attributions and/or stronger dispositional inferences have been shown to be likely when the actor's behavior is out of role (e.g., Jones, Davis, & Gergen, 1961), or otherwise violates normative expectations (e.g., Jones & Harris, 1967), or is highly salient to the perceiver (e.g., Taylor & Fiske, 1975).

Stereotyping is said to occur when a perceiver makes inferences about a person because of that person's membership in some group. Thus, when a person's ethnicity serves as a cue which increases the likelihood of the perceiver making certain internal attributions about the person, then stereotyping has occurred. Until recently, relatively little was known about the cognitive processes involved in stereotyping. The recent surge of interest in a cognitive analysis of person perception has resulted in a number of studies which have increased our understanding of this issue. In this chapter I review this growing research literature in terms of three major topics. The first section summarizes evidence indicating that cognitive biases can *result in* the perceiver holding stereotypic conceptions of social groups; that is, cognitive mechanisms alone may be the foundation of perceived intergroup differences. The second topic concerns cognitive biases which *result from* the perceiver's holding stereotypic conceptions of social groups; that is, the existence of a stereotype in the perceiver's cognitive structure may bias his processing of information about, and hence attributions about, a member of the stereotyped group. The third section considers the question of what behavioral consequences result from the perceiver holding a stereotype of a particular group.

II.   Cognitive Biases *Resulting In* Stereotypic Conceptions

Historically, stereotyping has been discussed not in terms of cognitive processes but as a consequence of motivational, dynamic factors and/or of social-learning and acculturation processes (cf. Brigham, 1971; Hamilton, 1976). As noted by Ashmore and Del Boca (in press), the major metatheoretical orientations reflected in the stereotyping literature have been the psychodynamic orientation and the sociocultural orientation. The psychoanalytic approach, with its focus on the unconscious needs and drives of the individual, emphasizes the defensive, anxiety-reducing functions of stereotypic beliefs. Holding derogatory beliefs about members of some group, it is argued, can serve a psychic function for the perceiver, warding off anxieties and frustrations regarding the self through such mechanisms as projection and displacement. The sociocultural approach, in contrast, views stereotypic beliefs as a reflection of the culture or social milieu which has shaped one's experience and learning history. Stereotypes, then, are culturally conditioned.

The cognitive approach which underlies this contribution represents a somewhat different orientation. The notion that biases in the way we process information about others may, by themselves, result in the perception of intergroup differences is of relatively recent vintage. In this section I describe several studies which indicate means by which our normal cognitive functioning can produce differential perceptions of groups. This discussion is organized in terms of two central aspects characteristic of our cognitive processing mechanism whose importance in understanding social perception has only recently been fully recognized: the categorization of objects into groups and our responsiveness to salient or distinctive stimuli.

A.   CONSEQUENCES OF THE CATEGORIZATION PROCESS

It seems almost inherent in us to lump others we encounter into social groups: females and males; blacks and whites; Catholics, Protestants, and Jews; high occupational status and low occupational status others; those we find attractive and unattractive. As many writers have noted (e.g., Allport, 1954; Ehrlich, 1973), the categorization process is an essential component of stereotyping. Obviously differential perception of and response to different ethnic groups is not possible without first categorizing persons as belonging to one group or another. In the psychodynamic approach, this differentiation of persons according to their

ethnicity serves certain psychic needs of the perceiver. The sociocultural orientation views these categorizations, and the beliefs associated with them, as being
learned through the acculturation process. Thus, in and of itself, a recognition of
the importance of the categorization process is not new.

In the cognitive approach the perceiver's grouping of objects into equivalence
classes is viewed as a means of reducing the enormous complexity of the
stimulus world with which he is confronted. This categorization process is in
large part highly functional: It lends organization to our social world and probably facilitates retention of information about individual others. Moreover, to the
extent that persons grouped into the same class are in fact similar, such categorization increases our ability to anticipate what a particular member of that group is
like and how he is likely to behave. However, the cognitive assimilation of an
individual into a group can have distorting effects as well: It can lead us to "see"
things about the person that are not there and not to see other things that are there.
Several studies reported within the last few years demonstrate the consequences
of this process.

1.   Categorization into Ingroup and Outgroup

The effects of the mere categorization of persons into an "ingroup" and an
"outgroup" on interpersonal perception and behavior have been demonstrated in
a number of experiments. Since a thorough review of this research literature has
recently been published (Brewer, 1979), only the findings most relevant to the
present discussion are summarized here. In a number of studies (e.g., Allen &
Wilder, 1975; Billig & Tajfel, 1973; Tajfel, Billig, Bundy, & Flament, 1971)
subjects were divided into two groups, allegedly on the basis of their preferences
for paintings by different artists, but actually by random assignment. Subsequently, when subjects were asked to distribute monetary rewards to members
of their own and the other group, there was a strong bias favoring the ingroup at
the expense of the outgroup members: subjects not only allocated greater
amounts of money to their own group members but did so following a strategy
that would maximize the difference between groups in the amount of money
received. This differential responding to own- and other-group members was
based solely on group membership information, since no interaction either within
or between groups transpired and information about individual persons was minimal. Thus, merely identifying others as being in the same or a different group
can result in intergroup differentiation and discriminatory behavior.

This ingroup favoritism also exists at the perceptual/attributional level. For
example, Doise, Csepeli, Dann, Gouge, Larsen, and Ostell (1972) found that
individuals who were assigned to groups on an arbitrary basis rated members of
their own group more favorably than outgroup members on a variety of evaluative personal characteristics and even attributed more desirable physical characteristics to them. Using a similar procedure, Allen and Wilder (in press) found
that subjects attributed greater belief similarity to ingroup than to outgroup mem-

bers. The observed differences were quite pronounced, despite the fact that there was no information basis for these differential judgments. In another recent study, Howard and Rothbart (1978) arbitrarily created two groups of subjects on the basis of a dot estimation task, telling them they were either "underestimators" or "overestimators" and suggesting that this difference was related to some unspecified personality variables. Subjects were then given a set of 24 positive and 24 negative statements which presumably were self-descriptions made by previous subjects in the study. Subjects were asked to indicate whether they thought each of the self-descriptive statements had been made by an underestimator or by an overestimator. Howard and Rothbart (1978) found that subjects assigned significantly more of the positively valued items to their ingroup. On the whole, then, the findings of these studies indicate that ingroup favoritism is not dependent upon intergroup hostility, competition, etc., but is likely to occur (at least in mild form) simply as a result of the categorization process.

Wilder and Allen (1978) have shown that categorization into ingroup and outgroup is likely to influence what one subsequently learns about the others, as well. In this study subjects were either categorized into two groups (again on the basis of preferences for paintings), or not assigned to groups at all. Subjects were told that they would be having a discussion with the other participants. Prior to the discussion, each subject was given the opportunity to see information regarding the attitudes (relative to his own) of the other subjects, presumably based on an attitude survey subjects had completed earlier. In the "group" condition, the subject could choose to see information regarding his similarity to other members of his group, his dissimilarity with the ingroup, his similarity with the outgroup, or his dissimilarity with the outgroup. In the "aggregate" (no group assignment) condition this information was simply in reference to other individual subjects. The results showed that subjects in the group condition (but not in the aggregate condition) preferred to see information indicating their similarity with the ingroup and their dissimilarity with the outgroup. Thus, even a rather arbitrary basis for group composition is sufficient to create a cognitive structure of the social situation which the perceiver attempts to maintain by seeking information in support of the differentiation on which it is based.

2. Categorization of Others into Groups

The findings of Wilder and Allen's (1978) study suggest a mechanism by which the categorization process may produce biased perceptions of group members, such that within-group similarities and between-group dissimilarities would be exaggerated. While such intragroup assimilation and intergroup contrast effects have been suggested and/or assumed by many writers, good experimental evidence of the phenomenon in social perception is difficult to find.

Results of a study by Tajfel, Sheikh, and Gardner (1964) are suggestive. They had college students ask questions of two members of each of two ethnic groups regarding their views on films and books and then rate each of the four persons on a series of descriptive scales. Members of the same ethnic group were rated similarly on attribute scales reflecting the stereotype of that group.

More recent research by Taylor, Fiske, Etcoff, and Ruderman (1978) provides evidence that one consequence of this categorization process is that it makes within-group differentiations more difficult than between-group discriminations. Subjects in this experiment listened to a tape recording of a discussion among six men. As each person spoke, a slide showing that person was projected onto a screen. Three of the discussants were black and three were white. Following the group discussion, subjects were asked to identify which of the six participants had made various comments and suggestions during the discussion. Subjects made significantly more intrarace than interrace errors; i.e., they were somewhat accurate in remembering the race of the person who made most of the comments but had greater difficulty remembering which individual, black or white, had made each comment. Similar effects were obtained in a second experiment in which the stimulus group was half male and half female: subjects made more intrasex than intersex errors in recalling who had said what during a group discussion. Together, these studies provide compelling evidence that categorization according to salient social groupings is an important encoding strategy used by perceivers, one which can influence the processing and retention of information acquired about individuals (see also Taylor, in press).

The attributional consequences of categorizing others into groups has been shown in some recent experiments by Wilder (1976). In these experiments, subjects viewed a videotape of four persons discussing an issue. The participants were identified as belonging to one group (e.g., "discussion group J"), two groups ("discussion group J," "discussion group K"), or no group identification information was given (the participants were presented as an aggregate of individuals). In the discussion, after one individual expressed his opinion on the issue, the tape was stopped and subjects were asked what opinion they thought another of the discussants would express. In comparison with both the aggregate and the two-groups case (in which the first and second discussants belonged to different groups), significantly more subjects in the one-group condition predicted that the second stimulus person would express the same position as the first. They also rated the second person as more likely to have opinions similar to the first discussant. In contrast, subjects expected members of different groups to hold differing opinions, even though no indication was given that the distinction between the two groups would be reflected in the member's opinions. Thus, the subjects anticipated greater similarity among persons if they were members of the same group than if they were in an aggregate or belonged to different groups. In a similar experiment, subjects viewed the entire videotape in which all four discussants expressed their opinions. Subjects were told to pay particular attention to one of the participants, about whom questions would be asked subsequently. The target person either expressed the same position as the other three stimulus persons or advocated the alternative viewpoint, in opposition to the other three. Again, he was presented as being either a part of an aggregate or a member of a group. When a "group" member agreed with the other participants his behavior was perceived as being externally caused to a greater extent that the same behavior in the "aggregate" condition. However, subjects perceived the group member as more internally motivated than the "aggregate" person when he dissented from the view of others. Thus, the extent to which the perceiver construes an individual to be a part of a larger social entity can influence his causal attributions in understanding that person's behavior.

Any given person can be classified into any number of categories, depending on the criteria that are used. For example, at various times I might construe a friend of mine as belonging to the set of persons who are (a) males, (b) divorced, (c) psychologists, (d) extraverts, (e) tennis players, or (f) easy for me to work with. Obviously I do not use the same categorization scheme under all circumstances, yet the findings summarized above indicate that the person categories I employ at any given time influence what information I retain and what kinds of inferences I make about the persons I group into those categories. It therefore becomes important to understand the factors that determine what categories are likely to be employed by the perceiver, the conditions under which various alternative groupings are likely to be used, and the variables that influence the perceiver to change the basis of his social categorization process. This question has received little research attention to date, although it is clear that both stimulus properties and contextual cues have an influence on this process (Taylor *et al.*, 1978). One factor which has an important bearing on the categorization process, in addition to being important in its own right, is discussed in the next section.

B. THE POWER OF STIMULUS SALIENCE

Social psychologists have only recently become aware of the extent to which perceivers are responsive to the salient or distinctive elements of the stimulus field (McArthur, in press; Taylor & Fiske, 1978). The evidence is now rather convincing that, at the very least, perceivers are differentially attentive to salient or distinctive stimuli and that such differential attention can have pronounced influences on social perception.

The characteristics which differentiate significant social groups (such as sex or race) are often physically prominent and hence salient to an observer. In fact, without easily perceivable distinguishing cues, identification of group members would be difficult and use of stereotypic schemas would be inhibited. The easy availability of such cues is crucial to the categorization process discussed above. Certainly the sex, race, and age of another person are difficult to ignore; in addition, any kind of stigma, the clothes one wears (e.g., a uniform), and a host of other personal features are quite visible, and any of them, in the context of a number of other persons who do not share such a feature, constitutes a highly distinctive characteristic. If perceivers are differentially responsive to distinctive stimuli, it becomes important to consider the implications of this fact for the case when the salient stimulus is a group-identifying characteristic (race, sex, etc.). Such perceptual consequences have been explored in a number of recent studies.

1. Differential Attention to Salient Stimuli

The fact that perceivers attend more to a novel, distinctive stimulus than to a familiar, nondistinctive stimulus has been well known to cognitive psychologists for some time. Although interest in the implications of this fact for social perception is of more recent vintage, the evidence available indicates quite clearly that the same conclusion holds for the perception of persons. This point is clearly demonstrated in a series of studies by Langer, Taylor, Fiske, and Chanowitz (1976). They argued that a stigmatized other constitutes a novel stimulus for the perceiver and, therefore, that if the usual normative sanctions against staring at such persons were removed, persons would look at a stigmatized person more than at a "normal" person. Subjects were provided with an opportunity to look at a stigmatized person (a woman with a leg brace, a hunchbacked man, a pregnant woman) or a nonstigmatized person while either observed or unobserved by another person. The amount of time spent looking at the stimulus person was unobtrusively recorded. The presence of another person invoked a norm against staring at stigmatized others and resulted in subjects looking at the nonstigmatized person longer. However, when no others were present, and hence these sanctions were removed, subjects spent significantly more time looking at the stigmatized person.

The results of Langer et al. (1976) suggest that almost any novel, distinctive feature of a person will result in increased attention to that person, except when normative pressures preclude such staring. Since most stereotyped minority groups are characterized by what, for majority-group members, are unfamiliar and therefore distinctive features (a different skin color, a foreign accent, etc.), we may expect them also to be the object of differential attention from majority-group perceivers. Such an effect should be even more pronounced when, as is commonly true, the physically distinctive minority-group member is outnumbered in a social context by majority-group persons, thereby making his or her presence all the more salient.

It then becomes important to determine the perceptual and attributional consequences of the perceiver's differential attention to a distinctively identifiable person. Recent research by Taylor, Fiske, Close, Anderson, and Ruderman (1977) provides evidence on this point. Taylor et al. explored the consequences of a minority group member's being a "solo" or "token" member of a small group, for example, a black member of an otherwise all white group or a female in an otherwise all male group. Subjects listened to a tape recording of a discussion among six males. While a person was talking, a slide of that person was projected. By using the same tape but varying the race of the persons shown in the slides, Taylor *et al.* were able to compare observers' perceptions of a black when he was the only black member of the group with perceptions of him (i.e., same voice, same picture) when he was one of three blacks in the group (i.e., a fully integrated group). In the former case, his status as a "solo" in the group makes him more salient to the perceiver. In contrast to when he was in a fully integrated group, the solo black was perceived as having been more prominent in the group discussion, received more extreme ratings on evaluative trait scales, and was more likely to be perceived as having played a special role within the group. These findings were replicated in a second study in which perceptions of male and female solos were compared to reactions to the same person in a sexually integrated group. Thus the salience of a distinctively identifiable person, due to his/her solo status within a group context, can have profound effects on majority group perceptions of that individual. Other findings (Rooks & Jones, 1978) that white subjects make more polarized ratings of black, as compared to white, stimulus persons are consistent with this salience effect.

The findings of these studies demonstrate the power of highly salient stimuli in their influence on interpersonal perceptions. Subjects generally directed more attention at and made stronger inferences about a stimulus person who was made salient by some means. Given that members of most minority groups are identifiable by distinctive characteristics, and that they are often solos in social situations, these studies provide evidence for a cognitive processing mechanism by which minority persons are differentially perceived by majority-group observers.

2. *Illusory Correlations Based on Distinctive Stimuli*

Stereotypic statements about social groups usually are correlational. That is, they express the speaker's belief in the relationship between two variables, one having to do with group membership and the other being a psychological attribute (e.g., blacks are lazy, Jews are shrewd, accountants are perfectionistic, Italians are emotional). There has been surprisingly little research investigating the cognitive processes by which humans intuitively develop correlational concepts (Peterson & Beach, 1967), but the evidence that has accumulated indicates that these processes are subject to considerable bias (e.g., Chapman & Chapman, 1967, 1969; Jenkins & Ward, 1965; Smedslund, 1963; Ward & Jenkins, 1965). Forming a correlational concept requires an accumulation of instances of cooccurrence between variables, storage of this information over time, and accurate judgment as to the resulting degree of association. Given the complexity of the process, it is perhaps not surprising that such judgments are often erroneous. The accumulated evidence suggests that certain kinds of cooccurrences are noticed and encoded (if, for example, they confirm expectations or are salient for other reasons), while we appear to be insensitive to other kinds of evidence equally relevant to the assessment of covariation (for example, the occurrence of one variable and nonoccurrence of the other). Furthermore, subjective estimates of degree of association are based on retrieval of relevant instances from memory, a process also subject to distortion (Tversky & Kahneman, 1973). Several of these biases have been shown to operate in such a manner that the observer overestimates the strength of the relationship between two variables. If stereotypic attributions are in effect correlational judgments, then it becomes important to determine the extent to which these cognitive biases can result in distorted beliefs about members of social groups.

Hamilton and Gifford (1976) have provided evidence for one cognitive mechanism which can result in differential perceptions of majority and minority groups. Building on Chapman's (1967) work on illusory correlations, these authors reported two experiments showing that subjects overestimated the frequency of cooccurrence of stimulus categories which themselves were distinctive. In this case, distinctiveness was operationalized simply as the relative infrequency of certain categories of stimulus information. In both studies, subjects read a series of sentences describing behaviors performed by members of two groups, which were simply identified as Group A and Group B. For example, "John, a member of Group A, visited a sick friend in the hospital" is representative of the kind of sentences used. In both studies there were twice as many statements about members of Group A as there were about members of Group B; by its infrequency, then, Group B became a novel or distinctive stimulus characteristic. The behaviors described in the sentences were either moderately desirable or moderately undesirable. In the first study, desirable behaviors occurred much more frequently, while in the second experiment there were twice as many undesirable as desirable behaviors. Thus, in each study, the relative infrequency of one type of behavior would presumably make it more salient than the other, and the two studies differed primarily in whether desirable or undesirable behavior was thereby made distinctive. However, in each experiment the ratio of desirable to undesirable behaviors was the same for both groups, and because of this, no actual relationship existed between membership in a particular group and the desirability of the behaviors describing that group. Because of the hypothesized salience of the cooccurrence of distinctive stimulus categories, however, we expected that subjects would overestimate the frequency with which Group B—the smaller group—had been described by the infrequently occurring category of behavior.

After the series of sentences had been presented, subjects were given a list of the behavior descriptions and were asked to indicate the group membership of the person who had performed each behavior. From these data we could determine the extent to which subjects attributed the undesirable and desirable behaviors to the two groups, A and B. The results from this task, shown in Table I, provided strong support for our hypotheses. The upper part of the table shows, for each

TABLE I

COMPOSITION OF STIMULUS SETS AND ATTRIBUTIONS OF GROUP MEMBERSHIP FOR EXPERIMENTS 1 AND 2[a]

	Experiment 1			Experiment 2	
Behaviors	Group A	Group B	Behaviors	Group A	Group B
(a) Distribution of stimulus sentences					
Desirable	18	9	Desirable	8	4
Undesirable	8	4	Undesirable	16	8
(b) Mean attributions of group membership (conditional probabilities in parentheses)					
Desirable	17.52 (.65)	9.48 (.35)	Desirable	5.87 (.49)	6.13 (.51)
Undesirable	5.79 (.48)	6.21 (.52)	Undesirable	15.71 (.65)	8.29 (.35)

[a] Adapted from Hamilton and Gifford (1976).

experiment, the number of desirable and undesirable behaviors that described members of Groups A and B. The data obtained from the subjects are summarized in the lower part of the table. It can be seen that subjects grossly overestimated the extent to which the infrequent group—Group B—performed the "uncommon" type of behavior—undesirable behavior in Experiment 1, desirable behavior in Experiment 2. That is, while subjects' assignments of the "frequent" behaviors to the two groups closely approximated the actual distribution of stimulus sentences (two-thirds to Group A, one-third to Group B), in both experiments over half of the "uncommon" behaviors were attributed to Group B, despite the fact that only one-third of those behaviors had in fact described members of that group. These findings (and others discussed by Hamilton and Gifford) support the interpretation that the pairing of distinctive stimuli had particular salience for the subjects which resulted in their overestimating the frequency of occurrence of those stimulus events.

These results demonstrated that an illusory correlation was established, that is, subjects erroneously perceived a relationship between group membership and behavior desirability that did not exist in the information presented to them. Furthermore, other results from these studies indicated that this illusory correlation influenced the subjects' perceptions of the two groups. On a variety of trait scales, members of Group B were rated less favorably than members of Group A in Experiment 1 but more favorably than Group A in Experiment 2. Thus, a cognitive bias in the way information was processed resulted in differential perceptions of the two groups.

As Hamilton and Gifford (1976; Hamilton, in press) point out, these findings have implications for stereotype formation. Majority-group members usually have infrequent contact and experience with minority-group members, and certain forms of behavior (e.g., most undesirable behaviors) occur infrequently. Hamilton and Gifford's studies indicate that, even though the "uncommon" behavior may actually be no more characteristic of one group than the other, perceiver biases may result in the misattribution of these behaviors to the minority group, with consequent differential perceptions of the groups. The specific content of those differential perceptions presumably would depend on the nature of the "uncommon" behaviors which become perceived to be associated with the minority group. Those differential perceptions would then constitute the basis for stereotyping.

C. CONCLUSION

In this section we have discussed several biasing factors in our cognitive processing systems which, by themselves, can produce differential attributions about members of different groups. The differential perception of groups is the foundation on which the development of stereotypes is based. We have seen that certain cognitive biases may be sufficient, at least under some circumstances, to provide that foundation.

We do not presume to argue that all stereotypic conceptions of groups are based solely on such cognitive factors. Certainly, many of our beliefs about ethnic groups have been acquired through social-learning processes in the course of development. The extent to which these cognitive biases play a determining role in the creation of intergroup differentiations remains to be determined. Given that children are responsive to group-distinguishing features at a quite young age (Katz, 1976), the possibility that early conceptions of groups are significantly influenced by such cognitive factors seems quite plausible. While the resolution of this issue awaits further research, it appears likely that the contribution of these cognitive biases to the development of stereotypic concepts has been underestimated.

III.   Cognitive Biases *Resulting From* Stereotypic Conceptions

Regardless of their origins, it is clear that by the onset of adulthood all of us hold a diversity of stereotypic beliefs about various social groups. In this section we examine the consequences, for attributional and cognitive representational processes, of a perceiver's having a stereotypic conception of a particular group. It is obvious that the stereotypes we hold influence our perceptions of members of the stereotyped groups; indeed, this seems almost inherent in the concept of stereotype itself. The questions of importance for understanding the nature of stereotyping is how this influence comes about and how it is maintained.

The term "stereotype" is in essence a cognitive structural concept, referring to a set of expectations held by the perceiver regarding members of a social group. It is, then, similar to an implicit personality theory, in this case one's group membership being the stimulus cue on which a number of inferences about the person are based (Schneider, 1973). A stereotype can also be thought of as a structural framework in terms of which information about another is processed and hence has the properties of a schema, a concept of importance in recent research on attribution processes (e.g., Kelley, 1972) and related topics (e.g., Cantor & Mischel, 1977; Markus, 1977; Taylor & Crocker, in press). In the discussion that follows we review some of the research which has investigated these processes.

A. INFLUENCE OF STEREOTYPES ON CAUSAL ATTRIBUTIONS

If stereotypes bias the way in which we perceive members of social groups, it seems likely that such an influence would be manifested in our causal attributions regarding the behavior of such persons. As noted in the introduction to this contribution, attribution researchers have made a basic differentation between internal attributions, in which an actor's behavior is explained in terms of his or her dispositional characteristics, and external attributions, in which situational influences are perceived as causing the actor's behavior. It seems highly plausible that our stereotypic evaluations of and expectations about others influence the way in which we interpret such behavioral "evidence," and, if so, this would have implications for the maintenance and change of stereotypes. Consider, for example, the possibility that behaviors which confirm stereotypic expectations are attributed to the actor's dispositional characteristics, but that behaviors inconsistent with one's stereotype tend to be attributed to external factors. Since the stereotype reflects the perceiver's assumptions about the dispositional attributes of members of a particular group, this attributional bias would essentially prevent the perceiver from having to confront and cope with disconfirming evidence; after all, according to this attribution scheme, such behaviors are due to situational influences and do not reflect anything about the person. If such a perceptual distortion were present, as intuitively seems likely, the extreme persistence of stereotypes would be understandable.

A few studies investigating the attributional bias have been reported, although their number is surprisingly small. Taylor and Jaggi (1974), in an experiment conducted in India, investigated the effect of stereotype-based evaluative biases on causal attributions. Their subjects, all of whom were of the Hindu religion, rated the concepts "Hindu" and "Muslim" on a set of trait scales. These ratings showed that subjects have much higher evaluations of their own group than of the Muslims. Subjects were then given a series of stimulus paragraphs, each of which described an actor performing some behavior in a social context. In these descriptions the ethnic identification of the actor (Hindu or Muslim) and the desirability of his behavior were systematically varied, making four possible combinations which were represented an equal number of times in the stimulus series. For each descriptive paragraph, several possible reasons were presented for the actor's behavior, and subjects were asked to choose the best alternative. Analysis of the subjects' responses indicated that these Hindu subjects attributed the desirable behavior of Hindu actors to internal factors and their undesirable acts to external causes. In contrast, when the actor was identified as a Muslim, the opposite pattern of attributions occurred. Thus, salient ingroup–outgroup distinctions can influence one's attributions regarding the behavior of members of these groups.

The influence of stereotypic expectations on causal attributions has been further investigated in studies of sex stereotypes. Recently Deaux (1976) has discussed such effects in terms of a model formulated by Weiner, Frieze, Kukla, Reed, Rest, and Rosenbaum (1972). According to this framework, causal attributions vary in terms of two major dimensions—an internal/external dimension and a temporary/stable dimension. The type of causal attribution likely to be made is a function of the nature of the information available, in terms of these two dimensions. Combining the two dimensions into a 2×2 table yields four major categories of attribution, as shown in Table II. For example, behavior which was viewed as relatively stable and as due to internal factors would be explained in terms of the actor's ability; performance which was considered unstable (inconsistent) and influenced by internal causes would be viewed as reflecting the actor's effort or motivation; and so forth. This model has proved quite useful in research investigating achievement behavior (Weiner et al., 1972).

Building on this framework, Deaux (1976) has proposed that the successful or unsuccessful performance of an actor is evaluated by the perceiver in terms of the expectancies held by the perceiver regarding males and females, and that these combine in influencing the perceiver's attribution regarding that behavior. Specifically, she proposed that behavior which is consistent with expectations (success by a male on a masculinity-related task, such as one requiring mechanical skills) will be attributed to a stable rather than a temporary cause (usually ability). In contrast, performance inconsistent with stereotypic expectations will be attributed to a temporary cause (luck or effort). Results of several studies (e.g., Deaux & Emswiller, 1974; Feldman-Summers & Kiesler, 1974), summarized by Deaux (1976), have provided partial support for this interpretation, and the model warrants further investigation.

Ashmore and Del Boca (1976) have suggested an interesting interpretation of recent changes in stereotypic conceptions of blacks, an interpretation which is also easily understood in terms of the framework represented in Table II. Historically, the fact that disproportionate numbers of blacks are found at the lower

TABLE II

CLASSIFICATION OF CAUSAL ATTRIBUTIONS ACCORDING TO
STABILITY AND INTERNALITY/EXTERNALITY

	Internal	External
Stable	Ability	Task difficulty
Unstable	Effort	Luck

socioeconomic levels (i.e., they fail to succeed) was commonly interpreted as due to their innate intellectual inferiority. Public opinion surveys and studies of stereotypes, conducted over the past several decades, have shown that the number of whites subscribing to this belief in the innate inferiority of blacks has decreased considerably. However, since blacks continue to be overrepresented at the bottom of the socioeconomic ladder, among the unemployed, on welfare rolls, etc., the same behavioral fact remains and, according to attribution theory, needs to be "explained." In terms of the model shown in Table II, two options seem to be available to the naive theorist. One may recognize that, in order to achieve socioeconomic success, blacks face greater "task difficulty" than do whites, a quite plausible assumption in view of the discriminatory barriers, educational disadvantages, and poor "starting position" that are commonly experienced by blacks. This explanation emphasizes the role of relatively stable, external factors that can make success difficult to achieve. Alternatively, one may maintain the belief that the failure of blacks to rise socioeconomically is due to internal factors, but that these factors are of a motivational rather than an intellecual nature. According to this view, black poverty would not be viewed as a consequence of any innate difference from whites in their capability, or as a consequence of discriminatory practices which blacks face, but would be attributed to their lack of effort and the low aspirations they set for themselves. Since perceivers are inclined to make internal, dispositional attributions, even when credible situational explanations are readily available, it is perhaps not surprising that the belief that "blacks are lazy" continues to be a prominent characteristic in stereotypes of blacks. While this intuitive analysis within the framework of this model of causal attributions seems quite plausible, the author knows of no studies which have empirically tested this line of reasoning.

The concepts and findings discussed in this section suggest that stereotypic expectations about social groups may bias considerably the perceiver's attributions regarding the causes of a person's behavior when his or her membership in a particular group has been made salient. If, as some of these findings indicate, perceivers are more likely to make dispositional inferences (and less likely to make situational attributions) when the observed behavior is consistent with stereotypic expectations, this bias would in the long run result in subjective confirmation of those expectancies, even in the absence of actual support in the observed behavior. This, in turn, would contribute to the maintenance and persistence of the stereotype.

A full understanding of this relationship requires empirical investigation of the cognitive mediating processes that might underlie this effect; that is, if the schema-based expectancies do bias the perceiver's use of the information available to him, then it is important to determine at what point(s) in the cognitive processing system this bias is occurring. Recently, social psychologists have begun to directly investigate these mediating processes, adapting the techniques and methodologies of cognitive psychology in studying these cognitive mediators. Despite the "newness" of this research in social cognition, a number of recent findings bear directly on this issue, and in the next two subsections we examine this emerging literature.

B.   INFLUENCE OF STEREOTYPES ON PROCESSING INFORMATION ABOUT PERSONS

Stereotypic schemas conceivably could influence the processing of information about an individual member of a social group in any of several possible ways. For example, such expectancies may focus one's attention on a particular aspect of the person's behavior, thereby making that aspect of the stimulus field more salient; or they may lead the perceiver to interpret certain behaviors in a biased manner; or they may result in a selective retrieval of information from that which is stored in memory. Any of these is a reasonable possibility, as is any combination of them; such effects need not be limited to one stage of the process.

In addition to these influences on the processing of the information per se, stereotypic schemas may also lead the perceiver to go beyond that information in certain specifiable ways. As "prototypes" called up in response to certain stimulus cues, well-developed stereotypes may result in the perceiver "seeing" certain things which were not a part of the stimulus configuration, "filling in the gaps" in terms of the schema-based expectancies.

The notion that cognitive schemas can influence the learning and retention of the available material is far from new. Bartlett's (1932) early work was concerned specifically with this question. The current interest in social cognition has resulted in renewed investigation of these issues.

A number of recent studies have been concerned with the kinds of processes enumerated above. Some of them have focused on how such biases can influence the perception of members of stereotyped groups; other studies have not dealt specifically with this content but have reported findings that have clear implications for the effect of stereotypes on these processes. In this section I attempt to bring together these studies and evaluate their significance for understanding how stereotypes function.

The potentially important role of stereotypic schemas in the encoding process is suggested in an experiment by Duncan (1976). In this study white college student subjects watched a videotape in which two males discussed possible solutions to a problem. The subjects were led to believe that they were observing, over closed-circuit television, a "live" interaction taking place in another room. They were told that their job was to code, each time the experimenter gave a signal, the behavior which had just occurred according to a Bales-like category system. Several such signals were given during the interaction, the last one coming immediately after the discussion had become heated and one actor had given an "ambiguous shove" to the other. At that point the television screen went blank and the experiment was terminated.

The major independent variables were the race—black or white—of the two actors in the videotape, the protagonist and the victim. Four coding categories were used in categorizing the "shoving" incident—playing around, dramatizes, aggressive behavior, and violent behavior. How this behavior was interpreted by the observers was almost totally a function of the race of the protagonist: if he was white, the shove was viewed as playfulness or dramatization; if he was black, it was interpreted as aggressive or violent behavior. If these results are valid,[2] they have considerable significance for understanding the important influence of stereotypes on information processing. Stereotypic expectations influenced the manner in which the same behavior was interpreted. However, once a behavior has been interpreted and encoded in a particular way, its meaning for the perceiver is determined, the stereotypic expectation has been "confirmed," and the perceiver has received "evidence" that would support and maintain the preexisting conception of the stereotyped group.

While Duncan's (1976) research suggests a biasing effect of stereotypes on the encoding of information about others, other studies have focused on the influence that stereotypic schemas can have on what is retained about others. Cohen (1977) had subjects view a videotape of a woman, whom they had been told was either a waitress or a librarian, having dinner with her husband. Several characteristics stereotypic of librarians and of waitresses (e.g., appearance and clothing, food preferences) were incorporated into the stimulus tape. For example, according to previously obtained data regarding stereotypic expectations, perceivers expect a librarian to be more likely than a waitress to wear glasses, but they

[2]There is, unfortunately, a serious problem in the interpretation of these findings. It is difficult to guarantee that the behaviors portrayed in different stimulus tapes are equivalent in all importnat respects. The possibility remains, for example, that the "shove" given by the white actors was in fact more timid than that given by the black actors. In that case, the subjects' judgments might simply reflect actual behavior differences. To assure that the results are due to interpretational processes, evidence that the crucial behaviors were equivalent in all stimulus tapes is essential. Since none is provided, these results provide only tentative support for the hypothesis.

consider waitresses more likely than librarians to drink beer with a meal. Following the videotape, subjects were asked a number of factual questions regarding the content of the tape. For example, one item asked what the woman had to drink with her dinner, and subjects were to choose between two options, wine and beer. In each case, one of the two choices was stereotypic of librarians, the other of waitresses; and of course, only one was correct. Cohen predicted that subjects would be more likely to be accurate if the correct alternative was also stereotypic of the "occupational set" they had been given (i.e., instructions that the woman was a librarian or a waitress). The results provided partial support for the hypothesis. The predicted effect was quite strong for subjects given the "waitress" set, and this memory bias persisted for up to 1 week. Unexpectedly, subjects who were told that the woman was a librarian showed no differential recognition accuracy in an immediate test, although the results for subjects who were not tested until 1 week later followed the predicted pattern. While Cohen's predictions received only partial support, the findings are nevertheless suggestive and, like Duncan's study, indicate that further research investigating stereotype-based biases in the observation of ongoing behavior is warranted.

Though not concerned with stereotyping per se, a series of studies by Zadney and Gerard (1974) is quite germane to this issue. In these experiments subjects were shown a videotape in which a number of the behaviors enacted and statements made by the participants could be readily interpreted in terms of several possible intentions which might be attributed to the actors. Different groups of subjects were given instructions which attributed one or another of the possible intentions to the actors. The results of these studies showed a tendency for intent-related information to be recalled better then behaviors and statements which were relevant to the other possible interpretations. One of the experiments demonstrated that this effect was observed only when the intention-inducing instructions were given prior to viewing the videotapes; when this manipulation followed presentation of the tape there was little evidence of biased recall. This pattern of findings suggests that the biasing effect of attributed intentions occurred primarily during the encoding phase rather than during the retrieval of information from memory.

Several recent papers have discussed the manner in which cognitive schemas influence the processing of information about persons. While these studies have not been concerned with stereotyping per se, they have straightforward implications for this topic since the cognitive structures investigated in them are conceptually similar to stereotypes. These studies have to do with the effect of "prototypes" (e.g., Cantor & Mischel, 1977, 1979), "schemas" (e.g., Markus, 1977; Taylor & Crocker, in press), or "scripts" (e.g., Abelson, 1976) on the processing of information about others.

Cantor and Mischel (1977, 1979, in press) have suggested that people hold well-developed conceptions of certain personality types (such as "extraverts") which they refer to as prototypes. A prototype consists of a network of traits and behavior patterns characteristic of that type, as well as situations in which that type of person is likely to manifest those behaviors. Cantor and Mischel argue that information acquired about others is coded, structured, and stored in terms of these prototypes, with the consequence that information consistent with a prototype is most likely to be remembered, while information inconsistent with these prior expectations is least likely to be retained. Results from their experiments support this notion. On a free-recall task subjects recalled more information consistent with the prototype (Cantor & Mischel, in press), and on a recognition memory task subjects made more errors in the "recognition" of items that were prototypic but which had not been presented (Cantor & Mischel, 1977). Findings similar to these reflecting the role of self-schemas in processing information about oneself have been reported by Markus (1977).

If we recognize that a prototype of, for example, extraverts is conceptually the same as a stereotype of an ethnic group, then the implications of these findings for stereotyping becomes clear. As was true in Cohen's (1977) research, the prototype biased the perceiver's cognitive representation of a person in a direction consistent with the prior expectations based on that prototype. As a result, the perceiver has gained subjective "evidence" for the validity of the prototype.

The exact locus of the effects reported in these studies remains unclear. To mention just two of the possibilities cited earlier, stereotypes may bias the encoding process, such that the information which "fits" with the prototypic conception is more likely to enter the cognitive system. This suggests that some information is not being attended to or acquired. Alternatively, it may be that all of the information is registered but that a stereotype has its primary influence on the retrieval of information, a process that would also bias recall and judgment measures. Of course, both processes may occur.

While most discussions imply the former process (e.g., Duncan, 1976; Zadney & Gerard, 1974), there is also some evidence that the latter bias may also exist. Kanungo and Dutta (1966; Dutta, Kanungo, & Freibergs, 1972) have shown that subjects are more likely to remember desirable information about their own group and undesirable information about an outgroup. They report evidence suggesting that this bias occurs during retrieval of information from memory. In a more direct examination of a retrieval bias, Snyder and Uranowitz (1978) had subjects read an extensive "case history" of a female character named Betty. The case history spanned Betty's childhood, education, and adult career and included material regarding her home life, relations with her parents, social life, and so on. Subjects returned a week later and were given a recognition memory test on various details of the character description. Before this test was given, half of the subjects were told that Betty was now living a lesbian lifestyle, while the other half were told she was living a heterosexual lifestyle. This information had a significant effect on subjects' performance on the recognition memory task. Subjects' memory for the details of Betty's life were biased in the direction consistent with this instruction. Assuming that subjects had differing stereotypic conceptions of lesbian versus heterosexual females, it appeared that subjects reconstructed the information they had received in a manner consistent with the prototype which had been activated prior to this task. This evidence indicates that retrieval processes can be biased in the same manner as the initial processing of information.

C. INFLUENCE OF STEREOTYPES ON PROCESSING INFORMATION ABOUT GROUPS

The research described in the preceding two sections was concerned with how a stereotype about a particular group could influence a perceiver's cognitive representation of and attributions about individual members of that group. A question of obvious importance for understanding stereotyping concerns how stereotypes influence the cognitive processes involved in making judgments about groups. That is, one might observe or acquire information about a number of individuals who belonged to a particular social group. If one has certain stereotypic expectations about that group, does that conception of the group influence the processing of the information about individual group members in such a way that subsequent judgments are biased? The findings of some recent studies suggest an affirmative answer to this question.

Hamilton and Rose (1978; Hamilton, 1977) have reported evidence bearing on this issue. This work was based on research on illusory correlations in judgment processes, and as such, focused on processes which result in errors in an observer's perception of the degree of relationship between two variables. In an earlier section, research by Hamilton and Gifford (1976) was described, in which an illusory correlation based on the cooccurrence of distinctive or salient events was demonstrated. Hamilton and Rose have investigated the role of associative relationships between variables as a basis for an illusory correlation.

Several studies have shown that subjects tend to overestimate the frequency with which associatively linked stimulus pairs have occurred in a stimulus list (e.g., Chapman, 1967; Chapman & Chapman, 1967, 1969; Tversky & Kahneman, 1973). For example, in a study in which each pair in a series of word pairs was shown to subjects an equal number of times, subjects consistently estimated that pairs having a meaningful or associative relationship (e.g., "bacon–eggs") had occurred more frequently than unrelated pairs (Chapman, 1967). Hamilton and Rose (1978) suggest that this pattern is conceptually the same as the effects of stereotypic associations on processing information about members of social groups (see also Hamilton, in press). That is, if one has acquired the belief that blacks are more likely than whites to be lazy, then information consistent with that expectation is likely to be salient and hence be more available (Tversky & Kahneman, 1973) for recall and therefore influential in judgment processes.

Thus, even in the absence of any actual difference between blacks and whites in the extent to which laziness is manifested in their behavior, the perceiver would "see" a relationship between race and this category of behavior.

To investigate this possibility, Hamilton and Rose (1978) showed subjects a series of sentences, each of which described a person, identified by first name and occupation, as having two personality attributes; for example, "Sue, a waitress, is attractive and loud." On the basis of pretesting, traits rated as highly descriptive of one occupational group, but not of the others included in the sentences, could be identified. In one study, the 24 sentences described members of three groups, e.g., librarians, stewardesses, and waitresses. Within the set of sentences, each group occurred eight times, and each of eight traits described a member of each group twice. Thus, in the stimulus materials there were no actual relationships between trait characteristics and group membership. Among the eight trait words, two had been rated as highly characteristic of librarians, two of stewardesses, two of waitresses, and two were unrelated to any of the three groups. After they had viewed the sentences, subjects were given a questionnaire asking how many times each trait adjective had described each group. The results, shown in Table III, indicate that stereotypic expectations significantly influenced these frequency estimates. In this table, the rows represent the three occupational groups and the columns represent the grouping of adjectives according to their stereotypic association. The data are collapsed across the two traits of

TABLE III

MEAN FREQUENCY ESTIMATES OF OCCUPATION-ASSOCIATED TRAITS FOR EACH OCCUPATIONAL GROUP

(a) Replication 1: Female occupations

Occupational group	Occupation-associated traits			
	Librarian	Stewardess	Waitress	None
Librarians	2.83	2.01	2.39	2.24
Stewardesses	2.13	2.65	2.42	2.08
Waitresses	2.13	2.42	2.81	2.03

(b) Replication 2: Male occupations

Occupational group	Occupation-associated traits			
	Accountant	Doctor	Salesman	None
Accountants	2.50	1.96	2.18	2.44
Doctors	2.29	2.67	2.40	2.11
Salesmen	1.75	1.82	3.07	2.58

each type. The values shown are the mean number of times an adjective of each type was estimated to have described a particular group. The correct answer for every cell in the table is 2.00. Our prediction was that the italicized entries would be the largest values in that row and column; that is, that subjects would overestimate the frequency with which stereotypically expected descriptions had occurred. The results provide strong support for this hypothesis.

As noted above, the trait characteristics were totally uncorrelated with group membership in the stimulus sentences used in this study, a situation which probably is rare in "real" social information. Would this bias also be observed if some attributes were in fact related to the group membership variable? To answer this question, Hamilton and Rose (1978) conducted a second experiment in which the trait descriptors were correlated with group membership. The findings show that when an attribute describes one group more frequently than another, subjects are much more likely to recognize that relationship if that attribute is consistent with stereotypic expectations than if the trait is unrelated to the group stereotype. Thus, while the preceding study shows that stereotypes can lead a perceiver to "see" a nonexistent relationship, this study indicates that when an actual relationship exists it will be perceived as stronger if it confirms stereotypic expectations. Finally, results of a third experiment showed that, at least under some conditions, subjects underestimated the frequency with which information incongruent with a group stereotype occurred in a stimulus set, relative to attributes unrelated to the stereotype.

Similar findings have been reported by Rothbart, Evans, and Fulero (in press). Rather than utilizing groups about whom subjects would likely share stereotypic expectancies, Rothbart induced specific expectancies in subjects by telling them that the members of the stimulus group were either "more intellectual than average" or "more friendly and sociable than average." Subjects then read a series of sentences describing members of the group. In the set of sentences, "intelligent" and "friendly" behaviors were equally frequent. Similar to Hamilton and Rose's findings, subjects given the "intelligent" set estimated that more "intelligent" than "friendly" behaviors had described group members, while the opposite pattern was shown by subjects given the "friendly" instructions. In addition, on a free-recall task, subjects were able to remember more sentences congruent with the instruction-based expectations. Thus, this rather simple "set" manipulation resulted in substantial differences in the subjects' conceptions of the group, despite the fact that both groups of subjects read the identical set of descriptive sentences.

Taken together, the findings of these experiments by Hamilton and Rose and by Rothbart *et al.* clearly reveal the extent to which a group stereotype can bias the processing of information about members of that group. Subjects overestimated the frequency with which the information they received confirmed their stereotypic expectations and underestimated the frequency of occurrence of disconfirming evidence. Thus, as in other studies described earlier, these subjects were "seeing" evidence that would confirm their stereotypes and "not seeing" incongruent information, even when there was no relationship between the pattern of trait descriptions and the group memberships.

An interesting study by Gurwitz and Dodge (1977) indicates that the pattern of confirming and disconfirming information received about group members can influence its impact on stereotypic inferences. Subjects in this experiment learned information about three friends of a target person, about whom they were then asked to make inferences. The four persons were members of a stereotyped group. Some of the information describing the target persons' friends either confirmed or disconfirmed the stereotype, and that information was either distributed across the descriptions of the three friends or was confined to the description of one of the friends. The extent to which subjects made stereotypic attributions about the target person was determined. Confirming evidence increased stereotyping more when it was dispersed across the three descriptions, but disconfirming evidence had greater impact (i.e., reduced stereotypic inferences) when it was concentrated in one of the descriptions. Thus, the pattern of information, as well as its confirming or disconfirming nature, can influence the extent to which perceivers make stereotypic attributions.

D. CONCLUSION

In this section we have summarized research evidence elucidating a number of cognitive biases in our processing of information which result from the stereotypic schemas we hold about significant social groups. In reviewing studies concerned with causal attributions, processing information about individuals, and making judgments about groups, we have consistently found evidence indicating that stereotypic expectations bias the processing and interpretation of information in the direction of confirming those expectations. The consistency of this finding across numerous studies focusing on different processes is impressive and suggests that stereotypic schemas can have powerful and widespread consequences.

Yet, it would be unwise to conclude that information is always bent, folded, and spindled in the direction of schematic confirmation. Behavioral evidence which is not congruent with expectations cannot always be ignored or dismissed; in fact, under some conditions the very incongruency of information with expectancies may increase its salience and hence its impact, resulting in a change in one's cognitive structure.

Such an interpretation was proposed by Hamilton and Bishop (1976) to account for the reactions of white suburban home owners to the integration of their neighborhoods. In this study, residents of white neighborhoods into which a new family (in some cases black, in other cases white) had just moved were interviewed at various times over the course of a year. A variety of attitudinal and

behavioral measures obtained from the interviews indicated that an initial negative reaction to new black neighbors changed over time into an acceptance of this
family's living in their area and more favorable racial attitudes. Since the extent
of actual interracial interaction was unrelated to attitude change, the contact hypothesis could not account for these findings. Hamilton and Bishop (1976) suggested that the observed changes over time were due to a disconfirmation of
expectancies:

> This interpretation would hold that white suburban residents oppose the integration of their
> neighborhoods and expect and fear such integration to have undesirable consequences.
> Many of their expectations are probably stereotypic in nature and based on widely-shared
> myths—that blacks will not take care of their property, that their yards will be messy, that
> they pose a threat to personal safety, that their children will be "rough," that property
> values will decline, etc. Over time, the experience of having black neighbors serves to
> disconfirm many of these expectations—the appearance of the neighborhood has not
> changed, physical assault and other forms of violence have not occurred, real estate prices
> have continued to climb as in similar neighborhoods, etc. The disconfirmation of these
> negative expectancies thus results in a change in the residents' beliefs about and attitudes
> towards blacks and towards neighborhood integration. (p. 66)

A pattern of findings based on a variety of dependent measures supported this
interpretation.

While the Hamilton and Bishop (1976) study was not concerned with
stereotypes per se, its findings are useful in demonstrating that information
inconsistent with expectancies can have rather dramatic effects on one's cognitions. Thus, disconfirming evidence will have differing effects, depending on the
circumstances. A delineation of the conditions under which we can expect
stereotype-incongruent information to have lesser and greater influences on our
cognitive representations is an important issue that future research needs to
address.

IV. Behavioral Consequences of Stereotypes

The discussion to this point has focused almost exclusively on processes and
phenomena which function or reside in the head of the perceiver. In the picture
drawn so far, the human being has been portrayed as a busy, if not totally
accurate, cognizer of the stimulus world around him. Little has been said about
interpersonal behavior, yet an issue which obviously is of crucial importance
concerns the relationship of these cognitions to real world behavior. In their
enthusiasm for studying the cognitive dynamics which underly the attribution
process, social psychologists have perhaps been too willing to simply assume
that these cognitive contortions do in fact have behavioral consequences. As a
result, cognitive social psychologists have been open to criticism (e.g.,
Thorngate, 1976), and the reader will note the relative paucity of research de-

scribed in this, compared to the two preceding sections. Nevertheless, I discuss here several recent experiments which clearly illustrate some processes by which stereotypic attributions are translated into significant behavioral consequences.

The notion that a person's expectancies can unintentionally influence one's behavior is not new and has been the subject of a considerable amount of research in recent years (e.g., Rosenthal, 1966; Rosenthal & Jacobson, 1968). The possibility that expectancies based on racial stereotypes can result in differential behavior toward blacks and whites was investigated by Rubovits and Maehr (1973). They had female undergraduates enrolled in a teacher training course teach a lesson to four junior high school students of comparable ability. Immediately prior to the session, each teacher was given a seating chart which provided each student's first name and IQ score and indicated whether the student was from the school's gifted program or from the regular track. Each session included two black and two white students, and one student of each race was randomly assigned a high IQ score and the "gifted" label. During the 40-min teaching session an observer coded the teacher's behavior according to several categories of student–teacher interaction. Analyses of these codings indicated that "black students were given less attention, ignored more, praised less and criticized more" (Rubovits & Maehr, 1973, p. 217). Moreover, these effects were somewhat augmented in the case of the gifted black student. The results of this field experiment provide rather dramatic evidence of the effect of racial cues on interpersonal behavior.

Three recent experiments provide compelling evidence of how stereotypes can be maintained through the self-fulfilling nature of their influence on social interaction. In a study by Word, Zanna, and Cooper (1974), white college students acted as job interviewers with either black or white confederates as job applicants. They found that the nonverbal behavior of the interviewer/subjects reflected less positive affect and friendliness in the presence of the black than the white confederates. That is, in comparison to the white confederate condition, subjects interacting with a black applicant maintained greater interpersonal distance, made more speech errors, and terminated the interview sooner. In a follow-up experiment, white confederates were trained to act as interviewers and to reproduce the nonverbal behavior patterns which in the first study had been expressed toward the black and the white applicants. Subjects in this experiment, all of whom were white, played the role of job applicants and were videotaped during the interview sessions. From these videotapes, judges later rated the adequacy of the subject/applicant's performance and his composure during the interview. Subjects who received the less positive pattern of nonverbal behavior from the interviewer (as had the black applicants in the first experiment) received significantly lower ratings of both performance and demeanor from the naive judges. Taken together, these experiments nicely demonstrate that the differential nonverbal behavior of whites in the presence of black and white others can produce behavior in those others which results in lower evaluations of the blacks.

In other words, the nonverbal behavior of the white interviewer would itself produce reciprocal behavior in the black, which would confirm the white's stereotypic expectancies.

More recently, Snyder, Tanke, and Berscheid (1977) have reported a similar demonstration of the self-fulfilling nature of stereotypes. They had male subjects interact with female target persons in a study purportedly concerned with the acquaintance process. One male and one female subject reported to separate experimental rooms. The male was given a snapshot of either an attractive or an unattractive female and was told that it was a picture of the other subject. In actuality, the same pictures were used throughout the experiment. Consistent with a considerable amount of research showing perceivers assume that "beautiful people are good people" (cf. Berscheid & Walster, 1974), the male subjects given the picture of an attractive female made much more favorable trait ratings of their partner than did those given the picture of an unattractive female. Thus, differing patterns of stereotypic expectations were created by this manipulation. The two subjects then carried on a "get acquainted" conversation over the telephone, during which each participant's voice was separately recorded on a tape recorder. Independent judges, unaware of the hypotheses or manipulations, rated the conversational behavior of the female on a variety of scales. Female targets whom their male partners had been led to believe were physically attractive were rated as having manifested more animation, confidence, and enjoyment in their conversation and greater liking for their male partners than did women whose perceivers believed they were unattractive. They were also rated as more sociable, poised, sexually warm, and outgoing than were the targets whose male partners perceived them to be unattractive. Thus the females behaved in such a way that would confirm the artificially induced expectations of their male partners. Subsequent analyses suggested that the males' expectations about their partners (based on physical attractiveness stereotypes) influenced their own behavior (i.e., males who thought they were talking with an attractive female were more animated, sociable, etc.), and that this in turn produced in the targets the very behaviors that would be expected from the males' stereotypic conceptions.

A somewhat different self-fulfilling mechanism has been demonstrated by Zanna and Pack (1975). In this experiment, female subjects expected to interact with a male subject in a study of impression formation. From information provided about their partner, subjects were led to believe that he would be either desirable or undesirable as a potential date, and that he held either a traditional or a nontraditional stereotype of the "ideal woman." On both attitudinal and behavioral indicators of self-presentation, when the partner was desirable, subjects portrayed themselves as being conventional or unconventional with regard to sex roles, depending on whether the males' stereotype of women was traditional or not. Thus, as in the Word et al. (1974) and Snyder et al. (1977) studies, the behavior of one person has been indirectly influenced in such a way as to confirm a stereotype held by another person.

There is, however, a difference between Zanna's and Pack's and the two previous demonstrations of the self-fulfilling nature of social stereotypes. In the Word *et al.* and Snyder *et al.* experiments, the stereotype holder's expectations presumably influenced his own behavior, which in turn created the stereotype-confirming behavior in the target person. In contrast, subjects in the Zanna and Pack (1975) study modified their own behavior in accordance with their perceptions of the stereotypic beliefs of a valued other.

Of course, it is not always the case that a person's expectancies will bring about confirming behavior in another person. There are instances when another's behavior clearly violates our stereotypic beliefs. How the perceiver reacts in these circumstances has not been extensively investigated. Earlier we suggested that disconfirmation of stereotypic expectancies might, under some conditions, result in a revision of one's beliefs (Gurwitz & Dodge, 1977; Hamilton & Bishop, 1976). A quite different possibility is suggested by the research of Costrich, Feinstein, Kidder, Marecek, and Pascale (1975). They report a series of three experiments in which subjects interacted with, listened to a tape of, or read about a male or a female stimulus person who acted in a passive or an aggressive manner. They reasoned that the passive male and the aggressive female represented instances of sex-role reversals and hence violated the stereotypic expectancies of the subjects. Costrich *et al.* (1975) report evidence showing that these stimulus persons were liked less, judged less popular, and rated as more likely to need therapeutic help than those whose behavior conformed to sex-role stereotypes. Thus, the person whose behavior does not "fit" into well-established, and therefore expected, patterns can receive rather harsh judgment from the typical perceiver.

The studies summarized in this section have shown that stereotypic beliefs can have an effect on social interaction in several ways. Stereotypic expectations can influence the perceiver's own behavior toward a member of the stereotyped group (Rubovits & Maehr, 1973; Snyder *et al.*, 1977; Word *et al.*, 1974); that behavior, which has been affected by stereotypic beliefs, can have an influence on the nature of the behavior manifested by the target person (Snyder *et al.*, 1977; Word *et al.*, 1974); and the target's behavior can be modified by his or her perception of the stereotypic expectations held by the perceiver (Zanna & Pack, 1975). Finally, one's stereotypes, when used as a basis for judging others, can result in negative evaluations of one who manifests counterstereotypic behavior (Costrich *et al.*, 1975).

V. Summary

The cognitive–attributional analysis of stereotyping presented in this contribution has revealed the significant role of cognitive mechanisms at several possible points in the overall attribution process. We have discussed evidence indicating that cognitive processing factors alone can result in the perceiver making differential attributions about members of different groups, attributions which could be the basis of stereotypic conceptions of those groups. We have seen that stereotypes, as cognitive schemas, can influence the encoding, interpretation, retention, and retrieval of subsequently obtained information about members of stereotyped groups, as well as the perceiver's causal attributions regarding the target person's behavior. The cognitive biases evidenced in these processes were consistently of such a nature that the perceiver would "see" evidence that confirmed his stereotypic expectations, even in the total absence of such confirming evidence. And finally, we have seen that the perceiver's stereotypic conceptions of another person can bring about behavior in the other that in fact confirms his expectations based on that stereotype.

One of the primary characteristics of stereotypes is their rigidity, persistence over time, and resistance to change (Ashmore & Del Boca, in press; Brigham, 1971). As construed from the psychodynamic perspective, this rigidity can be understood in terms of the functional value of the stereotypic beliefs for the perceiver. To the extent that they provide gratification for unconscious needs or reflect the ego-defensive processing of the perceiver, they are likely to be highly resistant to change. According to the sociocultural approach this persistence is understood in terms of the cultural basis of the stereotypic beliefs. As long as the stereotype remains a part of the person's culture or subculture, the individual is reinforced for holding those beliefs. Since cultural mores are slow in changing, it is not surprising that stereotypes are so stable.

The cognitive orientation presented in this chapter provides a new perspective for understanding why stereotypes are so persistent over time and resistant to change. Throughout this chapter we have discussed a number of cognitive biases which have bearing on the stereotyping process. In virtually every case the nature of these biases has been such that their effect is to maintain the stereotypic belief; that is, the perceiver "sees" or creates evidence which seemingly indicates that the stereotypic schema employed is indeed useful and appropriate. Thus, use of the stereotype serves to reinforce its apparent usefulness. A stereotype's persistence, then, is a natural consequence of the biases inherent in its employment.

The cognitive viewpoint is a functional viewpoint. That is, the cognitive mechanisms we use continue to be employed because, in some sense, they work. The biases we have discussed help reduce the complexity of a stimulus world which may otherwise be overwhelming and hence are in many circumstances quite adaptive. Recognition of this fact presents a rather depressing dilemma: If these biases are so functionally useful in the sense just noted, how will we be able to change them in those instances when they have undesirable consequences, as in stereotyping? A cognitive mechanism which in general has adaptive value would seem to be extremely resistant to change. This is an obviously important issue for which there is no answer at present. The major reason for our inability to address this question lies, we believe, in the newness of this field of research.

The development of social cognition as an area of investigation has, to this point, focused on demonstrations of the kinds of biases which characterize us as information processors. One of the primary challenges facing researchers in this field is the question of how these biases can be altered or modified in those cases where they yield consequences which reduce, rather than facilitate, our effectiveness as social beings. It is our hope that this question will receive the research attention it warrants in the near future.

REFERENCES

Abelson, R. P. Script processing in attitude formation and decision making. In J. S. Carroll & J. W. Payne (Eds.), *Cognition and social behavior*. Hillsdale, N.J.: Erlbaum, 1976.

Allen, V. L., & Wilder, D. A. Categorization, belief similarity, and intergroup discrimination. *Journal of Personality and Social Psychology,* 1975, **32**, 971–977.

Allen, V. L., & Wilder, D. A. Group categorization and attribution of belief similarity. *Small Group Behavior,* in press.

Allport, G. W. *The nature of prejudice*. Cambridge, Mass.: Addison-Wesley, 1954.

Ashmore, R. D., & Del Boca, F. K. Psychological approaches to understanding intergroup conflict. In P. A. Katz (Ed.), *Towards the elimination of racism*. New York: Pergamon, 1976.

Ashmore, R. D., & Del Boca, F. K. Conceptual approaches to stereotypes and stereotyping. In D. L. Hamilton (Ed.), *Cognitive processes in stereotyping and intergroup behavior*. Hillsdale, N.J.: Erlbaum, in press.

Bartlett, F. C. *Remembering*. Cambridge, England: Cambridge University Press, 1932.

Berscheid, E., & Walster, E. Physical attractiveness. In L. Berkowitz (Ed.), *Advances in experimental social psychology* (Vol. 7). New York: Academic Press, 1974.

Billig, M., & Tajfel, H. Social categorization and similarity in intergroup behavior. *European Journal of Social Psychology,* 1973, **3**, 27–52.

Brewer, M. B. Ingroup bias in the minimal intergroup situation: A cognitive-motivational analysis. *Psychological Bulletin,* 1979, **86**, 307–324.

Brigham, J. C. Ethnic stereotypes. *Psychological Bulletin,* 1971, **76**, 15–38.

Cantor, N., & Mischel, W. Traits as prototypes: Effects on recognition memory. *Journal of Personality and Social Psychology,* 1977, **35**, 38–48.

Cantor, N., & Mischel, W. Prototypes in person perception. In L. Berkowitz (Ed.), *Advances in experimental social psychology* (Vol. 12). New York: Academic Press, 1979.

Cantor, N., & Mischel, W. Prototypicality and personality: Effects on free recall and personality impressions. *Journal of Research in Personality,* in press.

Chapman, L. J. Illusory correlation in observational report. *Journal of Verbal Learning and Verbal Behavior,* 1967, **6**, 151–155.

Chapman, L. J., & Chapman, J. P. Genesis of popular but erroneous psychodiagnostic observations. *Journal of Abnormal Psychology,* 1967, **72**, 193–204.

Chapman, L. J., & Chapman, J. P. Illusory correlation as an obstacle to the use of valid psychodiagnostic signs. *Journal of Abnormal Psychology,* 1969, **74**, 271–280.

Cohen, C. *Cognitive basis of stereotyping*. Paper presented at the meeting of the American Psychological Association, San Francisco, August 1977.

Costrich, N., Feinstein, J., Kidder, L., Marecek, J., & Pascale, L. When stereotypes hurt: Three studies of penalties for sex-role reversals. *Journal of Experimental Social Psychology,* 1975, **11**, 520–530.

Deaux, K. Sex: A perspective on the attribution process. In J. H. Harvey, W. J. Ickes, & R. F. Kidd (Eds.), *New directions in attribution research* (Vol. 1). Hillsdale, N.J.: Erlbaum, 1976.

Deaux, K., & Emswiller, T. Explanations of successful performance on sex-linked tasks: What is skill for the male is luck for the female. *Journal of Personality and Social Psychology,* 1974, **29,** 80–85.

Doise, W., Csepeli, G., Dann, H. D., Gouge, C., Larsen, K., & Ostell, A. An experimental investigation into the formation of intergroup representations. *European Journal of Social Psychology,* 1972, **2,** 202–204.

Duncan, B. L. Differential social perception and attribution of intergroup violence: Testing the lower limits of stereotyping of blacks. *Journal of Personality and Social Psychology,* 1976, **34,** 590–598.

Dutta, S., Kanungo, R. N., & Freibergs, V. Retention of affective material: Effects of intensity of affect on retrieval. *Journal of Personality and Social Psychology,* 1972, **23,** 64–80.

Ehrlich, H. J. *The social psychology of prejudice.* New York: Wiley, 1973.

Feldman-Summers, S., & Kiesler, S. B. Those who are number two try harder: The effect of sex on attributions of causality. *Journal of Personality and Social Psychology,* 1974, **30,** 846–855.

Gurwitz, S. B., & Dodge, K. A. Effects of confirmations and disconfirmations on stereotype-based attributions. *Journal of Personality and Social Psychology,* 1977, **35,** 495–500.

Hamilton, D. L. Cognitive biases in the perception of social groups. In J. S. Carroll & J. W. Payne (Eds.), *Cognition and social behavior.* Hillsdale, N.J.: Erlbaum, 1976.

Hamilton, D. L. *Illusory correlation as a basis for social stereotypes.* Paper presented at the meeting of the American Psychological Association, San Francisco, August 1977.

Hamilton, D. L. The role of illusory correlation in the development and maintenance of stereotypes. In D. L. Hamilton (Ed.), *Cognitive processes in stereotyping and intergroup behavior.* Hillsdale, N.J.: Erlbaum, in press.

Hamilton, D. L., & Bishop, G. D. Attitudinal and behavioral effects of initial integration of white suburban neighborhoods. *Journal of Social Issues,* 1976, **32**(2), 47–67.

Hamilton, D. L., & Gifford, R. K. Illusory correlation in interpersonal perception: A cognitive basis of stereotypic judgments. *Journal of Experimental Social Psychology,* 1976, **12,** 392–407.

Hamilton, D. L., & Rose, T. *Illusory correlation and the maintenance of stereotypic beliefs.* Unpublished manuscript, University of California at Santa Barbara, 1978.

Heider, F. *The psychology of interpersonal relations.* New York: Wiley, 1958.

Howard, J. W., & Rothbart, M. *Social categorization: Biasing of memory for ingroup and outgroup information.* Paper presented at the meeting of the American Psychological Association, Toronto, August 1978.

Jenkins, H. M., & Ward, W. C. Judgment of contingency between responses and outcomes. *Psychological Monographs,* 1965, **79** (1, Whole No. 594).

Jones, E. E., & Davis, K. E. From acts to dispositions: The attribution process in person perception. In L. Berkowitz (Ed.), *Advances in experimental social psychology* (Vol. 2). New York: Academic Press, 1965.

Jones, E. E., Davis, K. E., & Gergen, K. J. Role playing variations and their informational value for person perception. *Journal of Abnormal and Social Psychology,* 1961, **63,** 302–310.

Jones, E. E., & Harris, V. A. The attribution of attitudes. *Journal of Experimental Social Psychology,* 1967, **3,** 1–24.

Jones, E. E., & McGillis, D. Correspondent inferences and the attribution cube: A comparative reappraisal. In J. H. Harvey, W. J. Ickes, & R. F. Kidd (Eds.), *New directions in attribution research* (Vol. 1). Hillsdale, N.J.: Erlbaum, 1976.

Jones, E. E., & Nisbett, R. E. The actor and the observer: Divergent perceptions of the causes of behavior. In E. E. Jones, D. E. Kanouse, H. H. Kelley, R. E. Nisbett, S. Valins, & B. Weiner (Eds.), *Attribution: Perceiving the causes of behavior.* Morristown, N.J.: General Learning, 1972.

Kanungo, R. N., & Dutta, S. Retention of affective material: Frame of reference or intensity? *Journal of Personality and Social Psychology,* 1966, **4,** 27–35.

Katz, P. A. The acquisition of racial attitudes in children. In P. A. Katz (Ed.), *Towards the elimination of racism*. New York: Pergamon, 1976.

Kelley, H. H. Attribution theory in social psychology. In D. Levine (Ed.), *Nebraska symposium on motivation*. Lincoln, Neb.: University of Nebraska Press, 1967.

Kelley, H. H. Causal schemata and the attribution process. In E. E. Jones, D. E. Kanouse, H. H. Kelley, R. E. Nisbett, S. Valins, & B. Weiner (Eds.), *Attribution: Perceiving the causes of behavior*. Morristown, N.J.: General Learning, 1972.

Langer, E. J., Taylor, S. E., Fiske, S., & Chanowitz, B. Stigma, staring, and discomfort: A novel-stimulus hypothesis. *Journal of Experimental Social Psychology*, 1976, **12**, 451-463.

McArthur, L. Z. What grabs you? The role of attention in impression formation and causal attribution. In E. T. Higgins, C. P. Herman, and M. P. Zanna (Eds.), *Social Cognition: The Ontario symposium on personality and social psychology*. Hillsdale, N.J.: Erlbaum, in press.

Markus, H. Self-schemata and processing information about the self. *Journal of Personality and Social Psychology*, 1977, **35**, 63-78.

Peterson, C. R., & Beach, L. R. Man as an intuitive statistician. *Psychological Bulletin*, 1967, **68**, 29-46.

Rooks, P. L., & Jones, E. E. *Polarized evaluation of out-group members: A cognitive approach to stereotyping*. Paper presented at the meeting of the American Psychological Association, Toronto, August, 1978.

Rosenthal, R. *Experimenter effects in behavioral research*. New York: Appleton, 1966.

Rosenthal, R., & Jacobson, L. *Pygmalion in the classroom: Teacher expectation and pupils' intellectual development*. New York: Holt, 1968.

Rothbart, M., Evans, M., & Fulero, S. Recall for confirming events: Memory processes and the maintenance of social stereotypes. *Journal of Experimental Social Psychology*, in press.

Rubovits, P. C., & Maehr, M. L. Pygmalion black and white. *Journal of Personality and Social Psychology*, 1973, **25**, 210-218.

Schneider, D. J. Implicit personality theory: A review. *Psychological Bulletin*, 1973, **79**, 294-309.

Smedslund, J. The concept of correlation in adults. *Scandinavian Journal of Psychology*, 1963, **4**, 165-173.

Snyder, M., & Uranowitz, S. Reconstructing the past: Some cognitive consequences of person perception. *Journal of Personality and Social Psychology*, 1978, **36**, 941-950.

Snyder, M., Tanke, E. D., & Berscheid, E. Social perception and interpersonal behavior: On the self-fulfilling nature of social stereotypes. *Journal of Personality and Social Psychology*, 1977, **35**, 656-666.

Tajfel, H., Billig, M. G., Bundy, R. P., & Flament, C. Social categorization and intergroup behavior. *European Journal of Social Psychology*, 1971, **1**, 149-178.

Tajfel, H., Sheikh, A. A., & Gardner, R. C. Contents of stereotypes and the inference of similarity between members of stereotyped groups. *Acta Psychologica*, 1964, **22**, 191-201.

Taylor, D. M., & Jaggi, V. Ethnocentrism and causal attribution in a South Indian context. *Journal of Cross-Cultural Psychology*, 1974, **5**, 162-171.

Taylor, S. E. A categorization approach to stereotyping. In D. L. Hamilton (Ed.), *Cognitive processes in stereotyping and intergroup behavior*. Hillsdale, N.J.: Erlbaum, in press.

Taylor, S. E., & Crocker, J. Schematic bases of social information processing. In E. T. Higgins, C. P. Herman, & M. P. Zanna (Eds.), *Social cognition: The Ontario symposium on personality and social psychology*. Hillsdale, N.J.: Erlbaum, in press.

Taylor, S. E., & Fiske, S. T. Point of view and perceptions of causality. *Journal of Personality and Social Psychology*, 1975, **32**, 439-445.

Taylor, S. E., & Fiske, S. T. Salience, attention, and attribution: Top of the head phenomena. In L. Berkowitz (Ed.), *Advances in experimental social psychology* (Vol. 10). New York: Academic Press, 1978.

Taylor, S. E., Fiske, S. T., Close, M., Anderson, C., & Ruderman, A. J. *Solo status as a psycholog-ical variable: The power of being distinctive.* Unpublished manuscript, Harvard University, 1977.

Taylor, S. E., Fiske, S. T., Etcoff, N. L., & Ruderman, A. J. Categorical and contextual bases of person memory and stereotyping. *Journal of Personality and Social Psychology,* 1978, **36,** 778–793.

Thorngate, W. Must we always think before we act? *Personality and Social Psychology Bulletin,* 1976, **2,** 31–35.

Tversky, A., & Kahneman, D. Availability: A heuristic for judging frequency and probability. *Cognitive Psychology,* 1973, **5,** 207–232.

Ward, W. C., & Jenkins, H. M. The display of information and the judgment of contingency. *Canadian Journal of Psychology,* 1965, **19,** 231–241.

Weiner, B., Frieze, I., Kukla, A., Reed, L., Rest, S., & Rosenbaum, R. M. Perceiving the causes of success and failure. In E. E. Jones, D. E. Kanouse, H. H. Kelley, R. E. Nisbett, S. Valins, & B. Weiner (Eds.), *Attribution: Perceiving the causes of behavior.* Morristown, N.J.: General Learning, 1972.

Wilder, D. A. Perceiving persons as a group: Effects on attributions of causality and beliefs. *Social Psychology,* 1978, **41,** 13–23.

Wilder, D. A., & Allen, V. L. Group membership and preference for information about others. *Personality and Social Psychology Bulletin,* 1978, **4,** 106–110.

Word, C. O., Zanna, M. P., & Cooper, J. The nonverbal mediation of self-fulfilling prophecies in interracial interaction. *Journal of Experimental Social Psychology,* 1974, **10,** 109–120.

Zadney, J., & Gerard, H. B. Attributed intentions and informational selectivity. *Journal of Experimental Social Psychology,* 1974, **10,** 34–52.

Zanna, M. P., & Pack, S. J. On the self-fulfilling nature of apparent sex differences in behavior. *Journal of Experimental Social Psychology,* 1975, **11,** 583–591.

SELF-MONITORING PROCESSES[1]

Mark Snyder

UNIVERSITY OF MINNESOTA
MINNEAPOLIS, MINNESOTA

I. Introduction 86
  A. The Conceptual Ancestry of Self-Monitoring 87
  B. The Construct of Self-Monitoring 88
II. The Identification of Self-Monitoring 89
  A. The Self-Monitoring Scale 89
  B. Construct Validity 90
  C. Discriminant Validity 92
III. The Consequences of Self-Monitoring 93
  A. The Situational Specificity of Self-Presentation 93
  B. The Situational Variability of Social Behavior 95
  C. The Creation of Consistencies in Expressive Behavior 96
  D. The Links between Attitudes and Behavior 97
  E. The Dynamics of Social Relationships 98
IV. The Processes of Self-Monitoring 100
  A. Conceptions of the Self 101
  B. From Thought to Action: Person-in-Situation Scenarios 101
  C. The Building Blocks of Person-in-Situation Scenarios 104
  D. The Cognitive Construction of Person-in-Situation Scenarios 106
  E. The Behavioral Enactment of Person-in-Situation Scenarios 106
  F. The Strategies of Self-Monitoring 109
V. The Individual in Social Psychology 111
  A. In Search of Behavioral Consistency 111
  B. The Individual and the Situation 115
  C. The Reciprocal Influence of Individuals and Situations 118
  D. Self-Monitoring and the Self 123
  References 124

[1]Research on self-monitoring processes and the preparations of this manuscript have been supported by National Institute of Mental Health Grant MH 2499 and National Science Foundation Grants SOC 75-13872 and BNS 77-11346 to Mark Snyder. For helpful advice and constructive commentary on the manuscript, my thanks to Daryl Bem, Ellen Berscheid, Eugene Borgida, William Ickes, Edward E. Jones, and Anne Locksley.

ADVANCES IN EXPERIMENTAL SOCIAL
PSYCHOLOGY, VOL. 12

Copyright © 1979 by Academic Press, Inc.
All rights of reproduction in any form reserved.
ISBN 0-12-015212-6

> The image of myself which I try
> to create in my own mind in
> order that I may love myself
> is very different from the image
> which I try to create in the
> minds of others in order that
> they may love me.
>
> W. H. Auden

I. Introduction

That individuals often strive to influence the images that others form of them has been noted time and again by observers of human nature. All the world, we have been told, is a stage; and, so the story goes, all the people are merely players in a theatrical performance in which they act out many different parts in their lifetimes. In the theater of life, appearances and outward images often are more important than reality itself. Indeed, it has been said that: "The world is governed more by appearances than by realities, so that it is fully as necessary to seem to know something as to know it."[2]

All the world may or may not be a stage. Appearances may or may not be more important than reality. Nonetheless, this "life as theater" metaphor does—at the very least—sensitize us to the possibility that gaps and contradictions may exist between public appearances and private realities. The public appearances of an individual's words and deeds may not—as conventional wisdom would have it—be accurate reflections of and meaningful communications about underlying beliefs, attitudes, and intentions. Instead, what people say and do may be the products of deliberate and strategic attempts to create images appropriate to particular situational contexts, to appear to be the right person in the right place at the right time.

To what extent do individuals actively attempt to control the images and impressions that others form of them during social interaction? Of what consequence is the adoption of such a strategic and pragmatic orientation to interpersonal relationships? These questions define the central concerns of theory and research on self-monitoring processes. At the core of the self-monitoring formulation is the proposition that individuals can and do exercise control over their expressive behavior, self-presentation, and nonverbal displays of affect. Moreover, these self-monitoring processes meaningfully channel and influence our world views, our behavior in social situations, and the unfolding dynamics of our interactions with other individuals. It is the intent of this essay to trace the origins and development of the social psychological construct of self-monitoring (Sec-

---

[2]This assertion has been attributed to Daniel Webster by Edwards (1927).

tions I and II), to chart the behavioral and interpersonal consequences of self-monitoring (Section III), and to probe the cognitive and psychological processes of self-monitoring (Section IV). Perhaps most importantly, however, it is also the intent of this essay to place self-monitoring processes within a larger theoretical perspective on the role of the individual in social psychology and, in so doing, to provide some guidelines for conceptualizing and investigating the interplay of individuals and their situations (Section V).

A. THE CONCEPTUAL ANCESTRY OF SELF-MONITORING

The self-monitoring construct traces its intellectual roots to classic pragmatic theories of the self. Accordingly, it is there that this essay begins. That individuals can and do exercise control over their self-presentation is a basic tenet of most, if not all, theories of the self in social interaction. Consider, for example, the early observations of William James:

> *a man has as many social selves as there are individuals who recognize him* and carry an image of him in their mind. . . . But as the individuals who carry the images form naturally into classes, we may practically say that he has as many different social selves as there are distinct *groups* of persons about whose opinions he cares. He generally shows a different side of himself to each of these different groups. Many a youth who is demure enough before his parents and teachers swears and swaggers like a pirate among his "tough" young friends. We do not show ourselves to our children as to our club companions, to our masters and employers as to our intimate friends. From this there results what practically is a division of the man into several selves; and this may be a discordant splitting, as where one is afraid to let one set of his acquaintances know him as he is elsewhere; or it may be a perfectly harmonious division of labor, as where one tender to his children is stern to the soldiers or prisoners under his command. (James, 1890, Vol. 1, p. 294)

James' notions of the situational specificity of self-presentation have been echoed by successive generations of self-theorists (for a review, see Gordon & Gergen, 1968). Such processes of impression management have formed the core of diverse analyses of the strategic presentation of self in everyday life. Thus, Goffman (1955, 1959, 1963, 1967) has likened social interaction to a theatrical performance in which each person acts out a "line." A line is a set of carefully chosen verbal and nonverbal acts that express one's self. Lines, however, can and do shift from situation to situation as different social roles and social expectations become differentially salient. Moreover, when individuals appear before others, they may have many motives for trying to control the impressions that others receive of them and of the nature of their interaction. Similarly, Alexander has proposed that there is for each social setting or interpersonal context a pattern of social behavior that conveys an identity that is particularly appropriate to that social situation (e.g., Alexander & Knight, 1971; Alexander & Lauderdale, 1977; Alexander & Sagatun, 1973). This behavioral pattern is called a "situated identity.'' Alexander claims that people strive to create the most favorable situated identities for themselves in their social encounters.

From the perspective of the impression management theorists, social interaction requires knowledge of the interpretations that others place upon our acts, a desire to maintain situationally appropriate identities, a wide range of self-presentational skills, and the willingness to use this repertoire of impression management strategies. In short, social interaction requires the ability to manage or control our verbal and nonverbal self-presentation to foster desired images in the eyes of our beholders. These abilities, incidentally, are precisely those abilities that have been attributed to the successful stage actor (Metcalf, 1931). This convergence is, of course, just what is to be expected from a theoretical framework that reflects a ''life as theater'' metaphor (for a review of this ''dramaturgical'' perspective, see Brissett & Edgley, 1975).

Indeed, individuals do strive to influence and control the images that others form of them during social interaction. Empirical researchers have meticulously and exhaustively catalogued the strategies and techniques often used (and sometimes exploited) by those who practice the arts of impression management. To greater or lesser extent, individuals seem to know what behaviors on their part will create what impressions in the eyes and minds of their beholders. At times, individuals seem to be able to convincingly and naturally perform precisely those verbal and nonverbal acts that create desired images, often in the service of winning friends and influencing people (for reviews, see Gergen, 1971, 1977; Jones, 1964; Snyder, 1977). Apparently, impression management is a basic fact of social life.

B. THE CONSTRUCT OF SELF-MONITORING

There are, however, striking and important differences in the extent to which individuals can and do control and manage their self-presentation, expressive behaviors, and nonverbal displays of affect. Clearly, professional stage and screen actors can do what I cannot. Successful politicians long have practiced the art of wearing the right face for the right constituency. One-time mayor of New York, Fiorello LaGuardia, was so skilled at adopting the expressive mannerisms that were characteristic of diverse ethnic groups that it is easy to guess whose vote he was soliciting by watching silent films of his campaign appearances.

Of course, entertainers, politicians, and silver-tongued confidence artists are the exception rather than the rule. Nevertheless, people do differ in the extent to which they can and do exercise control over their verbal and nonverbal self-presentation. These differences may be conceptualized in terms of the social psychological construct of self-monitoring (Snyder, 1972, 1974). It is perhaps easiest to convey the defining characteristics of self-monitoring with descriptions of the prototypic high self-monitoring individual and the prototypic low self-monitoring individual.

The prototypic *high self-monitoring individual* is one who, out of a concern for the situational and interpersonal appropriateness of his or her social behavior, is particularly sensitive to the expression and self-presentation of relevant others in social situations and uses these cues as guidelines for monitoring (that is, regulating and controlling) his or her own verbal and nonverbal self-presentation. By contrast, the prototypic *low self-monitoring individual* is not so vigilant to social information about situationally appropriate self-presentation. Neither does he or she have such well-developed repertoires of self-presentational skills. In comparison with their high self-monitoring counterparts, the self-presentation and expressive behavior of low self-monitoring individuals seem, in a functional sense, to be controlled from within by their affective states and attitudes (they express it as they feel it) rather than molded and tailored to fit the situation.

How can one meaningfully capture these proposed differences in self-monitoring? What are the behavioral and interpersonal consequences of these differences in self-monitoring? What are the processes that underlie the characteristic behavioral orientations of individuals who differ in their self-monitoring propensities? Empirical research has attempted to provide concrete answers to these abstract questions. Theoretical activity has attempted to probe the implications of these answers for choosing appropriate strategies for understanding the thoughts, feelings, and actions of individuals in social situations.

II.   The Identification of Self-Monitoring

Empirical research on self-monitoring processes began with the construction and validation of the Self-Monitoring Scale, an instrument designed to translate the self-monitoring construct into an instrument that reliably and validly identifies it.

A.   THE SELF-MONITORING SCALE

The Self-Monitoring Scale (Snyder, 1972, 1974) is a set of 25 true–false self-descriptive statements that describe: (a) concern with social appropriateness of one's self-presentation (e.g., "At parties and social gatherings, I do not attempt to do or say things that others will like"); (b) attention to social comparison information as cues to situationally appropriate expressive self-presentation (e.g., "When I am uncertain how to act in social situations, I look to the behavior of others for cues"); (c) the ability to control and modify one's self-presentation and expressive behavior (e.g., "I can look anyone in the eye and tell a lie [if for a right end]''); (d) the use of this ability in particular situations (e.g., ''I may deceive people by being friendly when I really dislike them''); and (e) the extent to which one's expressive behavior and self-presentation are tailored and molded to fit particular social situations (e.g., ''In different situations and with different people, I often act like very different persons''). For details of the psychometric construction of the Self-Monitoring Scale, as well as its items and instructions for its administration and scoring, see Snyder (1972, 1974).[3]

B. CONSTRUCT VALIDITY

Does the Self-Monitoring Scale validly capture differences in the extent to which individuals can and do monitor or regulate their expressive behavior and self-presentation? The convergence of diverse methods of measuring self-monitoring has provided validity evidence according to the strategy of construct validation (Cronbach & Meehl, 1955).

1. Self-Monitoring and Peer Ratings

A sociometric study of peer ratings provided a first source of validity evidence for the Self-Monitoring Scale (Snyder, 1974). This method assumes that people who have good control of their expressive self-presentation and who are sensitive to social appropriateness cues should be seen as such by others who have known them in a wide variety of social situations. Indeed, according to their peers, individuals with high scores on the Self-Monitoring Scale are good at learning what is socially appropriate in new situations, have good self-control of their emotional expression, and can use this ability effectively to create the impressions they want.

2. Self-Monitoring and Criterion Groups

Another means of establishing the validity of an instrument is by predicting how predetermined groups of individuals would score when the instrument is administered to them. According to this strategy, groups of individuals known to be particularly skilled at controlling their expressive behavior (e.g., actors, mime artists, and politicians) ought to score higher on the Self-Monitoring Scale than an unselected comparison sample. Indeed, professional stage actors have substantially higher scores on the Self-Monitoring Scale than do comparison samples of university undergraduates (Snyder, 1974).

The behavior of hospitalized psychiatric patients is less variable across situations than is that of normals (Moos, 1968). One interpretation of this finding is that psychiatric ward patients are unable or unwilling to monitor their social behavior to conform to variations in specifications of situational appropriateness.

[3]Information about the internal structure of the Self-Monitoring Scale is available from the author.

Indeed, the average Self-Monitoring Scale score of hospitalized psychiatric patients is markedly lower than that of undergraduate comparison samples (Snyder, 1974).

Finally, it appears that obese people may be higher in self-monitoring than their nonobese counterparts (Younger & Pliner, 1976). These differences may be a reflection of the hypersensitivity to external cues thought to be characteristic of obese individuals (e.g., Schachter, 1971; Schachter & Rodin, 1974). Alternately, a deviant or stigmatizing status may motivate the obese to monitor their social behavior more carefully in order to secure and maintain social acceptance (cf. Krantz, 1978).

3. Self-Monitoring and Expressive Self-Control

If the Self-Monitoring Scale meaningfully identifies differences in the self-control of expressive behavior, this should be reflected behaviorally in the ability to accurately and naturally communicate arbitrary affective states by means of expressive behavior. In fact, individuals with high scores on the Self-Monitoring Scale are much better able than those with low scores to intentionally express and communicate a wide variety of emotions (e.g., happiness, sadness, anger, fear, surprise, disgust, remorse) in both the vocal and facial channels of expressive behavior (Snyder, 1974).

Moreover, compared with low self-monitoring individuals, those high in self-monitoring can effectively and convincingly adopt the expressive mannerisms of a "reserved, withdrawn, and introverted" individual and then with chameleon-like skill shift colors and convincingly portray themselves as "friendly, outgoing, and extraverted" (Lippa, 1976). High self-monitoring individuals can also exploit their self-presentational skills to successfully practice the arts of deception in face-to-face interviews (Krauss, Geller, & Olson, 1976).

4. Self-Monitoring and Attention to the Behavior of Others

According to the self-monitoring construct, high self-monitoring individuals ought to be particularly vigilant and attentive to social comparison information that could guide their expressive self-presentation. Indeed, when given the opportunity in a self-presentation task, high self-monitoring individuals consult information about the modal self-presentation of their peers more often and for longer periods of time than do low self-monitoring individuals (Snyder, 1974).

Moreover, given the opportunity to observe another person with whom they anticipate social interaction, individuals high in self-monitoring are more likely than those low in self-monitoring to later remember accurately information about that person (Berscheid, Graziano, Monson, & Dermer, 1976). That high self-monitoring individuals are actively investing cognitive time and effort in attempting to "read" and understand others is manifested further in their keen attention to the subtle interplay between an actor's behavior and its context, and their use of this information in inferring that actor's intentions (Jones & Baumeister, 1976). At times, high self-monitoring individuals actually will go so far as to "purchase," at some cost to themselves, information that may aid them in guiding and managing their own self-presentation in forthcoming social interaction with another person (Elliott, 1977).

Another set of cues for guiding self-monitoring is the nonverbal expressive behavior of other individuals. Accordingly, high self-monitoring individuals ought to be particularly skilled at "reading" others to correctly infer their affective experience and emotional states. At least two empirical investigations have provided empirical confirmation of this "sensitivity" hypothesis (Geizer, Rarick, & Soldow, 1977; Krauss, Geller, & Olson, 1976).

C. DISCRIMINANT VALIDITY

From this series of converging investigations emerges an image of the prototypic individual identified by a high score on the Self-Monitoring Scale. He or she is one who, out of a concern for the situational appropriateness of his or her social behavior, is particularly sensitive to the expression and self-presentation of others in social situations and uses these cues as guidelines for regulating his or her own self-presentation and expressive behavior. Might not such an individual be identified equally well by existing measures of related psychological constructs? Is there any difference between the high self-monitoring individual and the person with a high need for approval (Crowne & Marlowe, 1964)? Is the high self-monitoring individual simply a Machiavellian (Christie & Geis, 1970) in disguise? In contrast, is he or she perhaps best characterized as an extravert (Eysenck & Eysenck, 1968)?

To demonstrate discriminant validity (Campbell & Fiske, 1959), direct comparisons have been made between self-monitoring and each of need for approval (Snyder, 1972, 1974), extraversion (Lippa, 1976, 1978; Snyder & Monson, 1975), and Machiavellianism (Jones & Baumeister, 1976; Krauss, Geller, & Olson, 1976) in the prediction of a variety of external criterion variables. In each case, strong and reliable relationships between self-monitoring and the criterion measure emerged. By contrast, the effects of need for approval, Machiavellianism, and extraversion were trivial and statistically insignificant. Evidently, self-monitoring is not just need for approval, Machiavellianism, or extraversion.

Moreover, the list of measures with which self-monitoring is not correlated includes: need for approval, Machiavellianism, locus of control, inner-directed versus other-directed social character, social chameleon, field-dependence, MMPI Pd (Psychopathic Deviance Scale), hypnotic susceptibility, neuroticism, repression–sensitization, achievement anxiety, intelligence, academic achievement, public self-consciousness, private self-consciousness, social anxiety, MMPI L (Lie Scale), MMPI Ma (Mania Scale), MMPI Si (Social Introversion Scale), vocational interests, and others. It has become increasingly clear that self-monitoring exists as a social psychological construct that can be measured reliably and validly with the Self-Monitoring Scale.

III.   The Consequences of Self-Monitoring

Clearly, individuals differ markedly in the extent to which they can and do exercise control of their expressive behavior, self-presentation, and nonverbal displays of emotion and affect. However, of what consequence are these differences in self-monitoring for understanding the behavior of individuals in social situations and interpersonal contexts? Empirical efforts to chart the behavioral and interpersonal consequences of self-monitoring have been guided by a theoretical formulation derived from knowledge of the psychological construct of self-monitoring and the evidence for its validity. According to the self-monitoring formulation, an individual in a social setting actively attempts to construct a pattern of social behavior appropriate to that particular context. Diverse sources of information are available to guide this choice, including (a) cues to situational or interpersonal specifications of appropriateness and (b) information about inner states, personal dispositions, and social attitudes.

However, evidence for the construct validity of self-monitoring suggests that individuals may differ in the extent to which they characteristically rely on either source of information. For those individuals who monitor or regulate their behavioral choices on the basis of situational information (high self-monitoring individuals), the impact of situational and interpersonal cues to social appropriateness ought to be considerable. These individuals ought to demonstrate considerable situation-to-situation specificity in their self-presentation and social behavior. Moreover, for high self-monitoring individuals, correspondence between behavior and attitude ought to be minimal. By contrast, persons who monitor or guide their choices on the basis of salient information from relevant inner states (low self-monitoring individuals) ought to be less responsive to situational and interpersonal specifications of behavioral appropriateness. Their social behavior ought to manifest substantial cross-situational consistency and temporal stability. Furthermore, for low self-monitoring individuals, covariation between behavior and attitude typically ought to be substantial. Empirical evidence from investigations of social behavior in diverse domains provides documentation for these theoretical propositions.

A.   THE SITUATIONAL SPECIFICITY OF SELF-PRESENTATION

The evidence for the validity of the self-monitoring construct suggests that high self-monitoring individuals have all the requisite skills to successfully mold and tailor their self-presentation to their situations. They are attentive to the actions of others in social situations and they actively seek out relevant social comparison information. Moreover, they are sufficiently skilled actors that they can successfully translate their beliefs about what constitutes a situationally appropriate self-presentation into a set of verbal and nonverbal expressive actions that convincingly portrays the ''right'' person for the situation. By contrast, low self-monitoring individuals seem to eschew such a strategic impression management orientation to social interaction and interpersonal relationships. It would seem, then, that the behavior of high self-monitoring individuals ought to be more sensitive to social and interpersonal cues to situational appropriateness than that of low self-monitoring individuals. Several empirical investigations have probed the links between self-monitoring and sensitivity to situational influences.

In one investigation of the behavioral consequences of self-monitoring, group discussion conditions sensitized individuals to different reference groups that could provide cues to social appropriateness of self-presentation (Snyder & Monson, 1975). In the ''public'' condition, the experimenter led the group members to a room furnished with a one-way mirror, two videotape cameras, a microphone, a videotape monitor, a table, and chairs. Before the discussions began, these participants watched as the experimenter turned on the videotape monitor. The two cameras were situated such that members of the group were visible on the monitor, which was itself within easy view of all group members. Participants in the public condition then signed release forms to allow videotape recording of their discussion for possible presentation to their own undergraduate psychology class. The videotape cameras, the feedback on the monitor, and the explicit consent form all highlighted the public nature of the group members' behavior and helped make salient membership in the larger reference group of undergraduate students with its norms favoring autonomy in response to social pressure. In the ''private'' condition, the discussions took place in a room furnished only with a table and chairs. In these discussion conditions, the most salient social comparison cues to normative appropriateness of self-presentation most likely were provided by the group. Accordingly, in the private condition, group consensus probably would seem to be the most socially appropriate self-presentation.

High self-monitoring individuals were keenly attentive and sensitive to the differences between the situations in which the discussions occurred. They were conforming in the private discussion condition, where conformity was the most appropriate interpersonal orientation, and nonconforming in the public discussion condition, where reference group norms favored autonomy in the face of social pressure. Low self-monitoring individuals were virtually unaffected by these differences in social settings. Presumably, their self-presentations were more accurate reflections of their personal attitudes, dispositions, and self-conceptions within the domain of conformity.

In this social context, self-monitoring moderated sensitivity to situational and interpersonal influences on self-presentation. It was not that high self-monitoring individuals were any more or less conforming than low self-monitoring individuals. Neither did the public discussion condition produce reliably more or less conformity than the private one. Rather, it was the case that in order to define and specify the relationship between situational influences (here, reference group norms made salient by the situational context of the discussions) and social behavior (here, conformity and autonomy) one had to know "for whom" these factors would have an impact. Moreover, it was self-monitoring that made it possible to perform this "for whom" task of identifying those persons whose social behavior was either very sensitive to situational influences or quite autonomous of such social forces.

B. THE SITUATIONAL VARIABILITY OF SOCIAL BEHAVIOR

How broadly applicable is the conceptual analysis that links self-monitoring to sensitivity to situations? Can one distinguish persons whose social behavior is stable across differing situations from those for whom it is more variable in such diverse domains as altruism, honesty, and self-restraint? Do high self-monitoring individuals manifest considerably greater cross-situational variability in their social behavior than their low self-monitoring counterparts?

The ideal strategy for answering these questions would be to observe the behavior of individuals (for whom scores on the Self-Monitoring Scale were available in advance) across a wide variety of situations. Furthermore, one would wish to observe numerous criterion behaviors in these situations. Clearly, this would be a monumental undertaking. The methodological burden would be eased considerably if an investigator could rely, instead, on self-reports of behavior in each of these domains. Of course, this would be an acceptable strategy only if it were known that individuals who reported themselves to be consistent in a particular domain actually behaved more consistently across situations than those who identified themselves as more variable. Fortunately, this hypothesis has already received support from the empirical work of Bem and Allen (1974).

The marked convergence between self-reports of cross-situational consistency and actual behavior consistency identified by Bem and Allen (1974) suggested the use of a similar measure of reported cross-situational variability in an investigation of the links between self-monitoring and cross-situational variability in social behavior. In this investigation, individuals judged what behaviors they would display in each of a variety of situations differing in the situational and contextual factors relevant to the display of generosity, honesty, and hostility (Snyder & Monson, 1975). Specifically, they read a series of three hypothetical everyday situations, each with nine specific contextual variations. They then estimated the likelihood that they would perform the given behavior in the specific situation described.

In this task, the variance in the behaviors reported for the self constitutes an index of each participants' perceived cross-situational variability within the domains of generosity, honesty, and hostility. This measure assumes larger values as the individual reports greater situation-to-situation variability in social behavior. In accord with the self-monitoring construct, high self-monitoring individuals reported considerably more variability across situations for themselves than did low self-monitoring individuals. This outcome was equally characteristic of reported cross-situational variability in the diverse behavioral domains of generosity, honesty, and hostility. In all cases, high self-monitoring individuals reported more cross-situational variability than did low self-monitoring individuals.

C. THE CREATION OF CONSISTENCIES IN EXPRESSIVE BEHAVIOR

Clearly, high self-monitoring individuals are quite flexible in their self-presentation. In different situations and with different people, they often act like very different persons. However, one ought not to infer that the only outcome of self-monitoring processes is a chameleon-like situation-to-situation tailoring of self-presentation to current settings. Indeed, one can readily imagine cases in which a self-monitoring orientation might generate marked consistency in self-presentation across situations and over time. Consider the case of a campaigning politician trying to appear equally attentive, involved, and statesperson-like in each of 10 different campaign appearances scheduled back-to-back in the same day. No doubt, the well-developed impression management skills of high self-monitoring candidates would allow them to more consistently project the same vote-getting image in each situation. By contrast, the self-presentation of low self-monitoring candidates might fall victim more readily to shifts in their moods and other inner states.

If self-monitoring processes can generate consistencies in self-presentation, where are these consistencies to be found? Empirical research suggests that the situation-to-situation shifts in self-presentation that are the hallmarks of high self-monitoring individuals are acted out against a consistent background of expressive behaviors that are common to a wide variety of interpersonal contexts. It is not unreasonable to assume that, in most social situations, most people would prefer to appear "friendly, outgoing, and extraverted" rather than "aloof, distant, and introverted." Similarly, in most social situations, most people would prefer to appear "calm and relaxed" rather than "worried and anxious." Across a wide variety of social situations, a consistently friendly and nonanxious image may provide the preferred common background self-presentation to be joined with foreground self-presentations specifically tailored to particular circumstances. A campaigning politician might strive for different images when courting the city vote and the farm vote, but in each situation he or she would also try to appear friendly and nonanxious. According to these notions, high self-monitoring individuals should, in general, appear to outside observers to be more "friendly, outgoing, and extraverted" but less "worried, anxious, and nervous" than their low self-monitoring counterparts. Exactly this pattern of results has been reported by Lippa (1976, 1978).

This research on expressive behavior augments the emerging characterization of the interpersonal orientations of individuals who differ in self-monitoring. In general, across a wide variety of social situations, high self-monitoring individuals strive to appear to be friendly and nonanxious. Against this common background, they construct specific self-presentations based upon their readings of situational and interpersonal cues to behavioral appropriateness. It is this strategic orientation that generates the pattern of cross-situational consistency in background self-presentation and cross-situational specificity in foreground self-presentation that characterizes the behavior of high self-monitoring individuals. By contrast, the social behavior of low self-monitoring individuals typically demonstrates relatively greater cross-situational consistency in foreground self-presentation coupled with greater fluctuation and cross-situational variability in background expressive behaviors.

D. THE LINKS BETWEEN ATTITUDES AND BEHAVIOR

Although the extensive repertoire of self-presentational skills of high self-monitoring individuals may give them the adaptiveness to tailor themselves to a wide variety of social roles and social situations, this flexibility may be purchased at some cost. In their continuing quests to appear to be the right person in the right place at the right time, their chameleon-like actions may reflect and communicate very little about their private attitudes, feelings, and dispositions.

Indeed, based upon their endorsement of Self-Monitoring Scale items, it appears that high self-monitoring individuals think that what they say and do may not necessarily reflect what they believe and feel (e.g., "I'm not always the person I appear to be"). In contrast, low self-monitoring individuals claim to value correspondence between their attitudes and their actions (e.g., "My behavior is usually an expression of my true inner feelings, attitudes, and beliefs"). It follows that consistency between attitudes and behavior should be moderated by self-monitoring: Low self-monitoring individuals should manifest substantially greater consistency than high self-monitoring individuals. To investigate this proposition, Snyder and Swann (1976) examined the relationship between measured attitudes toward affirmative action and verdicts 2 weeks later in a mock court case involving alleged sex discrimination.

Attitudes were measured with a psychometrically reliable set of items designed to tap the cognitive, affective, and intentional components of general attitudes toward affirmative action. Two weeks later, participants offered judicial judgments in the case of "Ms. C. A. Harrison versus the University of Maine." Participants read summary *curricula vitae* of two biologists, Ms. C. A. Harrison and Mr. G. C. Sullivan, both of whom had applied to the University of Maine for a position as assistant professor of biology. The University of Maine appointed Mr. Sullivan to the position. Ms. Harrison filed suit: She insisted this decision reflected a bias against females. All participants then considered the arguments advanced in court on behalf of the plaintiff (Ms. Harrison) and on behalf of the defendant (University of Maine). After reaching their verdicts, participants communicated them in written essays explaining and justifying their decisions. These essays then were read by raters who assessed the favorability toward Ms. Harrison of each participant's judicial decision-making behavior.

What was the relationship between general attitudes toward affirmative action and verdicts in the specific sex discrimination court case? Overall, for all participants, the correspondence between initial attitudes and judgment behavior was, at best, modest. However, when the relationship between attitudes and behavior was considered separately for high self-monitoring and for low self-monitoring individuals, the following pattern emerged. Covariation between attitude and behavior was substantially larger for low self-monitoring individuals than for high self-monitoring individuals.

Not only is it possible to predict accurately the future behavior of low self-monitoring individuals from measures of their present attitudes, but also it is possible to forecast the attitudes that they will express in the future from knowledge of their current actions (e.g., Snyder & Tanke, 1976). However, there may be costs associated with the low self-monitoring individuals' concern that their behavior accurately reflect their personal attitudes. When low self-monitoring individuals are induced to engage freely in behaviors that are discrepant from their attitudes (in the classic forced-compliance situation familiar to dissonance researchers), they are particularly likely to accept their counterattitudinal behavior as representative of their true attitudes (Snyder & Tanke, 1976). By contrast, high self-monitoring individuals, who regard what they do and what they believe as not necessarily equivalent, are relatively unaffected by their attitude-discrepant behavior. Their private attitudes tend to remain stable despite changes in their public behavior.

Finally, there exists some empirical evidence for a correlary of the theoretical proposition linking attitudes and behavior. If the behavior of low self-monitoring individuals characteristically reflects their attitudes and feelings, then their actions should reflect shifts and changes in these inner states. Consider again the case of the hypothetical campaigning politicians. As the day wears on, high self-monitoring candidates ought to be more skilled than low self-monitoring candidates at preventing their growing tiredness and fatigue from showing through in their repeated campaign appearances. Indeed, the self-presentations of low self-monitoring individuals seem to be quite sensitive to transitory fluctuations in distracting mood states; high self-monitoring individuals seem better able to ignore such inner distractions (e.g., Ickes, Layden, & Barnes, 1978).

E.   THE DYNAMICS OF SOCIAL RELATIONSHIPS

The consequences of self-monitoring are also reflected in the domains of social interaction and interpersonal relationships. Empirical research has been

successful in charting links between self-monitoring and both the cognitive and behavioral activities associated with the initiation and the development of social
relationships.

1. Cognitive Processes and the Initiation of Social Relationships

With few exceptions, most students of social cognition have endorsed the
view that cognitive activities serve to stabilize, make predictable, and make manageable the individual's view of the social world (e.g., Brunswik, 1956; Heider,
1958; Kelley, 1972). From this perspective, there is clear functional value to the
individual in construing others largely in terms of traits and dispositions. To do
so implies that their social behavior will be consistent across diverse situations
and stable over time. These characteristics would facilitate prediction and potential influence of the behavior of others. To do so would also allow those who are
so motivated to use their beliefs about other people as cues to managing and
regulating their own self-presentational behaviors in social relationships. "Those
who are so motivated" are, of course, high self-monitoring individuals. For
those individuals, perceiving the behavior of another person as dispositionally
organized would facilitate the use of their perceptions of that person as cues to
monitoring their own expressive self-presentation in social interaction with that
person (Snyder, 1976).

The empirical work of Berscheid (Berscheid, Graziano, Monson, & Dermer,
1976) provides support for the theoretical analysis that joins self-monitoring to
the initiation and unfolding of attributional processes in social relationships.
Given the opportunity to observe another person whom they expected to date
socially, men and women high in self-monitoring were more likely than their low
self-monitoring peers to notice and accurately remember information about that
person, infer her or his traits and dispositions, and think favorably of and express
liking for their prospective dates. Evidently, for high self-monitoring individuals, the prospect of social interaction may initiate perceptual and cognitive processes that predictably channel the search for potentially relevant information,
the interpretation of that information, and the form and substance of the images
constructed of those with whom they anticipate further social contact. It is as if
high self-monitoring individuals actively work to construct for themselves a
stable and predictable cognitive reality well-suited to adopting a strategic orientation to social relationships: a stable, predictable, phenomenological world populated by other individuals whose actions appear to consistently reflect stable
attitudes and enduring dispositions.

2. Behavioral Processes and the Development of Social Relationships

These cognitive activities are reflected in the behavioral contributions of
self-monitoring processes to the development of social relationships. To investigate the impact of self-monitoring on the unfolding dynamics of social interaction and acquaintance processes, Ickes and Barnes (1977) arranged for pairs of

strangers to spend time together in a room. They then surreptitiously audio- and videotaped the verbal and nonverbal behaviors of both individuals over a 5-min observation period. These conversational dyads represented all possible pairings of same-sex undergraduates at high, moderate, and low levels of self-monitoring. Ickes and Barnes (1977) scrutinized their tapes for evidence of the impact of self-monitoring on the interactional dynamics of these spontaneous encounters between strangers.

The channeling influences of self-monitoring on the unfolding patterns of social interaction were evident. In these encounters, as in so many other areas of their lives, high self-monitoring individuals suffered little or no shyness (cf. Pilkonis, 1977). Early in the course of social interaction, individuals high in self-monitoring actively took an initiatory and regulatory role in the conversation: The higher self-monitoring members of the dyads were inclined to talk first and to initiate subsequent conversational sequences. They also felt, and were seen by their partners to have, a greater need to talk. Their partners also viewed them as having been the more directive member of the dyad. It was as if high self-monitoring individuals were particularly concerned about managing their social behavior in order to create, facilitate, and maintain a smooth and pleasing flow of conversation throughout the course of the social interaction. In the service of these goals, high self-monitoring individuals took an active and continuing role in initiating and maintaining the conversations. It is perhaps this regulatory orientation to interpersonal relationships that accounts for the frequent emergence of high self-monitoring individuals as leaders of groups (e.g., Garland & Beard, 1978).

IV. The Processes of Self-Monitoring

The behavioral consequences of self-monitoring seem to be quite clearly defined: In regulating their social behavior, high self-monitoring individuals appear to be relatively situationally guided individuals; low self-monitoring individuals appear to be relatively dispositionally-guided individuals.[4] What, however, are

[4]High self-monitoring individuals purposely are not characterized as "situationally controlled." Similarly, low self-monitoring individuals purposely are not characterized as "dispositionally controlled." This is because the notion of situational "control" implies that the situation is in control of the individual and that the individual is responding in accordance with its specifications. However, social behavior may covary with situations and be situationally specific not because the individual is being buffeted around willynilly by situations but because the individual pays particular attention to situational characteristics and uses that information to studiously choose patterns of social behavior and self-presentation appropriate to that particular situation. It is in this latter sense that the high self-monitoring individual is a "situational" individual. Similarly, it is all too easy to construe dispositional "control" to mean control by dispositions, traits, and impulses that are fixed within us and drive us to behave as they dictate. By contrast, one can readily imagine a process of self-

the psychological processes that underlie and generate the differing behavioral orientations of individuals high and low in self-monitoring? Part of the answer may be found in the self-conceptions held by individuals of differing self-monitoring propensities. Empirical research has suggested that high self-monitoring individuals and low self-monitoring individuals construe themselves in ways that are meaningfully related to their respective behavioral orientations.

A. CONCEPTIONS OF THE SELF

Based upon their endorsement of items on the Self-Monitoring Scale, it appears that high self-monitoring individuals regard themselves as rather flexible and adaptive individuals who shrewdly and pragmatically tailor their social behavior to fit situational and interpersonal specifications of appropriateness. Indeed, in investigations of attributional processes, they tend to offer relatively situational explanations for their own behavior (e.g., Brockner & Eckenrode, 1977; Snyder, 1976). Moreover, high self-monitoring individuals tend to define their identities in terms of characteristics of the situations in which they find themselves (Sampson, 1978); in particular, their self-conceptions reflect a high degree of relationship and involvement with other people (Ickes, Layden, & Barnes, 1978).

By contrast, low self-monitoring individuals seem to cherish images of themselves as rather principled individuals who wish to live their lives according to the maxim "believing means doing." They claim to value congruence between "who they are" and "what they do." In fact, in investigations of attributional processes, low self-monitoring individuals prefer to construct relatively dispositional accounts of their actions (e.g., Brockner & Eckenrode, 1977; Snyder, 1976). They also tend to construe their identities in terms of enduring attributes that reside within themselves (Sampson, 1978).

B. FROM THOUGHT TO ACTION: PERSON-IN-SITUATION SCENARIOS

Clearly, high self-monitoring individuals and low self-monitoring individuals think of themselves in terms that meaningfully parallel their characteristic behavioral orientations. Within the domain of self-conception, it is as if the sense of self for high self-monitoring individuals is a flexible "me for this situation." By contrast, for low self-monitoring individuals, the sense of identity seems to be an enduring "me for all times." What, however, are the processes that join thought to action? How do high self-monitoring individuals translate their self-images of

---

regulation of behavior based upon the acting out of information read from salient and relevant inner states, attitudes, and dispositions. It is in this sense that the low self-monitoring individual is a "dispositional" individual.

pragmatic and adaptive creatures into self-presentations molded and tailored to fit each specific situation that confronts them? How do low self-monitoring individuals translate their self-images of principled and consistent beings into actions that faithfully mirror their true attitudes and dispositions?

The following theoretical account of the psychological operations that might produce the behavioral orientations known to be characteristic of high self-monitoring individuals and low self-monitoring individuals is an attempt to understand the processes of self-monitoring. Consider these processes first from the perspective of a hypothetical high self-monitoring individual and, then, from that of a hypothetical low self-monitoring individual.

1.   The Case of High Self-Monitoring

According to this theoretical analysis, when confronted with the task of choosing actions in a social situation, the high self-monitoring individual cognitively asks and behaviorally answers the question ''Who does this situation want me to be and how can I be that person?'' In so doing, the high self-monitoring individual reads the character of the situation to identify the type of person called for by that type of situation, constructs a mental image or representation of a person who best exemplifies that type of person, and uses that prototypic person's self-presentation and expressive behavior as a set of guidelines for monitoring his or her own verbal and nonverbal actions.

Thus, for example, Mike (a hypothetical high self-monitoring individual) might survey the situation at an early-evening cocktail party and read its character as being within the domain of extraversion. For Mike, the domain of extraversion may be exemplified best by his rather extraverted friend, Jim. Mike then would cope with that situation by putting on his most friendly, sociable, and outgoing mask, just as, in his mind's eye, Jim would. In contrast, when Mike reads the character of the situation presented by a departmental faculty meeting, it is quickly apparent to him that the extraverted type as exemplified by his good buddy Jim provides a rather inappropriate prototype, and he proceeds to draw upon an image of his appropriately professorial colleague Jack as the prototype of the right person for this situation. So too does Mike become the perfectly serious, reserved, and thoughtful academic, as dictated by his image of Jack, the prototypic academic. Although, in these hypothetical scenarios, Mike has used particular friends and acquaintances as his prototypes, he could equally well have drawn upon generalized images of the ''ideal extravert'' or the ''perfect academic'' as his prototypes. In either case, to the extent that Mike successfully acts out his image of the prototypic person for each situation, his chameleon-like behavior will reflect marked situation-to-situation specificity at the same time as it communicates little about his own true personal dispositions. These characteristics are, of course, the calling cards of the high self-monitoring individual.

2. The Case of Low Self-Monitoring

By contrast, this theoretical analysis proposes that the activities of the low self-monitoring individual can be characterized best as the cognitive asking and behavioral answering of the question "Who am I and how can I be me in this situation?" Just as the high self-monitoring individual first read the character of the situation and then constructed a representation of a person to guide his or her actions in the current situation, so too does the low self-monitoring individual. However, rather than creating a representation of the prototypic person for the situation, the low self-monitoring individual draws upon an enduring self-image or self-conception that represents knowledge of her or his characteristic actions in the behavioral domains most relevant to this situation. This self-image then serves as the low self-monitoring individual's operating guidelines for monitoring her or his actions.

Thus, for example, Emma (a hypothetical low self-monitoring individual) might survey the scene at the same early-evening cocktail party attended by our Mike, read the character of the situation as extraverted, and retrieve information from memory about her standing in the domain of extraversion. She might learn that "I'm much less sociable and talkative than the average person and, at parties, tend to blend into my surroundings as I let others take the social initiative." The next day at the faculty meeting, Emma again might scrutinize her enduring representation of her self in search of knowledge relevant to the serious and academic character of her current situation. She might retrieve the knowledge that "I'm much more serious and thoughtful than the average person and, at faculty meetings, tend to listen attentively and choose with great care the few words that I do speak." If Emma is successful in acting out her very shy and reserved self-image in both situations, she will display the consistency in behavior across situations and the correspondence between act and disposition that are the hallmarks of the low self-monitoring individual.

3. Person-in-Situation Scenarios

It is now possible to provide a more formal account of the processes of self-monitoring. Of critical importance in this theoretical analysis are the processes of the cognitive construction and the behavioral enactment of "person-in-situation scenarios."

According to this theoretical analysis, individuals plan their actions in social settings by, first, reading the character of the situation to learn what self-presentational attributes are most relevant to a situation of that type and, then, constructing cognitive scenarios in which a person expresses and manifests those attributes in a fashion appropriate to that situation. These cognitive scenarios represent knowledge of the unfolding pattern and sequence of verbal and nonverbal actions, instrumental and expressive behaviors, of that person in particular social situations. As such, cognitive scenarios are members of the same conceptual family as scripts, plans, and other cognitive representations of meaningfully ordered sequences of events involving an individual (e.g., Miller, Galanter, & Pribram, 1960; Schank & Abelson, 1977).

High self-monitoring individuals and low self-monitoring individuals are thought to differ in the identity of the person who is the central character in their cognitive scenarios. High self-monitoring individuals are thought to construct their person-in-situation scenarios by reading the character of each situation that confronts them to identify a prototype of the ideal person (either a specific prototypic example of a generalized ideal image) called for by situations of that type. Low self-monitoring individuals also construct their person-in-situation scenarios by first reading the character of the situation, but then using stored information about those enduring self-conceptions relevant to that type of situation to create an image of a person acting in accord with their characteristic natures. These person-in-situation scenarios, whether they involve images of prototypic others or characteristic selves, then may provide the operating guidelines for constructing and enacting patterns of social behavior.

With this theoretical overview as a guide, consider now a more finely grained analysis of the set of operations that constitute the cognitive construction and the behavioral enactment of the person-in-situation scenarios that may constitute self-monitoring processes.

C. THE BUILDING BLOCKS OF PERSON-IN-SITUATION SCENARIOS

Defining the cognitive processes of self-monitoring requires a precise specification of the kinds of knowledge and cognitive skills that the analysis requires of the individual. In reading the character of the situation, individuals must be able to identify particular behavioral domains that are relevant to particular situations. Also, they must have access to knowledge of themselves and/or other people that is structured in ways that permit and facilitate the construction of cognitive person-in-situation scenarios. Empirical evidence from diverse sources suggests that each of these knowledge requirements is well fulfilled.

1. Reading the Character of Situations

Do individuals have well-worked-out notions of the appropriate behavioral domain for particular situations? There does exist considerable empirical evidence that people can reliably assess the appropriateness of particular behaviors for particular situations (cf. Price & Bouffard, 1974). Moreover, it has been suggested (cf. Argyle, 1977; Mischel, 1977; Pervin, 1977) that people often choose to enter particular situations precisely because these situations allow them to express particular self-attributes. It is, therefore, not difficult to imagine that people do, in fact, have well-developed notions about the kinds of behaviors that are appropriate to particular situations.

2. Knowledge of Self

Do individuals have well-articulated knowledge about their own characteristics in various trait domains, the type of information that is thought to be used characteristically by low self-monitoring individuals to plan and guide their actions? The efforts of cognitive social psychologists have suggested that knowledge of one's own actions and dispositions is organized and represented by conceptual frameworks, cognitive structures, or schemata (e.g., Markus, 1977; Rogers, Kuiper, & Kirker, 1977; Tesser, 1978). Such self-schemata are defined as "cognitive generalizations about the self, derived from past experience, that organize and guide the processing of self-related information contained in the individual's social experience" (Markus, 1977, p. 64).

In a series of converging investigations, Markus (1977) and Rogers et al. (1977) have demonstrated the ways in which such self-schemata guide, facilitate, and channel the processing of information about the self. Self-schemata contain easily retrievable behavioral evidence, provide a basis for confident self-prediction of behavior in schema-related domains, and make individuals resistant to counterschematic information. These schematic cognitive structures easily could provide the basis for constructing a cognitive scenarios in which the individual acts in accord with characteristic personal dispositions in a specific situation.

3. Knowledge of Others

Finally, do individuals also possess well-articulated knowledge about the characteristics of a wide variety of ideal types of people, the type of information that is thought to be used characteristically by high self-monitoring individuals to plan and guide their social behavior? Investigations of personality prototypes (cf. Cantor & Mischel, 1977), of occupational stereotypes (cf. Cohen, 1977), and of implicit personality theory (cf. Rosenberg & Sedlak, 1972), all suggest that individuals, in fact, do possess well-developed notions about the traits and behaviors that go together in characterizing certain types of people (e.g., the prototypic extravert, the ideal librarian).

Such prototypes provide internally consistent descriptive descriptions of the defining example of a personality type. For example, most people conceive of the prototypic extravert as a typically confident, dominating, sociable, entertaining, and talkative creature (Cantor & Mischel, 1977). These prototypes can and do serve as standards that guide the processing of information about other individuals. To the extent that the pattern of another person's actions and attributes match well with a prototype, that person will be thought of in terms of that prototype and information about that person will be easily encoded, retrieved, and elaborated on the basis of information contained in the prototype (Cantor &

Mischel, 1977; in press). It is not unreasonable to infer from this research on the role of prototypes in thinking about others that people can form images of the right type of person for particular situations and that these images then may allow the individual to choose an appropriate set of behaviors for the situation.

D. THE COGNITIVE CONSTRUCTION OF PERSON-IN-SITUATION SCENARIOS

Evidently, individuals do possess the types of knowledge about persons and situations that are the building blocks of person-in-situation scenarios. If the theoretical assertions about the construction of person-in-situation scenarios are correct, then low self-monitoring individuals ought to be particularly skilled at constructing images of themselves and their characteristic actions in particular trait domains. By contrast, high self-monitoring individuals ought to be particularly adept at constructing images of other individuals who are prototypic examples of particular trait domains.

In their empirical research, Snyder and Cantor (1979) have attempted to chart the links between self-monitoring and images of characteristic selves and prototypic others. In accord with the theoretical analysis of the cognitive processes of self-monitoring, they have found that low self-monitoring individuals have richer, better articulated, and more informative self-images in a wide variety of behavioral domains than do high self-monitoring individuals. Moreover, they also have found that high self-monitoring individuals have richer, better articulated, and more informative images of prototypic persons in the same large set of behavioral domains than do low self-monitoring individuals.

Clearly, then, low self-monitoring individuals are particularly knowledgeable about their characteristic selves in particular behavioral domans. High self-monitoring individuals, by contrast, are particularly knowledgeable about other types of people who are prototypes or best examples of particular behavioral domains. These self-images and prototype images could then be used by low and high self-monitoring individuals, respectively, to form the basis of appropriate person-in-situation scenarios. Moreover, these cognitive scenarios may provide sets of behavioral guidelines for different situations.

E. THE BEHAVIORAL ENACTMENT OF PERSON-IN-SITUATION SCENARIOS

The behavioral orientations of individuals who differ in their self-monitoring propensities may be reflections and manifestations of their characteristic modes of thought. Specifically, person-in-situation scenarios involving characteristic selves or prototypic others may be involved fundamentally in the processes by which individuals plan and guide their actions in social contexts. Low self-monitoring individuals seem to be particularly skilled at constructing cognitive images involving their characteristic selves. Their self-images seem to be particularly rich sources of information that would be of considerable utility in choosing behaviors in social situations. In fact, as research on the behavioral consesequences of self-monitoring makes clear, their social behavior demonstrates precisely the correspondence between public behavior and private self-conception and the cross-situational consistency (see Sections III,A, B, and D) that the habitual enactment of such scenarios would produce. High self-monitoring individuals, in contrast, seem to be particularly skilled at constructing informative cognitive images involving other individuals who are prototypic examples of a wide variety of behavioral domains. Indeed, their social behavior reflects the marked cross-situational specificity (see Sections III,A, B, and D) that the continuing behavioral enactment of such scenarios would generate.

How are cognitive scenarios actively translated into corresponding patterns of social behavior? What are the processes that join thought to action? One possibility is that the individual, having constructed the appropriate person-in-situation scenario, puts himself or herself "into the picture," uses the unfolding pattern of events represented in the scenario as operating guidelines, and behaviorally becomes the person in his or her cognitive scenario.

However, just what constitutes this process of putting oneself into the picture? The notion that a cognitive image of a sequence of actions can initiate and guide performance of that sequence of actions should evoke a *déjà vu* reaction in those readers familiar with William James' ideomotor theory of the links between thought processes and motor action:

> We may then lay it down for certain that *every representation of a movement awakens in some degree the actual movement which is its object; and awakens it in a maximum degree whenever it is not kept from so doing by an antagonistic representation present simultaneously to the mind. . . .* We do not have a sensation or thought and then have to *add* something dynamic to it to get a movement. . . . Try to feel as if you were pricking your finger, while keeping it straight. In a minute, it will fairly tingle with the imaginary change of position; yet it will not sensibly move, because *its not really moving* is also a part of what you have in mind. Drop *this* idea, think of the movement purely and simply, with all breaks off; and presto! it takes place with no effort at all (James, 1890, Vol. 2, pp. 526–527)

To be sure, an action image need not automatically evoke a corresponding action sequence. From the perspective of ideomotor theory, a response image is a necessary but not a sufficient condition for ideomotor performance. One must, so to speak, release the brakes, engage the transmission, and allow the cognitive representation of movement to take command of the motor machinery of action.

The value of an ideomotor linkage in understanding the behavioral enactment of person-in-situation scenarios should be readily apparent. Such scenarios are dynamic cognitive representations of the unfolding pattern and sequence of verbal and nonverbal actions, instrumental and expressive behaviors of a person in a particular social situation. To the extent that response images can initiate and guide corresponding patterns of motor action, this ideomotor linkage may provide the machinery that translates imagined behavior into actual behavior. For example, a high self-monitoring individual who (for whatever reason) wanted to convincingly and accurately portray the expressive mannerisms of a sociable and gregarious individual might first clearly and vividly imagine the actions of a characteristically extraverted individual and then allow that scriptlike imagined scenario to "give life" to his or her musculature.

As intellectually appealing as an ideomotor linkage may seem, it has taken its share of hard knocks. It is an idea that was dismissed out of hand by behaviorists of the early twentieth century. Consider the harsh words of Thorndike:

> The idea of throwing a spear or pinching one's ear, or of saying "Yes" tends to produce the act in question no more than the idea of a ten dollar bill or of an earthquake tends to produce that object or event. (Thorndike, 1913, p. 94)

Fortunately, empirical evidence and not rhetorical arguments are the rules of the game in behavioral science. For, over the years, considerable empirical evidence has been offered in support of the ideomotor principle (for a review, see Greenwald, 1970).

Much of the evidence in support of an ideomotor linkage has been provided by demonstrations of the impact of thoughts of movement on electromyogram recordings of movement of the muscles and limbs. Thus, when Jacobson (1932) instructed participants to imagine lifting 10-lb weights with their right forearms, electrical impulses of the type produced by muscular activity were detectable in the biceps of their right arms. When participants thought of pounding two nails with a hammer, two sequential bursts of electrical activity occurred. However, when they thought of hammering nails with the left hand, no action currents could be detected in the right arm. Similarly, Jacobson (1932) was able to detect muscular activities in the tongue and throat in individuals as they imagined that they were talking to their friends, singing a song, or reciting a poem. Moreover, these action currents were strikingly similar to those that were involved in actually saying the relevant words.

Perhaps even more impressive are the demonstrations of Max (1935, 1937). He reasoned that deaf-mutes who talk in sign language ought to show more electrical action potentials in their hands and arms when they were thinking than would a comparison group of individuals who could both hear and speak. Indeed, in one investigation, deaf-mutes performed a series of arithmetic problems in their heads. Fully 80% of these individuals manifested action currents in their hands; by comparison, only 30% of the group of individuals who could both speak and hear showed such muscular activity. Moreover, the average intensity of the muscular responses recorded in the hands of the deaf-mutes was approximately four times as great as that for the speaking and hearing individuals. In another demonstration, Max recorded electromyographic activity of the hands during dreams. Once again, muscle potentials occurred with greater frequency in the hands of deaf-mutes than in the hands of dreamers who could speak and hear. No doubt, the dreams of deaf-mutes are particularly likely to involve thoughts of expressing themselves and communicating with hand movements.

The demonstrations of Jacobson and Max are consistent with the notion that thoughts of movement can actually initiate actual corresponding movements. Perhaps, too, the formation of a rich and vivid cognitive scenario of a person's self-presentational behaviors and expressive mannerisms may organize and guide the motor programming of actual expressive self-presentation. From this perspective, the behavioral enactment of person-in-situation scenarios may very well be a process of "putting one's self into the picture" precisely because the processes of imagining a sequence of actions may be fundamentally equivalent to the processes of organizing and programming the motor machinery of action.

F.   THE STRATEGIES OF SELF-MONITORING

One way of viewing this inquiry into the processes of self monitoring is in terms of two different sets of operational guidelines or "rules of thumb" that individuals in social settings might follow in constructing patterns of social behavior appropriate to their circumstances. It is as if, by classifying individuals according to their self-monitoring propensities, one may identify classes of individuals who best exemplify each of two strategies for actively planning and guiding actions in social contexts.

1.   The High Self-Monitoring Strategy

In the strategy characteristically practiced by high self-monitoring individuals, the individual deliberately strives to pragmatically create an image appropriate to the social forces and interpersonal pressures of the situation, to appear to be the right person in the right place at the right time. This high self-monitoring strategy gives the individual the flexibility to cope quickly and effectively with the shifting situational demands of a diversity of social roles.

In the high self-monitoring strategy, individuals plan and guide their actions with person-in-situation scenarios involving other individuals who are prototypic examples of the type of person called for by specific types of situations. However, this assertion is not meant to imply that personal dispositions and affective states have no necessary influence on the self-presentation and social behavior of a practitioner of the high self-monitoring strategy. Thus, one may turn to the situation and read it as one calling for a high level of gregariousness and sociability ("It's a party"). One must, nonetheless, "read" dispositional information from within to know just how high a level of extraversion one can realistically portray ("I'm, at best, moderately extraverted"), and one must retrieve information about one's personal style of expressing sociability and gregariousness ("I smile and laugh a lot, but I don't prance around"). Thus, although the decision to "be extraverted" may have been made on the basis of a reading of the character of the situation, decisions about just what constitutes a personally appropriate expressive self-presentation of a high level of extraversion must necessarily come from within. In the high self-monitoring strategy, situational information is figural against the ground of dispositional information as the person attempts to behaviorally answer the fundamental question: "Who does this situation want me to be and how can I be that person?"

2. The Low Self-Monitoring Strategy

In the strategy characteristically practiced by low self-monitoring individuals, the individual conscientiously attempts to choose precisely those words and deeds that most accurately reflect and meaningfully communicate relevant attitudes, feelings, and personal dispositions. Practitioners of this low self-monitoring strategy would manifest substantial congruence between "who they are" and "what they do."

In the low self-monitoring strategy, social behavior is a consequence of the cognitive construction and the behavioral enactment of person-in-situation scenarios involving the self manifesting characteristic attitudes, dispositions, and other self-attributes. However, this assertion is not meant to imply that situational factors will not be important in the generation and regulation of the social behavior of individuals who utilize the low self-monitoring strategy. For, even when an enduring self-image and its behavioral implications have been carefully articulated, any behavioral manifestations of this self-image nevertheless must be molded and shaped to fit a specific situational context. Thus, if I know that I am a generous person and want to express my generous self-image, I must still survey my current situation and see how generosity may be expressed in this situation and, within the constraints of this situation, decide what would be an appropriately high level of generosity for this situation. Similarly, the gregarious individual who is studiously true to his or her self-image must nevertheless express that image in different ways in different situations. Thus, one expresses a high level of gregariousness very differently on the telephone and face-to-face, with one's parents and with one's peers, and one ought not to confuse the different contexts. In the low self-monitoring strategy, when one is guiding one's actions on the basis of salient and relevant self-images, these representations of characteristic self-attributes serve as figure against the ground of information about the current situational context as the individual behaviorally answers the fundamental question "Who am I and how can I be me in this situation?"

3. Situations and Strategies

Although these strategies have been characterized in terms of the characteristic orientations of high self-monitoring individuals and low self-monitoring individuals, they need not be linked uniquely and exclusively with differences between individuals in their self-monitoring propensities. In fact, as Section V,A,2 indicates, it is possible to identify social environments and interaction contexts that promote the strategic orientation that characteristically is adopted by high self-monitoring individuals. Moreover, it also is possible to identify other social environments that foster the strategy that typically is practiced by low self-monitoring individuals.

Furthermore, viewing the processes of self-monitoring as strategies for planning and guiding one's actions in social situations may provide added perspective on the nature of self-monitoring. From this perspective, the processes of self-monitoring are those by which information gathered from current social situations and information provided by relatively enduring representations of "self" are integrated constructively and translated actively into patterns of social behavior. The processes of self-monitoring are, quite literally, those that link thought to action. From this perspective, the activities of all individuals (whether they are high or low in their self-monitoring propensities) are engaged in active constructive self-regulatory processes. What differs is which of situational or dispositional information is figure and which source of information is ground in these processes.

V. The Individual in Social Psychology

Of what consequence are self-monitoring processes for a theoretical understanding of human nature? It appears that individuals differ meaningfully in the extent to which they can and do exercise control over their expressive behavior, self-presentation, and nonverbal displays of affect. Moreover, it appears that these self-monitoring processes predictably channel and influence behavior in social situations and interpersonal contexts. The time has come to place this knowledge of self-monitoring processes into a somewhat larger theroetical framework. To do so, however, requires that contemporary research on self-monitoring be viewed from the perspective of the historical search for consistencies in social behavior.

A.   IN SEARCH OF BEHAVIORAL CONSISTENCY

Behavioral scientists long have tried to chart the links between an individual's actions in life situations and relevant attitudes, traits, and dispositions. Similarly, students of human behavior long have examined the consistency of an individual's social behavior across diverse situational contexts and its stability over extended periods of time. These searches for behavioral consistency have permitted an assessment of the utility of conceptualizing human social behavior in terms of such psychological constructs as attitudes, dispositions, and other inner states and personal characteristics.

The search for pervasive consistencies between social behavior and underlying self-conceptions has been not only a long one but also a frustrating one. Personality researchers have time and again found that trait measures were distressingly poor predictors of actual behavior, that actions were unreliable clues to underlying dispositions, and that the observed cross-situational correlation coefficients were often minimal (e.g., Mischel, 1968). Social psychologists all too often have reported weak and inconsistent relationships between verbal measures of attitudes and observations of relevant social behavior (e.g., Wicker, 1969) and equally often have been disappointed to find that hard-won changes in attitude are not always translated into corresponding changes in behavior (e.g., Festinger, 1964).

Perhaps the lesson to be learned from generations of research in social psychology and personality is a negative one. Longstanding assumptions to the contrary, there may be no necessary consistencies between the private realities of attitudes and dispositions and the public realities of behavior and action. Perhaps, it may be the case that knowing what people think and believe about themselves has little or no relevance for understanding what they actually say and do. Instead, human social behavior may be sufficiently sensitive to even subtle differences in situational influences to preclude the existence of close ties between behavior and attitudes, dispositions, and other inner states.

In the face of the theoretical and empirical crises that have plagued the concepts of "attitude," "disposition," and "trait," it is certainly understandable that one may be tempted by such a "situationist" view of human nature. However, critical scrutinies of the relevant empirical evidence have indicated that the evidence for the situational determination of social behavior is no better overall than the evidence for the dispositional determination of behavior (e.g., Block, 1976; Bowers, 1973; Jaccard, 1974; Wachtel, 1973). Whenever direct comparisons of the amount of variance in self-report, self-rating, or actual behavior attributable to "person" variables and "situation" variables are made, rarely does either account for sizeable amounts of variance. Thus, Bowers (1973) has reported that, across 18 comparisons, the average variance due to persons was 12.71%, that due to situations was 10.17%, and that due to person by situation interactions was 20.77%. Although both "persons" and "situations" do account for meaningful (but modest) amounts of variance, it is probable that the person-oriented ("behavior is a function of the person") and the situation-oriented ("behavior is a function of the situation") perspectives each have captured only a part of reality, and that neither viewpoint is a full and adequate characterization of the origins of human social behavior.

1. Consistency: Some People More Than Others

Research on self-monitoring processes, however, helps make clearer why the empirical searches for consistencies in social behavior has produced only modest yield. For, it is only some of the people who manifest such behavioral consistencies. As research on the behavioral consequences of self-monitoring processes indicates, people differ in the extent to which their behavior is sensitive to situational factors and in the extent to which their social behavior covaries with measures of relevant attitudes.

High self-monitoring individuals are particularly sensitive to social and interpersonal cues to situational appropriateness. However, their attitudes and behavior are virtually uncorrelated with each other. To predict their actions, one would seek information about characteristics of their situations. To influence their behavior, one would seek control of their situations. It is as if the psychology of high self-monitoring individuals is the psychology of their situations.

By contrast, one would adopt a rather different strategy for predicting and influencing the behavior of low self-monitoring individuals. Their behavior is typically a reflection of corresponding social attitudes, affective states, and personal dispositions. They are, at the same time, relatively unresponsive to situational specifications of appropriateness. Thus, it should be possible to predict their future behavior from measures of relevant present attitudes. Similarly, it ought to be possible to influence their behavior by changing relevant underlying attitudes. It is as if the psychology of low self-monitoring individuals is the psychology of their attitudes, dispositions, and other salient and relevant inner states.

2. Consistency: Some Situations More Than Others

Moreover, research on self-monitoring processes not only demonstrates that it is possible to specify for whom situational and dispositional guides to action are particularly influential but also suggests that it may be possible to specify when situational and dispositional information is particularly salient and relevant to the individual actor. At the same time as it is possible to identify individuals who differ in their self-monitoring propensities, so too may it be possible to partition social situations and interaction contexts according to their self-monitoring characteristics.

Perhaps some social environments more than others stress the relevance and utility of attitudes, feelings, and dispositions as guides to action. These settings should foster the behavioral orientation that is characteristic of low self-monitoring individuals. In such settings, covariation between measures of inner states and observations of social behavior should be substantial and the impact of situational and interpersonal cues to appropriateness of social behavior should be minimal. Behavior in these low self-monitoring environments should be well predicted from knowledge of personal dispositions, attitudes, and affective states.

Similarly, it may be possible to identify other social environments that promote the behavioral orientation that is characteristic of high self-monitoring individuals. In the presence of clear and unambiguous social or interpersonal cues to situational appropriateness, correspondence between social behavior and these situational factors should be substantial. At the same time, covariation between measures of inner states and observations of behavior might be minimal. Behavior in these high self-monitoring environments ought to be well predicted from knowledge of situational factors.

As a test of this conceptual formulation that social settings and interaction contexts may differ in self-monitoring, Snyder and Swann (1976) constructed social environments that differed in: (a) the extent to which they contained potentially relevant interpersonal cues to situational appropriateness of self-presentation (high self-monitoring environment), and (b) the extent to which relevant attitudes were made available as potential guides to action (low self-monitoring environment). Students participated in a judicial decision-making task (the same one described in Section III,D) in which they prepared written communications about their judgments of liability in a court case in which a female plaintiff alleged that she had been a victim of sex discrimination.

To construct a high self-monitoring environment that would provide salient and relevant interpersonal cues that could serve as guides to choosing a situationally appropriate verdict, some participants anticipated discussing their decisions with a partner who disagreed with them on the issue of affirmative action. In such circumstances, participants adopted a "moderation" strategy of strategic self-presentation and offered "middle of the road" judgments, favorable neither to the plaintiff nor to the defendant. As a strategy of impression management, such middle-ground decisions allow individuals to draw supportive arguments from both sides of the issue. Moreover, moderate positions are likely to create the impression of openness and rationality. Accordingly, by strategically choosing a moderate decision, individuals increase their chances both of making a favorable impression and of having their verdicts prevail in discussion. However, as expected in this high self-monitoring environment, there was no relationship whatsoever between the favorability of these judgments and previously measured general attitudes toward affirmative action.

To construct a low self-monitoring environment that would increase the salience of relevant attitudes, some participants were encouraged to think over, reflect upon, and privately articulate their general attitudes toward affirmative action and the implications of their viewpoints before considering the specific court case. This "thought manipulation" procedure markedly enhanced the covariation (in fact, it created a large and substantial relationship) between favorability of judgments toward the female plaintiff and previously measured general attitudes toward affirmative action.

Evidently, it is possible to construct social environments that promote the behavioral orientations that are characteristic of high self-monitoring and low self-monitoring individuals. Accordingly, behavioral scientists ought to be able to use knowledge of salient and relevant situational and interpersonal characteristics in their attempts to predict and understand social behavior in high self-monitoring environments. By contrast, behavioral scientists ought to be able to use reliable and valid measures of attitudes and other self-attributes in their efforts to predict social behavior in low self-monitoring environments.

B. THE INDIVIDUAL AND THE SITUATION

When viewed from the perspective of research and theory on self-monitoring, the difficulty of identifying pervasive consistencies between actions in life situations and underlying attitudes and self-conceptions becomes somewhat easier to understand. For it is only some individuals who manifest such consistencies. Moreover, it is only some environments that foster such consistencies. As long as observers do not identify in advance those individuals and those environments, then the observed consistencies in human social behavior will be minimal. So too will be the ability of either personal or situational variables alone to predict behavioral events in the general population.

⁎ Of course, the notion that social behavior is a function of both the individual and the situation is hardly a new one. It dates back historically at least to the writings of Lewin (1935). The focal point of the present strategy is the identification of moderating influences that determine both the existence and the nature of the relationships among situational influences, personal attributes, and social behavior. This knowledge then may indicate when predictions of situational influences will be confirmed and when applications of these principles will be appropriate. Similarly, this knowledge then may indicate when predictions of personal influences will be confirmed, and when applications of these principles will be appropriate. Moderating influences may be either attributes of the person or attributes of the situation.

1. Identifying Personal Moderating Influences

With the aid of personal moderating variables, one can identify classes of individuals whose social behavior is particularly sensitive to situational influences and classes of individuals whose behavior characteristically reflects relevant underlying attitudes and dispositions. These moderating influences are of interest not so much for whatever variance in human social behavior that they explain of their own power. They reveal their full potency when considered in combination with appropriate situational and personal variables to specify when and how situational or personal factors will influence social behavior.

Self-monitoring is, of course, one such moderating influence. Thus, for example, in research on conformity and autonomy in groups (see Section III,A), self-monitoring permitted the identification of that class of individuals (i.e., high self-monitoring individuals) whose self-presentation would be particularly sensitive to shifts in reference group norms and that class of individuals (i.e., low self-monitoring individuals) whose self-presentation would be relatively insensitive to these situational influences. Similarly, in research on attitudes and behavior (see Section III,D), self-monitoring permitted the identification of those individuals (i.e., low self-monitoring individuals) for whom covariation between measured attitudes and observed behavior would be substantial and those individuals (i.e., high self-monitoring individuals) for whom covariation between attitudes and behavior would be minimal. Self-monitoring permitted the specification, in the first case, of the relationship between situational influences and social behavior; and, in the second case, of the relationship between personal attitudes and social behavior. In statistical terms, the moderating influences of self-monitoring appear as interactions between self-monitoring and appropriate situational or dispositional variables, rather than as main effects of self-monitoring. Indeed, the potential of the moderating variable approach has been recognized and acknowledged by even the staunchest critics of traditional "main effects" approaches to the study of individual influences (e.g., Mischel, 1968, pp. 32–33).

The potential of the strategy of identifying personal moderating variables has proved itself in a variety of contexts. Within the domain of sex-role behaviors, Bem (1975) has demonstrated that androgynous individuals (as identified by the Bem Sex Role Inventory) are better able than sex-typed individuals to perform either traditionally "masculine" or traditionally "feminine" behaviors as one or other is more appropriate and functional in specific situations. Within the domain of altruism, Schwartz (1973) has found that measures of personal norms could be used successfully to predict helping behavior only for those individuals who (according to their scores on his Ascription of Responsibility Measure) claimed personal responsibility for their actions. Within the domain of aggression, Scheier (1976) has observed that overt acts of aggression are more meaningful reflections of aggressive predispositions for individuals who are highly self-conscious (as identified by his Self-Consciousness Scale) than for individuals who are low in self-consciousness. Moreover, in other research with the Self-Consciousness Scale, Scheier and Carver (1977) have shown that individuals high in self-consciousness are more responsive to their transient affective states than persons low in self-consciousness.

Each of these moderating variables seems to have its own terrain. Psychological androgyny seems to possess territorial rights in the domain of sex-role behaviors, self-monitoring has proved itself in investigations of self-presentational processes, and so on. One is, not surprisingly, tempted to ask "When all is said and done, how many moderating variables will there be?" It is, at this time, impossible to forecast any answers to this question. It is, however, possible to specify some of the criteria that are most likely to characterize "successful" attempts to identify personal moderating variables. A psychological construct will perform successfully as a moderating variable to the extent that it reliably and validly taps those processes by which information about persons and situations are actively translated into patterns of social behavior. Self-monitoring "works" as a moderating variable precisely because it reliably separates those individuals who believe that "In different situations and with different people, I often act like very different persons" from those individuals who believe that "My behavior is usually an expression of my true inner feelings, attitudes, and beliefs," and because these differences in self-conception are meaningfully reflected in the domain of action. Other moderating variables will succeed to the extent that they focus on the preferential use of dispositional or situational information as guides to action in particular behavioral domains.

2. *Identifying Situational Moderating Influences*

Situational moderating influences are those characteristics of social settings and interaction contexts that specify when individuals are likely to turn to salient and relevant attitudes, feelings, and dispositions as guides to action, and when they are likely to monitor their behavioral choices on the basis of social and interpersonal cues to situational appropriateness.

In the empirical research described in Section V,A, researchers constructed social environments that promoted the behavioral orientations characteristic of high self-monitoring and low self-monitoring individuals. Increasing the availability of relevant attitudes created a low self-monitoring environment. Structuring an interaction context that promoted a strategic "impression management" orientation created a high self-monitoring environment. Further, it may be possible to construct a taxonomy of social situations and interpersonal contexts based upon the extent to which they provide salient and relevant "dispositional" and "situational" guides to action. Toward this end, the following lists of potential situational moderating influences may constitute small steps in this taxonomic enterprise.

Individuals may be particularly likely to regulate their behavioral choices on the basis of information about their attitudes, dispositions, and other relevant inner states in environments that:

a. Encourage a reflective, contemplative orientation to action (cf. Snyder & Swann, 1976)

b. Enhance either one's sense of commitment or one's personal responsibility for one's actions (cf. Kiesler, 1971; Schwartz, 1973)

c. Heighten one's awareness of self as a potential cause of behavior, as in studies of objective self-awareness (cf. Carver, 1975; Pryor, Gibbons, Wicklund, Fazio, & Hood, 1977; Wicklund, 1975)

d. Cut short the processes of avoiding and reinterpreting commitment (cf. Kiesler, Roth, & Pallak, 1974) and therefore make it impossible to define one's beliefs and attitudes as irrelevant to one's actions

e. Provide normative support for congruence between behavior and belief (cf. Kiesler, Nisbett, & Zanna, 1969)

By contrast, individuals may be particularly likely to monitor their behavioral choices on the basis of available situational cues in environments that:

a. Are novel, are unfamiliar, and contain relevant sources of social comparison (cf. Festinger, 1954; Sherif, 1937)

b. Make individuals uncertain of or confused about their inner states (cf. Schachter & Singer, 1962)

c. Suggest that one's attitudes are socially undesirable (cf. Dutton & Lake, 1973) or deviant (cf. Freedman & Doob, 1968)

d. Sensitize one to the perspective of others and motivate concern with social evaluation and conformity with reference group norms (cf. Charters & Newcomb, 1958; Zimbardo, 1969)

e. Motivate individuals to adopt a strategic impression management or ingratiation orientation to self-presentation (cf. Jones, 1964; Snyder, 1977)

Not only may these lists of potential situational moderating influences constitute first steps in constructing a taxonomy of social situations, but also they may provide clues about the developmental origins of the characteristic behavioral orientations of individuals who differ in their self-monitoring propensities. The same sets of attributes that, in the short run, induce individuals to monitor their behavioral choices in particular social environments on the basis of relevant situational or dispositional guidelines may, in the long run, characterize the socialization backgrounds and developmental life histories that produce individuals who characteristically and habitually rely on one or the other source of information to guide their actions.

C. THE RECIPROCAL INFLUENCE OF INDIVIDUALS AND SITUATIONS

If correspondence between actions and underlying self-conceptions (e.g., attitudes and dispositions) is a question of "some individuals more than others" and "some situations more than others," then any empirical searches for behavioral consistency will be successful to the extent that they accurately identify "those individuals" and "those situations." As promising as this strategy of identifying relevant moderating influences may be, the ability to witness the impact of attributes of the individual nevertheless may be limited by inherent constraints of the characteristic methodology of psychological inquiry.

The psychological experiment, with its defining characteristics of random assignment of participants to different experimentally created situations, is a research methodology that tends to minimize the impact of the individual at the same time as it tends to maximize the impact of the situation on the outcome. Investigators conduct experiments to observe the impact of manipulated independent variables on measured dependent variables. It is in practice, if not in principle, easier to control and manipulate characteristics of the situation than it is to manipulate and control attributes of the individual. Accordingly, independent variables typically are manipulations of the situation. Moreover, investigators typically exercise great care to make sure that the different levels of the independent variable are sufficiently distinct to guarantee noticeably different effects on the comparison groups. Typically, investigators also tailor their manipulations to fit characteristics shared by their participant populations; for example, one would hardly arouse cognitive dissonance in the same way with adults and with children. Finally, investigators tend to recruit their participants from fairly homogeneous participant populations (most notably, college students, who are much less variable in personal, intellectual, social, and demographic attributes than the population at large). All of these factors effectively increase the extent to which social behavior in experiments will be particularly sensitive to situationally manipulated independent variables (cf. Cook & Campbell, 1976; Raush, Dittman, & Taylor, 1959), for the stage has been set to maximize sensitivity to the situational manipulation and to minimize the potential influence of personal attributes of the individual participants.

More importantly, however, experiments—as they are typically conducted, but not as they need be conducted—guarantee that virtually the most important contributions of the individual may not have any impact on the outcome. Experiments, by definition, are designed to isolate and measure the potential effects of the independent variable. Therefore, investigators manipulate and control that factor to occur in fixed and preprogrammed fashion and subject their participants to one or other level of the independent variable. This procedure effectively prevents the participants from doing two very important things: (1) They cannot choose whether or not to be exposed to the treatment or experimental situation to which they have been assigned and (2) they cannot interact with the experimenter and the stimulus factors to exercise any control over the interpersonal situation. There is literally nothing that they can do to alter those events that define the manipulated independent variable. All that they can do is react, respond, and attempt to cope with the surrounding situation.

This is, of course, precisely how it must be if investigators are to be able to make confident statements about the impact of the situational independent variable on the person's behavior, for these procedures are precisely those needed to conduct a valid experimental investigation of a "situation influences individual" hypothesis. Yet life situations rarely involve such predetermined stimulus events over which the individual has no influence. Individuals normally have considerable freedom to choose where to be, when, and with whom. Moreover, once in a social situation—whether of one's choosing or not—much of what transpires is determined by the individual's own actions. Thus, the social situations that influence my behavior are partially of my own choosing. Further, once in social situations, how other people treat me is often, if not usually, partially determined by my own actions. Although I may be reacting to and molding my behavior to fit the actions of others, what I am reacting to may have been a product of my own actions. Accordingly, in many—if not most—life circumstances, the situational factors to which the individual responds are often of his or her own making (cf. Mischel, 1977; Wachtel, 1973). The situation that appears to be a "cause" of the individual's subsequent behavior may also be an "effect" of that individual's prior actions. This interplay between individual and situation is understandably ruled out in most traditional procedural paradigms.

Thus, by their very nature, procedural paradigms that employ fixed situational stimuli as independent variables produce outcomes that maximize the impact of the situation on the individual but minimize the impact of the individual on the situation. Indeed, such procedural paradigms are ideally suited to confirm "situation influences individual" hypotheses but are woefully inadequate to generate "individual influences situation" outcomes. In fact,

> A survey of the literature . . . confirms the extent to which we have become captives of a one-sided paradigm to map a bidirectional process. Environmental control is overstudied, whereas personal control has been relatively neglected. (Bandura, 1974, p. 866)

1. Investigating the Impact of Individuals on Situations

Is it possible to structure experimental research paradigms that permit the study of the mutual interplay and reciprocal influence of individuals and their situations? Is it possible to design procedural paradigms that permit the evaluation of "individual affects situation" hypotheses as well as "situation affects individual" hypotheses? There is no doubt that experimental research methodologies provide our surest inoculation against threats to internal validity (Campbell & Stanley, 1963). There is also no doubt that experimentation has been profitably used to investigate "situation affects individual" hypotheses (e.g., Carlsmith, Ellsworth, & Aronson, 1976). Yet, there are reasons to believe that it is possible to investigate experimentally the influence of individuals on their situations.

How, then, might one investigate experimentally "individual affects situation" hypotheses? To do so would, of necessity, require casting the individual in the role of independent variable and the situation in the role of dependent variable. Consider the following example from the domain of person perception. A traditional "situation affects individual" experiment might investigate the effects of a target's behavior on a perceiver's impressions of the target. The researcher might find, for example, that if he or she arranges for the target to behave in a friendly and sociable manner, then the perceiver will infer that the target has a friendly and sociable temperament. If so, the researcher would have witnessed the impact of events in the situation (here, the target's behavior) on events in the individual (here, the perceiver's beliefs).

What if the researcher were to attempt to reverse the direction of causal influence? What if he or she were to manipulate and control the beliefs of the perceiver, allow perceiver and target to interact with each other, and observe the impact of the perceiver's beliefs on the actual behavior of the target? He or she might observe that when perceivers interact with targets whom they believe (erroneously, as a result of the experimental manipulation) to have friendly and sociable natures, those targets actually come to behave in friendly and sociable fashion. If so, the researcher would have witnessed an instance of the impact of events in the individual (here, the perceiver's beliefs) on events in the situation (here, the target's behavior). Indeed, it is possible to investigate experimentally the processes by which a perceiver's initial beliefs about a target exert powerful channeling influences on subsequent social interaction between perceiver and target. Actions of the perceiver based upon beliefs about the target can and do cause the behavior of the target to confirm and validate even erroneous beliefs of the perceiver. For demonstrations of such "behavioral confirmation" processes in social interaction, see Snyder and Swann, 1978a; Snyder and Swann, 1978b; Snyder, Tanke, and Berscheid, 1977.

Consider another example of the impact of the individual on the situation. This time, however, the example is drawn from the domain of self-perception. It goes without saying that some people regard themselves as more competitive than others and endorse a competitive orientation to social relationships. Of what consequence are these self-perceptions? As it happens, individuals with competitive orientations to social relationships believe that the world is composed homogeneously of competitive individuals; by contrast, those with cooperative orientations construe the world to be more heterogeneously composed of both cooperative and competitive people (Kelley & Stahelski, 1970). One consequence of these stereotypes is that competitive individuals are highly likely to elicit competitive responses from others with whom they interact, whether these others have cooperative or competitive dispositions (Kelley & Stahelski, 1970). Effectively, these competitively disposed individuals create for themselves a world that not only confirms the validity of their stereotyped beliefs that all people are competitive, but also justifies their own competitive dispositions. One can readily imagine similar scenarios. For example, a cool and aloof individual may treat others in ways that cause them to behave as if they too were cool and aloof creatures. By contrast, a warm and friendly individual, by acting out that friendly and sociable disposition, might construct a world populated by equally warm and friendly beings.

2. Understanding Individuals in Terms of Their Situations

The notion that situational factors are often a product of the individual's social behavior suggests a new approach to conceptualizing and assessing stable traits and enduring dispositions of the individual. Consider the case of sociability. If one assumes that some people are more sociable than others, how is one to identify these differences in sociability? One might identify those behaviors that are manifestations of sociability and tabulate the frequency with which individuals engage in these actions. It might even be acceptable to trust individuals to accurately report the frequency with which they perform sociable actions. One could then identify as sociable individuals those who perform (or claim to perform) relatively many sociable behaviors. Such an approach is, of course, very similar to traditional assessment strategies in personality psychology.

However, a consideration of the impact of individuals on situations suggests a fundamentally different approach that focuses on the processes of choosing and influencing situations. Instead of defining sociable individuals as those who perform sociable actions, one would define sociable individuals as those who: (1) When given the choice, choose to enter situations that foster the expression of sociability and (2) once in a situation, act in ways that increase the sociability of that situation. Thus, sociable individuals are those who, when given the choice of going to a party or going to the library, will choose to go to the party. Similarly, when sociable individuals find themselves with groups of people, these sociable individuals will actively work to mold their situations into ones conducive to the display of sociability. From this perspective, sociability is defined as the process of choosing whenever possible to enter sociable situations, and acting to maximize the sociability of one's situations. In so doing, sociable persons would be actively attempting to construct social worlds most conducive to the expression and manifestation of their sociable dispositions.

3. Understanding Situations in Terms of Individuals

If one can understand individuals in terms of the situations that they choose, can one also understand situations in terms of the individuals who choose them? It is not uncommon for individuals to characterize situations in terms of the prototypic individual to be found in such situations. Thus, if I were to tell you that Andy's Bar is the type of place that Archie Bunker would frequent, you would readily appreciate just what type of place Andy's Bar really is. Indeed, as discussed in Section IV,C, individuals do seem to have well-worked-out notions about the types of people who would be well suited to particular situations.

Moreover, Bem and Funder (1978) have proposed just such a strategy for "assessing the personality of situations." Their approach perhaps is characterized best by their own favorite example of how one might describe Stanford University to a prospective student. One might characterize Stanford in terms of a set of prototypic individuals: "Students who are hardworking but somewhat shy tend to get good grades but don't have much interaction with the faculty; students who are bright and assertive often get involved in faculty research projects but as a consequence sometimes have little social life and get lower grades than they should; students who . . . ." Rather than describing the situation represented by Stanford University in terms of enrollment, size of classes, reputation of the faculty, and background of the students, they have instead defined it in terms of sets of "template–behavior" pairs that specify how particular types of individuals will react to that situation. In so doing, they have described a situation in the language that typically is used to characterize a person. In their empirical research, they have translated this notion of "template–behavior" pairs into a procedure for empirically assessing the personality of situations.

D.   SELF-MONITORING AND THE SELF

This conceptualization of the individual in social psychology, with its emphasis on the reciprocal influences of individuals and their situations, should have a familiar ring to readers and students of Lewin (1935). Yet, the present approach suggests an important extension of Lewin's famous dictum: At the same time as we regard behavior to be a function of the individual and the social environment, so too must we recognize that the social environment is a function of the individual and his or her social behavior.

Moreover, this treatment of the individual in social psychology should also evoke knowing nods from those readers familiar with the themes that characterize the writings of the classical pragmatists and self theorists (e.g., Mead, 1934), who emphasize the active role that individuals play in shaping their social environments and their destinies. It is, of course, no accident that this emerging conceptualization of individuals as active agents who both influence and are influenced by their circumstances should reflect the themes of classical theories of the self in social interaction, for this conceptualization of the interplay of persons and their situations draws in part on theory and research on self-monitoring processes. Moreover, theory and research on self-monitoring processes themselves draw in part on concerns with the self in social interaction. Accordingly, it is with an explicit definition of the relationship between self-monitoring and the self that this essay concludes.

The concept of self is one of the oldest and most enduring in psychological and philosophical considerations of human nature. Traditionally, students of the self have been concerned with the processes by which individuals gain knowledge about themselves; in particular, with understanding how individuals identify and define those attributes of their behavior and their experience that they regard as "me." Social psychologists typically have focused on the social origins and interpersonal antecedents of self-knowledge; in particular, on the extent to which self-knowledge is a product of social interaction and relationships with others. Indeed, both classical (e.g., Cooley, 1902; James, 1890; Mead, 1934) and contemporary (e.g., Bem, 1972; Gergen, 1977; Schachter, 1964) treatments of self and identity emphasize the inferential nature of self-knowledge. From this perspective, individuals come to know their own social attitudes, personal traits, and enduring dispositions partially by inferring them on the basis of observations of their own behavior, their physiological reactions, and the social circumstances in which these events occur.

As inquiries into the nature and processes of the self, theory and research on self-monitoring reflect a somewhat different perspective. Rather than focusing on the antecedent processes by which individuals gain self-knowledge, theory and research on self-monitoring have turned their attention toward answering the question: "Of what consequence is this self-knowledge for what the person subsequently does?" Theory and research on self-monitoring have attempted to chart the processes by which beliefs about the self are actively translated into patterns of social behavior that reflect those self-conceptions. Indeed, as suggested in this essay, the processes of self-monitoring may be regarded as those by which self-knowledge provided by relatively enduring representations of "self" and information gathered from current social situations are constructively integrated and actively translated into meaningful patterns of social behavior. From this perspective, the processes of self-monitoring are the very processes of the self—a system of operating rules that translate self-knowledge into social behavior.

REFERENCES

Alexander, C. N., Jr., & Knight, G. W. Situated identities and social psychological experimentation. *Sociometry,* 1971, **34,** 65–82.

Alexander, C. N., Jr., & Lauderdale, P. Situated identities and social influence. *Sociometry,* 1977, **40,** 225–233.

Alexander, C. N., Jr., & Sagatun, L. An attributional analysis of experimental norms. *Sociometry,* 1973, **36,** 127–142.

Argyle, M. Predictive and generative rules models of PXS interaction. In D. Magnusson & N. S. Endler (Eds.), *Personality at the crossroads: Current issues in interactional psychology.* Hillsdale, N.J.: Erlbaum, 1977. Pp. 353–370.

Bandura, A. Behavior therapy and the models of man. *American Psychologist,* 1974, **29,** 859–869.

Bem, D. J. Self-perception theory. In L. Berkowitz (Ed.), *Advances in experimental social psychology* (Vol 6). New York: Academic Press, 1972.

Bem, D. J., & Allen, A. On predicting some of the people some of the time: The search for cross-situational consistencies in behavior. *Psychological Review,* 1974, **81,** 506–520.

Bem, D. J., & Funder, D. C. Predicting more of the people more of the time: Assessing the personality of situations. *Psychological Review*, 1978, **85**, 485–501.

Bem, S. L. Sex role adaptability: One consequence of psychological androgny. *Journal of Personality and Social Psychology*, 1975, **31**, 634–643.

Berscheid, E., Graziano, E., Monson, T., & Dermer, M. Outcome dependency: Attention, attribution and attraction. *Journal of Personality and Social Psychology*, 1976, **34**, 978–989.

Block, J. *Recognizing the coherence of personality*. Unpublished manuscript, University of California, Berkeley, 1976.

Bowers, K. S. Situationism in psychology: An analysis and a critique. *Psychological Review*, 1973, **80**, 307–336.

Brissett, D., & Edgley, C. *Life as theater: A dramaturgical sourcebook*. Chicago: Aldine, 1975.

Brockner, J., & Eckenrode, J. *Self-monitoring and the actor-observer bias*. Unpublished manuscript, State University of New York at Brockport, 1977.

Brunswik, E. *Perception and the representative design of experiments*. Berkeley: University of California Press, 1956.

Campbell, D. T., & Fiske, D. W. Convergent and discriminant validation by the multitrait-multimethod matrix. *Psychological Bulletin*, 1959, **56**, 81–105.

Campbell, D. T., & Stanley, J. C. *Experimental and quasi-experimental designs for research*. Chicago: Rand McNally, 1963.

Cantor, N., & Mischel, W. Traits as prototypes: Effects on recognition memory. *Journal of Personality and Social Psychology*, 1977, **35**, 38–48.

Cantor, N., & Mischel, W. Prototypicality and personality: Effects on free recall and personality impressions. *Journal of Research in Personality*, in press.

Carlsmith, J. M., Ellsworth, P. C., & Aronson, E. *Methods of research in social psychology*. Reading, Mass.: Addison-Wesley, 1976.

Carver, C. S. Physical aggression as a function of objective self-awareness and attitudes toward punishment. *Journal of Experimental Social Psychology*, 1975, **11**, 510–519.

Charters, W., Jr., & Newcomb, T. Some attitudinal effects of experimentally increased salience of a membership group. In E. Maccoby, T. Newcomb, & E. Hartley (Eds.), *Readings in social psychology*. New York: Holt, 1958.

Christie, R., & Geis, F. L. (Eds.). *Studies in Machiavellianism*. New York: Academic Press, 1970.

Cohen, C. *Cognitive basis of stereotyping*. Paper presented at the meeting of The American Psychological Association, San Francisco, August 1977.

Cook, T. D., & Campbell, D. T. The design and conduct of quasi-experiments and true experiments in field settings. In M. D. Dunnette (Ed.), *Handbook of industrial and organizational research*. Chicago: Rand McNally, 1976.

Cooley, C. H. *Human nature and the social order*. New York: Scribner, 1902.

Cronbach, L. J., & Meehl, P. E. Construct validity in psychological tests. *Psychological Bulletin*, 1955, **52**, 281–302.

Crowne, D. P., & Marlowe, D. *The approval motive*. New York: Wiley, 1964.

Dutton, D. G., & Lake, R. A. Threat of own prejudice and reverse discrimination in interracial situations. *Journal of Personality and Social Psychology*, 1973, **28**, 94–100.

Edwards, T. (Ed.), *The new dictionary of thoughts*. Charlotte, N.C.: Britkin, 1927.

Elliott, G. C. *Pretending to be someone: The effects of deception and level of self-monitoring on planning and reacting to a self-presentation*. Unpublished manuscript, University of Maryland, 1977.

Eysenck, H. J., & Eysenck, S. B. G. *Manual for the Eysenck personality inventory*. San Diego: Educational & Industrial Testing Service, 1968.

Festinger, L. A theory of social comparison processes. *Human Relations*, 1954, **7**, 117–140.

Festinger, L. Behavioral support for opinion change. *Public Opinion Quarterly*, 1964, **28**, 404–417.

Freedman, J. L., & Doob, A. N. *Deviancy: The psychology of being different.* New York: Academic Press, 1968.

Garland, H., & Beard, J. F. *The relationship between self-monitoring and leader emergence across two task situations.* Unpublished manuscript, College of Business Administration, University of Texas at Arlington, 1978.

Geizer, R. S., Rarick, D. L., & Soldow, G. F. Deception and judgment accuracy: A study in person perception. *Personality and Social Psychology Bulletin,* 1977, **3**, 446-449.

Gergen, K. J. *The concept of self.* New York: Holt, 1971.

Gergen, K. J. The social construction of self-knowledge. In T. Mischel (Ed.), *The self: Psychological and philosophical issues.* Totowa, N.J.: Rowman & Littlefield, 1977.

Goffman, E. On face-work: An analysis of ritual elements in social interaction. *Psychiatry,* 1955, **18,** 213-221.

Goffman, E. *The presentation of self in everyday life.* Garden City, N.Y.: Doubleday-Anchor, 1959.

Goffman, E. *Stigma: Notes on the management of spoiled identity.* New York: Prentice Hall, 1963.

Goffman, E. *Interaction ritual: Essays on face-to-face behavior.* Garden City, N.Y.: Doubleday-Anchor, 1967.

Gordon, C., & Gergen, K. J. (Eds.). *The self in social interaction.* New York: Wiley, 1968.

Greenwald, A. G. Sensory feedback mechanisms in performance control: With special reference to the ideomotor mechanism. *Psychological Review,* 1970, **77,** 73-99.

Heider, F. *The psychology of interpersonal relations.* New York: Wiley, 1958.

Ickes, W. J., & Barnes, R. D. The role of sex and self-monitoring in unstructured dyadic interactions. *Journal of Personality and Social Psychology,* 1977, **35,** 315-330.

Ickes, W. J., Layden, M. A., & Barnes, R. D. Objective self-awareness and individuation: An empirical link. *Journal of Personality,* 1978, **46,** 146-161.

Jaccard, J. J. Predicting social behavior from personality traits. *Journal of Research in Personality,* 1974, **7,** 358-367.

Jacobson, L. E. The electrophysiology of mental activities. *American Journal of Psychology,* 1932, **44,** 677-694.

James, W. *The principles of psychology* (Vols. 1, 2). New York: Holt, 1890.

Jones, E. E. *Ingratiation.* New York: Appleton, 1964.

Jones, E. E., & Baumeister, R. The self-monitor looks at the ingratiator. *Journal of Personality,* 1976, **44,** 654-674.

Kelley, H. H. Attribution in social interaction. In E. E. Jones, D. Kanouse, H. H. Kelley, R. E. Nisbett, S. Valins, & B. Weiner (Eds.), *Attribution: Perceiving the causes of behavior.* New York: General Learning, 1972.

Kelley, H. H., & Stahelski, A. J. The social interaction basis of cooperators' and competitors' beliefs about others. *Journal of Personality and Social Psychology,* 1970, **16,** 66-91.

Kiesler, C. A. *The psychology of commitment: Experiments linking behavior to belief.* New York: Academic Press, 1971.

Kiesler, C. A., Nisbett, R. E., & Zanna, M. On inferring one's beliefs from one's behavior. *Journal of Personality and Social Psychology,* 1969, **11,** 321-327.

Kiesler, C. A., Roth, T., & Pallak, M. S. The avoidance and reinterpretation of commitment and its implications. *Journal of Personality and Social Psychology,* 1974, **30,** 705-715.

Krantz, D. S. The social context of obesity research: Another perspective on its place in the field of social psychology. *Personality and Social Psychology Bulletin,* 1978, **4,** 177-184.

Krauss, R. M., Geller, V., & Olson, C. *Modalities and cues in perceiving deception.* American Psychological Association, Washington, D.C., 1976.

Lewin, K. *A dynamic theory of personality.* New York: McGraw-Hill, 1935.

Lippa, R. Expressive control and the leakage of dispositional introversion-extraversion during role-played teaching. *Journal of Personality,* 1976, **44,** 541-559.

Lippa, R. The effect of expressive control on expressive consistency and on the relation between expressive behavior and personality. *Journal of Personality*, 1978, **46**, 438–461.

Markus, H. Self-schemata and processing information about the self. *Journal of Personality and Social Psychology*, 1977, **35**, 63–78.

Max, L. W. An experimental study of the motor theory of consciousness: III. Action-current responses in deaf-mutes during sleep, sensory stimulation and dreams. *Journal of Comparative Psychology*, 1935, **19**, 469–486.

Max, L. W. Experimental study of the motor theory of consciousness: IV. Action-current responses in the deaf during awakening, kinaesthetic imagery and abstract thinking. *Journal of Comparative Psychology*, 1937, **24**, 301–344.

Mead, G. H. *Mind, self, and society.* Chicago: University of Chicago Press, 1934.

Metcalf, J. T. Empathy and the actor's emotion. *Journal of Social Psychology*, 1931, **2**, 235–238.

Miller, G. A., Galanter, E., & Pribram, K. H. *Plans and the structure of behavior.* New York: Holt, 1960.

Mischel, W. *Personality and assessment.* New York: Wiley, 1968.

Mischel, W. On the future of personality measurement. *American Psychologist*, 1977, **32**, 246–254.

Moos, R. H. Situational analysis of a therapeutic community milieu. *Journal of Abnormal Psychology*, 1968, **73**, 49–61.

Pervin, L. A. The representative design of person-situation research. In D. Magnusson & N. S. Endler (Eds.), *Personality at the crossroads: Current issues in interactional psychology.* Hillsdale, N.J.: Erlbaum, 1977, Pp. 371–384.

Pilkonis, P. A. Shyness, public and private, and its relationship to other measures of social behavior. *Journal of Personality*, 1977, **45**, 585–595.

Price, R. H., & Bouffard, D. L. Behavioral appropriateness and situational constraint as dimensions of social behavior. *Journal of Personality and Social Psychology*, 1974, **30**, 579–586.

Pryor, J. B., Gibbons, F. X., Wicklund, R. A., Fazio, R., & Hood, R. Self-focused attention and self-report validity. *Journal of Personality*, 1977, **45**, 513–527.

Raush, H. L., Dittmann, A. T., & Taylor, T. J. Person, setting, and change in social interaction. *Human Relations*, 1959, **12**, 361–378.

Rogers, T. B., Kuiper, N. A., & Kirker, W. S. Self-reference and the encoding of personal information. *Journal of Personality and Social Psychology*, 1977, **35**, 677–688.

Rosenberg, S., & Sedlak, A. Structural representations of perceived personality trait relationships. In A. K. Romney, R. Shepard, & S. B. Nerlove (Eds.), *Multidimensional scaling* (Vol. 2). New York: Seminar Press, 1972.

Sampson, E. E. Personality and the location of identity. *Journal of Personality*, 1978, **46**, 552–568.

Schachter, S. The interaction of cognitive and physiological determinants of emotional state. In L. Berkowitz (Ed.), *Advances in experimental social psychology* (Vol. 1). New York: Academic Press, 1964.

Schachter, S. Some extraordinary facts about obese humans and rats. *American Psychologist*, 1971, **26**, 129–144.

Schachter, S. & Rodin, J. (Eds.). *Obese humans and rats.* Hillsdale, N.J.: Erlbaum, 1974.

Schachter, S., & Singer, J. E. Cognitive, social, and physiological determinants of emotional state. *Psychological Review*, 1962, **69**, 379–399.

Schank, R., & Abelson, R. *Scripts, plans, goals and understanding: An inquiry into human knowledge structures.* Hillsdale, N.J.: Erlbaum, 1977.

Scheier, M. F. Self-awareness, self-consciousness, and angry aggression. *Journal of Personality*, 1976, **44**, 627–644.

Scheier, M. F., & Carver, C. S. Self-focused attention and the experience of emotion: Attraction, repulsion, elation, and depression. *Journal of Personality and Social Psychology*, 1977, **35**, 625–636.

Schwartz, S. H. Normative explanations of helping behavior: A critique, proposal, and empirical test. *Journal of Experimental Social Psychology*, 1973, **9**, 349–364.

Sherif, M. An experimental approach to the study of attitudes. *Sociometry*, 1937, **1**, 90–98.

Snyder, M. Individual differences and the self-control of expressive behavior (doctoral dissertation, Stanford University, 1972). *Dissertation Abstracts International*, 1972, **33**, 4533A–4534A (University Microfilms No. 73-4598).

Snyder, M. The self-monitoring of expressive behavior. *Journal of Personality and Social Psychology*, 1974, **30**, 526–537.

Snyder, M. Attribution and behavior: Social perception and social causation. In J. H. Harvey, W. J. Ickes, & R. F. Kidd (Eds.), *New directions in attribution research*. Hillsdale, N.J.: Erlbaum, 1976.

Snyder, M. Impression management. In L. S. Wrightsman (Ed.), *Social psychology*. Belmont, Ca.: Brooks-Cole, 1977.

Snyder, M., & Cantor, N. *Thinking about ourselves and others: Self-monitoring and social knowledge*. Unpublished manuscript, University of Minnesota and Stanford University, 1979.

Snyder, M., & Monson, T. C. Persons, situations and the control of social behavior. *Journal of Personality and Social Psychology*, 1975, **32**, 637–644.

Snyder, M., & Swann, W. B. Jr. When actions reflect attitudes: The politics of impression management. *Journal of Personality and Social Psychology*, 1976, **34**, 1034–1042.

Snyder, M., & Swann, W. B., Jr. Behavioral confirmation in social interaction: From social perception to social reality. *Journal of Experimental Social Psychology*, 1978, **14**, 148–162.   (a)

Snyder, M., & Swann, W. B., Jr. Hypothesis-testing processes in social interaction. *Journal of Personality and Social Psychology*, 1978, **36**, 1202–1212.   (b)

Snyder, M., & Tanke, E. D. Behavior and attitude: Some people are more consistent than others. *Journal of Personality*, 1976, **44**, 510–517.

Snyder, M., Tanke, E. D., & Berscheid, E. Social perception and interpersonal behavior: On the self-fulfilling nature of social stereotypes. *Journal of Personality and Social Psychology*, 1977, **35**, 656–666.

Tesser, A. Self-generated attitude change. In L. Berkowitz (Ed.), *Advances in experimental social psychology* (Vol. 11). New York: Academic Press, 1978.

Thorndike, E. L. Ideomotor action. *Psychological Review*, 1913, **20**, 91–106.

Wachtel, P. Psychodynamics, behavior therapy, and the implacable experimenter: An inquiry into the consistency of personality. *Journal of Abnormal Psychology*, 1973, **82**, 324–334.

Wicker, A. W. Attitudes versus actions: The relationship of verbal and overt behavioral responses to attitude objects. *Journal of Social Issues*, 1969, **25**, 41–78.

Wicklund, R. A. Objective self-awareness. In L. Berkowitz (Ed.), *Advances in experimental social psychology* (Vol. 8). New York: Academic Press, 1975.

Younger, J. C., & Pliner, P. Obese-normal differences in the self-monitoring of expressive behavior. *Journal of Research in Personality*, 1976, **10**, 112–115.

Zimbardo, P. G. The human choice: Individuation, reason and order versus deindividuation, impulse and chaos. In W. J. Arnold & D. Levine (Eds.), *Nebraska Symposium on Motivation*. Lincoln, Neb.: University of Nebraska Press, 1969.

PART II
SOCIAL INFLUENCES AND
SOCIAL INTERACTION

ARCHITECTURAL MEDIATION OF RESIDENTIAL DENSITY AND CONTROL: CROWDING AND THE REGULATION OF SOCIAL CONTACT[1]

Andrew Baum

UNIFORMED SERVICES UNIVERSITY
OF THE HEALTH SCIENCES
BETHESDA, MARYLAND

and

Stuart Valins

STATE UNIVERSITY OF NEW YORK
AT STONY BROOK
STONY BROOK, NEW YORK

I. Introduction 132
   A. Architecture and Social Behavior 132
   B. The Study of Density and Crowding 136
II. Density and the Arousal of Crowding Stress 139
   A. Group Size and Excessive Stimulation 139
   B. Crowding and Control 141
   C. Response to Anticipated Crowding 143
III. Architectural Mediation of Residential Density 149
   A. Social Density in Residential Settings 150
   B. Residential Experience 155
   C. Social Use of Space 157
   D. Persistent Stress and Social Withdrawal 160
   E. Reactance and Helplessness 165
   F. Group Development and the Modification of Stress 169
   G. Density, Crowding, and Pathology 170
   References 172

[1]The authors would like to thank John R. Aiello, Irwin Altman, Carlene S. Baum, Glenn E. Davis, Paul J. Hopstock, David S. Krantz, Judith Rodin, Jerome E. Singer, Susan Solomon, and Daniel Stokols for their critical readings of this paper and their contributions to the development and interpretation of this research. Some of this research was supported by a grant from the National Institutes of Child Health and Human Behavior (HD07545-01).

ADVANCES IN EXPERIMENTAL SOCIAL
PSYCHOLOGY, VOL. 12

I. Introduction

People have always been interested in their environment, but only recently has our attention focused on the social and behavioral effects of our surroundings. During the early part of this century, some psychologists studied the influence of the physical environment, but their concern was largely limited to the effects of climate, weather, seasons, and other aspects of the natural world. Lewin (e.g., 1935, 1946) noted the role of environment in determining behavior, but this was most often interpreted as the social environment (e.g., the family, reference groups). Starting about 30 years ago, however, research on the effects of the physical environment on interpersonal behavior was initiated. With Festinger, Schachter, and Back's (1950) report of the effects of arrangement of space on friendship formation and the development of social networks, attention turned to the features of the built environment and its effects of social behavior. Barker and his associates began to study the interactive nature of physical, social, and psychological variables (e.g., Barker, 1963, 1968; Barker and Gump, 1964), and others (e.g., Craik, 1970; Wohlwill, 1968) addressed the environment as an important source of behavior influence. Coinciding with an upsurge of interest in crowding as an interpersonal process, the study of the physical environment has become increasingly more sophisticated and widespread during the past decade. Our research is a product of these recent developments and it is the purpose of this article to illustrate the relationships among physical variables, such as architecture, social stressors, such as crowding, and behavior.

A. ARCHITECTURE AND SOCIAL BEHAVIOR

The role of architecture in determining behavior is best understood in terms of the effects of the arrangements of space imposed by the buildings in which we live. By virtue of their placement in relation to one another, buildings limit the ways in which exterior space may be laid out and used. Similarly, the interior design of these structures dictates certain arrangements and uses of interior space. As we shall see, these effects are insufficient to account for behavior alone. The architectural design of our surroundings provides us with different behavioral options and limits the appropriateness or likelihood of varying life styles. It is the interaction of architectural arrangements of space with ongoing social and psychological processes that determines behavior.

The impact of the natural environment is at once more apparent and dramatic than that of the built environment. The more obvious effects of environment on evolution and the sometimes overwhelming effects of natural disaster (e.g., floods, severe weather) bespeak this point. However, there is no reason to assume that more subtle influences derived from the built environment are any less important. The conditions of modern civilization constantly confront us with changes to which we must adapt, and the buildings and structures of the cities and towns in which we live limit the range of adaptations that is possible. Just as climate restricts behavior, the buildings and spaces of the architectural environment make some responses more likely than others. As Fitch (1972) has noted, we have created a third environment that intervenes between natural and psychosocial realms. By manipulating our natural surroundings we can influence the development of our social surroundings and affect the ways in which social and physical conditions influence our personal style of response.

The influences of the built environment have been studied in a number of ways. The most interesting for our purposes are those investigations addressing (1) the congruence of building spaces and user needs, (2) the influence of the distribution of valuable resources on the continuing satisfaction of the users, and (3) the role of architectural features in determining the impact of one person on another. Yancey (1972), for example, has described the Pruitt–Igoe housing complex as an instance of a poor fit between the needs of the residents and the arrangement of residential space in the complex. Semiprivate spaces in the project (space outside the apartment unit that local residential groups could use and control) was poorly arranged and distant from most residents. Since other research had suggested that people need space outside of the home for achieving social goals, Yancey reasoned that requirements for comfortable neighboring and casual interaction were not met. The failure of the interior architect to support social expectations and preferred responses by providing proximal space that could be used for social interaction was reflected in the "atomization" of social networks. Consequent social isolation and dissatisfaction were associated with a general decline in physical conditions so that the housing complex was eventually razed.

Newman (1972) has considered the role of defensible space, defined as space with well-defined boundaries easily controlled by residential groups, in determining the quality of life in residential settings. The degree to which the interior arrangement of residential space provided areas that could be surveyed, controlled, and comfortably used for casual interaction among neighbors was related to group development, to residents' feelings of security, and to rates of victimization. Long, undifferentiated hallways were not used by residents as interaction spaces and did not facilitate the development of group norms governing use of this space. Hallways broken by doors that formed small clusters of apartments were more likely to lead to casual interaction. As the neighbors in these latter hallways became better acquainted, they began to exert control over the use of hallway space. Strangers were more apt to be challenged in these buildings than in those with the long, undifferentiated, and uncontrolled hallway areas, and social networks seemed better developed. Lack of congruence between needs for

134ANDREW BAUM AND STUART VALINS

group development and spaces appropriate for such development created problems for residents. At the same time, the manner in which resources (e.g., neighbors, public and private spaces, access routes) were distributed in these buildings was important. By clustering residents in small groups and providing them with suitable semiprivate space, some buildings created a more positive residential experience.

The distribution of resources in architectural settings refers to the arrangement of a number of aspects of the environment. Consider distribution of space. If people are not provided with enough space to satisfy their needs, discomfort and dissatisfaction are likely. Thus, a single resident of a small efficiency apartment may feel cramped if the apartment is too small and may find it difficult to engage in socially desirable activities. The arrangement of this space is also important. If the apartment is large enough but the arrangement of its space is such that parts of it are virtually unusable, problems may also arise. As a case in point, we may encounter problems as we try to fit our belongings into small dormitory rooms or apartments or may have difficulty in decorating poorly designed space to achieve the effect we desire. These nonsocial thwartings[2] (Stokols, 1976) can be disruptive and discomforting and may lead to decreased residential satisfaction.

While spatial inadequacy can be stressful, especially when it occurs in primary residential or work settings, socially mediated problems are likely to cause more stress and require greater behavioral adjustment. Nonsocial variables, such as spatial variability, often have a greater and more complex impact under certain social conditions. The introduction of additional people into spatially restricted settings, for example, obviously can strain an individual's ability to adapt and adversely influence group development, maintenance of personal control, and satisfaction. When students are housed three to a room in units designed for double occupancy, arousal, stress, and social disruption have been observed (Aiello, Epstein, & Karlin, 1975; Baron, Mandel, Adams, & Griffin, 1976). Preliminary data from a series of studies that we have been conducting also suggest that overassignment (tripling) in double-occupancy dormitory rooms lessens residents' sense of personal control and is aversive, but that this effect is mediated by the relationships that develop among the three residents. When one resident felt that he or she was "left out" of things by the other two roommates, problems in the dormitory intensified; socially mediated personal thwartings created by an interaction among spatial and social conditions (i.e., the need to

[2]Stokols (1976, 1978) has considered the role of personal and neutral thwartings in the arousal of crowding stress. Briefly, personal thwarting refers to social interference or goal blocking by other people. These thwartings are usually deliberate or personally directed. Neutral thwartings, in contrast, are "unintentional." The neutral thwartings produced by other people or by the environment are less stressful than personal thwartings.

share limited amounts of primary space with two others who have formed an "exclusive" group) were related to the perception of crowding and control.

In a sense, Festinger, Schachter, and Back (1950) considered the distribution of social and architectural resources in their now classic studies of spatial and functional proximity. Studying homogenous student populations, they found that the distribution of people, buildings, walkways, stairways, and the like was related to the development of friendship networks and community involvement. This "physical layout" of space, people, and facilities seemed to determine the number of people the residents met and interacted with on a casual basis. The number of passive contacts among the residents was a function of where they lived, how close other people lived, and the spaces that they shared. Proximity was important, as the distance between residences was inversely related to the likelihood of passive contact. However, physical distance was mediated by architectural features that increased or decreased the likelihood of contact; sharing stairways or entrances with others, for example, increased the probability of meeting them. Thus, whether or not one resident was likely to interact with another "by chance" was determined by the distribution of physical resources.

Since the development of friendships and groups depended on passive contact and casual neighboring, Festinger et al. concluded that the design of housing and arrangement of units and residents in space could determine social relationships among residents and individual residents' attitudes and opinions. Subsequent research with more heterogeneous populations (Nahemow & Lawton, 1975) has supported the notion that the physical configuration of space and the distribution of people within it affect friendship formation. While similarity was influential in determining friendship patterns, proximity was associated with social networks among dissimilar residents.

Other studies have examined the ways in which architectural features affect interpersonal relations. While these investigations have focused on more isolated processes and secondary settings, they are of some interest here. Baum, Riess, and O'Hara (1974) noted the role of design features in reducing the aversiveness of spatial invasion, and Stokols, Smith, and Prostor (1976) have considered the ways in which different partitions increase and decrease the aversiveness of waiting in line. Desor (1972) found that responses to scaled-down rooms were a joint function of social orientations and physical features, such as barriers, doors, and the shape of the room. When "people" were more visually intrusive, judgments of crowding and indications of developing problems were more likely.

As noted earlier, a mounting body of research on the problems of population expansion and crowding has paralleled the increase in concern with environmental and architectural matters. Not unexpectedly, there has been a blending of these interests in crowding and the physical environment, and our research represents such a mixture. Our concern with architecture has largely been focused on the architectural mediation of population density and the consequences of social density and crowding. The next section describes our interest in the phenomena of crowding and personal control, and subsequent sections consider the ways in which the architectural issues discussed above are related to the experience of high density.

B. THE STUDY OF DENSITY AND CROWDING

Interest in density and crowding has been marked by a number of issues and controversies, many of which reflect basic differences in approach (see Altman, 1978, for a review of this subject). Psychological analyses of the processes by which density may lead to social pathology usually attempt to identify the antecedents of crowding stress and the ways in which people cope with this stress. Most of these conceptions have been merely descriptive, however, so that it is not easy to reconcile the divergent approaches. On the one hand, contradictory findings and perspectives may be due to different levels of analysis. Research has been conducted at molar and molecular levels, in the field and in the laboratory, and at the societal, group, and individual levels. The issue here is not "which level is best" but which is appropriate for the question under study (cf. Karlin, Epstein, & Aiello, 1978) and how movement among these levels can produce conceptual and methodological refinement.

On the other hand, there are also definitional problems. Studies of urban density (e.g., Schmitt, 1966; Winsborough, 1965) tended to equate the two terms, density and crowding. Studies of high-density animal populations (e.g., Calhoun, 1962) also used these words interchangeably. In the first series of experimental studies of human subjects, crowding was defined in the language of physical density (cf. Freedman, 1975). Shortly thereafter, however, Stokols (1972) drew a distinction between crowding and density, defining the former as the psychological experience of the physical conditions described by the latter. Further, he noted that this experience was mediated by environmental, social, and psychological parameters of situations and setting occupants. The significance of this distinction is immediately obvious, since density clearly causes a number of phenomena that are not generally considered crowding and may result in positive experiences that are not stressful. Stokols' distinctions between physical density and crowding experience have now been elaborated so that crowding has been variously defined in terms of inadequate privacy, loss of control over interpersonal contact, intensification of affect and behavior, and as a label for arousal (e.g., Altman, 1975; Baron & Rodin, 1978; Worchel and Teddlie, 1976).

It has become fairly clear that it is problematic to equate density and crowding when large, heterogenous units, such as census tracts, are studied; variations in density are generally not considered in such analyses, and the interpersonal nature of crowding may not be adequately considered (e.g., Galle, Gove, & McPherson, 1972). Similarly, field research has suggested that density and crowding do not always occur together (e.g., McCarthy & Saegert, 1979). Since high population density is associated with a number of problems that cannot be defined as crowding nor expected to generate crowding stress (e.g., noise, deindividuation, excitement, diversity of behavior options), we often have to study the psychological resultants, such as crowding. Because psychological experience is mediated by other variables, the use of physical indices of density as operationalizations of experienced crowding may not be sufficient.

In light of these considerations, we feel it is important to define crowding as a subjective state, *the stressful experience of limited space and/or of too many people*. Density, on the other hand, is best viewed as an objective condition, *the number of persons per unit of space*. As available space decreases or as the number of people in a constant amount of space increases, density increases. Increasingly high density is accompanied by a number of potential constraints, inconveniences, or threats (such as interference with ongoing activity, social overload, reduction of available privacy, or restriction of behavioral freedom). However, these problems are not always salient when density is great; physical or social structure can minimize interference and overload in a high-density situation. By organizing behavior, by providing norms and expectations governing interaction, or by reinforcing control over social experience, some kinds of social structures may allow people to live and work under high-density conditions without discomfort or stress. These intervening relationships can reduce the salience of density-related problems by mitigating their effects and reducing the likelihood that they are perceived as inconvenience or threat. If high density does not pose problems for people, it is unlikely that crowding will be experienced. If, however, problems associated with high density are salient, crowding is likely.

Crowding is viewed as psychological stress that is sometimes caused by high density. Whether or not stress is experienced is dependent upon mediation by situational and psychological variables. Our research has been based upon these definitions, and the overall formulation of density and crowding is based upon and consistent with Stokols' distinctions and subsequent theoretical development (e.g., 1972, 1976). Further, the findings of our research are explicable using these conceptualizations, while other definitions equating density and crowding have more difficulty in accounting for our data.

Our approach is multimethod and multilevel; our research has used experimental, quasiexperimental, observational, and survey strategies and has considered molar and molecular responses of groups and single individuals. We have used laboratory studies of people expecting to feel crowded, for example, to clarify the dynamics of phenomena observed in natural settings. Our housing research, in contrast, is based on an architectural variation of social density analogous to an experimental treatment. The strength of this variation arises from the many hours and days that subjects are exposed to the "treatment." Data on the participants' experience and behavior while in these residential environments are conceptualized as manifestations of the "independent manipulation," and data on the subjects' responses to conditions in the laboratory are seen as persistent or enduring effects of residential conditions, i.e., the "dependent" measures. By combining strategies and levels of analysis, assuring random assignment to residence where possible, and demonstrating comparability of resident populations where randomizations was not possible, we feel that we have maintained a good deal of experimental rigor in our study of naturally occurring phenomena. As Singer, Lundberg, and Frankenhaeuser (1978) suggest, the balance between the greatest possible rigor in situations that "consistently defy" attempts to maintain experimental control and the maintenance of the integrity of the setting under observation represents a crucial aspect of our attempt to understand the effects of density, architectural design, and crowding.

In the next section, we take our definition of crowding a step further. Following from control-based formulations of crowding (e.g., Altman, 1975; Baron & Rodin, 1978; Stokols, 1978), we propose that crowding is experienced when high density inhibits individuals' ability to regulate the nature and frequency of their social interaction with others. As our research developed, the utility of personal control constructs in examining and predicting the effects of crowding became ever more obvious to us. Our use of these constructs has primarily reflected what may be termed selective or regulatory control, i.e., an individual's ability to determine to what or whom he/she attends and when others are encountered. However, the relationship between control and crowding is considerably more complex; crowding may interfere with people's abilities to predict social events and choose among response options and may affect people's perception that outcomes are contingent upon behavior. Thus, our use of control may be interpreted within the framework of personal control, defined as the ability to establish correspondence between intent and the consequences of one's actions (Baron & Rodin, 1978).

We have interpreted many of our findings in terms of conditions associated with high density that are presumably relevant to the sense of personal control. However, as will become apparent, we have very little direct evidence regarding the role of perceived control in the arousal of crowding stress. Control was not directly manipulated, and we did not begin to measure perceptions of control until late in our research program. As a consequence, we do not have sufficient data to adequately demonstrate the operation of these perceptions. However, we feel that our interpretations are reasonable in light of the data we have collected. The direct investigation of perceived personal control as a mediator of crowding stress should be pursued further.

II. Density and the Arousal of Crowding Stress

A. GROUP SIZE AND EXCESSIVE STIMULATION

Density, as a physical condition, involves both spatial and social phenomena. Our initial interest was in the effects of increasing group size and, as a result, our original thinking was guided primarily by conceptualizations of density based on numbers of people. We therefore considered those analytic models primarily concerned with the complexity of the social environment, the regulation of social contact and information, and the effects of unpredictable and uncontrollable interaction.

In considering the urban experience, Milgram (1970) used the concepts of system overload and social complexity to link the quality of urban life to demographic circumstances, such as residential density and frequency of social contact. Milgram reasoned that at any given time, people have a vast amount of information available to them, derived from both internal and external sources. In constructing their individual realities, they selectively attend to some information impinging on them. Most persons neither want nor need to deal with all of the information available to them, and by actively disregarding information judged to be unimportant, they are able to function more comfortably and productively. As the amount of available input increases, the amount that is disregarded must also increase. Milgram argued that when a substantial portion of the overall increase is social, the result may be withdrawal from other people. In cities we are continually exposed to situations in which the number of potential encounters with others is far greater than we desire. We therefore may be forced to limit our involvement with unimportant others and confine attention to a small number of primary relationships.

If people can maintain control in their selection of persons with whom they interact (and in when and where this interaction occurs), their response to information overload will be orderly. Low-priority inputs will be discarded in favor of more important information, and perceptual screening will permit involvement only with those persons considered important (e.g., friends, more "valuable" associates). Further, interaction will tend to occur primarily at times during which contact is desired, and in places where they feel relatively comfortable. Such adaptations are costly, resulting in the proliferation of superficial relationships, the development of norms legitimizing noninvolvement, and a certain degree of withdrawal from the environment. However, they appear to make the surfeit of information in urban settings more tolerable. If selective control were not maintained, screening would probably become more arbitrary; if involvement cannot be allocated on the basis of some predetermined schema, withdrawal will become more pervasive and indiscriminate.

Milgram's description of city life suggests that high density is a primary determinant of the complexity of the urban environment. Because of the large number of people in cities, we are exposed to many more potential interactions than we may like. Thus, urban life may represent a more or less continuous encounter with social overload, straining our capacity to structure the environment and to deal with it in a satisfying and comfortable way. When this overload is experienced as stress (i.e., when the ability to selectively reduce frequency of contact is taxed), people begin to feel crowded and to orient themselves toward simplifying the social environment. They do so in an attempt to maximize meaningful social experience at the expense of less important or "new" social interactions. As noted above, role structuring and development of norms legitimizing "streamlined" and superficial relationships help an individual to optimize the number and intensity of social encounters. Such strategies may also be responsible for the observed unresponsiveness of the urban "bystander" (e.g., Latane & Darley, 1970). When these strategies fail, people will be forced to make an excessive number of social adjustments (e.g., Calhoun, 1970), and persistent stress and withdrawal are more likely.

Calhoun (1962, 1970) assumes that people must regulate their interactions with others in order to maintain a healthy balance between frustrating and gratifying social encounters. As group size and the number of others with whom interaction is likely increase beyond optimal levels, people may find it difficult to control and regulate their encounters with others. This overloaded social environment leads to a general breakdown of the individuals' ability to influence the frequency and nature of their social interactions. They may experience too many interactions at times when such contact is inappropriate, or with others with whom interactions is unwanted. Since the selective screening mechanisms developed to deal with social overload may not be effective in such situations, contact with the social environment may be generally reduced in order to minimize further overload.

As these accounts and our own research suggest, crowding stress is to a large extent a function of the consequences of having to deal with too many others. The experience of crowding may be thought of in terms of excessive stimulation (Desor, 1972), increased social complexity (Saegert, 1978), or a syndrome of social overload (Milgram, 1970) and unwanted, uncontrolled interaction (Calhoun, 1970). To the extent that these conditions are experienced (regardless of whether or not they are labeled as crowding), people will seek to reestablish control over their interactions. If successful, stress will be reduced and coping behaviors will persist. If these coping behaviors fail, however, the stress will continue and may form the foundation for the development of pathology. The large numbers of people in cities and other high-density environments require the development of social screening techniques which permit individuals to control the number and nature of their interactions with others.

Glass and Singer (1972) suggest that interaction controls similar to those discussed by Milgram and Calhoun can be conceptualized as "... long term consequences of adaption to the overload inherent to urban life . . . the coping process of not attending to social stimuli produces a sustained lack of reaction to the environment . . .'' (Glass & Singer, 1972, p. 11). Because successful coping with the large numbers of people may lead to the reduction of social encounters and lessen sensitivity to social stimuli, this withdrawal often succeeds and may become a modal response to the social environment.

B.   CROWDING AND CONTROL

As these accounts suggest, the effects of large group size may be most severe when they affect one's ability to regulate social interaction and selectively attend to the information provided by the given setting. High density is a rich source of information and is associated with a number of conditions that may present us with problems or otherwise interfere with desired behavior. Many of these conditions have been used as central constructs in analyses of crowding. Most notably, spatial restriction, behavioral constraint, overload, and interference have been proposed as products of high density that can cause people to feel crowded (e.g., Freedman, 1975; Saegert, 1978; Stokols, 1972; Sundstrom, 1975). It may be possible to reconcile these different schemes if we can identify the ways in which these antecedent conditions affect one's sense of control over social experience. Our attempt at such a synthesis has been facilitated by previous discussion of boundary regulation and interaction control in high-density settings (Altman, 1975; Baron & Rodin, 1978).

Altman (1975) focused on crowding as an extreme consequence of failure to achieve desired levels of privacy. In doing so, he considered the role of social and spatial conditions in the regulation of privacy and interpersonal contact. Similarly, Baron and Rodin (1978) have discussed the role of social and spatial conditions of high density as they threaten maintenance of personal control, and Stokols (1976) has noted the effects of density-related loss of control that inhibits the attainment of desired goals and the exercise of behavioral freedom. We feel that these approaches are promising, both in terms of generating interesting new questions and in facilitating our understanding of crowding.

In our research on density, we are assuming that perceived loss of desired control can be aversive, stressful, and debilitating. Based upon discussions of people's needs for control and their belief in self-determination (e.g., Kelley, 1971; Lerner, 1970; Wortman & Brehm, 1975), many researchers have employed similar reasoning and have demonstrated the variety of ways in which loss of control can be experienced (e.g., Averill, 1973). Helplessness arising from repeated exposure to uncontrollable outcomes has been associated with psychological depression (e.g., Seligman, 1975) and impaired adaptive abilities (e.g., Glass & Singer, 1972; Janis & Leventhal, 1968; Rodin, 1976). Research has also suggested that perceived loss of control can arouse reactance (Brehm, 1966), withdrawal (e.g., Seligman, 1975), and aggression (e.g., Zimbardo,

1969). Perceived loss of control apparently does have effects on mood and behavior and, to the extent that it is engendered by high density, may be active in the arousal of crowding stress.

1. Spatial Regulation of Dyadic Interaction

Framing spatial conditions of high density in terms of degree of perceived control, one may argue that spatial limitation becomes aversive as it threatens the desired sense of personal control. Numerous studies have demonstrated that people attempt to control the intimacy of their social contacts, regulating the distance between themselves and others by adjusting their behaviors, such as eye contact and body lean, that signal psychological closeness (e.g., Aiello, 1977; Argyle & Dean, 1965; Kaplan & Greenberg, 1976). Regulation of intimacy with others may be a way of controlling one's social experience. When spatial limitation makes adjustment of actual or perceived interpersonal distances difficult, intimacy regulation may be impaired. To the extent that small spaces are seen as responsible for spatial intrusion or inappropriate intimacy, high density may threaten one's sense of control and arouse stress.

The constraining influence of others in relatively small spaces can also threaten behavioral freedom. Because of limited amounts of space, the number of possible behavioral options may be low and the freedom to choose among those available may be limited. The close proximity of others can inhibit certain responses; close physical presence may make even the most routine behaviors more difficult (e.g., stretching without bumping into someone else). This spatially induced problem may arouse reactance, which appears to be involved in crowding stress (e.g., Stokols, 1972, 1976). Closely related to this problem is the matter of interference; the presence of others in a small setting may block goal attainment, physically disrupt behavior, and otherwise make purposeful behavior more frustrating and less effective (Schopler & Stockdale, 1977; Sundstrom, 1975). Both of these conditions, restrictions on freedom of action and thwartings, can also inhibit and sense of individual control and arouse crowding stress.

It should be noted that although spatial limitations may be disruptive when only one person is involved, this type of limitation does not lead to the experience of crowding unless other people are present. Providing a single individual with inappropriately small amounts of space may constrain his or her behavior and reduce his or her perceived control over instrumental behaviors, but this condition is probably considered "cramped" rather than crowded. As we have already mentioned, when one's sense of control is threatened by the presence of others or when control over interpersonal events is reduced we are especially apt to label our experience "crowding." In accord with Stokols' (1976) discussion of personal and neutral thwartings, we believe that the socially mediated loss of control is particularly aversive and potentially quite disruptive.

Also consistent with Stokols' formulations, we think that the value and significance of personal control varies from situation to situation. The value of maintaining and exercising control should increase when highly desirable goals are being sought or when operating in primary settings (places where one spends a relatively large amount of time and relates to others on a personal basis). Thus, the maintenance of control over one's social experience in primary residential settings should be more important than achieving control over events in a laboratory.

2. Social Regulation of Dyadic Interaction

Density is also related to the number of people involved in a situation. As the number of people active in the setting increases, the amount of social stimulation, frequency of social contact, and desirability of social contact may be affected. Both Milgram (1970) and Calhoun (1970) consider ways in which high density affects the individual's ability to regulate and selectively attend to his or her social environment. Other writers have also alluded to the social interference caused by increasingly dense concentrations of people (e.g., Baum & Koman, 1976; Schopler & Walton, 1974). Large numbers of people may also lead to decreasing familiarity with those people whom one encounters routinely; highrise living seems to produce more frequent contact with people who are not known (e.g., McCarthy & Saegert, 1979) and increases in this contact with unfamiliar others may reduce the predictability of one's social encounters. Increasingly large group size can therefore have negative consequences for mood and behavior when desired social control or regulation of social contact is restricted.

Up to this point we have assumed that the consequences of exposure to social and spatial conditions of high density are similar. In both cases, we believe, a loss of the desired sense of control gives rise to stress. However, the effects of social and spatial conditions accompanying high density appear to be very different. Those conditions made salient by situational and psychological variables appear to determine the kinds of responses that are likely.

C. RESPONSE TO ANTICIPATED CROWDING

Our studies of response to anticipated crowding have provided some relevant evidence. Originally designed to avoid the problems that are created by only brief exposure to high density, our procedure focuses on the behavior and affect displayed by people preparing to spend an undetermined period of time under high-density conditions (e.g., Baum & Greenberg, 1975). Although limited in that subjects are never exposed to actual high-density situations, this method is particularly well suited for research into the cognitive aspects of the crowding process. By convincing subjects that they will be crowded and by observing their preparatory behavior and feelings, we have been able to identify some conditions that people expect to be associated with high density, the ways in which they expect these conditions to affect them, and the coping strategies they have developed from prior experience with crowding.

The procedures in these studies were designed to convince subjects that they would be exposed to high-density conditions. Subjects arrived for the session expecting to participate in a group. The expected group size was manipulated through the instructions provided and the number of materials (e.g., pencils, clipboards, experimental forms) in the room that were visible to the subjects. As they waited for the group to gather, same-sex confederates posing as subjects began to arrive, and subjects overheard them receiving the same instructions they had received. Subjects were observed during this waiting period, and self-report data were obtained by asking subjects to complete a preexperimental questionnaire after two confederates had arrived. Upon completion of the questionnaire, the sessions were terminated and subjects were debriefed.

Initial use of these procedures revealed interesting parallels between the reactions exhibited in these ''preparatory'' situations and responses to actual conditions of high density (Baum & Greenberg, 1975). Subjects expecting to participate in 10-person groups felt more uncomfortable and crowded than did subjects expecting to be in four-person groups, even though all subjects made these ratings in the same room and in the presence of only two other people. Further, subjects expecting large groups chose more socially isolated seat positions and avoided contact with the confederates, while subjects expecting small groups were less likely to show this avoidance. Subjects appeared to be anticipating conditions associated with large group size. Their withdrawal was evidently an adaptive preparation that sought to minimize their social encounters and increase their sense of control over their social contacts. By assuming a noninteractive stance, the subjects may have believed that they could discourage interaction or escape it during the session, thereby reducing the impact of those social conditions that they anticipated.

Social and Spatial Density

Our initial studies suggested that preparatory responses to anticipated crowding reflect those conditions associated with high-density that people expect to experience. As we have argued, density may be described in terms of a number of physical conditions, each of which may affect an individual's ability to regulate social experience. However, the ways in which these conditions are experienced and the nature of one's response to them should be different. Loss of control over the distances from others that one may maintain should result in responses directed toward increasing interindividual distances, gaining dominance over larger amounts of space, or otherwise reasserting one's ability to choose freely among those behavioral options available. Loss of regulatory control over frequency of interaction, in contrast, should be oriented toward avoiding unwanted contact or minimizing that which is inescapable.

These differences were addressed by a second study of anticipated crowding (Baum & Koman, 1976) in which social and spatial antecedents were varied independently. Social density, manipulated by varying group size, can be viewed as a way of operationalizing potential problems with interaction frequency caused by physical density. As group size increases, the number of people with whom one may interact also increases. Thus, increasing social density refers to the heightened saliency of numerosity effects in a setting and to threats to control produced by large groups. Individuals in high social density settings may anticipate or even experience social or cognitive overload, unwanted interactions, social interference, or excessively high levels of social stimulation. These experiences should be mediated by variables, such as group structure and goals, that influence one's ability to regulate the frequency and nature of interpersonal contacts (e.g., see Schopler & Walton, 1974). The response to social density should be directed toward minimizing contact, reestablishing regulatory control over social experience, or reinforcing one's ability to predict and avoid interaction with others.

Spatial density, in contrast, is manipulated by varying room size and has to do with the ways in which diminishing amounts of available space affect mood and behavior. Increasing spatial density refers to the increasing salience of the threats to one's sense of control that arise from small spaces. These threats may involve loss of control over the intimacy of interpersonal contacts, interference and behavioral disruption, or proximity-caused behavioral constraints. These experiences should be mediated by properties of the setting that make the amount of space available appear larger or more appropriate or that relieve spatially induced constraints on behavior (e.g., Baum & Davis, 1976; Stokols, 1972; Worchel & Teddlie, 1976). Further, the response to spatial density may be more aggressive than the response to social density. For example, people may respond to spatial limitation by aggressively attempting to ''enlarge their spatial holdings.'' If one assumes that controlling more space will enable people to regain control over how close others may approach, restore their control over interpersonal intimacy, and alleviate the constraining aspects of the situation, aggression may be a productive response.

In order to assess the relative effects of room size and group size and to determine whether these effects are mediated by different social or psychological variables, two levels of social and spatial density were crossed with two levels of structure and sex-of-subject variables in a $2 \times 2 \times 2 \times 2$ experimental design. Subjects were told to expect a five- or a 10-person group session and were seated in either a large (2.7×4.6 m) or a small (1.5×4.1 m) room. Half of these groups were to be composed of college men and the other groups were to be college women. Further, half of the subjects were told to expect a high degree of externally determined social structure ("Once everyone arrives, a group leader will be selected and rules governing behavior in the session will be explained"), while remaining subjects were not given any information about social structure. Procedures in this experiment were similar to those used previously, and subjects' seat position, facial regard (looking at the face or eyes of the confederates), willingness to talk with confederates, and discomfort were again assessed. Ratings of the experimental room and the expected session were also collected.

It was predicted that subjects would respond differently when high social densities were perceptually salient (expectation of a 10-person group) than when spatial densities were salient (expectation of five-person groups in the small room), or when neither was seen as too great (five-person groups in the large room). When the salient stimulus features of the setting aroused expectation of inadequate space and threats to distancing, behavioral freedom, and intimacy regulation, subjects should assume more central seat positions (thereby taking an offensive position and signifying a desire to be dominant). However, since men seem to prefer interacting with each other at greater distances than do women (e.g., Aiello, 1977; Aiello & Jones, 1971), the effects of small spaces were expected to vary with sex; men would respond more aggressively than women and would report greater discomfort and crowding. When the nature of the setting emphasized the imminent presence of many others, response was not expected to be aggressive or dominance oriented. If subjects felt that groups of 10 would provide too much interaction, they should withdraw. Thus, we expected them to assume more peripheral seat positions. Further, the presence of structure (providing a leader and rules governing group interaction) should make the amount of contact in 10-person groups seem more reasonable or controllable. While having a leader and knowing when one will interact with others should affect preparation for a session in which frequent contact is expected, it should not affect response to expectations that others will be very close, in the way, or otherwise intrusive.

Our findings confirm these predictions, suggesting that social and spatial density are mediated by different conditions and that they evoke different responses. The effects of anticipated group size were qualified by an interaction with expected structure; subjects expecting 10-person groups reported more discomfort and crowding during the anticipatory period and withdrew from the center of the group by selecting more peripheral seat positions than did subjects expecting five-person groups. The sex of the subjects did not influence these reactions, but rules governing interaction did. Those people expecting structured sessions in a large group did not differ from those anticipating smaller groups, while those subjects expecting an unstructured session with 10 participants reported more crowding and discomfort and assumed more peripheral seat positions than did subjects in the other conditions.

Effects of group size were relatively strong and consistently mediated by structure. The effects of room size were less pervasive and varied with the sex of the subject. Room size did not affect subjects' reaction to the anticipated 10-person groups. Apparently, the expectation of a large group is sufficient to generate discomfort and crowding and the size of the room did not appreciably relieve or intensify this response. However, the size of the room produced the predicted effects when only a small group was anticipated. The people expecting

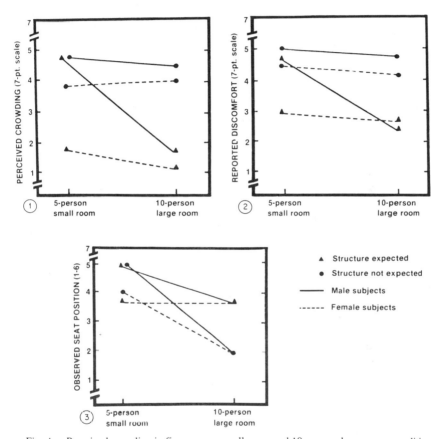

Fig. 1.   Perceived crowding in five-person, small-room and 10-person, large-room conditions.

Fig. 2.   Reported discomfort in five-person, small-room and 10-person, large-room conditions.

Fig. 3.   Observed seat position in five-person, small-room and 10-person, large room conditions. (Figures 1, 2, and 3 from Baum, A., & Koman, S. Differential response to anticipated crowding: psychological effects of social and spatial density. *Journal of Personality and Social Psychology*, 1976, **34**, 526–536. Copyright 1976 by the American Psychological Association. Reprinted by permission.)

five-person groups reported more crowding and discomfort in the small room than in the large room and sat in more centrally located chairs when space was relatively limited. This tendency, however, was primarily exhibited by men. Room size did not affect the women's responses to any of the conditions in the study; a comparison of the reactions to five-person groups in the different size rooms indicated that decreasing amounts of available space only affected men's responses. Decreasing room size led to feelings of crowding and discomfort and increased the choice of central seat positions among males but not females.

These findings suggest a number of things. First, behavioral reactions to anticipated large-group experience are different from the responses to expected participation in small spaces. Second, these responses are affected by different variables, suggesting that the appraisal of and reactions to high social density are governed by different processes from those associated with high spatial density. Further, our results indicate that numbers of people have a greater impact than do small spaces; when 10 people were expected, the subjects' responses were was more likely to be withdrawal oriented and affected by anticipated degree of external regulation of interaction. Room size did not affect this pattern.

Additional support for this analysis may be obtained by comparing the reactions to the five-person, small-room condition and to the 10-person, large-room condition. Because both room size and expected group size were varied on a ratio of 2 : 1, anticipated physical densities in these two conditions were comparable. Had the appropriate number of subjects actually been present, both conditions would have provided each subject with about 1.2 m^2 of space. If the absolute level of physical density in the setting rather than the perceived locus of threats to personal control is the primary determinant of response to these anticipated conditions, the reactions to these two situations should be comparable. However, as can be seen in Figs. 1–3, there were very different responses to these two conditions. In the 10-person, large-room condition, the anticipated experience appears to be dominated by expectation of large numbers of people. Response seemed to be directed more toward withdrawal than toward "annexation" of additional space and was determined largely by structure rather than by sex. By comparison, the participants' response to the small room when only five people were expected and spatial restrictions were pronounced depended on their sex. When salient conditions aroused perceptions of inadequate space, experiential and behavioral responses were different from those caused by stimulus features promoting frequent contact with a large number of people.

These findings are interesting for a number of reasons. First they help us explain the contradictory findings in studies of crowding. Some of the investigations, for example, have yielded consistent sex differences similar to those observed in our small-group, small-room conditions (e.g., Freedman, 1975; Ross, Layton, Erickson, & Schopler, 1973; Stokols, Rall, Pinner, & Schopler, 1973). Other studies have not obtained these sex differences (e.g., Baum & Valins,

1977; Griffitt & Veitch, 1971). For the most part, studies reporting sex differences involved variation of room size, while those that did not yield sex differences manipulated group size. In light of our study, these divergent findings appear to reflect differences between the operationalizations used. Because previous research has not considered the same antecedent conditions, their divergence is predictable and consistent.

More importantly, our findings suggest that the ways in which social and spatial conditions threaten subject's sense of personal control are different. Large numbers of people present threats to interaction regulation because (1) the number of potential interactions is great, (2) individuals' ability to predict encounters is low, (3) interaction is more likely when it is unwanted, and (4) social contacts become difficult to avoid or terminate. Consistent with Baron's and Rodin's discussion of crowding and personal control, crowding experienced in the context of more than optimal numbers of people is caused by an increase in the amount of social information available and the frequency of contact. Ability to effectively manage the number of interactions experienced and to predict and regulate when or where they occur is therefore reduced.

The effects of small amounts of space, however, can be considered in light of the nature of interactions experienced. Inadequate amounts of space threaten one's sense of control by (1) making it more difficult to regulate the intimacy of each encounter, (2) interfering with goal-oriented behavior, and (3) constraining behavior by reducing the number of options available. Physical closeness of others, then, should not increase the frequency of contact so much as reduce an individual's ability to regulate the quality of the interaction.

We have considered the role of regulatory control in the arousal of crowding stress. So far, however, this has been limited to the laboratory, where the freely occurring dynamics of crowding may be suppressed. We are confident that these laboratory studies have identified conceptual linkages in determining the effects of high density, but we do not feel that specific characters of this equation have been isolated. Clearly, the way to do this is to study the experience of density and mediation of crowding stress in naturally occurring environments and to apply as many of the controls of experimental psychology to this investigation as is possible. In the next section, we begin to explore the mediating role of architectural variables in the density–crowding relationship. Interior design is viewed as influencing the salience of some aspects of high density.

III. Architectural Mediation of Residential Density

The operation of physical, social, and psychological variables in arousing crowding stress and determining coping responses was the focal point of our research in college dormitories. Architectural variables determining the arrangement of residents around shared spaces were studied. Despite initial population comparability and equivalent physical densities characterizing all dormitories, variation along architectural dimensions was associated with stress and reported crowding. Dormitories clustering large numbers of residents around undifferentiated, shared spaces exposed residents to relatively high social density in which regulation of social experience was difficult. Residents readily used "crowding" as a label for stress associated with loss of regulatory control over social contact and frequent unwanted interaction. Coping responses, adaptive in the dormitory environment to the extent that they reduced unwanted interaction and attentuated threats to control, were found to persist in laboratory settings where they were counterproductive. This persistence was seen as a consequence of an inability to restore comfortable regulatory control over social experience and may reflect the foundations of density-related pathology.

In this section we intend to review the mediation of high-density conditions by architectural design and discuss behavioral and affective consequences of long-term exposure to excessive social stimulation and large residential group size. By reviewing these findings, we hope to further demonstrate the role of regulatory control over social contact in arousing stress, in evoking judgments of crowding, and in determining responses to a variety of situations.

A. SOCIAL DENSITY IN RESIDENTIAL SETTINGS

As we have noted, social density can be thought of in terms of numerosity-based threats to regulation of social contact. As the number of people in a setting increases, the number of interpersonal adjustments required of each also increases. Higher levels of information and the increasing complexity of the social environment caused by high social density present demands that strain individual ability to selectively attend to other people. Unwanted interaction becomes an important dynamic in such situations; when screening mechanisms fail, people are no longer able to control the intensity of interactions or determine when and with whom they will interact.

When the duration of exposure to social density is brief and the setting relatively unimportant, these problems may not be severe and successful coping may be relatively easy. Brief exposure to large numbers of people in a waiting room or building lobby, for example, may not seriously threaten personal control; the interpersonal adjustments required can be minimized by directing one's gaze away from the people in the setting or by focusing one's attention exclusively on a small group of associates. Most of the information provided by the setting can be ignored without significant penalty, and norms legitimizing noninvolvement in public, secondary settings should reduce unwanted contact. However, when perceived mastery over the environment is important, as it is in primary residential and office settings, and when exposure to high social density is prolonged, the costs of these kinds of responses may be too great and successful coping more difficult.

In a residential context mastery of interpersonal relationships and information provided by the setting are important concerns. Under benign conditions, people adjust their behavior toward each other in ways that lead to variable amounts of gratifying and frustrating experience. As their behavioral adjustments unfold, people extract information about the relationships between behavior and social outcome and learn behaviors that produce desirable and undesirable results. In a college dormitory, for example, residents will learn how to deal with each of their neighbors and how to communicate varying levels of desired involvement. Particular people become comfortable with one another and see one another as linked to positive experience. These people should, therefore, seek each other out. Hierarchical friendship networks develop as residents assign different "values" to their associates.

Thus, the process of becoming comfortable with one's neighbors is based on recognition of behavior—outcome contingencies. One must learn what to expect and how to behave with other residents. As the size of an interacting group increases, this process may become more time consuming and more difficult. Because more people are routinely encountered, more relationships must be learned and involvement with others may be more dispersed. At some point in their development, for example, large residential groups present individuals with dyadic interactions that are both unpredictable and unfamiliar. Neighbors are not as sure of what to expect from each other as when groups are smaller, and more extensive contact with each neighbor is possible. As a result, residents living with a large number of others may not know how to behave in a given interaction, more frequently encountering people with whom comfortable modes of interaction have not evolved. Involvement-noninvolvement and friend-stranger categories for each neighbor are less likely to have been established, leading to more unpredictable and uncomfortable encounters with neighbors and rendering social outcomes more independent of behavior.

These regulatory difficulties associated with social density, however, are not a simple function of numbers of people. Situational mediation of density will determine the likelihood and severity of these threats to regulatory control. If, for example, architectural designs provide semiprivate spaces that facilitate small-group formation and strengthen an individual's ability to regulate social experience, the arousal of stress, crowding, and withdrawal should be minimal. In a sense, externally supported social control can counteract the potential threat posed by high social density. If, however, large numbers of residents are housed in settings in which the arrangement of interior space does not provide appropriate semiprivate space or facilitate social groupings that support individual control, selective screening mechanisms may fail and the ability to predict, approach, or avoid specific encounters should be impaired. Under these conditions, the potential threats to control posed by social density are realized, and stress attributable to crowding should be likely.

Our research has considered the experiential and behavioral consequences of college residential environments in which interior architectures varied in the degree to which they provided spaces that supported expectations for and experience with regulation of social experience. One group of dormitories grouped large numbers of residents around common areas, and the design of these buildings differentiated only between private bedroom areas and more public hall facilities. A second group of buildings provided physical distinctions among private, semiprivate, and public spaces and structured social contact by grouping residents in smaller clusters around shared space. Since the physical density (space per person) was comparable for both types of buildings (approximately 153 and 156 ft^2 per person), we had the opportunity to observe the effects of architecturally induced variation of social density (number of people sharing common areas).

Basic to this research was the assumption that comparison of relatively homogeneous and comparable resident populations housed in buildings varying in design would yield information reflecting the impact of the different designs. Experimental treatments were inferred from architectural variation, and assessments of these treatments were conducted in much the same way as if they were generated in the laboratory.

The Dormitory Design

Of the designs studied, the corridor design was more traditional. Dominated by a long, undifferentiated central hallway, these dormitories housed about 34 residents on a floor. Physical structure did not provide groupings or subdivisions of this large group beyond that afforded by the two-person bedroom unit. Instead, 17 double-occupancy bedrooms, a central bath area, and an end-hall lounge were arranged along a double-loaded corridor. Residents shared these living areas and the hallway provided social space as well as access to facilities and to the rest of the building (see Fig. 4).

The 32 or 34 residents of a floor in the suite-design dormitories were not required to share many resources with all their neighbors. Instead, the design of these residential environments dispersed people in small four- to six-person suites, each containing its own bath and lounge. The only area shared by the larger group in these buildings was the hallway space, and because shared bathroom and lounge spaces were inside the suites, the need to use the hallway was reduced. Thus, that space shared by all residents of a floor was less likely to be used, and unfamiliar neighbors were encountered less frequently. Suite units arranged along this hallway were relatively self-sufficient, and use of the hallway seemed to be restricted to access to other suites and to the rest of the building (see Fig. 5).

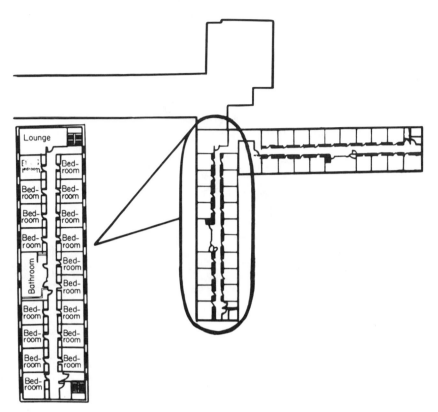

Fig. 4.   Floor plan of corridor-design dormitory. (From Baum, A., & Valins, S. *Architecture and Social Behavior: Psychological Studies of Social Density*. Erlbaum, 1977.)

Considering our discussion of threats to regulatory control created by high social density, one might expect residents of the corridor design dormitories to experience greater difficulty regulating social contact in the dormitory. Both suite and corridor residents share bathroom and lounge spaces. However, access to these areas is different. Corridor residents must use the hallway to reach these areas, while suite residents do not. Thus, corridor residents are more likely to be using the hallway and to encounter others in this space. As we shall see, the hallway space in which corridor residents "collide" is relatively uncontrolled space in contrast to the group-regulated suite interior.

More importantly, the greater number of people sharing corridor dormitory facilities should result in contact with more different people, while the group size in suites creates a situation in which contact is with fewer different people. The corridor resident leaving his or her bedroom is likely to encounter any of the 33 people sharing this space with him or her. As a result, interaction is likely to

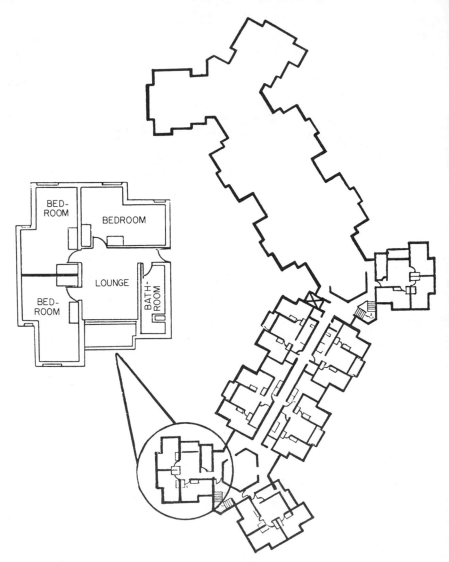

Fig. 5.   Floor plan of suite-design dormitory. (From Baum, A., & Valins, S. *Architecture and Social Behavior: Psychological Studies of Social Density.* Erlbaum, 1977.)

occur between people for whom comfortable modes of interaction have not evolved. By nature, these interactions are unpredictable and, if so frequent that one's ability to selectively avoid them is impaired, they may be unwanted. While suite residents are equally likely to be unfamiliar with many residents of their floor, they do not routinely encounter these neighbors. Rather, contact for suite residents is likely to be with any of the five others sharing the suite. Presumably, these residents are known, and interaction styles governing contact have been established. Corridor residents should be less likely to have developed comfortable interaction patterns with those routinely encountered in the dormitory and less able to avoid or predict these contacts.

During our observations of these residential environments, we collected extensive background data that suggested that residents of corridor- and suite-design housing were comparable prior to entering college. Our studies focused on new freshmen residents of these dormitories and considered students who had chosen and been assigned to their residences. We have conducted research indicating that corridor and suite residents do not differ in their sensitivity to group size and tolerance for crowding before living in these settings but diverge in predicted directions after a semester of residence. We have also found that students who were assigned to dormitory rooms did not differ in response to the dormitory from those who chose their housing. Dormitory populations were comparable on a number of background variables (e.g., family size, socioeconomic status, personality) and these dimensions were statistically unrelated to our dependent measures. Subsequently, some of this research was successfully replicated with different populations who were randomly assigned to residence in conceptually similar dormitories. We were also satisfied that the dormitories were generally comparable; furnishings were similar, and surroundings were not very different. The primary difference between the designs was the way in which they arranged interior space and distributed social resources on the floor.

B. RESIDENTIAL EXPERIENCE

Initially, our research relied heavily on self-report by residents of the dormitories. Students were surveyed and observed in the dormitory settings, and findings were used to verify original assumptions and generate additional assessments and hypotheses. Generally, these data provided evidence for our conceptualization of the effects of these environments.

Self-report data obtained from questionnaires distributed to residents of both dormitory complexes indicated that corridor residents more frequently complained of unwanted interaction and numbers of neighbors and were more likely to judge the size of their residential grouping as too large than were suite residents. The effective level of social density appeared greater in the corridor-design settings, and this seemed to be exerting an effect on residential experiences. As can be seen in Table I, corridor residents were more likely to feel crowded than were residents of suite-design dormoritories.

This experience varied with proximity to shared spaces in the dormitory environment. If perceptions of crowding were related to the within-unit sharing of common living areas, one would expect these feelings to vary with resident

TABLE I

REPRESENTATIVE PERCEPTIONS OF DORMITORY EXPERIENCE REPORTED BY DIFFERENT SAMPLES OF
CORRIDOR AND SUITE RESIDENTS (PERCENT RESPONDING)

Dormitory design	Crowded	Not crowded	Have privacy	Do not have privacy	Desire to avoid others often	Desire to avoid others seldom	Crowding[a]
Corridor	61	39	41	59	84	16	3.219
Suite	16	84	72	38	38	62	1.375

[a]Mean responses; 1 = not crowded, 5 = very crowded.

bedroom location. Those living near the bathroom, for example, may be seen as occupants of functionally and spatially central areas. Since more residents were likely to be in the hallways outside shared areas, the probability of interaction for these residents should be greater. Similarly, residents living near shared lounge areas should also experience more contact and crowding. Analysis of responses of one sample of 39 freshmen residents of corridor housing confirmed these expectations. Residents in bedrooms adjacent to or across from bathroom and lounge areas felt more crowded than did residents living at the far end of the hall. This finding provided support for our interpretation of the impact of high social density; crowding seemed to result from increased frequencies of social contact and unwanted interaction in the corridor-design dormitories. Considered with findings indicating that suite residents felt that they could exert more control over what happened on their floor, it became clear that the dynamics of the corridor environments posed threats to residents' ability to regulate social contact.

Questionnaire data also provided information about the ways in which corridor residents attempted to cope with these threats. When asked how many neighbors they would rather avoid than interact with, corridor residents reported an average of more than six neighbors (suite residents reported an average of fewer than two). They were also more likely than were suite residents to indicate that there were others living on their floor with whom interaction was not wanted and that they wished that they could avoid seeing of talking with neighbors. The frequency of contact with neighbors was perceived as excessive; corridor residents reported more unwanted interaction and contact with unknown or unfamiliar neighbors and expressed greater avoidance motivation than did suite residents, who did not perceive the frequency of contact with neighbors as excessive.

The degree to which residential conditions reduced students' ability to selectively attend only to important others was also considered. Corridor residents reported frequent contact with unfamiliar neighbors and expressed a desire to avoid both friends and strangers. If, in the spirit of Milgram's (1970) analysis, these residents were maintaining selective control in dealing with social overload, we should have observed a disparity between their treatment of friends and strangers. Apparently, these screening mechanisms were less effective in the corridor setting, and residents experienced unwanted interaction with important and unimportant others.

These findings suggested that Calhoun's ideas about group size and crowding were applicable to people and that screening may break down at some point. Furthermore, they indicated that design variables which varied group size, even when physical density remained constant, were influential in determining response to other people. However, we had only survey data upon which to base our hypotheses; we still had no evidence that this syndrome of crowding was stressful or was associated with pathology. While we were confident that our description of life in these dormitories was accurate, we felt that we needed evidence of behavioral differences in order to extend our analysis.

A study by Pekarik (1977) provided some physiological evidence of corridor and suite residents' differing affective response to their dormitories. In order to study the relationship between cognitive appraisal and psychopathology, he developed a sensitive method of assessing evaluations of different situations. Subjects were placed in a situation in which galvanic skin response (GSR) was conditioned to the evaluative dimensions of good or bad. For half the subjects, the GSR response was associated with the concept of "good" and for the other half this training procedure linked response to the concept "bad." Conditioning was accomplished by pairing loud noise with positive or negative statements.

Following the training procedures, subjects were presented with statements that included several "objectively neutral" descriptions of different situations previously rated either positively or negatively. Conditioned GSR response generalized to these statements, producing a clear gradient of autonomic response.

Of interest here is the fact that about half of Pekarik's subjects were residents of the corridor- and suite-design dormitories. Items relevant to dormitory experience were included in the list of generalization statements. When conditioned to respond to the concept "bad," corridor residents showed greater autonomic response to the statement, "You have to deal with a lot of different people in your dormitory" than did residents of suite-style housing. Conversely, of those subjects conditioned to the concept "good," suite resident response to the statement, "You encounter many different people on your dormitory floor" was greater than GSR exhibited by corridor residents. Corridor residents responded to statements about the interaction patterns in their dormitories as if they were negative, while suite residents responded as if they were positive.

C. SOCIAL USE OF SPACE

Differences in the suitability of interior space for use as a semiprivate area were also observable in the two dormitory designs. If we assume that (1) both corridor and suite residents require additional space beyond their bedroom and

158ANDREW BAUM AND STUART VALINS

(2) the space immediately adjacent to bedroom units will be the likely target for such a need, we can easily see how the lack of physical structure provided by the corridor design creates problems for residents. Immediately adjacent to the bedrooms in a suite, the small lounge area is appropriate for use as an interaction territory. Suite residents have more control over interaction that occurs in the lounge; group norms regulating who may use the area as well as when different uses are appropriate reinforce individual control over interaction in this setting.

The long unstructured hallways in the corridor-design dormitories are not suitable for conversion to group-controlled territory. Immediately adjacent to and connecting bedroom units and shared facilities, the hallway space is geographically central and most appropriate for use as group territory. However, the corridor design requires too many people to use these areas and fails to structure them into more useable and manageable sizes. Consequently, group-reinforced control does not extend into these hallway areas. Although the hallways are heavily used, corridor residents exercise little control over what happens in them.

During our initial consideration of experimental tests of self-report findings, we conducted behavioral mapping of the two environments. A variant of controlled observation techniques, behavioral mapping provided us with a record of behaviors which occurred in these environments and allowed identification of their location. By mapping behavior on three corridor and three suite floors, we obtained further evidence of different behavior in the two settings.

The results of this effort provided evidence of social withdrawal and suggested an unexpected link with Calhoun's discussions of social velocity. *Social velocity* refers to the amount of time an individual spends in places where interaction is likely. Most social behavior that we observed occurred in the hallways of the corridor dormitories and in the small lounges of suite-style housing. Interaction was thus most likely to occur in central areas adjacent to bedroom units. When nonsocial behavior is considered, corridor residents were most frequently observed in their bedroom and suite residents were most often found in the lounge. Suite residents continued to use the lounge, where interaction was most likely, whereas corridor residents returned to their bedrooms, where interaction was considerably less likely. Similarly, when asked where they would prefer to interact with friends and neighbors, corridor residents indicated that they would rather interact in their bedrooms, while suite residents reported preference for the suite lounge. By avoiding those spaces in which interaction was most likely, corridor residents may have been attempting to reduce the frequency of contact experienced.

An alternative explanation of these findings, that corridor residents did not use the hallway space for nonsocial activities because these areas were less appropriate for things that people do alone, led to our first experimental study.

Yancey (1972) and Newman (1972) have described the impact of unsuitable or nondefensible spaces in residential environments, and it seemed clear that the long, undifferentiated hallways in the corridor-design dormitories were too public to be converted to semiprivate space. The suite lounges, in contrast, were physically removed from the public hallways and were interposed between these spaces and private bedroom areas. Access to the lounge was limited, and the small group clustered around it seemed to be able to use the lounge and to exert control over who used it and when different uses were appropriate. Furthermore, control over interpersonal contact seemed greater in these lounges than in the corridor hallways. Thus, the amount of social control available to residents in primary areas for social encounter and neighboring varied by design.

Frequent and unwanted social interaction in the corridor-design dormitories was viewed as being exacerbated by the lack of control available to the group in the hallway spaces where interaction was most likely. Corridor residents were not choosing to interact in these areas but seemed forced to do so by the arrangement of living space. Suite residents, however, were interacting with others in areas of their choice, and the features of the suite lounge provided the opportunity for group control over these shared spaces. A study was designed to test some of these hypotheses, assessing the relationship between sensitivity to numbers of people and control provided by the situation.

In this experiment, we used the model-room technique discussed by Desor (1972). Although these procedures were largely exploratory and not intended to be definitive, we felt that we could obtain valid projective indices of crowding and sensitivity to others. The model settings that we created lacked most non-visual cues that would be present in real-life environments, thereby exaggerating the visual aspects of the situations described. However, for our purposes, these additional cues were not crucial.

One hundred freshmen residents of the corridor- and suite-style dormitories were visited in their bedrooms and presented with three scale-model rooms representing a bedroom, lounge, and library reference room. Subjects were asked to place as many miniature people into each room as they could "before you would feel crowded." The assumption underlying this index was that subjects would arrive at a "threshold of crowding" and that the addition of another figure would cause the room to be perceived as crowded. The activities in the rooms were described so that the bedroom represented a space in which social interaction was very likely but proprietorship provided some control; the lounge, a room where interaction was again likely but control was not; and the library, a room where interaction was unlikely and external control high. It was expected that corridor and suite responses would diverge most when control was lacking and interaction was probable (lounge) and would diverge least when interaction was unlikely and control externally supplied by implicit behavioral norms.

The results of this and of subsequent model-room experiments provided general confirmation of these predictions. Unexpectedly, corridor residents did not respond to the control provided by the bedroom space; they placed fewer figures in the bedroom ($\bar{X} = 6.2$) and lounge ($\bar{X} = 20.2$) than did suite residents ($\bar{X}_B = 9.4$; $\bar{X}_L = 26.9$). As was expected, corridor residents placed more figures ($\bar{X} = 12.1$) in this room than did suite residents ($\bar{X} = 11.2$).

While these studies revealed differences in sensitivity to numbers of people as a function of dormitory residence, the degree of control afforded by the situation seemed to influence sensitivity only when extreme comparisons were made. When control was not provided, corridor residents placed fewer figures than did suite residents. When control was externally supplied, corridor residents placed more figures than did suite residents. However, when self-generated control was implied by proprietorship of one's own bedroom, corridor residents again placed fewer figures. These findings may have been caused by a number of factors. General feelings of helplessness involving resignation to the fact that one can rarely control interaction may have made corridor residents less sensitive to control cues (e.g., Rodin & Baum, 1978), causing them to respond only to rather strong descriptions of control. Alternatively, the rather limited nature of model-room procedures may have restricted realism to the point that control in the bedroom was not considered by subjects.

A third explanation is that the probability of interaction in the settings overwhelmed the effects of control provided by the nature of the space. Control provided by these rooms is largely normative and often subtle. The effects of excessive interaction, in contrast, appear to be more pervasive. Both the bedroom and the lounge models were presented in ways which made social interaction in them very likely, while the library model description implied relatively low levels of social interaction. It is possible that the effects of frequent and uncontrolled social contact were sufficiently strong to render interaction regulation through territorial control less effective. Corridor residents should respond negatively to increasingly likely social contact in settings other than those in which they experience unwanted social interaction, and only externally supplied control or social structure should ameliorate this negativity.

D. PERSISTENT STRESS AND SOCIAL WITHDRAWAL

In order to assess the relative strength and persistence of the impact of high social density and frequent and unregulated interaction, a series of laboratory studies was conducted. The scenarios in these studies were all similar. Subjects were asked to wait, either alone or with a confederate posing as a subject, while an experiment was being readied. By placing subjects in a waiting room and observing their responses to the setting that we had created, we were able to assess some of the persistent effects of prolonged exposure to high density.

Our use of the laboratory to study corridor residents' propensity for withdrawal was based on an important assumption—that this withdrawal would generalize beyond the dormitory. The data that we had collected up to this point provided strong but indirect evidence of avoidance and withdrawal from people and places where interaction was likely. Yet, withdrawal did not appear to be selective as Milgram had suggested. Rather than avoiding contact with unfamiliar neighbors and becoming involved with those neighbors with whom comfortable and predictable relationships had been established, they reported a desire to avoid neighbors whether they were friends or not. This suggested that selective withdrawal had broken down in the corridor environments, and that residents of these dorms engaged in an "across the board" withdrawal that might persist in other situations.

It is doubtful that avoidance and withdrawal strategies were useless in dealing with the problems encountered in the corridor-design housing. Each unwanted interaction that is successfully avoided should make dormitory life more tolerable and provide residents with an instance of achieved control over contact. However, its overall effectiveness can only be determined by considering how often successful avoidance is not possible. Given residents' continued complaints of frequent and unwanted interaction, it is possible that the success of their coping responses is outweighed by the frequency of its failure. Due to the nature of access to important spaces outside of their bedroom, corridor residents cannot avoid neighbors altogether. They still must routinely encounter them in the hallways and other shared spaces. The frequency of this contact may be excessive in spite of those contacts avoided, and those which are not avoided may be sufficient to generate stress. The number of others with whom areas must be shared makes regulation of contact difficult, but the necessity of using these areas makes withdrawal difficult and contact in the hallway inevitable.

Thus, the corridor-style dormitories create an environment in which reinforcement of withdrawal (successful avoidance of contact) is highly variable and far from continuous. In this light, one could consider avoidance as a well-learned coping response, elicited by the presence of other people. Highly resistent to extinction (but of only limited effectiveness), such a response strategy might generalize to nondormitory settings where interaction is likely. This response tendency may be so well learned that it approximates stereotypic responding (i.e., is independent of situational variables other than those affecting the likelihood of interaction). Persistence of withdrawal in situations in which it does not result in effective social adjustment nor produce adaptive behavior probably represents an "automatic" pattern of response rather than a deliberate strategy.

At the time that we began considering this possibility, we had no direct evidence of motivational decrements or nonadaptive persistence of withdrawal beyond the dormitory environment. However, our "feel" for the data suggested to us that withdrawal characterized much of the social experience of corridor residents. While they did maintain friendships and did engage in meaningful interaction with others, these relationships were maintained almost exclusively outside of the residential environment. Corridor residents were more likely to have friends in other dormitories and to maintain group memberships in other settings, while suite residents tended to belong to local groups. Similarly, corridor residents were more likely to report satisfying contact with nonneighbors than with neighbors. This seems to reflect a purposeful and adaptive way of satisfying one's need for meaningful social contact while living in overloaded residential settings. Still, these residents lived in overloaded residential settings and complained of unwanted interaction. They appeared to respond negatively to people other than those with whom friendships had been established, avoiding contact with unfamiliar students. Corridor residents seemed to be responding to others with whom interaction was probable as they would to a more generalized stressor.

Our first experiment considered the most basic manipulation of the probability of interaction; corridor and suite residents were brought to the laboratory and asked to wait either alone or with another student. It was predicted that corridor and suite residents would respond comparably when waiting alone, but that the introduction of another person would cause corridor residents to experience stress and to avoid or discourage interaction. Suite residents were not expected to respond to this situation as if it were stressful. A total of 47 corridor residents and 46 suite residents, randomly selected from freshmen housing lists, were considered and were tested during the first 2 months of either the fall or the spring semester.

The experiment was conducted in two adjoining rooms connected by a two-way mirror and a single door. The large room was sparsely furnished and its rear third was screened from view so as to suggest to subjects that some of the experiment was housed in that part of the room. The smaller adjoining room had seven attached and immovable chairs arranged in a row against the wall opposite the mirror, which appeared to be completely covered by a curtain. Actually, observation of the adjoining room was possible.

In the "alone" conditions, subjects were greeted by the experimenter, seated, and told that they were going to participate in a study of simple motor performance. They were asked to complete a one-page fact sheet asking for information such as their age, interests, family size, and ordinal position. When they had completed this form, subjects were informed that the experimental apparatus was not ready and were asked to wait in the adjoining room until it was properly prepared. The experimenter showed subjects into the adjoining room, motioned toward the seven chairs, and asked them to sit down. After subjects selected seats, the experimenter began observation.

In the "together" conditions, subjects encountered the experimenter and the confederate, who was busily completing the fact sheet. The experimenter greeted the subject and asked the confederate to stop working for a moment. Both were told that they were going to participate in a study of simple motor performance. The confederate was instructed to continue answering the questions on the sheet, and subjects were asked to begin completing the sheet. After 30 sec, the confederate informed the experimenter that he was finished. The experimenter took the sheet, explained that the experimental apparatus was not ready, and showed the confederate into the waiting room. When subjects finished answering all items, their sheets were collected, the explanation of why they were being asked to wait was repeated, and they were also shown into the waiting room. There they encountered the confederate, who always selected the second seat from the wall. Once subjects had selected seats, the experimenter, who was unaware of subjects' place of residence, began observation.

During observation, subjects' seat position, facial regard for the confederate, and conversation initiation were recorded. Following this 5-min period, the experimenter entered the waiting room and explained that it was customary to assess the preexperimental condition of subjects in order to control for potential error. Subjects were asked to complete a brief assessment form which asked questions regarding recent sleeping and eating habits and assessed subjective comfort. After completion of this form, subjects were told that the study was over and were debriefed.

As predicted, corridor and suite residents behaved comparably while waiting alone but diverged in predicted directions when another person was waiting with them (see Table II). The seat position selected by subjects yielded an index of interindividual distancing from the confederate in the together condition and a basal-type measure of seat preference in alone sessions. Thus, seat preference was not different among corridor and suite residents when there were no referent others, but distancing from the confederates was greater among corridor residents than among suite residents. Similarly, facial regard, interpreted as a measure of an individual's willingness to interact, was significantly greater among suite

TABLE II

RESPONSE TO WAITING ROOM SITUATION BY CORRIDOR AND SUITE RESIDENTS

Dormitory design	Seat position[a]		Seconds looking at confederate[b]		Discomfort following waiting period[c]	
	Alone	Together	Alone	Together	Alone	Together
Corridor	2.83	3.32	26.37	20.00	2.48	4.31
Suite	2.64	2.08	33.24	36.68	2.74	2.44

[a]Mean number of seats between subject and confederate (together conditions) or between subject and the second seat (alone conditions).
[b]Mean number of seconds subjects looked at the confederate (together conditions) or looked to their right toward the second seat (alone conditions).
[c]Mean ratings of discomfort, 1–7 scale.

residents than among corridor residents. Corridor residents seemed to be avoiding the confederate by maintaining greater distances from him (her) and by discouraging or not permitting eye contact and interaction. Conversation initiation, an index of actual interaction, showed a similar pattern for corridor ($\bar{X}$ = 1.4 conversations) and suite ($\bar{X}$ = 3.4) residents waiting with the confederate.

These data also provided support for the notion that other people, presumably because they represent potential interaction and interpersonal involvement, are experienced as stressors by students living in corridor-design housing. As with measures of avoidance, corridor and suite residents responded comparably when discomfort was assessed after waiting alone (see Table II). However, the presence of another person caused a dramatic increase in reported discomfort among corridor residents while not affecting comfort experienced by suite residents.

Interestingly, the semester during which data were collected did not influence these findings. Corridor residents avoided others and reported heightened discomfort when others were present from the second or third week of residence on. Further, this effect was no stronger or weaker following an entire semester of residence.

A second study was designed to separate the effects of the presence of others from the probability of interaction. Subjects were asked to wait with a confederate under involvement-enhancing (cooperative) expectations or with involvement-inhibiting (competitive) expectations. Procedures used in this study were comparable to those previously described, except that half of the subjects were told that they would be cooperating with the other participant and half were told that they could be competing. When interaction was made less likely by introducing an "adversary set" between subject and confederate, response to the waiting situation was comparable for corridor and suite residents. When interaction was more likely (cooperation expected), corridor residents again assumed greater distances from the confederate and expressed greater discomfort after waiting than did suite residents. Corridor residents responded selectively to the presence of another person, avoiding interaction and reporting discomfort only when interaction was likely.

All of the studies that we conducted using these procedures suggested that withdrawal and stress caused by frequent contact with dormitory neighbors generalized to neutral laboratory settings. Regardless of the nature of the manipulation, residents of the corridor design dormitories avoided or discouraged interaction with strangers when contact was likely. Similarly, they experienced stress when interaction was probable, whether or not they successfully avoided contact. Other findings have also lent support for these interpretations. Reichner (1974) found that when ignored, corridor residents experienced more positive affect than did suite residents. They also felt somewhat better when ignored than when not ignored. Apparently, the recognition that the others in the setting would not interact with them reduced discomfort typically experienced. For corridor residents the probability of interacting with strangers was more aversive than norm violations implicit in an ignoring situation. Further, we were able to replicate the waiting room experiments on a second college campus, where students were grouped in different sized residential groups (36- to 40-resident long corridors, 20-resident short corridors).[3] Withdrawal was again observed, and when the length of the waiting period was increased, discomfort still did not dissipate over time. Further, discomfort was not affected by whether or not interaction was actually avoided during the waiting period. Corridor residents experienced discomfort whenever interaction with strangers appeared likely, and this discomfort was persistent enough to generalize to nonresidential settings.

E. REACTANCE AND HELPLESSNESS

Our data presented us with a consistent and disturbing picture of the dynamics of corridor dormitory life. The residents of these dormitories (1) felt crowded, (2) complained of excessive and unwanted interaction in the dormitory, (3) expressed the desire to avoid social contact in the dormitory, and (4) withdrew from others in a laboratory setting and experienced discomfort when contact with them was likely. It seemed clear that we were observing situations in which high social density interfered with residents' ability to regulate social interaction. This loss of control appeared to cause residents to avoid people and seemed readily labeled as crowding. Other than reported difficulty on controlling interaction in the dormitories, however, we had no evidence of stressful loss of personal control in these settings.

Despite the purposeful nature of coping responses used by corridor and long-corridor residents, we suspected that prolonged exposure to conditions in these dormitories might condition helplessness. Residents' attempts to restore regulatory control over social contact were only partially successful; the number of times unwanted contact was successfully avoided appeared to be outweighed by those instances when contact was not avoided. Repeated failure to control environmental and social outcomes in these settings could lead to a sense of helplessness. When people learn that their outcomes are independent of responses and are therefore uncontrolled, they are less likely to behave adaptively, even when control over outcomes is offered or restored (e.g., Seligman, 1975).

[3] Approximately 40 residents, primarily freshmen, lived in two-person bedrooms arranged along a double-loaded hallway in the long-corridor dormitory. Two bath areas were available on each of the three floors, and a lounge area and a reduced number of residents were housed in the basement. Residents of the basement level were not studied. Approximately 60 residents, primarily freshmen, lived in two-person bedrooms arranged along three double-loaded hallways on each of the two floors of the short-corridor dormitory. Thus, residents lived in subgroupings of about 20; each subgrouping was furnished with a bath area and a building lounge was available. During one year, each section of 20 residents also had a lounge area, but the elimination of this lounge the next year did not have any noticeable effects on resident behavior. Residents of long- and short-corridor housing were randomly assigned to place of residence.

Helplessness training in the corridor and long-corridor dormitories may begin when residents recognize their inability to regulate social encounters on their floors. Their ineffectiveness in predicting and selectively attending to social contact with known and unknown neighbors may generate perceived independence of behavior and outcomes. Prolonged exposure to lack of regulatory control may lead residents to give up more readily and to stop trying to control or make active choices (Rodin, 1976).

Several studies were directed toward assessing the contribution of noncontingent social outcomes in the corridor and long-corridor dormitories. Davis (unpublished data) found that corridor residents were less persistent on unsolvable puzzles than were suite residents, and we have found evidence of this lack of persistence during solution of difficult but solvable anagrams. In another study, subjects were presented with an ambiguous choice situation in which they had the opportunity to seek information upon which they could base a decision. The experiment was conducted during the third and fourth months of residence in dormitory housing, and subjects were freshmen residents of long- and short-corridor housing. Of those long-corridor residents participating, only 17% sought information or signified that they were interested in pursuing the opportunity to make a choice, while about 50% of the short-corridor residents sought further information.

A third study, considering 40 freshmen residents of long- and short-corridor housing, was conducted during the spring semester following 6–7 months of dormitory residence. Subjects arrived at the laboratory alone, and the experimenter asked that he (she) be seated, explaining that a second subject would be playing the game as well. After approximately 1 min, a same-sex confederate arrived and the experimenter began to explain the experimental procedures. Subjects were told that they would be playing a prisoners' dilemma game. The probability of interaction was manipulated by telling half of the subjects that they were not allowed to talk with each other and telling the other half that they could talk with each other as long as they did not discuss the game.

The game was a modified, three-choice prisoners' dilemma game (see Fig. 6) similar to that used by Kurlander, Miller, and Seligman (1975). Players could make any of three responses, reflecting cooperative, competitive, or withdrawal strategies. Withdrawal was viewed as most reflective of helplessness, since it represented an inability to arrive at decisions or an unwillingness to participate in and meaningfully influence the game's outcome.[4]

---

[4]Kurlander et al. (1974) found that subjects exposed to solvable problems before playing this kind of game competed frequently and withdrew infrequently. Prior exposure to unsolvable problems, however, led to increased withdrawal and decreased competitiveness, suggesting that the withdrawal response reflects some form of motivational deficit. Further, we have found that students, after playing this game, report that the competitive response is associated with negative affect and avoidance, while the withdrawal response is associated with detachment from and lack of interest or motivation in the game.

PLAYER 2 PLAYS

	△	○	□
△	1 loses 5 pts. 2 loses 5 pts.	1 wins 15 pts. 2 loses 10 pts.	1 wins 1 pt. 2 loses 1 pt.
PLAYER 1 PLAYS ○	1 loses 10 pts. 2 wins 15 pts.	1 wins 5 pts. 2 wins 5 pts.	1 loses 1 pt. 2 loses 1 pt.
□	1 loses 1 pt. 2 wins 1 pt.	1 loses 1 pt. 2 loses 1 pt.	1 wins 0 2 wins 0

Fig. 6. Matrix of Prisoners' Dilemma game used to assess helplessness. (From Baum, A., & Valins, S. *Architecture and Social Behavior: Psychological Studies of Social Density.* Erlbaum, 1977.)

Participants were told the object of the game was simply to score as many points as possible. Subjects were not told to maximize the difference between their scores and their partner's, nor were they asked to cooperate with each other. Instead, they were told that at the end of the semester those players scoring in the highest 25% of all participants would share a monetary reward. In this way the possibility of both players in a given session winning a postexperimental prize was made clear.

As can be seen in Table III, rates of competitive, cooperative, and withdrawal responding during the game varied as a function of dormitory residence and the probability of interaction. Long-corridor residents were less cooperative than short-corridor residents, but the nature of their noncooperative strategy was determined by the manipulation of interaction probability. For long-corridor residents, competition was greater when interaction was allowed and withdrawal was greater when interaction was not allowed. Since students have indicated that competition in this game is a good way of discouraging interaction with the other player, it is likely that long-corridor residents were actively avoiding social

TABLE III

MEAN PERCENTAGE OF COOPERATIVE, COMPETITIVE, AND WITHDRAWAL RESPONSE[a]

	Cooperative		Competitive		Withdrawal	
Dormitory design	Interaction	No interaction	Interaction	No interaction	Interaction	No interaction
Long corridor	13	11	78	54	9	35
Short corridor	40	40	49	48	11	12

[a] From Rodin, J., and Baum, A. Crowding and helplessness. In A. Baum and Y. Epstein (Eds.), *Human Response to Crowding.* Lawrence Erlbaum Associates, Publishers, 1978.

contact when interaction was possible. When talking was not allowed, the need to avoid by competing was diminished and less purposeful withdrawal responding increased. While helpless withdrawal responsing was condition specific and did not represent the modal response to any situation, these findings suggested that long-corridor residents were experiencing a motivational deficit, at least in those situations studied.

Questionnaire data about dormitory experience also revealed that long-corridor residents expressed greater feelings of helplessness than did short-corridor residents, although these feelings were not overwhelming. Similarly, when asked about the value of trying to change things and of working toward making things better, long-corridor residents indicated less confidence in purposeful activity than did short-corridor residents. They also reported greater difficulty controlling social contact in the dormitory. Apparently, ineffective regulation of interaction in these dormitory settings reduced residents' feelings of control and conditioned a limited variant of helplessness.

We considered this helplessness limited because it did not appear to be complete. Given competitive responding when interaction was permitted, it appeared that helpless responding could not compete with well-learned avoidance motivation when interaction was likely. Long-corridor residents are not generally helpless. They actively avoid interaction when it is likely and attempt to create meaningful social relationships outside the residential area. However, they exhibit behavior symptomatic of helplessness when interaction is not very likely. Thus, one interpretation of our findings was that competition in this game represented a desire to discourage interaction, and avoidance motivation became salient when talking was permitted. When subjects were not allowed to interact, avoidance responding was not elicited and helpless behavior was observable.

An alternative hypothesis was that competitive responding represented reactance and that helplessness conditioning in the long-corridor dormitory followed a pattern similar to that described by Wortman and Brehm (1975). According to this interpretation, initial response to perceived loss of regulatory control would be aggressive, protest behavior directed toward reestablishing control over social experience. Assuming that students brought with them certain expectations of social control, initial disconfirmation of these expectations could be associated with reactance. As length of exposure increased and expectations of control diminished, responding would be more characteristic of helpless behavior.

Subsequent research (Baum, Aiello, & Calesnick, 1978) has indicated that both of these processes are active in the dormitory setting. Questionnaire data indicated that subjects felt that competitive responding in the game was well suited to discouraging interaction in the session or to expressing negative affect and gaining control of the game. Further, long-corridor residents playing the same prisoners' dilemma as in earlier studies (but not allowed to talk during the session) responded competitively during the first month of dormitory residence and increased withdrawal responding dramatically at the end of the second month of residence. Short-corridor residents did not exhibit this pattern and were less likely to indicate that their goals had been reactant or avoidance directed. Finally, questionnaire data indicated that long-corridor residents' feelings of control, motivation to structure interaction, and willingness to engage in purposeful behavior diminished as length of exposure increased.

These studies have begun to address the role of personal control in the arousal of crowding stress and in determining the impact of social density. Previous findings suggested that loss of social control was being perceived, labeled as crowding, and responded to with a sequence of withdrawal-oriented behaviors. If crowding is a function of loss of control or perceived regulatory failure, repeated exposure to it should lead to helplessness. These studies confirm this relationship. They also suggest that variants of learned helplessness, which are not of sufficient magnitude to compete successfully with well-learned coping responses and which follow a stage of reactance and control seeking behavior, may be more representative of naturalistically conditioned helplessness.

F. GROUP DEVELOPMENT AND THE MODIFICATION OF STRESS

The role of regulatory control in determining the dynamics of corridor and long-corridor dormitories can also be considered as it attentuates the consequences of high social density. Groups, for example, provide norms and reinforce individuals' ability to regulate encounter while shielding the individual member from unwanted contact. Thus, the development of small residential groups in the long-corridor and corridor settings should increase ability to regulate contact and decrease stress and withdrawal associated with crowding.

Our findings suggest that small-group development can mitigate the consequences of high social density. Groups form quite readily in the suite and short-corridor environments but do not appear with the same frequency in corridor and long-corridor settings. Apparently, large residential group size and the undifferentiated semipublic nature of shared space in these crowded buildings inhibits group development beyond the roommate dyad. Questionnaire data collected from sophomore residents of corridor and suite housing, all of whom had lived in corridor dormitories the year before, suggested that corridor residents were more concerned with structuring their floor by having friends living nearby than were new suite residents. However, the degree to which cohesive groups were actually achieved was independent of attempts to structure the floor and were not as successful in corridor as in suite settings. Those corridor residents who did report that they were members of cohesive residential groups did not feel as crowded as did those who were not members of local groups.

Experimental study indicated that corridor residents were less able to reach consensus following group discussion of a problem, and that this effect was strongest when subjects were participating in groups composed of immediate neighbors. Unlike suite residents who reached consensus in groups of strangers or neighbors, corridor residents could not come to agreement with neighbors. Considered with findings from more recent research (Baum, Mapp, & Davis, 1978), it appears that corridor residents are not likely to participate in a group with immediate neighbors or to desire a great deal of satisfying interaction with them. Rather, corridor residents appear to maintain appropriate friendship and reference group memberships in other dormitories. Again, corridor residents appear to cope with residential experience by withdrawing and shifting group affiliations to more controllable settings.

When groups did develop in the corridor and long-corridor dormitories, they were recognized by other residents and were able to exert some territorial control over their shared space. When residents were able to get together and function as a fairly cohesive group, evolving norms and structures reinforced individual members' ability to regulate social interaction. Well-established channels of communication, territorial "acquisition," and the resiliency of the "group membrane" allowed members to predict and control intragroup contact, discourage intrusion by nonmembers, and circumvent unwanted or uncontrollable interaction with known and unknown others.

G. DENSITY, CROWDING, AND PATHOLOGY

On the surface this research has been concerned with crowding as a dependent variable—an outcome of architectural mediation of conditions associated with high residential density. Two architectural designs clustered residents in relatively large groups and were associated with a loss of regulatory control over social experience, unwanted interaction, and inhibition of group development. By maximizing the impact of social density and the number of people with whom interaction was probable, these designs made high-density dormitory experience more aversive than did other designs. Residents used "crowding" to describe this experience, and their behavior was similar to that considered characteristic of response to crowding (e.g., Altman, 1975; Saegert, 1978; Sundstrom, 1978). The ways in which architectural designs arranged interior space in these dormitories were associated with reported crowding.

At another level, crowding can be viewed as a link between density and pathology. This connection has been tested largely through correlational studies of urban density and statistical indices of pathology. The findings of these studies have been inconsistent and difficult to interpret. Unfortunately, most of these studies did not assess residents' experience of density. One would not ordinarily expect high density to cause pathology unless the experience is negative; those unaffected by high density should not experience crowding stress nor should they behave as if they did. Correlational investigations have equated density and crowding and, as we noted earlier, this practice may create problems for meaningful analysis.

If we are to accept the notion that density and crowding are equivalent and interchangeable, we must seek an alternative explanation for our findings in laboratory and dormitory settings. In the dormitories density was comparable across comparison groups; numbers of residents on each floor were equivalent, buildings were similar, and all residents were provided roughly equal amounts of space. If density is expressed as the ratio of numbers of people and amount of space, residents of the corridor and suite (or short-corridor) dormitories should have felt equally crowded. Clearly, they did not. An architectural variable that provided another comparison, numbers of people to shared residential spaces, accurately predicted divergent experience. Physical density was not associated with crowding but social density, an experiential translation of social conditions associated with high density, was. Persistent withdrawal and problems related to reduction of regulatory control were similarly unrelated to physical density, but were consistent with analysis of residents per shared area. These findings suggest that one must consider architectural and social mediation of the experiences people have in high-density settings.

Our research has also provided evidence for the interpretation of crowding as the stressful perception of density-caused threats to one's sense of personal control. Our analysis of control-relevant problems of overload, unwanted interaction, and regulation of social contact was supported. Crowding appears to be linked to perceptions of excessive contact and social stimulation, but it also seems to be caused by failure to influence social outcomes in high-density settings. We have also found limited evidence of helplessness caused by high social density. Since crowding is therefore produced by the same conditions that condition helplessness in the dormitory environments, one can make a good case for the interrelatedness of these phenomena. Consistent with recent theoretical statements (e.g., Baron & Rodin, 1978), crowding is at least partially caused by loss of control over social experience.

While we have reported evidence of pathology associated with crowding, we have also found indications of relatively successful coping strategies. Clearly, people can cope with stress, and research has demonstrated our ability to adapt to environmental stressors (e.g., Glass & Singer, 1972). When adaptation to high density is successful, stress should be relieved and one should not expect to find behavioral problems. However, coping itself may be associated with psychological costs affecting tolerance for frustration and ability to deal with subsequent experiences of stress (e.g., Glass & Singer, 1972; Rodin & Baum, 1978; Sherrod, 1974). These costs appear to be most severe when individuals do not have adequate control over stressors. Exposure to uncontrollable aversive conditions should influence ability to cope with subsequent stress. With repeated or prolonged exposure to crowding experienced as a function of diminished regulatory control, one could find reduced tolerance for stress and impairment of ability to cope with crowding.

In our laboratory studies of resident behavior, crowded corridor residents displayed what appeared to be rather well-learned avoidance behaviors. These behaviors were dominant responses to situations in which interaction was likely, and secondary response patterns, such as helplessness, emerged only when the probability of interaction was reduced. Yet, these avoidance behaviors were relatively ineffective in reducing stress; despite the fact that these students were successful in avoiding contact,they remained uncomfortable when others were present. Similarly, levels of stress and crowding did not decrease over time. Furthermore, these behaviors generalized beyond the settings in which they could be considered adaptive. In neutral laboratory and field settings, corridor residents continued to shun social stimulation, even when such a strategy was clearly counterproductive. Continued and persistent stress exhibited by corridor residents, even when interaction in neutral settings was successfully avoided, suggests that withdrawal and helplessness are long-term costs of prolonged exposure to high social density.

Thus, if we assume that the socially dense corridor-design dormitories do not present problems that are initially beyond coping ability, we can still explain the breakdown of effective coping and discrimination in these settings. When individuals cannot cope with stress, dysfunction is likely. However, successive adaptations to stress can have costs which, among other things, make subsequent adaptations more difficult. Prolonged exposure to high social density and loss of regulatory control can therefore be expected to diminish residents' ability to cope.

REFERENCES

Aiello, J. A further look at equilibrium theory: Visual interaction as a function of interpersonal distance. *Environmental Psychology ard Nonverbal Behavior,* 1977, **1.**
Aiello, J., & Jones, S. Field study of the proxemic behavior of young school children in three subcultural groups. *Journal of Personality and Social Psychology,* 1971, **19,** 351–356.
Aiello, J., Epstein, Y., & Karlin, R. *Field experimental research on human crowding.* Paper presented to the Eastern Psychological Association, New York, 1975.
Altman, I. *The environment and social behavior.* Monterey, Calif.: Brooks/Cole, 1975.
Altman, I. Crowding: Historical and contemporary trends in crowding research. In A. Baum & Y. Epstein (Eds.), *Human response to crowding.* Hillsdale, NJ: Erlbaum, 1978. Pp. 3–29.
Argyle, J., & Dean, F. Eye contact, distance, and affiliation. *Sociometry,* 1965, **28,** 389–304.
Averill, J. Personal control over aversive stimuli and its relationship to stress. *Psychological Bulletin,* 1973, **80,** 286–303.
Barker, R. G. *The stream of behavior.* New York: Appleton, 1963.
Barker, R. G. *Ecological psychology.* Stanford, Calif.: Stanford University Press, 1968.

Barker, R. G., & Gump, P. *Big school, small school.* Stanford, Calif.: Stanford University Press, 1964.

Baron, R., & Rodin, J. Crowding and control. In A. Baum, J. Singer, & S. Valins (Eds.), *Advances in Environmental Psychology* (Vol. 1). Hillsdale, N.J.: Erlbaum, 1978.

Baron, R., Mandel, D., Adams, C., & Griffen, L. Effects of social density in university residential environments. *Journal of Personality and Social Psychology,* 1976, **34,** 434-446.

Baum, A., Aiello, J., & Calesnick, E. Crowding and personal control: Social density and the development of learned helplessness. *Journal of Personality and Social Psychology,* 1978, **36,** 1000-1011.

Baum, A., & Davis, G. Spatial and social aspects of crowding perception. *Environment and Behavior,* 1976, **8,** 527-544.

Baum, A., & Greenberg, C. Waiting for a crowd: The behavioral and perceptual effects of anticipated crowding. *Journal of Personality and Social Psychology,* 1975, **32,** 671-679.

Baum, A., & Koman, S. Differential response to anticipated crowding: Psychological effects of social and spatial density. *Journal of Personality and Social Psychology,* 1976, **34,** 526-536.

Baum, A., Mapp, K., & Davis, G. Determinants of residential group development and social control. *Environmental Psychology and Nonverbal Behavior,* 1978, **2,** 145-160.

Baum, A., & Valins, S. *Architecture and social behavior: Psychological studies of social density.* Hillsdale, N.J.: Erlbaum, 1977.

Brehm, J. *A Theory of Psychological Reactance.* New York: Academic Press, 1966.

Calhoun, J. Population density and social pathology. *Scientific American* 1962, **206,** 139-148.

Calhoun, J. Space and the strategy of life. *Ekistics,* 1970, **29,** 425-437.

Craik, K. M. Environmental psychology. In T. M. Newcomb (Ed.), *New directions in psychology* (Vol. 4). New York: Holt, Rinehart & Winston, 1970. Pp. 1-121.

Desor, J. Toward a psychological theory of crowding. *Journal of Personality and Social Psychology,* 1972, **21,** 79-83.

Festinger, L., Schachter, S., & Back, K. *Social pressures in informal groups: A study of human factors in housing.* Stanford, Calif.: Stanford University Press, 1950.

Fitch, J. *American building: The environmental forces that shape it.* Boston: Houghton Mifflin, 1972.

Freedman, J. *Crowding and behavior.* San Francisco: Freeman, 1975.

Galle, O., Gove, W., & McPherson, J. Population density and pathology: What are the relations for man? *Science,* 1972, **176,** 23-30.

Glass, D., & Singer, J. *Urban Stress.* New York: Academic Press, 1972.

Griffitt, W., & Veitch, R. Hot and crowded: Influences of population density and temperature on interpersonal affective behavior. *Journal of Personality and Social Psychology,* 1971, **17,** 92-98.

Janis, I., & Levanthal, H. Human reactions to stress. In E. Borgatta & W. Lambert (Eds.), *Handbook of personality theory and research.* Chicago: Rand McNally, 1968.

Kaplan, K., & Greenberg, C. Regulation of interaction through architecture, travel and telecommunication: A distance-equilibrium approach to environmental planning. *Environmental Psychology and Nonverbal Behavior,* 1976, **1,** 17-29.

Karlin, R., Epstein, Y., & Aiello, J. A setting specific analysis of crowding. In A. Baum & Y. Epstein (Eds.), *Human response to crowding.* Hillsdale, N.J.: Erlbaum, 1978. Pp. 165-179.

Kelley, H. *Attribution in social interaction.* Morristown, N.J.: General Learning Press, 1971.

Kurlander, H., Miller, W., & Seligman, M. Learned helplessness, depression and prisoners dilemma. In M. Seligman (Ed.), *Helplessness.* San Francisco: Freeman, 1975.

Latane, B., & Darley, J. *The unresponsive bystander: Why doesn't he help?* New York: Appleton, 1970.

Lerner, M. The desire for justice and reactions to victims. In J. Macaulay & L. Berkowitz (Eds.), *Altruism and helping behavior.* New York: Academic Press, 1970.

Lewin, K. *A dynamic theory of personality*. New York: McGraw-Hill, 1935.

Lewin, K. Behavior and development as a function of the total situation. In L. Carmichael (Ed.), *Manual of child psychology*. New York: Wiley, 1946.

McCarthy, D., & Saegert, S. Residential density, social overload, and social withdrawal. In R. Aiello & A. Baum (Eds.), *Residential crowding and design*. New York: Plenum, 1979.

Milgram, S. The experience of living in cities. *Science*, 1970, **176**, 1461-68.

Nahemow, L., & Lawton, M. Similarity and propinquity in friendship formation. *Journal of Personality and Social Psychology*, 1975, **32**, 205-13.

Newman, O. *Defensible space*. New York: Macmillan, 1972.

Pekarik, G. *The use of autonomic responses to assess idiosyncratic evaluations of personally relevant situations*. Unpublished doctoral dissertation, State University of New York at Stony Brook, 1977.

Reichner, R. *On being ignored: The effects of residential group size on social interaction*. Unpublished Masters' Thesis, State University of New York at Stony Brook, 1974.

Rodin, J. Density, perceived choice, and response to controllable and uncontrollable outcomes. *Journal of Experimental Social Psychology*, 1976, **12**, 564-578.

Rodin, J., & Baum, A. Crowding and helplessness: Potential consequences of density and loss of control. In A. Baum & Y. Epstein (Eds.), *Human response to crowding*. Hillsdale, N.J.: Erlbaum, 1978. Pp. 389-401.

Ross, J., Layton, B., Erickson, G., & Schopler, J. Affect, facial regard, and reactions to crowding. *Journal of Personality and Social Psychology*, 1973, **28**, 69-76.

Saegert, S. High density environments. Their personal and social consequences. In A. Baum & Y. Epstein (Eds.), *Human response to crowding*. Hillsdale, N.J.: Erlbaum, 1978. Pp. 257-281.

Schmitt, R. Density, health and social disorganization. *Journal of American Institute of Planners*, 1966, **32**, 38-40.

Schopler, J., & Stocksdale, J. An interference analysis of crowding. *Environmental Psychology and Nonverbal Behavior*, 1977, **1**, 81-88.

Schopler, J., & Walton, M. *The effects of expected structure, expected enjoyment, and participant's internality-extermality upon feelings of being crowded*. Unpublished manuscript, University of North Carolina, 1974.

Seligman, M. *Helplessness*. San Francisco: Freeman, 1975.

Sherrod, D. Crowding, perceived control, and behavioral effects. *Journal of Applied Social Psychology*, 1974, **4**, 171-186.

Singer, J., Lundberg, U., & Frankenhaeuser, M. Stress on the train: A study of urban commuting. In A. Baum, J. Singer, & S. Valins (Eds.), *Advances in environmental psychology*. Hillsdale, N.J.: Erlbaum, 1978.

Stokols, D. On the distinction between density and crowding: Some implications for future research. *Psychological Review*, 1972, **79**, 275-277.

Stokols, D. The experience of crowding in primary and secondary environments. *Environment and Behavior*, 1976.

Stokols, D. A typology of crowding experiences. In A. Baum & Y. Epstein (Eds.), *Human response to crowding*. Hillsdale, N.J.: Erlbaum, 1978. Pp. 219-255.

Stokols, D., Smith, T., & Proster, J. The perception of crowding as a function of architectural variations in naturalistic settings. *American Behavioral Scientist*, 1976.

Stokols, D., Rall, M., Pinner, B., & Schopler, J. Physical, social and personal determinants of the perception of crowding. *Environment and Behavior*, 1973, **5**, 87-115.

Sundstrom, E. Toward an interpersonal model of crowding. *Sociological Symposium*, Fall, 1975.

Sundstrom, E. Crowding as a sequential process: Review of research on the effects of population density on humans. In A. Baum & Y. Epstein (Eds.), *Human response to crowding*. Hillsdale, N.J.: Erlbaum, 1978. Pp. 31-116.

Winsborough, H. The social consequences of high population density. *Law and Contemporary Problems,* 1965, **30,** 120–126.

Wohlwill, J. Amount of stimulus exploration and preference as differential functions of stimulus complexity. *Perception and Psychophysics,* 1968, **4,** 307–312.

Worchel, S., & Teddlie, C. The experience of crowding: A two-factor theory. *Journal of Personality and Social Psychology,* 1976, **34,** 30–40.

Wortman, C., & Brehm, J. Responses to uncontrollable outcomes: An integration of reactance theory and the learned helplessness model. In L. Berkowitz (Ed.), *Advances in experimental social psychology* (Vol. 8). New York: Academic Press, 1975.

Yancey, W. Architecture, interaction, and social control: The case of a large-scale housing project. In J. Wohlwill & D. Carson (Eds.), *Environment and the social sciences.* Washington, D.C.: American Psychological Association, 1972.

Zimbardo, P. The human choice: Individuation, reason, and order versus deindividuation, impulse, and chaos. In W. Arnold and D. Levine (Eds.), *Nebraska Symposium on motivation.* Lincoln, Nebraska: University of Nebraska Press, 1969. Pp. 237–307.

A CULTURAL ECOLOGY OF SOCIAL BEHAVIOR[1]

J. W. Berry

QUEEN'S UNIVERSITY
KINGSTON, CANADA

I. A Cross-Cultural Perspective 177
II. An Ecological–Cultural–Behavioral Model 179
III. Some Studies of Social Behavior 185
    A. Implications of the Model 185
    B. Independence 190
IV. Applications 200
    A. Telecommunication Needs 200
    B. Housing Needs 201
V. Conclusions 202
    References 203

I. A Cross-Cultural Perspective

The conventional wisdom of the decade has assigned to social psychology a crisis stage (Elms, 1975; Gergen, 1973; Israel & Tajfel, 1972; McGuire, 1973; Smith, 1972; Strickland, Aboud, & Gergen, 1976). Lacking sound theoretical and methodological frameworks, the argument goes, social psychology is floundering, unable to define and follow a course of action. However, the problem may be morass rather than crisis, for we appear to have been suffering from a multitude of minor options.

[1] This research program has been supported, over a period of 15 years, by a variety of agencies. I wish to thank the Canada Council, the Australian Research Grants Committee, Communications Canada, and the research grants committee of the University of Sydney and Queen's University. I wish also to thank Walt Lonner, Harry Triandis, and the series editor, Leonard Berkowitz, for their helpful comments upon an earlier draft.

ADVANCES IN EXPERIMENTAL SOCIAL
PSYCHOLOGY, VOL. 12

Copyright © 1979 by Academic Press, Inc.
All rights of reproduction in any form reserved.
ISBN 0-12-015212-6

Major reorientations are called for (Strickland, Aboud, & Gergen, 1976); one which is increasingly identified is that based upon cross-cultural comparison (Faucheux, 1976; Pepitone, 1976; Triandis, 1977). It is also argued, however, that before cross-cultural comparisons are attempted, there must be some specification of the cultural or societal bases of ones understanding of social behavior (Berry, 1974a, 1978; Berry & Wilde, 1972; Diaz-Guererro, 1977; Moscovici, 1972). Thus, there appears to be a growing interest in relationships between social behavior and its sociocultural context, and in the cross-cultural generality of these relationships. This article attempts to illustrate how such studies may be done (a methodological emphasis), what one such study reveals (a substantive emphasis), and finally how such knowledge can be returned to the people (an applied emphasis).

The year 1972 seems to have been when social psychology first began to go "cultural" in earnest. The arguments of Moscovici (1972), in particular, established the point of view that "the social psychology that we ought to create must have an origin in our own reality" (p. 23). He observed that social psychology was largely developed in one society (the United States), which took "for its theme of research and for the contents of its theories the issues of *its own* society" (p. 19). He argued that social psychologists elsewhere "have the choice between building a social psychology appropriate to their society and culture, or to rest content with the application to their teaching and research of a model from elsewhere which is highly restricted" (p. 19). His choice for Europeans was clearly to "turn toward our own reality" on which to build one's own social psychology. Similarly, Berry and Wilde (1972) and Berry (1974a) argued for the importance of understanding the Canadian social and cultural context if ever the social behavior there was to be comprehended. In essence the argument demands local ethnographic (both anthropological and sociological) analysis prior to social psychological investigation.

Broad frameworks for the cross-cultural study of social behavior also began to appear in earnest in 1972. In his examination of "subjective culture" (a cultural group's characteristic way of perceiving its social environment, particularly its norms, roles, and values), Triandis employed samples from three cultures to obtain variation in antecendents and consequents of subjective culture. He later (1976, 1977, 1978) outlined a more extensive cross-cultural framework for investigating social behaviors which could be incorporated into a "universal social psychology." Pepitone (1976) has also been advocating the cross-cultural approach, arguing that "cross-cultural . . . research will need to become the stock in trade of social psychologists instead of the occasional research design" (p. 647). He considers three stages of comparative research: that which "maps and defines various value and belief systems"; that which studies "the structure and functioning" of these systems; and that which deals with their origins (pp. 647–649).

The cultural and cross-cultural thrusts may be seen, then, as sharing an interest in ethnographic analysis—the characteristic features of the indigenous sociocultural milieu must be incorporated into our research; but the cross-cultural or comparative approach goes further—it attempts to assemble these local understandings into a universal psychology of social behavior (Berry 1978; Triandis, 1978). Much of the earlier cross-cultural work, according to Faucheux (1976), largely ignored the local cultural realities and then illegitimately sought more universal statements on their basis. Furthermore much of this earlier work is charged (Faucheux, 1976) with being blindly atheoretical, hence lacking a framework for the comparative integration of the local realities. The one study found to be acceptable by Faucheux (1976, pp. 295–307) by these criteria was (luckily) the first stages of the research program reported in the balance of this chapter.

II.   An Ecological–Cultural–Behavioral Model

Over the past few years a model of ecological, cultural, and behavioral relationships has been proposed and elaborated (Berry, 1966, 1971a, 1976). This model has been operationalized and evaluated by employing data from a series of field studies and by a review of the literature (Witkin & Berry, 1975).

The general approach is one which views the development of individual behavior as a function of membership in a cultural group; and cultural characteristics are viewed as a function of both the ecological setting of the group and the acculturative influences which impinge upon the group. These functions are not necessarily undirectional, for cultures may be influenced by the growing individuals, and ecological and intergroup relationships may be altered by cultural patterns. Furthermore, the individual's behavior may exist as a direct function of ecological or acculturative factors (not mediated by his or her culture), and of course these direct relationships may exert influence from the developing individual. We are thus dealing with three levels of variables which are all potentially interacting: extracultural input (ecological and acculturational), cultural, and behavioral.

These variables have been incorporated into a model (Berry, 1976) which may be reviewed briefly here. In Fig. 1, six components are included within a single interacting framework. The two basic input components are ecology (interactions between human organisms and their habitat) and acculturative influences (influences, mainly via education and urbanization, from outside the culture). In adaptation to these, are two cultural components: the traditional culture (here limited to those aspects which may be conceived of as ecologically adaptive), and the contact culture (parallel to traditional culture, but now altered during acculturation). Finally, two behavioral components are illustrated: the

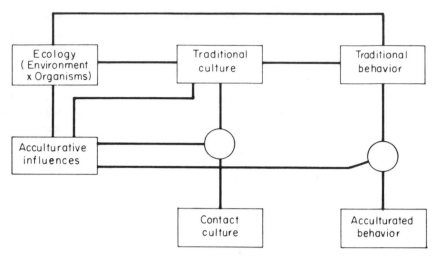

Fig. 1.   An ecological, cultural, and behavioral model.

traditional behavior component is viewed as being in adaptation not only to traditional culture but also to ecology, and the acculturated behavior component is considered as a function both of traditional behavior and of acculturation (acculturative influences and contact culture).

The content of these six components of the model, to be described next, are operationalized later. The ecology component is concerned with the basic interaction between a cultural group and its physical environmental setting. It includes such factors as the economic "exploitive pattern" typically used (for example whether in the group hunting, gathering, fishing, farming, or pastoral activities predominate), the "settlement pattern" of the group (for example, whether they are nomadic, moving daily, monthly and seasonally; or sedentary, staying put throughout their annual economic cycle), and the "demographic distribution" of the group (for example, whether they tend to be dispersed in small bands over a large territory or concentrated in large settlement units). Although these three elements are conceptually distinct, they are known (e.g., Murdock, 1967) to be consistently interrelated: for example, hunting and gathering people tend to be nomadic in settlement pattern and dispersed in small population units, while agricultural groups tend to be sedentary and to congregate in much larger settlements.

In the traditional culture component are included customary features of group life which are thought to be adaptive to their ecological setting. One element, that of social and political stratification, varies across groups quite widely. In those which have been termed "tight" by Pelto (1968) and "complex" by Murdock and Provost (1973), there is a good deal of vertical organization to the group, while in those which are "loose," a horizontal, more egalitarian organization predominates. In "tight" societies, an extended family structure is usual, while in "loose" societies, nuclear families are more common. Finally, in this component, it is now well established that child rearing tends to emphasize obedience and responsibility training in "tight" societies (often termed "compliance"), while it is more likely to emphasize independence and self-reliance (termed "assertion") in "loose" societies (Barry, Child, & Bacon, 1959). Thus, we may say that the authority pressures from the group tend to be pervasive in "tight" societies, from the time of initial child rearing through to later involvement in social and political life; in contrast, in "loose" societies the authority system is less encompassing of the individual through the course of his or her life. Most important for the purposes of the model is that there is a high probabilistic relationship between the ecology and the traditional culture components, such that in hunting nomadic societies "loose" sociocultural systems predominate, while in agricultural societies "tight" systems are most common.

Any number of behaviors could, in principle, be included in the traditional behavior component. In practice, until now only those subsumed under Witkin's notion of psychological differentiation (Witkin, Dyk, Faterson, & Goodenough; 1962) have been studied extensively (see Witkin & Berry, 1975; Berry, 1976), while some Piagetian work has also employed the model (see, e.g., Dasen, 1975). The basic set of behaviors studied has been those designated by the cognitive style dimension of field dependence–independence. This notion refers to the tendency for individuals to be self-consistent in their ways of interacting with the environment, both physical and social (Witkin & Goodenough, 1977b). A person operating at the field-dependent end of the dimension tends to accept the physical field as presented, to interact with it globally, and to be sensitive to social cues. A person operating at the field-independent end of the dimension tends to impose structure on the physical field, to perceive analytically, and to be socially insensitive and distant. Until recently the bulk of the evidence for the cognitive style derived from perceptual and cognitive studies, but the review by Witkin and Goodenough (1977a) has demonstrated that these social behaviors are an integral element of the style, at least within some western cultures.

At the second level of the model (acculturation), the acculturative influences component presents another major set of inputs. These all derive, not from the natural habitat of the group (as in the case of the ecological input), but from contact with other, often dominant cultures. The elements of acculturation which are considered are the experience of formal education (usually based upon western systems), the movement to larger settlements (usually referred to as urbanization), and an involvement in wage employment, often a major reorientation from traditional subsistence economic life.

Following this second level of the model, the contact culture represents the emergent cultural system in which the traditional culture is partially represented (that is, some features of the life style remain virtually unchanged), and new cultural forms emerge under the impact of the acculturative influences component.

Finally, the acculturated behavior component consists of two classes of behavior (Berry, 1979). One, termed "behavioral shifts," includes changes in rates or levels of previously existing behaviors in the group. For example, under the influence of technical training, it has often been found that analytical skills are increased over their original level (Witkin & Berry, 1975). The other, termed "acculturative stress," includes those behaviors which are socially disruptive and personally discomforting which often accompany the turbulence of social and cultural change (Berry & Annis, 1974).

With the structure and content of the model now outlined, we may proceed to its operationalization. It is apparent, even from this brief glance, that it is not possible to operationalize such a complex model unless some parameters are set. Moreover, of course, when these are set, the generality of the model becomes limited. These general limits are three in number: First, the model is intended to apply only to subsistence-level societies (and to those which were so until recently), for it is only at this level that ecological adaptation is likely to be meaningfully studied. Second, the content of the various components is narrow, being confined to the theoretical and empirical research interests of the present investigator (primarily cultural ecology and psychological differentiation). Third, the model is limited to the kind of a culture contact situation which typically has resulted from the period of European colonial expansion over the past 500 years.

The basic strategy for operationalizing the model was first to select cultural groups (from published ethnographies and archives) which ranged quite widely in terms of their ecological setting. Then, communities within these cultures were selected to represent differing levels of acculturation to European life style. Finally field work was conducted, during which psychological tests were administered to samples from these various communities. In terms of experimental design, the selection of cultures, communities, and samples represents a quasimanipulation of the "independent" variables, and the testing and interviewing provides the "dependent" behavioral data.

It is not possible to present here much of the details of the cultures and samples employed in the study (see Berry, 1976). However Table I provides the essential data needed to operationalize the model. In this table are listed 10 cultural groups, from which 17 samples were drawn (additionally four European samples were drawn from Scotland and Canada, but they lie outside the model). Also in the table are three indices which represent various components of the model.

These three indices have been derived primarily from the materials prepared by Murdock and others who have developed the cultural archives (Murdock,

TABLE I

Cultures, Samples, and Their Characteristics

Cultural group	Location	Sample name	N	Ecological index	Cultural index	Ecocultural index	Acculturation index
Temne	West Africa	Mayola	90	-1.98	-1.93	-1.96	-1.68
		Port Loko	32	-1.98	-1.48	-1.66	-0.02
Telefol	New Guinea highlands	Telefomin	40	-1.53	-1.48	-1.51	-1.47
Motu	Coastal New Guinea	Hanuabada	30	-0.39	-0.53	-0.49	+0.68
Koonganji	Coastal Australia	Yarrabah	30	-0.27	-0.53	-0.45	-0.38
Tsimshian	Coastal British Columbia	Hartley Bay	56	-0.27	-0.37	-0.34	+0.74
		Port Simpson	59	-0.27	-0.37	-0.30	+1.42
Carrier	British Columbia Mountain	Tachie	60	+0.18	-0.26	-0.11	+0.47
		Fort St. James	61	+0.18	+0.36	+0.30	+0.95
Ojibway	Northern Ontario	Aroland	39	+0.64	+0.64	+0.64	+0.34
		Long Lac	37	+0.64	+0.25	+0.38	+0.80
		Sioux Lookout	31	+0.64	+0.41	+0.49	+1.48
Arunta	Central Australia	Santa Teresa	30	+0.52	+0.80	+0.72	-1.26
Cree	Northern Quebec	Wemindji	61	+0.86	+0.75	+0.79	-0.69
		Fort George	60	+0.86	+0.64	+0.72	+0.26
Eskimo	Baffin Island	Pond Inlet	91	+1.09	+1.58	+1.43	-1.20
		Frobisher Bay	31	+1.09	+1.57	+1.36	-0.44

1967; Murdock & Provost, 1973; Pelto, 1968) but are supplemented by other ethnographic sources, including material collected during the field work itself. They follow the descriptions of elements in the model which have just been described. Each element is coded and rated in the cultural archives and has been extracted from these archives for use in these indices. To construct an index each element within a component is summed for each culture group, and then the distribution is standardized. This yields, for example on the ecological index, a range from −1.98 for a West African sedentary agricultural group to +1.09 for a nomadic Arctic hunting group. A negative score on this index, then, indicates a position toward the sedentary end of the ecological dimension, while a positive score indicates a position toward the nomadic end. Similarly on the cultural index, a negative score indicates a position toward the "tight" end, while a positive score indicates a position toward the "loose" end. On the acculturation index, a positive score indicates an experience of formal education, urbanization, and wage employment, while a negative score indicates a relative lack of these influences. The specific elements which enter into each index are:

   Ecological index. Ratings of "exploitive pattern," "settlement pattern," and "mean size of local community" from Murdock (1967)
   Cultural index. Ratings of "political stratification," "social stratification," and "family organization" from Murdock (1967), and ratings of "socialization compliance–assertion" from Barry, Child, and Bacon (1959) supplemented by respondent self-ratings on the same dimension
   Ecocultural index. A combination of the first two indices to provide a more general input variable.
   Acculturation index. Ratings of experience of European education combined with ratings of the degree of urbanization and wage employment in the communities

   It is apparent that the selection of cultures and samples for their variation on these dimensions has been moderately successful; there is a fair degree of spread on these indices which provide the quasimanipulation which was sought.
   Turning to an examination of relationships among these indices and their elements, we may consider them from two points of view: coherence of elements within indices and independence of the indices from each other. Ideally, of course, we should sample cultures which provide for relative independence between the two levels in the model (the ecological–cultural and the acculturational) but which allow for consistency within levels.
   Within the ecological component and within the cultural component, there is a pattern of coherence among the elements which justifies their summation into indices. The two sets of elements are highly related; a correlation of +.84 between the two indices led to the decision to incorporate both into a single ecocultural index, to represent the first adaptive level of the model.

Similarly, the three elements within the acculturation index cohere to a high degree. However, they do not correlate highly with elements in the ecological and cultural indices; this minimal relationship among these elements is supported by the low correlations between the acculturation index and the other three indices ($+.25$, $+.12$, and $+.16$). We may assert that we have met our aim of sampling societies which exhibit a high degree of coherence within components of the model but which maintain independence between the two major levels of the model.

A number of behaviors have now been systematically related to this model (Berry, 1976; Witkin & Berry, 1975). Most of these have been in the domains of perception and cognition, primarily those related to the concept of psychological differentiation (Witkin *et al.,* 1962) and the cognitive style dimension of field dependence–independence (Witkin & Goodenough, 1977b). Results of cross-cultural studies employing perceptual and cognitive tasks have shown that, as predicted from the model, those peoples who are nomadic and hunting based, who are "loose" in social and political structure, and who emphasize "assertion" in child socialization tend to develop a field-independent cognitive style. Conversely, those peoples who are sedentary and agriculture based, who are "tight," and who emphasize "compliance" tend to develop a field-dependent cognitive style (Berry 1976; Witkin & Berry, 1975). These results are taken as support for the model and for the theoretical links which tie it together.

III. Some Studies of Social Behavior

Behavior in the perceptual and cognitive domains has not been the sole focus of research stemming from the model. Earlier reports of independence and conformity in a few societies (Berry, 1967, 1974b) demonstrated that cultural group differences do exist and that they seem to be distributed in a way which can be predicted from the model; however, individual differences have been much more difficult to comprehend. This section focuses on some social behaviors which have been charted cross-culturally and upon their group and individual distributions.

A. IMPLICATIONS OF THE MODEL

As we have presented the model, our expectation is that in hunting and gathering societies settlement pattern will be more sedentary and population density will be high. Congruent with these ecological differences, the model predicts low social and political stratification ("loose" organization) at the migratory end, and high social and political stratification ("tight" organization) at the sedentary end of the dimension.

For understanding social behavior our first element of interest is population density and our second is the level of sociocultural stratification. From the first, we may argue that in living with many people, the development of a sensitivity to others is highly adaptive; and when they are permanent neighbors, a certain degree of attention to their views is required. Thus, in high-density and sedentary communities, we would expect to find developed a social sensitivity, and a social responsiveness, which are not present in lower density, nomadic groups. In the latter case, having fewer people around and the possibility of simply moving away when social interaction becomes problematic are both suggestive of a need for lower social sensitivity and responsiveness.

Continuing from this prediction, and based upon the second element (that of higher levels of social and political stratification in sedentary communities), we expect that in such sedentary communities, acceptance of social influence (conformity) will be higher than in migratory communities. That is, not only will individuals be more aware of and responsive to social stimuli, but they will acquiesce to them to a greater degree than in migratory "loose" communities. Social and political stratification, when they are high, bring greater authority pressures to bear upon individuals, and in such communities acceptance of authority is more likely to be adaptive than not. This situation of social pressure is reinforced by family structure; in the extended family, greater social pressure is likely to be exerted than in the nuclear family. Thus in sedentary "tight" communities, general social pressures from structured authority are likely to lead to the development of greater conformity in the society, while in nomadic, "loose" communities, lesser acceptance of social influence is likely to be found.

The crucial link between this set of background ecocultural features and the development of individual social behavior lies in the characteristic socialization practices employed by a society. Before we turn to a consideration of social learning, however, it is important to note that biological and cultural mechanisms may be operating as well. At the biological level, if there is any connection between social behavior and genetic action (Barash, 1977; Barkow, 1978; Wilson, 1975) it is possible that those very independent, socially unresponsive individuals in sedentary farming communities may be removed from the breeding population either by ostracism or by death. In hunting bands, also, highly dependent individuals may similarly be removed (Berry, 1974b). In either case the effect would be to change the gene pool in the direction of increased adaptation to the ecocultural setting.

For cultural mechanisms in addition to socialization, agents of social control and political authority may eliminate socially deviant persons as inappropriate role models for others in the group. Imprisonment or other forms of institutionalization may be used to simply remove the undesired social behavior from view. This is more likely to be done in a sedentary stratified community, where political authority is sufficiently well organized to effect such removal;

however, even in nomadic hunting bands, cultural mechanisms such as ridicule may be equally effective.

Considering the question of socialization, it is useful to remember that the practice of turning newcomers (whether neonate or immigrant) into fully functioning members of a cultural group is considered to be a universal feature of group life (see review by Lonner, 1979). As we have argued in the opening section of this chapter, such a common cultural feature must be present if cross-cultural comparison and integration are to be legitimate. In a classic presentation of the functional prerequisites for social existence (Aberle, Cohen, Davis, Levy, & Sutton, 1950), socialization is argued to be the key prerequisite since most of the others (e.g., shared modes of communication, normative control of behavior) are achieved by way of socialization.

Such functional prerequisites establish universal dimensions of social existence; what cross-cultural research can establish is the variations in cultural practice and social behavior which have been developed at different locations on these dimensions. Indeed, it may be possible to establish the systematic covariation between two or more of these variables. In essence this paper may be viewed as an attempt to trace the relationships between socialization (along with its ecocultural antecedents) and the normative regulation of behavior (represented by response to a test of independence–conformity).

The cross-cultural study of socialization is now well advanced. One line of research is represented by the use of cultural archives, such as the Human Relations Area Files (e.g., Whiting & Child, 1953), and another by the deployment of field workers for specific studies of socialization (e.g., Minturn & Lambert, 1964; Whiting & Whiting, 1975). In the former, where an anthropologist has made notes on socialization and incorporated them into an ethnography, data on socialization can be coded, rated, and analyzed comparatively (e.g., Barry, Bacon, & Child, 1957; Barry, Child, & Bacon, 1959; Barry & Paxson, 1971; and Barry, Josephson, Lauer, & Marshall, 1976). In the latter, specific research questions can be posed and hypotheses tested.

A socialization dimension which has emerged from the literature of the first type as we have seen has been given the bipolar label of "assertion–compliance" (Barry, Child, & Bacon, 1959). A similar dimension has also emerged from factor analyses of data collected during research of the second type (termed "responsibility demands" by Minturn-Triandis & Lambert, 1963). The "assertion–compliance" dimension places cultural groups on a scale of socialization practices which is anchored by independence, self-reliance, and achievement training at the "assertion" end and by obedience and responsibility training at the "compliance" end. These rating scales were derived from an earlier study (Barry et al., 1957) and are defined as follows:

1. Achievement training. Usually on the basis of competition or imposition of standards of excellence in performance.

2. Self-reliance training. Defined as training to take care of oneself, to be independent of the assistance of other people in supplying one's needs and wants.

3. General independence training. This was defined more generally, through self-reliance training, to include training not only to satisfy one's own needs but also toward all kinds of freedom from control, domination, and supervision. Ratings of general independence training were highly correlated with ratings of self-reliance training but were not identical to them.

4. Obedience training. Defined as training to accept the commands of those in some position of authority over the child.

5. Responsibility training. Usually on the basis of participation in the subsistence or household tasks.

The variable of "responsibility demands" appears to be virtually identical to that of "compliance." For our purposes, we will take these two studies as providing converging evidence that there is a universal dimension of socialization which ranges from an emphasis on setting children off early on a relatively independent life course through to an emphasis on surrounding children with a structured system of social demands.

The basic thrust of the Barry et al. study was to establish a link between socialization practices and other features of their culture, and in particular their ecological setting. They begin by asking the question (1959, p. 51): "Why does a particular society select child training practices which will tend to produce a particular kind of typical personality?" and they suggest that such an adult personality along with its child-training antecedents are functional for life in the society.

The basic hypothesis advanced by Barry et al. (1959, p. 52) is that adult economic roles should be consistent with the degree of "food accumulation" which is characteristic of the society. They distinguish between two extremes of food accumulation: In one, where animal husbandry predominates, the future supply of food "seems to be best assured by faithful adherence to routines designed to maintain the good health of the herd," or where agriculture predominates, "there might well be a premium on obedience to the older and wiser, and on responsibility in faithful performance of routine"; in the other, where hunting and gathering predominates, innovation and "variations in the energy and skill exerted in food-getting lead to immediate reward or punishment." The former (animal husbandry and agriculture) they refer to as "high food accumulating," while they term the latter "low food accumulating."

As a second hypothesis, Barry et al. argue that "in societies with low accumulation of food resources, adults should tend to be individualistic, assertive, and venturesome. By parallel reasoning, adults should tend to be conscientious, compliant, and conservative in societies with high accumulation of food resources." Finally, they argue that "the kind of adult behavior useful to the society is likely to be taught to some extent to the children, in order to assure the appearance of this behavior at the time it is needed."

In order to assess the argument, child-training practices (emphases in socialization) were compared, in a sample of societies, with the degree of food accumulation (defined in terms of exploitive patterns). No comparisons were made with "adult personality," since these data were not available to them in the ethnographic literature.

A classification of 79 societies was made on the food accumulation scale as follows: High food accumulation societies were those with exploitive patterns combining agriculture with animal husbandry or pastoralism ($n = 24$); medium food accumulation societies were those preserving root or grain cultivation, with animals unimportant ($n = 33$); while low food accumulation societies were those who relied upon hunting, gathering, or fishing ($n = 22$).

Relationships between degree of food accumulation and socialization emphases were calculated for boys and girls separately. For "responsibility," correlations were $+.74$ and $+.62$, respectively; for "obedience" they were $+.50$ and $+.59$ (all significant at the .01 level). For "achievement" correlations were $-.60$ and $-.62$, respectively; for "self-reliance," the correlations were $-.21$ and $-.46$; and for "independence" they were $-.41$ and .11, respectively.

When the more global measure of socialization ("pressure toward compliance vs. assertion") is employed, these relationships still hold. This global measure combines ratings on "responsibility" and "obedience" on the one hand, and ratings of "achievement" and "self-reliance," on the other. A difference score between the two pairs, if positive, indicates an emphasis upon "compliance," and, if negative, an emphasis upon "assertion" in socialization. The distribution of societies indicates that of the 23 societies above the median on the compliance–assertion rating, 20 are high food accumulating, while of the 23 societies below the median, 19 are low food accumulating.

This compliance to assertion dimension provides both a clear scale of variation for socialization cross-culturally and a link between the background ecocultural setting and the most adaptive adult behavioral characteristics. Some evidence for the latter can be found in the anthropological literature. The case for adaptive psychological characteristics of the hunter has been put eloquently by Hallowell (1946). Reviewing the historical and cultural material available, he concluded that independence, individualism, and emotional restraint characterize the early reports on the character of hunting Amerindians of northeastern North America. Quotations selected from early explorers and missionaries illustrate these characteristics: "... the savage does not know what it is to obey..."; "... In a word, they hold it as a maxim that each one is free: that one can do whatever he wishes; and that it is not sensible to put constraint upon men..."; "... The savages agree very readily with what you say, but do not, for all that, cease to act upon their own ideas" (Hallowell, 1946).

Such a pattern of independence in social behavior combined with restraint in emotional expression is referred to as "atomism" by Hallowell. This theme is taken up by Honigmann (1968), who extends the analysis to other hunting groups (the Eskimo and Athabascan Indians) and provides an ecological explanation for these behaviors. For Honigmann, such behavior "is congruent with the atomism of his community and directly adaptive in an environment that demands individual resourcefulness and independence" (1968, p. 226).

In summary, then, when the ecocultural model is employed as a predictive base for social behaviors, there are some fairly clear leads. The most apparent is in the domain of independent (as opposed to conforming) behavior, while there may also be variation in social and emotional self-restraint. Specifically, across a broad range of ecological adaptations, from hunting and gathering to agricultural pursuits, there should be found variation in social behavior: At the loose, nomadic end independence should be characteristic, while at the tight, sedentary end conformity should be more in evidence. In keeping with the acculturation features of the model, moreover, there should be observable changes ("behavioral shifts") from these traditional characteristics in the direction of the norms of social behavior of the dominant social or cultural communities.

B. INDEPENDENCE

Classical studies of independence and conformity in the Asch (1956) tradition have been conducted almost entirely with western, usually university student, samples; these studies are generally well known and are not reviewed here. A few cross-cultural studies have been conducted with Asch-type materials (e.g., Boldt, 1976; Chandra, 1973; Claeys, 1967; Milgram, 1961; Whittaker & Meade, 1967); and some other studies have been conducted using a variety of other estimates of conformity (e.g., Huang & Harris, 1973; Meade & Barnard, 1973; Munroe & Munroe, 1972, 1975; and Munroe, Munroe, & Daniels, 1973).

Even within the set of studies employing Asch-type materials, it is difficult to make detailed comparisons or to draw out precise generalizations (Faucheux, 1976). It is virtually impossible to draw together the other studies with any confidence. However, several of the studies do make some assessment of, or comment upon, the strength of the cultural surround. For example, reference is made to strong traditional group influence (Huang & Harris, 1973; Meade & Barnard, 1973), strong childhood compliance training (Munroe & Munroe, 1975), communal social organization (Boldt, 1976), or authoritarian social structure (Chandra, 1973). A reasonable interpretation of these various terms (strong, communal, authoritarian, etc.) is that they all point to the effect of a "tight" sociocultural context on the level of individual conformity exhibited.

These studies are generally consistent with the model proposed here. First, as we have noted, the authors interpret their results as indicative of a culture-to-behavior relationship: Tighter cultures yield greater conformity. Second, however, there is evidence in these studies that sedentary, agricultural-based groups exhibit generally higher levels of conformity than others (e.g., Rhodesians in Whittaker & Meade, 1967).

1. The Task

For the test of independence, the task is to make judgements of the lengths of lines after having been provided with a fictitious group norm. In the Asch prototype, the task was to indicate which of three clearly different length lines was the same as a standard; one of the three was obviously the correct one, while another of the three was unanimously indicated by a group of phoney subjects (confederates of the experimenter). For field purposes there are two difficulties with such a test, although the general nature of it seemed quite suitable. The first is that experimental confederates are not possible in settlements or villages; word about the deception would soon spread, and the test would be rendered useless. Second, the use of obviously right or wrong lines as alternatives makes plain the deception; the whole research effort would soon be discounted if one element were considered to be a trick.

To remedy these problems, a new task had to be designed which avoided the use of confederates and obvious deception. The second of these can be handled easily by increasing the ambiguity of the stimulus array. Thus, a set of eight lines, which differed minimally but perceptibly from each other, was offered to the participant; the selection of one was to be made on the basis of its similarity to the standard. However the first problem was more difficult and its solution had to make use of an early observation by Sherif (1935) that individuals in experimental settings accepted the norms of their group, even when members of the group were not present. Thus, it was decided that a group norm could be presented during the administration of the test by one line marked as "the one most . . . people chose." Pilot trials prior to field work indicated the acceptance of this manipulation.

Conceptually, such a task appears to be related to Witkin's notion of sensitivity to external influence, one of the social elements in his notion of cognitive style. Empirically, this task is relevant to the ethnographic descriptions of contrasting behavior of hunters and agriculturalists: The former are independent and self-reliant in early training (Barry, Child, & Bacon, 1959), while the latter are obedient and compliant in early training and live in more highly structured authority systems. Despite the relevance of such a task to descriptions of the life style of the people in these studies and its suitability for field use, there is now evidence (reviewed by Witkin & Goodenough, 1977a) which shows that the use of such inanimate or simulated "social" stimuli does not relate to perceptual or cognitive elements of cognitive style. When Asch-type situations are employed with real social stimuli, however, such relationships generally do emerge. We are thus faced, after the collection of these data, with the fact that we are dealing not with differentiation in the social domain, but perhaps only with a general independence–conformity measure.

Details of the task are presented in Table II. Although the task was used in all samples, it underwent an expansion in the number of test items during the

TABLE II
INDEPENDENCE TASK: TEST SPECIFICATIONS

	Differences in length between successive lines (mm)	Length of standard line (cm)	Line designated		Line correct	
			Rank	Length (cm)	Rank	Length (cm)
Version 1						
Sheet A	3	9.4	—	—	4	9.4
Sheet B	2	9.6	—	—	5	9.6
Sheet C	2	9.6	6	9.6	6	9.6
Sheet D	1	9.0	7	8.5	2	9.0
Sheet E	2	9.4	8	10.4	3	9.4
Sheet F	3	10.9	7	8.5	2	10.0
Version 2						
Sheet P1	3	9.9	—	—	6	9.9
Sheet P2	2	9.7	—	—	4	9.7
Sheet A	0.5	9.4	—	—	2	9.4
Sheet B	1	9.6	—	—	3	9.6
Sheet C	2	9.4	—	—	5	9.4
Sheet D	3	9.3	—	—	4	9.3
Sheet 1	0.5	9.4	7	9.15	2	9.4
Sheet 2	1	10.3	3	10.8	8	10.3
Sheet 3	2	10.1	7	9.1	2	10.1
Sheet 4	3	10.4	3	8.9	8	10.4

course of the research; thus, two sets of numbers appear in the table. An example (of sheet 3 from the second version) is given in Fig. 2.

In version 1, sheets A and B provided practice on the task without any group norm being suggested. Sheet C was presented with the correct line designated as the one most often chosen; this was an attempt to provide some credibility for the task and the norm. Sheets D, E, and F were presented with an incorrect line designated as the group norm and always five ranks (lines) away from the correct one. If the designated line were chosen, a score of 5 was assigned, and if the correct line were chosen, a score of 0 was assigned; intermediate choices were assigned the appropriate score between 0 and 5. Thus over the three test items, total scores per participant could range from 0 to 15.

In version 2, sheets P1 and P2 provided practice on the task, without any group norm being suggested. Sheets A, B, C, and D were then presented, also without any norm being suggested, so that basic ability on this kind of task might be assessed independently of initial practice and of distortions introduced by social influence. This series also introduces some element of control over the possible individual and group differences in line discrimination accuracy. Finally, sheets 1 to 4 were presented, with suggestions of the group norms, in a way comparable to the earlier version. In this case, since there are four test sheets, total scores could range from 0 to 20.

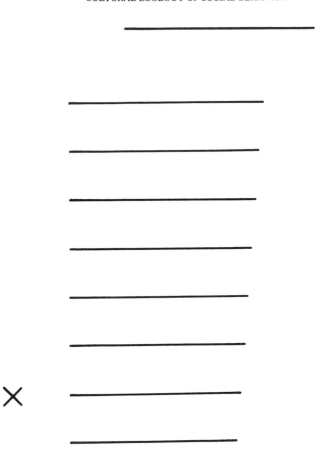

Fig. 2.   Example of independence task (sheet 3 of version 2).

In order to make scoring comparable between the two versions, a score is extracted which employs the three common items from each version (based upon items with 1 mm, 2 mm, and 3 mm differences): These are items D, E, and F from version 1 and items 2, 3, and 4 from version 2. In order to make the score in the appropriate conceptual direction (that is, a high score indicating high independence) the score is reversed (by subtracting it from 15) and then expressed as a percentage of the maximum.

2.   Results

Sample means for independence task versions 1 and 2, are provided in Tables III and IV. In Table III, each trial mean is provided first, followed by the mean total of items D, E, and F. Item C is reported as a partial check upon initial sample differences. However, because item C in version 1 did not really consti-tute an acceptable control, items A–D were added when version 2 was con-

TABLE III

INDEPENDENCE TASK MEANS: VERSION 1

Sample	Test series trial means				Total (ΣD, E, F)	
	C	D	E	F	M	sd
Mayola	1.12	3.50	2.91	2.63	9.04	3.3
Port Loko	1.16	3.62	2.82	2.17	8.61	3.2
Telefomin	1.21	3.30	2.14	1.46	6.90	3.8
Yarrabah	1.24	2.81	1.76	0.79	5.36	2.8
Hanuabada	1.11	2.64	1.28	0.61	4.53	2.8
Santa Teresa	1.19	2.80	1.68	0.74	5.22	3.0
Pond Inlet	1.27	1.31	1.15	0.29	2.75	2.9
Frobisher Bay	1.32	1.29	0.91	0.05	2.25	2.5
Inverkeilor	1.00	1.77	1.57	0.66	4.00	3.8
Edinburgh	1.05	1.93	1.42	0.50	3.85	3.0

structed. Table IV provides the mean total of pretest items A–D on version 2, followed by the four test items 1–4. As we have noted, only items 2–4 are employed to yield a score comparable to that derived from version 1.

An integrated table (Table V) then reports the independence task means, the reversed score, and the percentage score for all samples, including the four communities not at subsistence level. Internal relationships (item-to-item Pear-

TABLE IV

INDEPENDENCE TASK MEANS: VERSION 2

Sample	Pretest series (Σ A–D)		Test series trial means				Total (Σ 2–4)	
	M	sd	1	2	3	4	M	sd
Hartley Bay	6.07	3.4	2.04	2.41	2.26	1.96	6.63	3.9
Port Simpson	6.06	2.9	2.08	2.30	2.18	1.70	6.18	3.8
Tachie	5.66	2.9	2.03	2.16	2.04	1.73	5.93	3.4
Fort St. James	6.76	2.8	2.98	2.21	2.16	1.61	5.98	3.4
Aroland	7.24	2.8	3.23	2.24	2.20	1.57	6.01	3.7
Long Lac	7.42	3.3	3.18	2.27	2.19	1.58	6.04	3.1
Sioux Lookout	7.75	3.1	3.24	3.11	2.42	1.68	7.21	4.1
Wemindji	7.35	3.4	3.12	2.61	2.08	0.94	5.63	2.9
Fort George	7.13	3.2	3.20	2.89	2.03	0.87	5.79	3.0
Westport	6.18	3.6	3.16	2.51	1.63	0.68	4.82	2.8
Sioux Lookout	7.87	3.2	3.02	3.39	2.96	2.70	9.05	4.3

son product moment correlations) range from $+.21$ to $+.34$, while item-to-total correlations range from $+.61$ to $+.70$.

Our primary interest lies in the relationship between the level of independence indicated in Table V and the ecocultural index listed in Table I. The expectation is that those at the nomadic, hunting, "loose" end of the ecocultural dimension would exhibit the highest levels of independence, while those at the sedentary, agricultural, and "tight" end of the dimension would be least independent. The relationship is plotted in Fig. 3; it is clear that the 17 subsistence-level samples are distributed widely on the independence task, and that their scores are related to their position on the ecocultural dimension. In fact the Pearson correlation between the sample independence task mean and their score on the ecocultural index is $+.70$. When individual scores (rather than sample means) are employed in the correlation, the coefficient across the 780 individuals is $+.51$.

TABLE V

INDEPENDENCE TASK MEANS

Sample	Mean score	Reversed mean[a]	Percentage score[b]
Mayola	9.04	5.96	39.7
Port Loko	8.61	6.39	42.6
Telefomin	6.90	8.10	54.0
Hanuabada	4.53	10.47	69.8
Yarrabah	5.36	9.64	64.3
Hartley Bay	6.63	8.37	55.8
Port Simpson	6.18	8.82	58.8
Tachie	5.93	9.07	60.5
Fort St. James	5.98	9.02	60.1
Aroland	6.01	8.99	59.9
Longlac	6.04	8.96	59.7
Sioux Lookout	7.21	7.79	52.0
Santa Teresa	5.22	9.78	65.2
Wemindji	5.63	9.37	62.5
Fort George	5.79	9.21	61.4
Pond Inlet	2.75	12.25	81.7
Frobisher Bay	2.25	12.75	85.0
Inverkeilor	4.00	11.00	73.3
Edinburgh	3.85	11.15	74.3
Westport	4.82	10.18	67.9
Sioux Lookout	9.05	5.95	39.7

[a]Reversed mean $= 15 -$ mean score.

[b]Percentage score $= \dfrac{\text{Reversed mean}}{15} \times 100$.

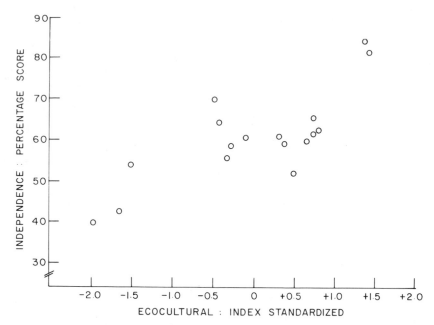

Fig. 3.   Independence task score of each sample as a function of sample position on the ecocultural dimension ($r = +.70$, $n = 17$).

In the four other samples (which are not at subsistence level) independence scores were spread over virtually the whole range of scores in the 17 samples in the 10 traditional cultures: The Scots and one Canadian sample are clearly toward the independent end, while one Canadian sample matches the West African sample which anchors the range at its conforming end. Thus, it is not possible to characterize Canadian or European levels of independence. Within the other cultural groups, however, there is fair homogeneity, the greatest sample-to-sample range being exhibited by the Ojibway (Aroland at 59.9 to Sioux Lookout at 52.0). This lack of variation between the traditional and acculturated samples is illustrated by the nonsignificant correlations with the acculturation index ($-.07$ across the 17 samples; $-.11$ across the 780 individuals).

3.   Discussion

Several issues require attention beyond the central question of how independence varies with the ecocultural and acculturation indices. One of these is the nature and structure of the task in relation to its cross-cultural use. We have argued earlier that the normative regulation of individual behavior is a cultural universal; we thus held the expectation that all groups would respond to the suggestion of the group norm and would do so in a fairly consistent fashion.

Evidence in Tables III and IV indicates that all groups responded with judgments in the direction of the group norm; the range was large (totals between 2.25 and 9.04) but all responded with yielding when the norm was indicated. Similarly the item–item and item–total correlations suggest that, within each sample, individual responses to test items covaried directly, yielding sufficient internal consistency to permit a summed total score. We may assert, then, that the test behaved in a way consistent with the universal status of the concept which underlies it.

Another issue to consider is the possible existence of group variation in pretest response. Version 1 did not permit a direct examination of this question, but inspection of sample means for test item C (where the suggested norm was in fact the correct answer) shows that cross-group variation is minimal (compared to items D, E, and F), and it is not systematic in relation to ecocultural features of the sample. Version 2 was developed, in part, to introduce such a pretest control; there the pretest score range is not great, and variation is unsystematic. For both versions, performance on the task is insignificantly correlated with such other visually based tasks as gap discrimination, reported in Berry (1976). Furthermore, all samples were screened for near (25 cm) and far (6 m) visual acuity, so that basic group sensory differences cannot account for any variation in independence task performance. However, it is clear from Tables III and IV that yielding to the group norm was systematically influenced (in all samples) by the item "difficulty" (in terms of the difference in length between successive lines). The ambiguity of the stimulus array did affect responses to both pretest items (in version 2) and the actual test items (in versions 1 and 2). In version 2, mean pretest scores declined from 2.31, to 2.15, to 1.43, to .93 as the pretest items "eased" from .5-, to 1.0-, to 2.0-, to 3.0-mm differences between successive lines. In version 1, mean test scores declined from 2.66, to 1.83, to 1.09 (for 1.0-, 2.0-, and 3.0-mm differences); and in version 2, they declined from 2.79, to 2.47, to 2.17, to 1.52 (for .5-, 1.0-, 2.0-, and 3.0-mm differences). It is clear that these test characteristics did contribute to task performance in a systematic way.

Turning to the fundamental question of the effect of suggesting a group norm, we can extract from Table IV actual differences between pretest and test scores. In all samples total pretest scores are lower than total (Σ 1–4) test scores. They range from a mean of 2.40 among the Tsimshian samples to a mean of 1.63 among the Cree samples, with the Carrier and Ojibway being intermediate. On version 2, a mean score increase of 2.12 points (over a mean pretest score of 6.83) represents an effect of about 31%; this is very similar in magnitude to that reported on other Asch-type studies for the percentage of trials on which yielding took place.

Although no pretest is available for version 1, it is interesting to consider the differing effect of the suggested group norm between trial C (where the correct line was suggested) and the mean of trials D, E, and F (Table III). The mean score on trial C was 1.20, while for trials D, E, and F it was 1.86; this represents a score increase of 55%, considerably greater than the increase found employing the more conventional control in version 2. However, whichever method is employed, it is clear that the suggestion of a group norm had an effect on responses over all groups. The question of the variation in this effect across the ecocultural and acculturational range can now be examined.

The samples in Table V have been arranged according to the position of the group on the ecocultural dimension. The expectation was that those peoples who were sedentary and tight in settlement and sociopolitical structure (top of Table V) would exhibit the higher mean score on the independence task; conversely, those who were nomadic and loose should exhibit lower scores. Translated into a percentage score, in which a high number indicates high independence, regression analysis has provided strong evidence for the direct covariation of independence and ecocultural position. Clearly, there is a characteristic level of independence in these groups which is predictable from an examination of their cultural ecology. Consistent with the ethnographic reports, nomadic hunters tend to be independent in dealing with normative influence, while sedentary agriculturalists tend to accept such influence. Moreover, those samples which fall in the intermediate ecocultural ranges tend to exhibit intermediate responsiveness to influence.

The process of acculturation, for all cultures in this study, has involved an increase in settlement size and the development of new social and political structures. In principle, it is possible that such acculturative influences could either raise or lower independence scores. On the one hand, settlement generally brings greater authority pressures to bear upon individuals (teachers, police, courts, administrators, bosses, etc.); but on the other hand, these being nontraditional sources of influence, such authority may be rejected. Considering interpersonal bonds, on the one hand increased settlement offers a greater opportunity for small-group formation (clubs, associations, gangs, etc.); but on the other hand, social disintegration has often been shown to accompany acculturation (Berry, 1979). Thus, whether the question is considered at the level of social and political structures or at the level of small groups, it is possible to expect either an increase or a decrease of independence in acculturation.

Evidence has been presented showing that, overall, there is no significant relationship between the acculturation index and the independence score. This general statistic may mask the presence of varying "behavioral shifts" in independence with acculturation; thus, a more detailed examination is warranted. Although most cultural groups show little difference between the independence scores of the traditional and acculturated samples, it is possible to consider the direction of these marginal trends. The two "tightest" cultural groups for which we have two samples (Temne and Tsimshian) both shifted toward greater independence with acculturation. In contrast, the looser Carrier, Ojibway, and Cree cultures shifted toward lesser independence. The emerging pattern of shifts toward a common norm is hampered, however, by the Eskimo pattern (least "tight" but shifting toward even greater independence with acculturation). With this exception, though, it is possible to suggest that acculturation weakens the traditional style or (put in other terms) leads to homogenization of independence cross-culturally.

In one field area, it is possible to examine scores across three indigenous samples and their relation to the Euro-Canadian sample in the same area. The northern resource-based town of Sioux Lookout has provided a score (39.7%) equivalent to that of the traditional Temne village (Mayola); this suggests the existence of a fairly tightly knit community, an assertion which is borne out by sociological field work (Beal, Berry, Franks, Harmsen, Herman, McKirdy, & Peppard, 1976). If we consider the three Ojibway samples as acculturating toward this town (indeed one Ojibway sample is living in the town itself), we can note that there is a consistent trend from the traditional Ojibway sample (Aroland) through the transitional sample (Longlac) to the town sample, all in the direction of the independence score of the Euro-Canadian town sample. This linear shift with acculturation is reminiscent of the findings by Hallowell (1955), in which other Ojibway samples exhibited evidence of personality change in a linear fashion as their camps were located closer to the Euro-Canadian trading post.

Finally, in this discussion we may consider the relationship between these data on independence and other cultural and psychological evidence. Foremost is their relationship with perceptual and cognitive tasks included by Witkin and his colleagues (Witkin & Berry, 1975; Witkin & Goodenough 1977b) within the field dependent–independent cognitive style. As we have noted earlier, one of the original purposes for investigating independence cross-culturally was the apparent relevance of such a task to social aspects of cognitive style; those who are field independent are reasoned to be independent in social behavior as well, while those who are field dependent are more sensitive to social information. However, as we have also noted, a recent review of the literature (Witkin & Goodenough, 1977a) clearly shows that relationships have not been found in most (western-based) studies where the social situation is not "live." In the present study, the social influence was not conveyed by a live social group but merely by an assistant indicating the group norm. In the present study, correlations between independence scores and performance on one indicator of cognitive style (Kohs Blocks) were generally positive but also generally insignificant (range $-.15$ to $+.32$ for version 1; $-.05$ to $+20$ for version 2), confirming the Witkin and Goodenough generalization.

However, in contrast to this general lack of significant individual-level correlation within samples, there is a strong relationship between mean independence scores and one perceptual–cognitive test of cognitive style; the correlation with mean Kohs scores across the 17 samples is +.86. Clearly, those samples exhibiting a field-independent cognitive style are also characterized by high independence scores; this is as expected from the model, despite low individual-level covariation.

IV. Applications

The demonstration of systematic covariation between a group's habitat and their characteristic level of independence has value as a basic finding about human development. However, the potential applications of such a discovery are perhaps even more valuable, especially when this knowledge is coupled with what is already known about the distribution of perceptual and cognitive characteristics (Witkin & Berry, 1975; Berry, 1976) in the same populations.

Earlier assessments of the applicability of social psychological research to questions facing northern native peoples in Canada (Berry, 1971b, 1973) were made while some applied projects were still being conducted. Since then, two projects have been completed (Beal *et al.*, 1976; Saladin-d'Anglure, Larochelle, Zrudlo & Berry, 1974) which considered, from an interdisciplinary perspective, the relevance of independence and other social behaviors to the areas of telecommunications and housing needs in northern Canada.

A. TELECOMMUNICATION NEEDS

A team of researchers has attempted to construct a dynamic systems model of northwestern Ontario, employing demographic, economic, political, sociocultural, and psychological data (Beal *et al.*, 1976). The purpose of this model was to assist in the development of a telecommunications policy for the region, which is composed of both Euro-Canadian and Ojibway populations; the model was also developed so that the impact of telecommunication changes could be assessed over the course of time.

The psychological component of the research was concerned with describing a broad range of attitudes, abilities, and traits which are theoretically relevant to the use of telecommunications systems: intergroup and interpersonal attitudes, perceptual and sensory characteristics, and independence. Samples were drawn (three Ojibway, from Aroland, Long Lac, Sioux Lookout; and one Euro-Canadian, from Sioux Lookout—see Table I), and field studies were conducted over a 2-year period.

Independence task data for these Ojibway samples have been reported (Tables IV and V) in the context of all samples in the study. With a percentage score in the 52–60 range, the Ojibway samples are toward the more independent end of the range, while the Euro-Canadian sample (at 40) is at the less independent end.

As we have already noted, across the three Ojibway samples, there is a decline in score with acculturation; the Sioux Lookout Ojibway sample lies intermediate between the traditional Aroland sample and the Sioux Lookout Euro-Canadian sample.

In terms of other psychological data, the Ojibway samples did not differ significantly among themselves, or from the Euro-Canadian sample, on a battery of sensory, perceptual, and cognitive-style tasks, in either the visual or the auditory modality. These results had been predicted on the basis of other work with hunting and gathering groups (Berry, 1976; Witkin & Berry, 1975), such skills being considered to be adaptive to their particular habitat.

In the domain of attitudes, the more traditional Ojibway sample was least interested in assimilating to Euro-Canadian life, while those Ojibway living in Sioux Lookout were more positive about it. Conversely, Sioux Lookout Ojibway were least interested in rejecting future influence from the Euro-Canadian life style, while the other two Ojibway samples tended more toward such a rejection. However, all three Ojibway groups were most accepting of an integration of life styles in which their cultural integrity would be respected while at the same time interacting with the larger Euro-Canadian society (cf. Berry, Kalin, & Taylor, 1977).

These findings hold a number of implications for telecommunications policy development. One is that the ability and skill substrate is clearly sufficient to operate, after appropriate specific technical training, a telecommunications system. Another is that the more traditional Ojibway wish to avoid assimilation into the larger Euro-Canadian society, and some even wish to reject the larger society. Combined with relatively high independence task scores, these findings suggest that serious consideration should be given to an Ojibway-controlled telecommunications system in that region. The ability base is in place, intergroup attitudes indicate a concern for cultural swamping and independence task scores suggest a relatively low inclination to accept social influence. Such a pattern of results is clearly in opposition to the uncontrolled extension of Euro-Canadian broadcasting into Ojibway areas.

B. HOUSING NEEDS

Traditional Eskimo housing, as is well-known, consisted of a single snow house (iglu) occupied by a single family. Occasionally during festivities or ritual occasions, a number of snow houses was constructed adjacent to one another and connecting arches were opened up between them. In contrast to this single multipurpose room, recent plywood houses (which were designed in and shipped from the south) were relatively direct copies of four- to seven-room southern bungalows. Considering the implications of earlier work on Eskimo space and independence (Berry, 1966, 1967), it was thought that Eskimo people would exhibit definite spatial interests and needs, as well as a concern for independence. This led to an attempt to elicit expressions of spatial requirements in housing by conducting an interdisciplinary field study in the settlement of Puvirnituuq in northern Quebec (Saladin-d'Anglure *et al.*, 1974).

A team consisting of anthropologists, an architect, and a psychologist established, by survey, the basic demographic, economic, sociocultural, and housing characteristics of the population. A sample of families was then drawn, and each family was invited to construct a model of both its previous house and its present house; then they were asked to create a model of the house they would like to have in the future. All models were constructed using cardboard panels (scale 1 inch = 4 ft) with pins in them, mounted on a 2 × 3 ft styrofoam base. Panels representing windows, doors, and internal partitions were all included, in addition to exterior walls. Models were constructed with care, and with an obvious excitement and pleasure. Typical household activities were then discussed, and human figures were placed in the model to represent their spatial arrangements during those activities. Photographs were taken of each household activity and were later analyzed for details of house size and design, room number and size, and human locations.

In contrast to their current houses (where interior space was divided into many nearly equal sized rooms), models of desired houses characteristically had a single large undifferentiated room with a few small semiseparated rooms arranged around the larger room. This appears to be a partial return to earlier spatial preferences in housing and is consistent with the traditionally high level of independence found in Eskimo samples. As a working hypothesis, we consider that several psychological techniques were probably employed in the iglu to maintain one's separateness. In addition to independence, the ethnographic field reports indicate, as we have seen, reserve, reticence, and intense emotional control in many hunting-based societies. In the absence of environmental means to regulate social encounters (such as walls or private spaces) psychological characteristics may be developed as effective privacy regulation devices (Altman, 1975; Altman 1977; Altman & Chemers, 1979).

The practical importance of such research is that housing may be designed which is psychologically and culturally appropriate (not to mention environmental appropriateness in such extreme temperature conditions). Indeed, three prototype designs were produced which were based upon the models and the spatial analysis, and they are now being inhabited and evaluated by the Eskimo families themselves.

V. Conclusions

The research program reported in this article has attempted to show that both cultural and cross-cultural dimensions of social behavior can be investigated. The pursuit of any such venture must be rooted in a universal and in a systematic theory if both the local cultural and the pancultural are to be validly studied. In the present case the social and cultural universal of normative influence and the systematic approach of a model derived from cultural ecology were employed. The second of these provided a base for understanding adaptive levels of independence, while the first provided an appropriate comparative dimension.

With such analytical tools available in the social sciences, there is no longer any reason for social psychologists to remain culture blind or culture bound in their studies of social behavior. If the aim of science is to make general statements, then the aim of social psychology is to make culturally universal statements about human social behavior. This cannot be done, obviously, by continuing to work only in a single society and by assuming that what holds there has general applicability to all human groups (Berry, 1978).

Cross-cultural social psychology has only begun. We have before us exhortations (e.g., Pepitone, 1976) and criticisms (e.g., Faucheux, 1976) to do it, and to do it thoughtfully. This paper has sought to provide an example; but clearly it can be done better, and it can be done with a wider range of social behaviors. Such stocks in trade as aggression, attitudinal consistency, competition, dependency, communication styles, and many more are likely candidates for comparative analysis. In making these, however, we must be careful not to overrun the local while in pursuit of the universal; indigenous conceptions of social behavior constitute a valuable cultural resource, and they demand our respect.

REFERENCES

Aberle, D. F., Cohen, A. K., Davis, A. K., Levy, M. J., & Sutton, F. X. The functional prerequisites of a society. *Ethics,* 1950, **60,** 100–111.

Altman, I. *The Environment and social behavior.* Monterey, Calif.: Brooks/Cole, 1975.

Altman, I. Privacy regulation: Culturally universal or culturally specific. *Journal of Social Issues,* 1977.

Altman, I., & Chemers, M. Cultural aspects of environment-behavior relationships. In H. C. Triandis & R. Brislin (Eds.), *Handbook of cross-cultural psychology* (Vol. 5). Boston: Allyn & Bacon, 1979.

Asch, S. E. Studies in independence and conformity: 1. A minority of one against a unanimous majority. *Psychological Monographs,* 1956, **70,** 416.

Barash, D. P. *Sociobiology and behavior.* New York: Elsevier-North Holland, 1977.

Barkow, J. H. Culture and sociobiology. *American Anthropologist,* 1978, **80,** 5–20.

Barry, H., Bacon, M., & Child, I. A cross-cultural survey of some sex differences in socialization. *Journal of Abnormal and Social Psychology,* 1957, **55,** 327–332.

Barry, H., Child, I., & Bacon, M. Relation of child training to subsistence economy. *American Anthropologist.* 1959, **61,** 51–63.

Barry, H., Josephson, L., Sauer, E., & Marshall, C. Traits inculcated in childhood: Cross-cultural codes. *Ethology,* 1976, **15,** 83–114.

Barry, H., & Paxson, L. M. Infancy and early childhood: Cross-cultural codes. *Ethnology,* 1971, **10,** 466–508.

Beal, J. C., Berry, J. W., Franks, C. E. S., Harmsen, R., Herman, K., McKirdy, J., & Peppard, L. E. *The Application of dynamic modelling to the study of telecommunications development in Canada.* Ottawa: Government of Canada, 1976.

Berry, J. W. Temne and Eskimo perceptual skills. *International Journal of Psychology,* 1966, **1,** 207-229.

Berry, J. W. Independence and conformity in subsistence-level societies. *Journal of Personality Social Psychology,* 1967, **7,** 415-418.

Berry, J. W. Ecological and cultural factors in spatial perceptual development. *Canadian Journal of Behavioural Science,* 1971, **3,** 324-336. (a)

Berry, J. W. Psychological research in the north. *Anthropologica,* 1971, **13,** 143-157. (b)

Berry, J. W. *Education, communication and housing in the Canadian north.* Paper presented to APA symposium on applications of cross-cultural research, Montreal, 1973.

Berry, J. W. Canadian psychology: Some social and applied emphases. *Canadian psychologist,* 1974, **15,** 132-139. (a)

Berry, J. W. Differentiation across cultures: Cognitive style and affective style. In J. L. M. Dawson & W. J. Lonner (Eds.), *Readings in cross-cultural psychology.* Hong Kong: University of Hong Kong Press, 1974. (b)

Berry, J. W. *Human ecology and cognitive style.* New York: Wiley, 1976.

Berry, J. W. Social psychology: Comparative, societal and universal. *Canadian Psychological Review,* 1978, **19,** 93-104.

Berry, J. W. Social and cultural change. In H. C. Triandis & R. Brislin (Eds.), *Handbook of cross-cultural psychology,* (Vol. 5). Boston: Allyn & Bacon, 1979.

Berry, J. W., & Annis, R. C. Acculturative stress: The role of ecology, culture and differentiation. *Journal of Cross-Cultural Psychology,* 1974, **5,** 382-406.

Berry, J. W., Kalin, R., & Taylor, D. M. *Multiculturalism and ethnic attitudes in Canada.* Ottawa: Government of Canada, 1977.

Berry, J. W., & Wilde, G. J. S. (Eds.), *Social psychology: The Canadian context.* Toronto: McClelland & Stewart, 1972.

Boldt, E. D. Acquiescence and conventionality in a communal society. *Journal of Cross-Cultural Psychology,* 1976, **7,** 21-36.

Chandra, S. The effects of group pressure in perception: A cross-cultural conformity study in Fiji. *International Journal of Psychology,* 1973, **8,** 37-40.

Claeys, W. Conforming behavior and personality variables in Congolese students. *International Journal of Psychology,* 1967, **2,** 13-24.

Dasen, P. Concrete operational development in three cultures. *Journal of Cross-Cultural Psychology,* 1975, **6,** 156-172.

Diaz-Guererro, R. A Mexican psychology. *American Psychologist,* 1977, **32,** 934-944.

Elms, A. C. The crisis of confidence in social psychology, *American Psychologist,* 1975, **30,** 967-976.

Faucheux, C. Cross-cultural research in experimental social psychology. *European Journal of Social Psychology,* 1976, **6,** 269-322.

Gergen, K. J. Social psychology as history. *Journal of Personality and Social Psychology,* 1973, **26,** 309-320.

Hallowell, A. I. Some psychological characteristics of northeastern Indians. In F. Johnson (Ed.), *Man in northeastern North America.* Boston, Mass.: Peabody Foundation, 1946.

Hallowell, A. I. Background for a study of acculturation and the personality of the Ojibway. In A. I. Hallowell (Ed.), *Culture and experience.* Philadelphia: University of Pennsylvania Press, 1955.

Honigman, J. Interpersonal relations in atomistic societies. *Human Organization,* 1968, **27,** 220-229.

Huang, L., & Harris, M. Conformity in Chinese and Americans: A field experiment. *Journal of Cross-Cultural Psychology*, 1973, **4**, 427-434.

Israel, J. & Tajfel, H. (Eds.), *The context of social psychology*. London: Academic Press, 1972.

Lonner, W. J. The search for psychological universals. In H. Triandis & W. Lambert (Eds.), *Handbook of cross-cultural psychology* (Vol. 1). Boston: Allyn & Bacon, 1979.

McGuire, W. The yin and yang of progress in social psychology: Seven koan. *Journal of Personality and Social Psychology*, 1973, **26**, 446-456.

Meade, R., & Barnard, W. Conformity and anticonformity among Americans and Chinese. *Journal of Social Psychology*, 1973, **89**, 15-25.

Milgram, S. Nationality and conformity. *Scientific American*, 1961, **205**, 45-51.

Minturn, L., & Lambert, W. W. *Mothers of six cultures*. New York: Wiley, 1964.

Minturn-Triandis, L., & Lambert, W. W. Pancultural factor analyses of reported socialization practices. *Journal of Abnormal Social Psychology*, 1962, **62**, 631-639.

Moscovici, S. Society and theory in social psychology. In J. Israel & H. Tajfel (Eds.), *The context of social psychology*. London: Academic Press, 1972.

Munroe, R., & Munroe, R. Obedience among children in an East African society. *Journal of Cross-Cultural Psychology*, 1972, **3**, 395-399.

Munroe, R., & Munroe, R. Levels of obedience among U. S. and East African children on an experimental task. *Journal of Cross-Cultural Psychology*, 1975, **6**, 498-503.

Munroe, R., Munroe, R., & Daniels, R. Relation of subsistence economy to conformity in three East African societies. *Journal of Social Psychology*, 1973, **89**, 149-150.

Murdock, G. P. Ethnographic atlas: A summary. *Ethnology*, 1967, **6**, 109-236.

Murdock, G. P., & Provost, C. Measurement of cultural complexity. *Ethnology*, 1973, **12**, 379-392.

Pelto, P. The difference between 'tight' and 'loose' societies. *Transaction*, 1968 (April), 37-40.

Pepitone, A. Toward a normative and comparative biocultural social psychology. *Journal of Personality and Social Psychology*, 1976, **34**, 641-653.

Saladin-d'Anglure, B., Larochelle, G., Zrudlo, L., & Berry, J. W. *Projet nunaturliq*. Québec: Récherches Inuksiutiit, Université Laval, 1974.

Sherif, M. A study in some social factors in perception. *Archives of Psychology*, 1935, **27**, (9, Whole No. 187), 1-60.

Smith, M. B. Is experimental social psychology advancing? *Journal of Experimental Social Psychology*, 1972, **8**, 89-96.

Strickland, L., Aboud, F., & Gergen, K. (Eds.), *Social psychology in transition*. New York: Plenum, 1976.

Triandis, H. C. Social psychology and cultural analysis. In L. Strickland, F. Aboud, & K. Gergen (Eds.), *Social psychology in transition*. New York: Plenum, 1976.

Triandis, H. C. Cross-cultural social and personality psychology. *Personality Social Psychology Bulletin*, 1977, **3**, 143-158.

Triandis, H. C. Some universals of social behavior. *Personality and Social Psychology Bulletin*, 1978, **4**, 1-16.

Triandis, H. C., Vassiliou, V., Vassiliou, G., Tanaka, Y., & Shanmugam, A. V. *The analysis of subjective culture*. New York: Wiley, 1972.

Whiting, B. B., & Whiting, J. *Children of six cultures*. Cambridge: Harvard University Press, 1975.

Whiting, J., & Child, I. *Child training and personality*. New Haven: Yale University Press, 1953.

Whittaker, J. W., & Meade, R. Social pressure in the modification and distortion of judgement: A cross-cultural study. *International Journal of Psychology*, 1967, **2**, 109-114.

Wilson, E. O. *Sociobiology: The new synthesis*. Cambridge: Belknap Press, 1975.

Witkin, H. A., & Berry, J. W. Psychological differentiation in cross-cultural perspective. *Journal of Cross-Cultural Psychology*, 1975, **6**, 4-87.

Witkin, H. A., & Goodenough, R. Field dependence and interpersonal behavior, *Psychological Bulletin,* 1977, **84,** 661–189. (a)

Witkin, H. A., & Goodenough, R. *Field dependence revisited.* ETS Research Bulletin, 1977, RB-77-16. (b)

Witkin, H. A., Dyk, R. Faterson, H., & Goodenough, D. *Psychological Differentiation.* New York: Wiley, 1962.

EXPERIMENTS ON DEVIANCE WITH SPECIAL REFERENCE TO DISHONESTY

David P. Farrington

INSTITUTE OF CRIMINOLOGY
UNIVERSITY OF CAMBRIDGE, ENGLAND

I. Deviance and Experimentation 208
  A. Definition of "Deviance" 208
  B. Definition of "Experiment" 210
  C. An Alternative Methodology 212
II. Operationally Defining and Measuring Deviance in Experiments 214
  A. Dishonesty as a Dependent Variable 214
  B. Other Dependent Measures of Deviance 219
  C. Dishonesty as an Independent Variable 224
  D. Other Independent Measures of Deviance 227
  E. Some Ethical Issues 229
III. Experiments on Dishonesty 230
  A. Factors Influencing Dishonest Behavior 230
  B. Evaluating and Reacting to Dishonesty 238
IV. Conclusions 241
  References 242

With comparatively few exceptions (e.g., Steffensmeier & Terry, 1975), the field of deviance is dominated by nonexperimental research. Most of this is by sociologists and can be described as hypothesis generating rather than hypothesis testing. The common methodologies used are participant observation, cross-sectional surveys, and case histories. Hypothesis-generating research is necessary for the advancement of knowledge, but it needs to be followed by hypothesis testing. These methodologies are unsuitable for testing hypotheses because of their low internal validity or the low extent to which they can demonstrate unambiguously that changes in one factor have produced changes in another (Campbell & Stanley, 1966). They can establish correlations between

ADVANCES IN EXPERIMENTAL SOCIAL
PSYCHOLOGY, VOL. 12

deviance and other factors, but they cannot establish causal relationships and they cannot decide between alternative explanations of observed findings.

The most conclusive methodology for testing hypotheses is experimentation, which distinctly characterizes research by psychologists. However, with comparatively few exceptions (e.g., Bickman & Henchy, 1972), psychological experiments have been carried out in rather artificial laboratory settings with undergraduate psychology students as subjects. This means that their external validity, and especially the extent to which their findings can be generalized to real life, is likely to be low. Gradually, however, naturalistic experiments are becoming more common, and psychological journals are becoming more concerned with external validity (e.g., Wyer, Dion, & Ellsworth, 1978).

The argument in this essay is that, by using the experimental method, psychologists can make a great contribution to our understanding of deviance. The major barriers which need to be overcome are the ethical and practical difficulties of devising operational definitions and methods of measuring deviance which enable experiments with high internal and external validity to be carried out. The first aim of this contribution is to review operational definitions of deviance which have been used so far in experiments, and to indicate which are the most satisfactory and where improvements may be made. The second aim is to review the advances in our knowledge about one specific kind of deviance—dishonesty—which have been achieved by experimental psychological research.

I. Deviance and Experimentation

A. DEFINITION OF "DEVIANCE"

Deviance may be defined as behavior which violates a norm or breaks a rule, but this is a rather unsatisfactory definition for research purposes. This is because different groups of people have different norms, and consequently the same act may be deviant by the standards of one group but not by the standards of another. Furthermore, an individual may simultaneously be a member of several different groups with different behavioral norms, and it may be difficult to discover the norms of any particular group. In order to study deviance, it is desirable to devise an unambiguous method of classifying any given act as deviant or not, assuming that deviant behavior is a category rather than a continuum.

This article concentrates on deviant behavior which is prohibited by the criminal law or which violates other widely recognized moral norms of Western society at the present time. This definition acknowledges that laws and norms vary with time and place. It is somewhat arbitrary and ambiguous, but it will serve as a guiding rule. In practice, the major focus of interest here is on various kinds of dishonesty (stealing, lying, and cheating) and on other illegal acts. It is hardly necessary to point out the practical importance for our society of understanding these kinds of deviant behavior and the social benefits which would follow from a decrease in their frequency. In order to reduce this contribution to a manageable length, no attempt is made to review experiments on aggression here.

Simmons and Chambers (1965) asked a quota sample of the United States population to list acts or types of persons which they regarded as deviant. While 252 different things were mentioned by the 180 subjects, the most frequent responses were homosexuals, drug addicts, alcoholics, prostitutes, murderers, criminals, lesbians, juvenile delinquents, beatniks, mentally ill people, and perverts. In all cases, the acts which characterize these types of persons would come within my definition of deviance. There is a difference, of course, between deviant acts and deviant persons. Hood and Sparks (1970, p. 129) have pointed out that calling someone a murderer because he has committed one murder is rather like calling someone a golfer because he has played one round of golf. Perhaps someone should not be called a deviant person unless he commits deviant acts with a certain degree of regularity. The emphasis here is on deviant acts, but some experiments studying deviant persons (e.g., drunks: Piliavin, Rodin, & Piliavin, 1969) are mentioned.

One important issue is the extent to which any empirical variable is a valid measure of the theoretical construct of deviance. This falls within the topic of external validity. What is needed is correlational research to investigate the strength of the relationship between the measure used in the experiment and some external criterion of the theoretical construct. Social psychologists have been much less concerned with this aspect of external validity than have users of psychological tests (e.g., Cronbach, 1970). It is particularly important to establish the relationship between verbal measures—for example, predicted behavior in hypothetical situations—and actual behavior. The reliability of verbal reports of mental processes is doubtful (e.g., Nisbett & Wilson, 1977), and there is a great deal of inconsistency between verbal reports and behavior (e.g., Deutscher, 1973). Even more inconsistency might be expected with deviance than with other topics, since frank admissions of deviant acts or tendencies are likely to attract social disapproval. In the interests of drawing general conclusions about deviance in real life, this article concentrates on experiments using behavioral measures.

So far, deviance has been discussed as if it were a single category or dimension. This seems unlikely, in view of the apparent heterogeneity of prohibited acts such as stealing, assault, vandalism, rape, and possessing drugs. However, the extent to which it is possible to generalize from one kind of deviance to another, and the extent to which all kinds of deviance obey the same causal laws, are empirical questions. One theoretical implication of generalization might be that each person can be placed at some point on a single dimension reflecting a tendency to commit deviant acts of all kinds.

In agreement with this, there is little evidence of specialization in the crimes committed by convicted delinquents. West and Farrington (1973, 1977) showed that most juveniles and young adults convicted of aggressive, damaging, and drug offences in England had other convictions for crimes of dishonesty. In the United States Wolfgang, Figlio, and Sellin (1972) found that the probability of committing any type of crime did not depend on the type of crime committed on the last occasion. Other indications of the versatility of delinquent behavior are obtained in research with self-reported delinquency questionnaires. Farrington (1973), in England, found that those who admitted theft and burglary also tended to admit aggressive and damaging offences and even minor deviant acts, such as playing truant from school and drinking under age. Similar results were obtained by Hindelang (1971) in the United States. There is some evidence that older and more experienced offenders do tend to specialize, for example, in violent as opposed to property crimes (Buikhuisen & Jongman, 1970; Peterson, Pittman, & O'Neal, 1962), but even here there is conflicting evidence that the majority of older offenders convicted for a violent crime also have convictions for property crimes (McClintock, 1963; Walker, Hammond, & Steer, 1967).

These questions about the generality or specificity of deviant behavior are very important in developing theories of deviance, but they are not discussed further in this contribution. The major theoretical concern (in Section III) is with dishonesty.

B. DEFINITION OF "EXPERIMENT"

An experiment, of course, is a study of the effect of changes in one or more independent variables on one or more dependent variables, its defining feature being the control of independent variables by the experimenter. There should also be some attempt to control extraneous variables that may influence the dependent variables, and the most satisfactory way of doing this is to randomly allocate subjects to different conditions of the independent variable. Another method is to give all the treatments to each subject in a random order, but this is beset with the problems of the effects of prior treatments and the interaction of treatments. Another possibility is to individually match the subjects in each condition in advance, but it is impossible to match for every factor which may affect the dependent variable. One of the least satisfactory experimental methods, because of the lack of control, is to give different treatments to different naturally occurring groups of subjects (e.g., classes in a school) and then to check subsequently to see if any of the preexisting differences between the groups reached statistical significance. Experiments using all these methods are included in this review but the selection bias is in favor of experiments which appear to have high internal validity, in randomly allocating subjects to conditions, and also high external validity, in being carried out in realistic field settings with members of the general public as subjects, rather than in the artificial conditions of the psychological laboratory with introductory psychology students as subjects.

From the point of view of internal and external validity, nonreactive field experiments using unobtrusive measures (cf. Webb, Campbell, Schwartz, & Sechrest, 1966) are especially desirable. If a subject does not know that he is serving in a psychological experiment, he is likely to behave typically rather than be affected by such reactive factors as experimenter expectancy and demand characteristics (e.g., Miller, 1972). These kinds of experiments raise ethical problems (see Section II,E). They also create methodological questions, particularly in regard to manipulation checks. It is very difficult to carry out a manipulation check during a nonreactive experiment without its becoming reactive. If the check is carried out after the experiment has been completed, the subject's response in the check might be influenced by the way he has just responded in the experiment (see also Kidd, 1976). The deviance literature indicates that persons who have committed deviant acts will seek to justify or defend them or to minimize their own responsibility (e.g., Sykes & Matza, 1957), in order to avoid disapproval or sanctions from other people. It would be possible to carry out a separate study to do a manipulation check, but, as mentioned above, there is no guarantee that subjects would be able or willing to make verbal statements in the check reflecting either their mental processes or their likely behavior in the experiment.

A manipulation check is just one kind of validity check. It is desirable to check that the independent variable in an experiment is a measure of the specified theoretical construct by correlating it with some other measure of the same theoretical construct, preferably obtained externally to the experiment. This is essentially what is done in a manipulation check, but demonstrating one significant correlation is not enough. The independent variable may actually be measuring some construct other than the intended one, a construct which is correlated with the intended one for some reason. It would be better to investigate the correlations between the independent variable and a variety of measures of different theoretical constructs, to demonstrate that the highest correlation is with the measure of the intended construct. It is also desirable to check that the dependent variable in an experiment is a measure of a specified theoretical construct, in the same way. However, both of these checks become less important as the independent and dependent measures become more similar to the theoretical constructs, which is usually true in naturalistic research. The desirability of manipulation checks should only be considered as part of the wider question of internal and external validity.

C. AN ALTERNATIVE METHODOLOGY

There are many hypotheses about deviant behavior which, for ethical and practical reasons, are difficult or impossible to test experimentally in Western society at the present time. The main argument in this paper is that, whenever possible, experiments should be carried out. However, when experiments are not possible the next best methodology, in terms of internal and external validity, is probably the quasiexperiment (Campbell & Stanley, 1966). This has been almost completely ignored by psychologists and sociologists alike, despite some interesting published demonstrations of its value (e.g., Campbell & Ross, 1968; Ross, Campbell, & Glass, 1970; Schnelle & Lee, 1974).

As an example of the use of the quasiexperimental methodology, Farrington (1977) tested a hypothesis derived from labeling theory (e.g., Becker, 1963; Lemert, 1972), namely that persons who are publicly labeled as deviants will become more deviant as a result. Public labeling was operationally defined and measured by convictions in court for criminal offenses, and deviant behavior was operationally defined and measured by self-reports of the commission of certain delinquent and socially disapproved acts. It would be difficult to test this hypothesis experimentally using these operational definitions, because it would be difficult to persuade the police and the courts to randomly allocate people either to a group who were to be found guilty in court or to a group who were not to be officially processed or labeled in any way. The hypothesis could be tested experimentally using other operational definitions of public labeling, but it might then be difficult to generalize the results to the real-life situation with which the labeling theorists were concerned.

The research described by Farrington (1977) was part of a longitudinal survey called the Cambridge Study in Delinquent Development (West & Farrington, 1973, 1977). Nearly 400 working-class London youths were given self-reported delinquency questionnaires (Farrington, 1973) successively at ages 14, 16, and 18 approximately, and their scores on these questionnaires were used as measures of their deviant behavior. Each youth was given a percentile rank score at each age, and it was found that the scores of the 53 youths who were first convicted between ages 14 and 18 had significantly increased by the later age, in agreement with the hypothesis.

This was a satisfactory outcome, but it was then necessary to systematically investigate a number of alternative explanations of the results, or threats to the internal validity of the quasiexperiment (Campbell & Stanley, 1966). First of all, the results could not have been caused by maturation (processes within the subjects operating as a function of the passage of time), history (events occurring between the first and second test), testing (the effects of taking one test on the scores in a second) or instrumentation (changes in the measuring instruments or scoring methods). Each of these factors would be expected to affect the whole sample equally, but the scoring method (percentile rank scores at each age) meant that the scores of the convicted youths increased relative to the scores of the whole sample. Second, the results could not have been caused by mortality (differential loss of subjects from the comparison groups), because the analysis was based on only the 383 youths who were interviewed at all three ages (over 93% of the original sample of 411 at age 8 years). Third, statistical regression to the mean could not explain the results, because the scores of the convicted youths became even more extreme at age 18 than they had been at age 14.

This left only two of Campbell and Stanley's factors, namely selection effects and the interaction between selection and other factors, especially maturation and history. It is plausible to suggest that the convicted youths differed from the remainder even before they were convicted, and that one of these preexisting differences rather than the conviction caused their relative increase in deviant behavior. In an attempt to counteract selection factors, the 53 convicted youths were individually matched at age 14 with 53 other youths not found guilty up to age 18, not only on their self-reported delinquency scores but also on an index of deviant behavior derived from teacher and peer ratings and on a combination of five nonbehavioral factors which were known to predict delinquency (parental criminality, low family income, large family size, low IQ, and a global index of poor parental behavior: see West & Farrington, 1973). It was hoped that this matching technique would produce two groups which were comparable in every factor except for the occurrence of a conviction. In the event, the scores of the convicted youths still increased significantly relative to the scores of the matched unconvicted youths, so the conclusion about the effect of convictions was unchanged.

There is another threat to internal validity which was not listed by Campbell and Stanley but which was tested in this research, namely the question of causal order. It is possible that the increased deviant behavior of the convicted youths caused rather than was caused by their convictions. This was investigated using the self-reported delinquency scores at age 16, and the fact that 26 of the 53 convicted youths were not found guilty until after they had been interviewed at 16. These youths had significantly higher scores at 18 than their matched unconvicted youths. If the increase in deviant behavior preceded the conviction, it might be expected that the convicted youths would already have had higher scores at age 16 than their matched unconvicted youths. If the conviction preceded the increase in deviant behavior, however, the two groups should have had similar scores at age 16, and this was in fact what was found. This result is in agreement with the hypothesis that the conviction caused the increase in the deviant behavior, rather than the reverse. Attempts were also made to elucidate intervening variables in the causal chain (see Farrington, 1977).

Since this work was done, a further analysis using self-reported delinquency scores at age 21 has been completed (Farrington, Osborn, & West, 1978). In agreement with the labeling prediction and with the earlier results, youths first convicted between ages 18 and 21 significantly increased their self-reported delinquency between these ages, in comparison with other youths. However, these demonstrations that being found guilty in court tends to increase deviance are by no means as conclusive as field experiments would have been. Where they are ethically and practically feasible, field experiments on deviance should be carried out, but the quasi-experimental methodology should be considered in other instances. It may be better to sacrifice some internal validity and carry out a quasiexperiment than to sacrifice some external validity and carry out a laboratory experiment.

II.   Operationally Defining and Measuring Deviance in Experiments

A.   DISHONESTY AS A DEPENDENT VARIABLE

In order to carry out an experiment with deviance as a dependent variable, it is necessary to give subjects an opportunity to commit deviant acts under controlled conditions. The most influential early research in which this was arranged was concerned with dishonesty. It was undertaken by Hartshorne and May (1928), although they did not carry out experiments. They devised a variety of methods of measuring cheating, lying, and stealing by children aged about 10–14, in school, in athletic contests, and in party games.

Cheating was operationally defined as achieving a falsely good performance on a test by disobeying instructions, reporting scores incorrectly, or making illegitimate use of an answer key. It was either detected directly, for example by comparing a child's test paper before and after he was allowed to score it himself, or indirectly, from improbably good performance. The indirect method was less satisfactory, since there was always some doubt, however small, about whether or not cheating actually had occurred. Two methods of measuring lying were used, one based on admissions or denials of cheating a week or more after the tests were taken, and the other based on improbable answers on a questionnaire (e.g., saying "Yes" to "Do you always do today things that you could put off until tomorrow?"). The disadvantage with the former method is that only the cheaters were exposed to the risk of lying, while the problem with the latter method is that a saint would appear to be a liar. Hartshorne's and May's tests of stealing involved children having opportunities to steal coins which were given to them for use in games or puzzles. Stealing was detected either by noting surreptitiously that a child failed to return a coin which he had been given or by giving the children coins in inconspicuously numbered boxes which were later checked.

The methods used by Hartshorne and May to study cheating have been used in experiments by many subsequent researchers. A favorite method has been to allow subjects to score their own tests after they have been secretly copied or scored by confederates of the researcher (e.g., Heisler, 1974; Keehn, 1956; Schachter, 1971; Stephenson & White, 1970; Tittle & Rowe, 1973). More ingenious methods of recording subjects' original answers have also been devised (e.g., Dienstbier & Munter, 1971; Mills, 1958). Cheating has also been studied by arranging for subjects to obtain a predetermined set of scores in a game and allowing them to score themselves (e.g., Grinder, 1962; Hill & Kochendorfer, 1969; Lepper, 1973). Improbably good reported performance has also been used as an index of cheating in tests (e.g., Stephenson & White, 1968; Vitro & Schoer, 1972) and in guessing games (e.g., Dmitruk, 1971; Kanfer & Duerfeldt, 1968). Disobeying instructions to achieve a good performance has also been studied (e.g., Aronson & Mettee, 1968; O'Leary, 1968). The research by O'Leary is especially interesting, as he is one of the few researchers actually to have observed and recorded cheating as it happened. In his experiment, 6-year-old boys were told to press a telegraph key to obtain a marble, which was exchangeable for a prize, only when a certain stimulus appeared on the screen. The experimenter watched through a one-way mirror to see whether each boy violated the rules and pressed the key when other stimuli were shown. Diener and Wallbom (1976) also used a one-way mirror to observe and record cheating, defined as disobeying instructions in a test by continuing after the time limit.

Lying has not been studied a great deal as a dependent variable in experiments, although the dividing line between cheating and lying is sometimes arbitrary. In some of the researches mentioned above, cheating consisted of telling lies about performance rather than making illegitimate use of an answer key. Two other studies in which subjects were given opportunities to tell lies were carried out by Medinnus (1966) and by Taylor and Lewit (1966). Medinnus presented children with a list of book titles, some of which were fictitious, and asked them to check those which they had read. Taylor and Lewit gave adolescents a dynamometer which was programmed to produce the same series of readings for each boy and asked them to report their grip strengths. Bleda, Bleda, Byrne, and White (1976) placed subjects in a situation where each had to tell a lie in order for a confederate to benefit from his or her cheating. In the research of Quigley-Fernandez and Tedeschi (1978), subjects were given the opportunity to tell lies about whether they had previously heard the answers to a test which they had to take.

Stealing has not been investigated under controlled conditions to any great extent, but in recent years a number of field experiments have been carried out. In most of these, subjects were given an opportunity to steal or dishonestly accept money in situations where the owner of the money was either unknown or absent or both. It is doubtful that some of these studies would conform to legal definitions of theft. For example, in England, the Theft Act of 1968 specifies that a person is not committing theft if he appropriates property in the belief that the person to whom the property belongs cannot be discovered by taking reasonable steps.

In a naturalistic study, Feldman (1968) pretended to pick up money in the street and offered it to members of the public, asking if they had dropped it. The subjects therefore had an opportunity to claim the money dishonestly. Feldman also gave cashiers and store clerks too much money when buying items, giving them an opportunity to keep the money dishonestly, and Korte and Kerr (1975) used the same method. Bickman (1971) carried out an experiment in which coins were left in telephone booths and the users of the booths were then asked whether or not they had picked them up. Again, the users had the opportunity to keep the money dishonestly, and Franklin (1973) and Kleinke (1977) used the same method. Lenga and Kleinke (1974) unobtrusively observed customers in a department store taking shopping bags without paying. Diener, Fraser, Beaman, and Kelem (1976), after telling children that they could take one candy from a dish in a house, observed the stealing of extra candies, or of money from an adjacent dish, using a peep hole in curtains. In a campus-bound experiment, Penner, Summers, Brookmire, and Dertke (1976) left unobtrusively coded dollar bills in various locations where students would find them and recorded whether the dollars were returned, ignored, or taken dishonestly. Steinberg, McDonald, and O'Neal (1977) gave female students the opportunity to steal shampoo in dormitory shower rooms.

Stealing has also been involved in experiments intended primarily to investigate helpful behavior. Hornstein, Fisch, and Holmes (1968); Hornstein (1970); and Tucker, Hornstein, Holloway, and Sole (1977) left a wallet containing $2 in cash in an envelope on the street for members of the public to pick up. While returning the envelope constituted helpfulness, keeping it constituted stealing. White (1972), in an experiment intended to investigate the donating of 5¢ gift certificates exchangeable at a local store, also observed children stealing these certificates, using a one-way mirror in a mobile laboratory. Mention should also be made of the experiments on stealing carried out by hypnotists. Beigel (1962) gave subjects a posthypnotic suggestion to steal a (marked) $10 bill from a book at the rear of a lecture theatre. Nineteen out of 20 subjects complied, in comparison with only one who thought he might in the waking state, and none out of 20 unhypnotized controls complied. Coe, Kobayashi, and Howard (1972) carried out an experiment in which subjects were given posthypnotic suggestions to steal a copy of a master's degree examination paper from a secretary's office for the graduate student experimenter.

The field experiments on stealing and financial dishonesty seem to me to be the nearest approach yet to the experimental study of delinquent behavior. Systematic observation and recording of delinquent behavior as it happens are rare but they may advance our knowledge of the reality of delinquency more than the official statistics, with all their known biases (e.g., Hood & Sparks, 1970). Furthermore, if it is possible to experimentally manipulate delinquent behavior, this holds out the likelihood of controlling it, at least in principle. McNese, Egli, Marshall, Schnelle, and Risley (1976) and Switzer, Deal, and Bailey (1977) carried out naturalistic experiments designed to reduce stealing. McNees et al. measured shoplifting in a department store by checking 25 key items each day and found a considerable decrease in stealing following the introduction of antishoplifting signs. Switzer et al. placed 10 items in a classroom each day and found that the theft of these items decreased after the children were made aware that the whole group would suffer if stealing occurred.

I have been involved in a number of researches which have investigated stealing or financial dishonesty under controlled conditions (see Farrington & Knight, 1979a). In the first of these, carried out in collaboration with William S. Knapp and Bonnie E. Erickson, 25 youths in Cambridge, England, were invited to participate in a survey about gambling and risk taking and were interviewed in a van parked in the street. During part of this interview, the youths were left alone in the van with a bag of money and were asked to sort the coins as fast as possible into a sorting box. They were given the (incorrect) impression that the interviewer did not know how many coins were in the bag, and had the opportunity to steal some of the coins. The number and value of coins stolen (if any) were ascertained later by the interviewer. This study indicated that stealing was not impulsive, since youths only stole when they knew in advance what was involved in the interview. Another result was that the behavioral measure of stealing was not closely related to verbal measures based on reports of past behavior or assessments of likely behavior in hypothetical situations.

The second study, carried out in collaboration with Robert F. Kidd (Farrington & Kidd, 1977), was based on the method used by Feldman (1968). The experimenter walked past a member of the public in the streets of Cambridge, England, pretended to pick up a coin, and then ran after the subject, offering him the coin and asking whether he had dropped it. The subject had the opportunity to dishonestly accept the coin. One problem in this study was the very marked experimenter effect, because subjects were nearly twice as likely to take the money from the male experimenter as from the female experimenter.

In view of this experimenter effect, the third study used a nonreactive paradigm and was based on the technique of Hornstein et al. (1968). It was carried out in collaboration with Barry J. Knight (see Farrington and Knight, 1979b). One hundred stamped, addressed, apparently lost, unsealed letters, each containing a handwritten note and also (apart from control conditions) a sum of money, were left on the streets of London, England, and were picked up by members of the public. The experimenter, who was blind to the condition of each letter, noted down the personal characteristics and behavior of each subject. Each subject was free to post the letter and money to the intended recipient or to steal the money. The results obtained in this experiment, and in another using the same paradigm, are discussed in Section III, A.

Virtually all the researchers mentioned so far in this section have used behavioral measures of dishonesty. Others have used verbal measures, as for example in the "ethical risk taking" studies of Rettig and his collaborators (e.g., Rettig, 1964, 1966; Rettig & Pasamanick, 1964; Rettig & Rawson, 1963; Rettig & Turoff, 1967) and later Krauss (e.g., Krauss & Blanchard, 1970; Krauss, Coddington, & Smeltzer, 1971; Krauss, Robinson, Janzen, & Cauthen, 1972). In some well-known recent research, West, Gunn, and Chernicky (1975) asked some students whether they would participate in a burglary and other students whether they thought they would agree to participate in a burglary in the hypothetical situation of being asked to do so.

The external validity of verbal statements about dishonesty in relation to real dishonest behavior is not securely established. In studying it, verbal and behavioral measures need to be obtained from the same people. Shotland and Berger (1970) lent pencils to female workers to fill in the Rokeach value scale and found that those who returned the pencils rated the value of honesty more highly than those who kept them dishonestly. In agreement with this result, Henshel (1971) found a negative correlation between the rated value of honesty and cheating on a spelling test, and Lepper (1973) found a negative correlation between cheating and self-perceived honesty. However, Santrock (1975) found little correlation between cheating and verbal measures of honesty (self-ratings and moral judgments) and, as mentioned above, Farrington, Knapp, and Erickson found little correlation between verbal and behavioral measures of stealing.

The final question which can be asked is whether it is reasonable to treat dishonesty as a unidimensional variable, or whether different theories are required for different kinds of dishonesty. Hartshorne and May (1928) found that their measures of cheating were significantly correlated with teachers' ratings of dishonesty in class, while Hill (1934) showed that institutionalized delinquents cheated more than nondelinquents, and Heisler (1974) found that cheating by students was significantly related to their self-reports of law violations. These results indicate that cheating in experiments is related to more serious kinds of dishonesty. They may seem surprising in the light of Hartshorne's and May's famous conclusion, based on the small positive correlations between their different tests, that dishonest behavior is largely determined by situational factors. However, in a reanalysis of their data, Burton (1963) found that most of the low correlations were contributed by tests with very low reliabilities and concluded that, although situational factors were very important, there was an underlying general factor of honesty. Nelsen and his collaborators (Nelson, Grinder, & Biaggio, 1969; Nelsen, Grinder, & Mutterer, 1969) gave six cheating tests to more than 100 children and came to much the same conclusion. Although there are not many studies intercorrelating different behavioral measures of dishonesty, the indications are that it is reasonable to suggest the existence of a single underlying dimension or general factor.

B.   OTHER DEPENDENT MEASURES OF DEVIANCE

In experiments on deviant behaviors other than dishonesty, the dependent variable of deviance has usually been measured by self-reports or official records. As mentioned earlier, deviant behavior has rarely been observed directly. This is true with sexual deviance, for example, and the few observational studies (e.g., Humphreys, 1970) have almost all been nonexperimental. There are obvious difficulties in observing sexual deviance under controlled conditions. Most types of it occur primarily in private, and those acts which take place in public tend to be relatively infrequent. Providing the ethical problems could be overcome, it would be possible in principle to study types of sexual deviance which occurred in public places with a reasonably high frequency, such as male homosexuality in certain public toilets.

Almost the only question in the area of sexual deviance which has been studied experimentally is the effect of pornography, but the occurrence of sexually deviant behavior before and after exposure to pornography has been measured by self-reports rather than by observation (e.g., Mann, Sidman, & Starr, 1970). Probably the nearest approach to a behavioral experiment on sexual deviance was carried out by Kline (1958, 1972). In this, a male student was hypnotized to indecently expose himself in what appeared to be a public place, although in fact the area had been sealed off by the police. In an interesting recent experiment using a verbal measure, Mathes and Guest (1976) asked students to say how willing they were to carry a sign saying "masturbation is fun!"

It is surprising that more experiments have not been carried out on deviant behaviors which occur frequently and which do not raise insurmountable ethical difficulties, such as dropping litter and traffic offences. As an example of what might be done, Buikhuisen (1974) studied the effect of a police and newspaper campaign on the incidence of worn tires on cars. Before and after the campaign, his students recorded the incidence of worn tires in two towns in Holland, by checking all cars parked in a representative sample of streets between 1:00 a.m. and 5:30 a.m. Fortunately for the research, few car owners in these towns had garages. The police and newspaper campaign was mounted in one town, and the other was used as a control. Because only one town was compared with one other town, rather than many towns being randomly allocated to the two conditions, this experiment was not high in internal validity. Sigelman and Sigelman (1976) also showed the possibility of experimenting with traffic offenses using observational measures, in investigating right turns by cars against a red light, and Lefkowitz, Blake, and Mouton (1955) observed the behavior of pedestrians in conforming to or violating traffic signals. Mention should also be made of the recent experiments on litter dropping, an illegal behavior (e.g., Baltes & Hayward, 1976; Burgess, Clark, & Hendee, 1971; Finnie, 1973; Kohlenberg & Phillips, 1973; Krauss, Freedman, & Whitcup, 1978).

With other kinds of deviance, there have been isolated examples of behavioral experiments. One of the best known was carried out by Zimbardo (1969), who left a car in the street with its hood open and license plates removed and filmed vandalism directed against it. Unfortunately, because of the inadequate control of independent and extraneous variables, this study would not come within my definition of an experiment. The research of Coe, Kobayashi, and Howard (1973) was more clearly experimental. They studied whether or not students sold heroin off campus to a confederate, in relation to the presence or absence of hypnosis and the presence or absence of a relationship with the experimenter.

Much more common are experiments in which official statistics are used to measure the dependent variable. For example, Törnudd (1968) studied the effect on drunkenness of a reduction in the likelihood of prosecution. The police in three towns in Finland cooperated by halving the proportion of arrested drunks who were prosecuted, and these towns were compared with three control towns in which this proportion did not change. The three experimental towns were chosen at random from the six towns participating, and all six towns were comparable in size. None of the six police forces was supposed to change the likelihood of arresting drunks, and the incidence of arrests for drunkenness was used as the dependent variable. However, it is difficult to be sure that police policies did not change in an experiment of this kind. In any experiment using official statistics, it is hard to disentangle changes in deviant behavior from changes in the behavior of the official agencies. This is less of a problem when the official agencies can be kept blind to the conditions of the experiment and where they play a less active role in the production of the official statistics. For example, Schwartz and Orleans (1967) studied the effect of threats of sanctions and appeals to conscience on income tax fraud. Their dependent variable, based on information supplied by the income tax authorities, was the total paid by randomly chosen groups of taxpayers in 1 year in comparison with the previous year. A relative increase in income tax paid, by experimental groups in comparison with a control group, was taken to indicate a decrease in the incidence of income tax fraud.

The Schwartz and Orleans study can be regarded as an experiment in the prevention of crime. It differs from the experiments by Buikhuisen (1974) and

Törnudd (1968) in that the preventive measures were applied to specific individuals rather than aimed at the community as a whole. This is true of most prevention experiments, but the dependent variable is usually general delinquency obtained from records held by criminal justice agencies, rather than a specific type of crime.

In the classic Cambridge–Somerville experiment, for example (McCord & McCord, 1959), boys were chosen at random to receive either regular friendly attention from specially appointed counselors or the usual resources of the community. The counseling began at age 11 and continued for 5 years, on the average, and the major dependent variable was whether each boy had been convicted by 15 years after the beginning of the project. As is usual in experiments on delinquency prevention and treatment, the experimental and control groups did not differ significantly in their conviction histories, suggesting that the counseling had been ineffectual in preventing delinquency. A further followup 30 years after the end of the treatment showed that, if anything, the treated group was more criminal (McCord, 1978). A more intended result was obtained in the prevention experiment of Bowman (1959), who found that low-achieving children taught in special classes having one sympathetic teacher had fewer recorded offenses during a 2-year period than low-achieving children taught in regular classes. The experiment by Reckless and Dinitz (1972), in which boys thought to be vulnerable to delinquency were randomly allocated to regular or special classes, is especially notable, because the police records of offenses were supplemented by self-reports. However, the experimental and control groups were not significantly different on either measure.

The dependent variable of general delinquency obtained from official records also predominates in experiments on the treatment of delinquency, which are more numerous than prevention experiments. One exception, in concentrating on a specific kind of delinquency, is the experiment of Berg, Hullin, and McGuire (1979). In this, boys brought before the courts for truancy were randomly allocated either to have their case adjourned or to be supervised by social workers, and the subsequent records of truancy for both groups were then investigated. The adjourned group showed less truancy, suggesting that social work supervision was less effective than adjournment in the treatment of truancy. In an experiment on a related, although nondelinquent, kind of deviance, Palmer (1967) showed that boys who were punished by detention for arriving late at school were more likely to repeat this offence than those who were reprimanded.

Most treatment experiments have been intended to investigate the relative efficacy of different methods of treating convicted persons, rather than their absolute efficacy in comparison with no treatment. However, there have been a few experiments which come close to being comparisons between treatment and no treatment. Venezia (1972) randomly allocated juveniles apprehended for crimes either to receive unofficial probation or to be released without further official action. Neither group was taken to court, and the groups were not significantly different in the dependent variable of re-referral to the probation service during a 6-month follow-up period. In a rather similar experiment, Rose and Hamilton (1970) randomly allocated juveniles either to be cautioned and supervised for 6 months or only to be cautioned and again found no difference in subsequent offenses known to the police.

Most treatment experiments compare what are essentially different varieties of the same treatment rather than different treatments, and this may be one reason why null results predominate in the literature. For example, Kassebaum, Ward, and Wilner (1971) randomly allocated offenders sent to a new prison to receive small or large group counseling or no counseling. There was little difference in reconviction rates between the groups, but it could be argued that the differences in treatment between the groups were negligible in comparison to the similarities resulting from the fact that they were all in the same prison. After all, the counseling sessions occupied only 1 or 2 hr/week. In other prison experiments, Berntsen and Christiansen (1965) and Shaw (1974) found that prisoners selected at random for special welfare treatment were less likely to be reconvicted than others, but Fowles (1978) did not find that prison welfare treatment was effective.

Experiments have also been carried out on institutional treatment for juveniles and young adults, and on probation and parole. Jesness (1971) randomly allocated boys entering a juvenile institution either to a small, well staffed living unit or to a larger, poorly staffed one, and found that, at least in the short term, those leaving the smaller unit had lower recidivism rates. Cornish and Clarke (1975) randomly allocated boys entering an approved school either to a unit run as a therapeutic community or to a more traditional unit and found no difference in reconvictions during a 2-year follow-up period. Williams (1975) randomly allocated Borstal boys to three institutions, one with a traditional regime and the other two dominated by casework and group counseling, respectively; he found that the boys in the casework Borstal had significantly lower reconviction rates. Folkard, Smith, and Smith (1976) randomly allocated men on probation either to probation officers with specially reduced caseloads or to regular probation officers and found no effect on reconviction rates. Similarly, Reimer and Warren (1957) randomly allocated parolees to officers with large or small caseloads without finding any effect on subsequent arrest rates, but Adams (1970) found that parolees who were given special intensive counseling were less likely to be returned to custody.

Very few treatment experiments have been carried out in which offenders were randomly allocated to radically different sentences. Empey and Erickson (1972) and Empey and Lubeck (1971) compared recidivist juvenile offenders allocated to regular institutions with those given special treatment in the community emphasizing guided group interaction. There was little difference between the groups in subsequent arrest rates. Palmer (1971) also compared regular institutional treatment with individualized community treatment and found that the juveniles receiving community treatment had lower recidivism rates. However, the dependent measure of recidivism was parole revocation, and Lerman (1975) showed that Palmer's groups did not differ in recorded offending but did differ in their likelihood of parole revocation. Lerman concluded that the community treatment program had changed the discretionary decision-making behavior of the adults but had not changed the delinquent behavior of the juveniles. This highlights once again the problems of using official records as a dependent measure of deviant behavior.

The review of research in this section may give the impression that experiments on delinquency prevention and treatment using random allocation are commonplace, but this is far from true. As in other areas of deviance, the majority of research on prevention and treatment is nonexperimental and hence has low internal validity. This is at least partly because of the difficulty of persuading judges and other people in the criminal justice system to randomly allocate offenders to different treatments. To many of these people, experimentation and justice seem incompatible. As a result, offenders are being allocated to treatments whose effects are essentially unknown. In my opinion, the social benefits consequent upon the advancement of knowledge from treatment experiments are likely to exceed the costs of injustice to the individuals concerned. If the medical profession had been as opposed to experimentation as the legal profession is now, we would know very little about the relative effectiveness of different medical treatments.

In theory, the kinds of experiments reviewed so far in this section should have high internal and external validity. Their internal validity is boosted by the random allocation of subjects to different conditions, which leads to the control of extraneous variables. Their external validity is boosted by the fact that they are concerned with real-life deviant behavior, rather than with the laboratory behavior of introductory psychology students. Furthermore, these kinds of experiments are likely to have important implications for theories of deviant behavior. Theories about the causes of delinquency are likely to lead to predictions about the prevention and treatment of delinquency and, conversely, the results of prevention and treatment experiments can be used in deciding between competing theories. Yet experimental social psychologists have shown little interest in carrying out these kinds of experiments and, partly because of this, the existing experiments are rather inadequate.

One of the major problems of the existing experiments is to specify the independent variable. Most treatments vary along many dimensions and, even if a positive result is obtained, it is difficult to know to which aspect of the treatment it can be attributed. Furthermore, most treatments are not based upon explicitly stated theories about the causes of deviant behavior, and hence the results of the experiments are difficult to use in testing theories. Another problem is that few researchers try to use a double-blind technique in which neither the subjects nor the criminal justice personnel know what is going on, making it impossible to control for the Hawthorne effect, for example. Finally, as mentioned before, the methods of measuring the dependent variable of delinquency leave much to be desired and lead to the kinds of problems highlighted by Lerman (1975).

On the basis of the experimental social psychology literature, it might be expected that prevention and treatment experiments designed and carried out by experimental social psychologists would try to avoid the above problems. This is one of the reasons why I have argued that they could make a great contribution to the field of deviance. However, they would have to face rather unfamiliar practical difficulties, such as the problem of obtaining the cooperation of criminal justice staff who have a well-founded suspicion that the results of the research will indicate that their work is ineffectual (cf. Clarke & Cornish, 1972). They would have to be prepared to carry out research over a much longer time period than the average laboratory experiment and would have to accept the associated threat to their productivity, at least in terms of quantity. They would also have to accept that results which fail to show a significant difference are worth reporting. Such results are conspicuous by their absence in the experimental social psychology literature, presumably because of the policies of journal editors. The selection of significant results for publication ensures that the proportion of spurious results in the literature is considerably greater than the $p = .05$ level.

One kind of deviance which has not been studied experimentally to any great extent is vandalism or property damage. This is puzzling, because it occurs frequently in public and is not such an ethically sensitive subject as sexual deviance, for example. Furthermore, it can usually be measured by unobtrusive, observational methods, and there is often a permanent record which is easier to measure than in the case of, say, shoplifting. Whereas experimenters might not wish to be victims of physical violence, it is more feasible that they should be victims of vandalism. After theft and other forms of dishonesty, this might be the deviant act which is most susceptible to real-life experimentation. It is usually regarded as a more serious crime, and a more serious social problem, than either dropping litter or traffic offenses.

C. DISHONESTY AS AN INDEPENDENT VARIABLE

In most experiments with deviance as an independent variable, the subject is exposed to the deviance of another person (usually a confederate) and is then expected to evaluate or react to this in some way. The other person's deviance is presented in real life, in a film or videotape, or in a written description. In a minority of experiments with deviance as an independent variable, the subject himself is induced to behave deviantly or to feel deviant, and the focus of interest is then on his subsequent behavior.

It has been argued above (Section II,B) that real-life experiments in which the subjects do not realize that they are participating in an experiment are likely to have the greatest internal and external validity. In studying dishonesty as an independent variable, a number of these kinds of experiments have been carried out, often involving staged thefts. Harari and McDavid (1969) had a confederate child steal money in a classroom while the teacher was called out, and then interviewed the children to see if they would report the "thief." Latane and Darley (1970) carried out two experiments to study the reporting of thefts. In the first, students waiting to be interviewed observed another student steal cash, while in the second members of the public in a beer store observed the theft of a case of beer. Gelfand, Hartmann, Walder, and Page (1973); Steffensmeier and Terry (1973); Bickman and Green (1975); Bickman (1976); and Bickman and Rosenbaum (1977) also staged thefts in shops to investigate reporting by members of the public. Moriarty (1975) staged thefts on a beach to investigate bystander intervention, and Harris and Samerotte (1976) staged thefts in restaurants to study the effect of transgression on altruism. Campus-bound experiments on reporting or bystander intervention were carried out by Dertke, Penner, and Ulrich (1974) and Bickman (1975), who staged thefts in university bookstores, and by Shaffer, Rogel, and Hendrick (1975), who staged thefts in a university library.

One of the major methodological problems in this kind of research is to ensure that the subjects observed the theft. It seems that little reliance can be placed on their statements about this in postexperimental interviews. Latane and Darley (1970) reported that observers watching the subjects through one-way mirrors were convinced that many of those who claimed that they had not noticed the theft had in fact done so. Bickman and Green (1975) included as subjects in their analysis people who said that they had not seen the theft, providing that their observers thought that the people had seen it. Many members of the public deliberately turn a blind eye to thefts in shops. Steffensmeier and Terry (1973) found that their shoplifting incident had to be carried out very blatantly and right next to the shoppers before anyone would report. All of the researchers appear to have been successful in avoiding damaging publicity during the course of their experiments. For example, Gelfand et al. (1973) staged shoplifting incidents in two drugstores over an 8-month period and gave every subject a printed handout explaining the study, but only one subject said that he suspected that the shoplifting had been staged. Apparently, no subject had learned about the research from a previous subject, and no subject gave the printed handout to his local newspaper.

Staged thefts have also been used in nonexperimental research on eyewitness testimony (e.g., Buckhout, Alper, Chern, Silverberg, & Slomovits,

1974) and in other correlational research. For example, Denner (1968) investigated the reasons given by students for reporting or not reporting a staged theft from a handbag. A staged cheating incident was used in an experiment by Savitsky and Babl (1976). In this, students witnessed a confederate cheating and later had the opportunity to deliver aversive noise to him as punishment for mistakes in a learning task. In the research of Heisler (1974), a confederate was apprehended for cheating, and the influence of this event on later cheating by students was studied. It is rare for subjects to be cheated out of money by experimenters, but this happened in the study of Fromkin, Goldstein, and Brock (1977). Members of the public riding in taxis were overcharged by a large or a small amount in an attempt to manipulate high or low frustration. It is less rare for subjects to be deceived by experimenters, of course (e.g., Carlson, 1971), and some researchers have tried to investigate the effects of being deceived on subjects' later behavior (e.g., Silverman, Shulman, & Wiesenthal, 1970).

Subjects have often been shown films or videotapes of dishonest behavior or have listened to dishonesty. Brickman and Bryan (1975, 1976) showed children a film in which a girl stole and then asked them to evaluate her, while people heard a violent theft occurring in the bystander intervention research of Schwartz and Gottlieb (1976). Savitsky, Muskin, Czyzewski, and Eckert (1976) showed incarcerated juvenile offenders a videotape in which a confederate cheated, again requiring evaluative decisions, while Lingle, Brock, and Cialdini (1977) also showed a videotape of cheating in a study of entrapment attempts. Films including thefts have been used in experiments on eye-witness testimony (e.g., Marshall, 1966) and on the perception of people and events (Tickner & Poulton, 1975). In an experiment on the detection of deception, Ekman and Friesen (1974) showed students videotapes of people telling lies or being honest. One problem is that it may not be possible to generalize from results obtained with videotapes of dishonesty to results obtained with real dishonesty, as Bickman (1976) found.

Written descriptions of dishonesty have also been used as independent variables. Mudd (1968) gave these to students in an experiment relating recommended sanction severity to the degree of behavior deviation and the relevance of the norm, while Efran (1974) gave students written descriptions of cheating in a simulated jury experiment. Maier and Lavrakas (1976) gave subjects written descriptions of lies and asked them to rate the lies for reprehensibility. Maier and Thurber (1968) studied the accuracy of detection of deception in relation to whether lies were presented in written descriptions or whether the subjects watched or listened to the deceivers. In real-life experiments on reactions to dishonesty, Buikhuisen and Dijksterhuis (1971) and Boshier and Johnson (1974) sent letters applying for jobs to companies, in some conditions including the information that the applicant had been convicted for theft. The applicant was less likely to be called for an interview in these conditions than when his letter included no mention of the conviction.

The simplest way of arranging experiments in which the subject himself behaves dishonestly is to instruct subjects to be dishonest. For example, Burns and Kintz (1976) instructed students to tell lies to a confederate and found that they gazed longer into the confederate's eyes when lying than when telling the truth. This method is difficult to distinguish from role playing, which has also been used. For example, Maier and Lavrakas (1976) measured the GSRs of subjects instructed to play honest or lying roles, and subjects have pretended to commit thefts in lie detection experiments (e.g., Lykken, 1959). One problem with role playing is that the subjects are aware of at least some of the aims of the experiment and can pretend to behave in a way that they would not actually behave in real life. For example, Shaffer et al. (1975) described the library theft to some students as a role-playing exercise. Many more of the role-playing subjects said that they would intervene to prevent the theft than actually did in the experiment (85% as opposed to 40%).

It is more satisfactory to induce the subject to act dishonestly in an experiment whose true purpose he does not know. However, it is difficult to avoid self-selection of subjects and to achieve experimental control over dishonesty, so that all subjects in one condition are dishonest, for example. This can only be achieved when the dishonest behavior is universal. Freedman, Wallington, and Bless (1967) and McMillen (1971) came close to this in experiments in which a confederate, posing as a previous subject, gave the subject information about a test the subject was about to take. When asked by the experimenter if they had heard anything about the test before, all subjects, except one in the Freedman et al. experiment, told a lie and denied this. The focus of interest in the two experiments was on compliance after transgressing, but they have important implications for the reliability of verbal measures obtained from subjects (e.g., in postexperimental questionnaires).

D. OTHER INDEPENDENT MEASURES OF DEVIANCE

It is very rare for subjects to be exposed to kinds of deviance other than dishonesty in naturalistic experiments. This is surprising, for it is possible in principle to stage acts of violence or vandalism, for example, in front of subjects. In a campus experiment, Shotland and Straw (1976) staged a fight between two actors in front of introductory psychology students and found that most believed it to be realistic. In contrast, when shown a videotaped fight, nearly half of the students said they did not believe that it was genuine and was really happening.

Most experiments with deviance as an independent variable have involved subjects being presented with written descriptions. This has happened, for example, in the large number of researches in which students have been asked to recommend a sentence for an offender on some interval scale convenient for statistical analysis (e.g., 1–25 years). The student subjects are often referred to as simulated jurors, but a more accurate term would be simulated judges, since with few exceptions (e.g., Sealy, 1975; Valenti & Downing, 1975) they have rarely discussed the case in groups and arrived at a group decision. Descriptions of many kinds of deviance have been used, including rape (e.g., Jones & Aronson, 1973; Scroggs, 1976) and murder (e.g., Hendrick & Shaffer, 1975; McGlynn, Megas, & Benson, 1976; Stephan, 1974). Similar descriptions have been used in experiments on attribution of responsibility (e.g., Hill, 1975) and on legal procedures (e.g., LaTour, Houlden, Walker, & Thibaut, 1976).

Few researchers have presented written descriptions to people who have to make legal decisions in real life, but Shea (1974) and Ebbesen and Konecni (1975) did. The research of Ebbesen and Konecni is especially notable, because they compared decisions made by judges in simulated cases with decisions made by the same judges in real cases. On the basis of a multiple regression analysis, it appeared that real decisions (about bail) depended only on the District Attorney's recommendation, whereas in the simulation experiment two other factors appeared to influence the decision as well. In another realistic study, Schwartz and Skolnick (1962) used the methodology mentioned in Section II,C in making job applications to employers. Some of the applications mentioned that the applicant had been convicted for assault, some that he had been tried for assault and acquitted, and some did not mention any court appearance. As before, the employers did not realize that they were participating in an experiment.

Written descriptions of deviance also have been used extensively in experiments on moral judgment. In a typical experiment, Bandura and McDonald (1963) presented children with pairs of stories, each contrasting a well-intended act resulting in material damage with a maliciously motivated act having only minor consequences. With each pair, the children were asked to say which act was the naughtier and why. Several other researchers have used these kinds of moral dilemmas in experiments (e.g., Birnbaum, 1972; Cowan, Langer, Heavenrich, & Nathanson, 1969; Dorr & Fey, 1974; Le Furgy & Woloshin, 1969; McManis, 1974; Walker & Richards, 1976). The experiment by Prentice (1972) is notable, because he compared moral judgments and delinquent behavior, as measured by official records. His subjects were convicted delinquents, and they were randomly allocated either to a control group or to experimental groups that were exposed to modeling techniques designed to change their moral judgments. Prentice succeeded in changing moral judgments as he intended, but he found no difference between the groups in recorded delinquency during a 9-month follow-up period. Few researchers have compared verbal and behavioral measures as he did, and fewer still have carried out experiments over a comparatively long period to investigate the persistence of experimentally induced changes (cf. Sternlieb & Youniss, 1975). However, both of these are desirable.

In other experiments using written descriptions of deviance, Walker and Argyle (1964), Berkowitz and Walker (1967), and Kaufmann (1970) studied moral evaluations of acts in relation to whether or not they were prohibited by the law. A number of experimenters (e.g., Bord, 1971; Kirk, 1974; Phillips, 1963; Schroder & Ehrlich, 1968) have studied the evaluation of persons displaying mentally abnormal behaviors in relation to the label given to the behavior (e.g., mentally ill, wicked, under stress) and the labeler (e.g., a psychiatrist, the person himself, his family, or sane people). Videotaped interviews have also been used in studying reactions to mentally abnormal behavior (e.g., Caetano, 1974). In the research by Lerner and Agar (1972), students were asked to evaluate drug addicts in relation to the perceived causes of their addiction, while Weissbach and Zagon (1975) studied reactions to homosexuals.

This brings us to the study of deviant persons rather than deviant acts. Field experiments are conspicuous by their absence in the present section, but a number have been carried out to investigate how members of the public react to deviant persons, such as hippies (e.g., Raymond & Unger, 1972) and drunks (e.g., Piliavin *et al.,* 1969). It is significant that the dependent variable in both of these experiments was helpfulness, because this is the one area of social psychology in which large numbers of field experiments have been carried out. As an example of experiments in which subjects were induced to feel deviant, Bramel (1962, 1963) made male subjects feel homosexual by showing them photographs of nude men and giving them false feedback about their GSRs to lead them to believe that they were sexually aroused.

E. SOME ETHICAL ISSUES

Many of the methods of operationally defining and measuring deviance described so far in this contribution may be considered unethical by some psychologists. Some methods may even be considered illegal by some lawyers (e.g., Nash, 1975; Silverman, 1975). Ethical problems arise in naturalistic field experiments, and these are magnified when the topic being studied is deviance. The ethical problems are likely to be greatest when the experimenter deliberately provides opportunities for people to commit deviant acts, rather than tries to influence a naturally occurring deviant behavior, such as shoplifting.

Most official statements about ethics by professional bodies in psychology suggest that the decision about whether or not to carry out an experiment should depend on the relationship between its costs (especially the harm suffered by subjects) and its benefits (especially the advancement of knowledge). Furthermore, it has been argued that ethical decisions should be informed by empirical research about the reactions of potential subjects, such as that carried out by Wilson and Donnerstein (1976). Perhaps rather surprisingly, subjects in experiments on deviance have not complained about their treatment. For example, even after being cheated out of money, no subject in the Fromkin *et al.* (1977) experiment expressed regrets or reservations about participating, and this has been a common finding (e.g., Schwartz & Gottlieb, 1976). As pointed out by West and Gunn (1978), follow-up research on even experiments employing highly stressful and deceptive procedures has uniformly failed to find that the subjects have suffered any long-term consequences. It seems unlikely that existing psychological research has had anything other than a negligible impact on the lives of the subjects. As Sullivan and Deiker (1973) discovered, psychologists are more concerned with ethics than are their subjects, but this is as it should be.

No one should embark lightly on research which may cause harm or stress to the subjects. However, real life is full of stresses, strains, and moral dilemmas for most people, full of opportunities to be deviant and to react to deviance. Anything done by psychologists in experiments on deviance will almost certainly be negligible in comparison with the harm caused by deviants to their victims, and with the harm caused by society to deviants. Being cheated out of a few cents pales into insignificance in comparison with being raped or mugged or in comparison with being incarcerated in degrading conditions for many years. If a psychologist sincerely believes that his experiment will have a negligible impact on the lives of his subjects and will advance our knowledge about deviance, is it not worth taking some small ethical risks in the hope of avoiding large social costs?

III.   Experiments on Dishonesty

A.   FACTORS INFLUENCING DISHONEST BEHAVIOR

In the remainder of this paper I shall discuss theories and experimental results on dishonest behavior, concentrating on experiments using behavioral measures. The focus of interest is on why people commit dishonest acts and on how people react to dishonesty. Numerically, crimes of dishonesty predominate in the official criminal statistics of most countries. This means that conclusions about delinquency in general will be similar to conclusions about dishonesty alone.

Most theories proposed in the area of deviance or delinquency have been intended to apply to deviance or delinquency in general rather than to a specific type of deviant or delinquent behavior. Furthermore, most have been dynamic or process theories, in which present behavior is explained by reference to a sequence of past events, rather than static theories, in which present behavior is explained in relation to the immediate influences of the moment. This is equally true of psychological approaches, such as social-learning theory (Trasler, 1973), and sociological perspectives, such as labeling or social reaction (Taylor, Walton, & Young, 1973). Another feature of the existing theories is that they treat delinquency as a dichotomous variable and try to explain why some people become "delinquents" and others remain "nondelinquents." This kind of approach emphasizes individual consistency over situations. By and large, the nonexperimental, empirical investigations follow the theories in treating delinquency as dichotomous and in studying historical factors. Typically, a group of officially convicted delinquents is compared with an unconvicted group on social background factors, such as broken homes and family size. This approach encounters problems both in the definition of the groups (e.g., the biases in official statistics) and in the measurement of historical factors (e.g., retrospective bias and faulty memory).

The experimental studies of dishonesty have very different theoretical foundations. No doubt because of the very short time scale within which they have been carried out and their static independent variable–dependent variable design, they have been concerned with immediate influences on dishonesty. Furthermore, their emphasis is on individual variability over situations, and hence the importance of situational factors. The situational factors which have been studied most are the costs and benefits of dishonesty, and several experiments have been inspired by the theory that dishonest behavior is largely determined by rational or hedonistic factors.

This theory has much in common with the theory of deterrence, dating back to Jeremy Bentham, which still has a great deal of influence on the sentencing practices of judges. Bentham thought that people acted rationally and hedonistically, weighing the pleasure of crime against the pain of the legal punishment, and that it was necessary to increase the severity of the punishment to tip the scales in favor of law-abiding behavior. However, he also realized that there was an interaction between the certainty and the severity of punishment and concluded that, as a punishment became less certain, it should be more severe to maintain its deterrent effect (Geis, 1955). The most popular method of investigating the theory of deterrence has been to correlate crime rates, usually in different states of the United States, with indices of the severity and certainty of punishment in each state (e.g., Chiricos & Waldo, 1970; Logan, 1972; Tittle, 1969). However, such studies can never be conclusive, partly because of their reliance on official statistics and partly because of the problem of drawing causal inferences in correlational research. In order to make unambiguous causal inferences, experimental research is needed.

If dishonesty depends on rational considerations, it should increase with the rewards which might be gained and with the increasing likelihood of a reward, and should decrease with the punishment which might follow and with the increasing likelihood of punishment. In general, the likelihood of cheating increases with the rewards which are consequential upon it. Mills (1958) found increased cheating with a more valuable prize at stake, Dmitruk (1971) found more cheating with more attractive incentives, and Vitro and Schoer (1972) found more cheating in a test when the results of the test were made more important to the subject. Farrington and Kidd (1977) did not find that financial dishonesty increased with the amount of money which could be gained, but it could be argued that the amounts involved in their research were too small to have a significant effect.

Most of the research studying the negative consequences of dishonesty has varied the likelihood of negative consequences rather than their severity. However, Heisler (1974) varied the severity of the penalty for cheating by students by negatively sanctioning a confederate in front of them and found that cheating decreased as the consequences became more severe. Mills (1958) found that cheating decreased when he increased the likelihood of detection by suggesting to children that their scores would be checked, and similar results were obtained by Burton, Allinsmith, and Maccoby (1966); Hill and Kochendorfer (1969); and Vitro and Schoer (1972). Tittle and Rowe (1973) found that cheating by students decreased when they were made aware of the likelihood of negative consequences, and Kanfer and Duerfeldt (1968) found that merely warning children not to cheat was effective in reducing cheating.

Despite the differing operational definitions of costs and benefits, most of the above experiments indicate that the likelihood of dishonesty varies with the costs and benefits which might follow from it. I shall now attempt to specify this theory more exactly. The theoretical variable of interest is the probability of committing a dishonest act, given an opportunity to do so. The importance of opportunity should not be neglected, despite individual variations in awareness of opportunity. For example, Wilkins (1964) showed that the number of thefts from cars increased over the years in direct proportion to the number of cars registered. It is suggested that this probability is transformed into actuality according to processes which can be regarded as random. In other words, whether or not a person commits a delinquent act in a certain situation, within the constraints of his probability of doing so, depends on a random process. Given the indeterminancy of human behavior, it seems more realistic to build probabilistic processes into the model than deterministic ones.

The most general theory suggests that the probability of committing a dishonest act in any situation depends on a large number of factors, only some of which correspond to costs and benefits. A very simple additive model might be specified as follows:

$$P = a_0 + a_1 x_1 + a_2 x_2 + a_3 x_3 + a_4 x_4 + a_5 x_5 + \cdots + a_n x_n \qquad (1)$$

In Eq. (1), P is the probability of committing a dishonest act, $x_1, x_2, \ldots, x_n$ are theoretical variables, and $a_0, a_1, a_2, \ldots, a_n$ are coefficients. [In order to ensure that P falls between 0 and 1, it would be better to have $\log (P/1 - P)$ on the left-hand side of this equation, as in a logistic regression. However, I will ignore mathematical complications of this kind, which do not affect the argument.] In

Eq. (1), x_1 might correspond to the costs of the dishonest act and x_2 to its benefits, assuming for simplicity that these can be expressed as unidimensional variables. However, x_3 then might correspond to some individual factor, such as strength of conscience, and x_4 and x_5 might correspond to other situational factors, such as the presence of a dishonest model and characteristics of the victim (again treated as unidimensional variables). It is easy to see how this equation could be extended to allow for theoretical variables which are not unidimensional (e.g., by putting in several x terms for each) or interactions (e.g., by having such terms as $a_5 x_5 x_6$). The problems come in operationally defining the theoretical variables in order to apply the equation to empirical variables.

The most specific theory would suggest that the probability of committing a dishonest act in any situation depended only on the costs and benefits present in that situation, and that all factors influenced this probability only insofar as they could be treated as costs or benefits. An equation is then required which relates the probability of committing a dishonest act to costs and benefits and their associated probabilities. One of the most obvious candidates is based on the subjectively expected utility model which has been so influential in explaining single-stage risky decision making (e.g., Becker & McClintock, 1967; Edwards, 1961; Rapoport & Wallsten, 1972; Slovic, Fischhoff, & Lichtenstein, 1977). The decision to commit a dishonest act is a risky decision, and theories of risky decision making should therefore have some relevance.

The subjectively expected utility (SEU) of an event or outcome is the product of the subjective probability of its occurrence and its utility, or subjective value, attractiveness, benefit, or cost. In a risky decision, each alternative choice has a certain SEU, which is the sum of the SEUs associated with each outcome of the choice. The SEU theory is deterministic and suggests that a person chooses the course of action with the greatest SEU. It is inspired by the fact that, in gambling, a person can maximize his winnings by choosing the bet with the greatest expected value (the product of objective probability and objective value). The SEU theory has been derived and tested in gambling experiments. Because of the maximization involved, it can be argued that the SEU theory prescribes the "rational" course of action. It is not suggested that subjective probabilities and utilities are calculated and combined at the conscious level, but only that people behave as if they are maximizing SEU.

Converting the SEU theory into a probabilistic theory yields the following rather general equation:

$$P = a_0 + a_1 \sum p_1 u_1 + a_2 \sum p_2 a_2 + \cdots + a_n \sum p_n u_n \qquad (2)$$

What Eq. (2) indicates is that the probability of committing a dishonest act depends on the SEU of each possible course of action. For example, imagine someone in a shop considering whether or not to steal something, and for simplicity imagine that he has two possible courses of action, stealing and not stealing. The SEU of stealing might be as follows:

$$\text{SEU} = p_{11}u_{11} - p_{12}u_{12} \tag{3}$$

In Eq. (3), u_{11} is the positive utility of the item which is stolen, and this is multiplied by the probability of stealing (p_{11}), which in this course of action is 1; u_{12} is the negative utility (cost) of an uncertain outcome, being caught by the store detective, and p_{12} is the subjective probability of this event. This is again a simplification, since only two possible outcomes have been included in the equation. The SEU of stealing is then compared with the SEU of not stealing, obtained by a similar process of multiplication, and the probability of stealing depends on the relative size of the two SEUs. The probability of stealing increases with the SEU of stealing.

In attempting to test either of the theories outlined here, the general theory and the more specific SEU theory, it would be necessary to simplify them by making restrictive assumptions. It is doubtful that the theories could be tested quantitatively at the present time, given our present ability to quantify human behavior. However, mathematical specification of theories is valuable, if only to force theorists to make all their assumptions explicit.

The SEU theory has been stated here deliberately in an extreme version. It seems implausible to suggest that dishonesty depends only on costs, utilities, and their associated probabilities or, alternatively, that all factors influence dishonesty only insofar as they are costs and utilities. However, it is valuable to begin with a very simple theory and to see which results cannot be included within it. The most useful theory is a simple theory which explains a large number of results. In trying to explain every possible result, it may be necessary to postulate a very complex theory which is less useful, and indeed less testable, than the simple theory. There is always the danger that the number of free parameters in the theory may approach the number of degrees of freedom in the data.

Some experiments on dishonesty have been designed to investigate factors other than costs and utilities, and some researchers have tried to compare cost factors with moral factors. Tittle and Rowe (1973) found that making students aware of the sanctions for cheating was more effective in reducing it than was a moral appeal, emphasizing the immorality of cheating. This result seems to conflict with that of Schwartz and Orleans (1967) showing that income tax fraud decreased more after taxpayers were interviewed and given moral reasons for compliance then after they were reminded of the possible penalties. However, moral factors, such as a sense of guilt or an uneasy conscience, could be regarded as costs which are taken into account in decisions about dishonesty.

Some other experimental results could also be explained from a cost–utility perspective. For example, Diener et al. (1976) found that children were more likely to steal in conditions of anonymity than when their names were known to the potential victim. This result could be explained by suggesting that the important theoretical construct being varied was probability of being caught, which was less in the anonymous condition. A similar explanation could be offered for another result obtained by Diener *et al.*, namely that children were more likely to steal in groups than alone, and for Penner's *et al.* (1976) demonstration that students were more likely to steal money which had no identifiable owner than money with an identifiable owner. Even Bickman's (1971) results, showing that members of the public were more likely to steal from someone in lower class dress than from someone in higher class dress, could be explained by reference to variation in the probability of legal consequences, since rich people are more likely to invoke the support of legal agencies than poor people are. The plausibility of these explanations could be tested in further experiments measuring both the probability of being caught and anonymity (for example), to see whether anonymity had an effect on stealing over and above the effect resulting from variations in the probability of being caught.

Other experimental results are less easy to explain on the extreme SEU theory outlined above. For example, Schachter (1971) found that students cheated more after being given chlorpromazine, which reduces arousal or fear, than after taking a placebo. This is understandable if arousal or fear tends to inhibit cheating. Dienstbier and Munter (1971) and Dienstbier (1972) gave students a placebo, but told them to expect side effects of either a pounding heart or yawning. They found more cheating in the pounding heart condition, and suggested that this was because the students could attribute their arousal to the effects of the drug rather than to the cheating. Just as arousal has been found to be an important factor in aggression (e.g., O'Neal & Kaufman, 1972; Zillman, 1971; Zillman, Katcher & Milavsky, 1972), it seems likely that it should be included in a theory of dishonesty.

Arousal might possibly be involved as an explanatory factor in the social facilitation of dishonesty. For example, Taylor and Lewit (1966) found that delinquent boys were most likely to tell lies in reporting their grip strengths when another boy would be aware of their performance, and several experimenters (e.g., Dmitruk, 1973; Hill & Kochendorfer, 1969; Shelton & Hill, 1969) found that children were more likely to cheat to do well in a test or to win a prize if they believed that their peers had done well.

Other experimental results are harder to explain in relation to either costs and utilities or arousal. Diener and Wallbom (1976) found less cheating when subjects were made aware of what they were doing by performing in front of a mirror, and O'Leary (1968) found that children cheated less when they were required to verbalize the task instructions. Cheating was also more likely among subjects who believed that they had done relatively badly on a test (Millham, 1974), or who believed that their responses were deviant from those of their peers

236 DAVID P. FARRINGTON

(Lepper, 1973), or who had lowered self-esteem for another reason (Aronson & Mettee, 1968). Children were also more likely to cheat if they had been justly privileged or unjustly deprived in comparison with their peers (Stephenson & Barker, 1972; Stephenson & White, 1968, 1970). In order to explain all these results, it seems likely that the more general theory is needed. However, it may also be valuable to investigate the range of applicability of the more specific SEU theory.

I have carried out two experiments, in collaboration with Barry J. Knight, inspired by the SEU theory. They were intended to investigate three basic hypotheses, namely that (a) the probability of stealing increases with increasing utility of the theft, (b) the probability of stealing decreases with increasing cost of the theft, and (c) the probability of stealing decreases with increasing probability of apprehension by the police. If these three hypotheses were not verified, the importance of costs, benefits, and probabilities in the explanation of dishonesty would require reconsideration. These hypotheses were investigated in nonreactive field experiments with members of the public unwittingly participating as subjects.

The experiments were based on the lost letter technique. This was originally used by Merritt and Fowler (1948) to study dishonesty. They showed that letters left on the street and containing a lead slug which felt like a 50¢ piece were less likely to be returned unopened than letters merely containing a message. As mentioned earlier, Hornstein *et al.* (1968), Hornstein (1970), and Tucker *et al.* (1977), in studies of helpfulness, also left money in an envelope on the street. In these experiments, failing to return the letter constituted stealing, but this was not true in later research on helping using this technique (e.g., Deaux, 1973; Gross, 1975; Hornstein, Masor, Sole, & Heilman, 1971; Korte & Kerr, 1975; Lowe & Ritchey, 1973; Sole, Marton, & Hornstein, 1975). The lost letter technique has been used primarily to measure political and social attitudes (e.g., Georgoff, Hersker, & Murdick, 1972; Himes & Mason, 1974; Jacoby & Aranoff, 1971; Milgram, Mann, & Harter, 1965; Wicker, 1969; Zelnio & Gagnon, 1977).

In the first experiment, 100 stamped, addressed, apparently lost, unsealed letters, each containing a handwritten note and in most cases also a sum of money, were left on the streets of London, England, and were picked up by members of the public. The experiment employed a $2 \times 2 \times 2$ between-subjects factorial design, with two levels of utility (low or high), two levels of cost (low or high), and two levels of probability of apprehension (low or high). The dependent variable was whether the letter and its contents were returned intact to the intended recipient (Barry J. Knight). Ten letters were dropped in each of the eight main conditions of the experiment, and 10 letters in each of two control (no money) conditions. The experimenter who dropped the letters was blind to the conditions.

An attempt was made to manipulate the utility of stealing by varying the amount of money contained in the letter, either 20p (low utility) or £1.00 (high utility). An attempt was made to manipulate the cost of stealing by varying the content of the note. In the low-cost condition, the intended recipient was the male secretary of a yachting association, and the note indicated that the sender was enclosing money for a yachting magazine. In the high-cost condition, the intended recipient was an old lady, and the note indicated that the sender was refunding money from a Senior Citizen's outing to her. It was thought that stealing in the low-cost condition would be more pleasant, because the victims were less deserving. The probability of apprehension was varied by the form in which the money came, either cash (low probability) or an uncrossed postal order (high probability). It is necessary to forge the signature of the intended recipient of a postal order to obtain the money, and it is possible that someone doing this might be asked for identification evidence and hence detected.

One problem with the operational definition of stealing as failure to return a lost letter containing money is that it is impossible to separate honesty and helpfulness. Those who return the letter are displaying both. The 20 control (no money) letters were intended to investigate helpfulness in the absence of dishonesty. Ten had a very similar note to that used in the low-cost condition, and 10 had a very similar note to that used in the high-cost condition. The 100 letters were made up in a random order, with the restriction that each of the 10 conditions occurred once in each block of 10 letters. A further 20 control letters, two in each condition, were made up and posted by the experimenters during the same period and in the same areas in which letters were dropped. These 20 letters were intended to check the efficiency of the Post Office, and all were delivered safely.

Twenty-three of the 80 letters in the main experiment were not returned. An analysis of variance showed that the main effects of cost and probability were statistically significant and that there was a significant interaction between cost and probability. The results are clear when simple percentages are presented. The nonreturn rates in the low-cost and high-cost control conditions were identical (20%), giving a base rate for unhelpfulness or carelessness in not returning letters. The nonreturn rate in the low cost–low probability condition, at 75%, was significantly greater than the control rate (15 out of 20 in comparison with 4 out of 20; $\chi^2 = 10.03$ with 1 d.f., $p < .002$). However, the nonreturn rates of other conditions were not significantly greater than the control rate. It can be concluded that a low cost and a low probability of apprehension produced a high level of stealing. The fact that the experimental manipulations of cost and probability had clear-cut effects shows that they were very powerful, in view of the many sources of variation which were controlled only by the random allocation.

The utility manipulation did not have a significant effect on stealing (32.5% nonreturn out of 40 in high-utility conditions, as opposed to 25% nonreturn out of

40 in low-utility conditions). This replicates the result of Farrington and Kidd (1977), who found no difference between 10p and 50p in inducing financial dishonesty. However, it could be argued that these utility manipulations were too weak, so that for the majority of subjects the difference between 20p and £1 was not sufficient to have a significant effect on stealing. The second lost letter experiment was carried out to investigate this. It was very similar to the first lost letter experiment, except that only utility was manipulated. Sixty letters were left on the streets of London, England, and picked up by members of the public. The note in each letter indicated that the intended recipient was an old lady, and each letter contained either no money, £1, or £5 (in cash).

The utility manipulation in the second experiment did have a significant effect. The proportion of letters not returned was 5% in the control condition, 25% in the £1 condition, and 45% in the £5 condition ($N = 20$ in all cases: $\chi^2 = 8.69$ with 2 d.f., p $<$ .025). Thus, taken together, the two lost letter experiments are in agreement with the hypotheses, in showing that the probability of stealing increases with increasing utility, with decreasing cost, and with decreasing probability of apprehension. In turn, this leads to increasing confidence in both of the theories outlined above, the general theory and the SEU theory. Given that stealing is influenced by costs, utilities, and probabilities, the next step is to carry out experiments which systematically investigate the importance of other factors, preferably in comparison with the above factors.

B. EVALUATING AND REACTING TO DISHONESTY

The process of reacting to crime by criminal justice agencies usually begins when a crime is officially recorded by the police and hence becomes an entry in the official criminal statistics. Before a crime can be recorded, some person must become aware that a criminal act has been committed and, unless that person is a policeman, he must decide to report it to the police. Most entries in the official statistics are initiated by citizen reports rather than by the police themselves (e.g., Black & Reiss, 1970). Therefore, citizens play an important role in defining and hence creating crime, and the study of factors influencing a person's decision to report a crime has important practical implications. Furthermore, some states of the United States have "Good Samaritan" laws requiring citizens to intervene to prevent crimes. It is clear that crime would be reduced if more citizens were to intervene in this way, and therefore the study of factors influencing citizens' intervention also has practical importance.

There have been a number of nonexperimental studies of crime reporting. Most of these have used the victim survey technique, which involves asking people about crimes which have been committed against them rather than about crimes they have observed. For example, Ennis (1970) reported the result of a victim survey based on a random sample of 10,000 American households, in which people were asked about crimes committed against them in the previous year. As is usual in such surveys, this victim survey revealed twice as much major crime as the official statistics in the Federal Bureau of Investigation *Uniform Crime Reports*. The rates of homicide and car theft in the victim survey were similar to those in the official statistics. In the case of car theft, the high rate of reporting to the police was at least partly caused by the requirements of insurance companies. For other major crimes, the victim survey rates were higher than those in the official statistics. The victim survey revealed four times as much forcible rape, three times as much burglary, twice as much theft over $50, twice as much aggravated assault, and 50% more robbery than the official statistics.

In general, the more serious crimes were more likely to be reported to the police. Whenever anyone was victimized and did not report to the police, he was asked to give the reason. Much the most common reason (55%) was the belief that reporting would be a waste of time, because the police would not want to be bothered or would not catch the offender. A further 9% did not want to take the time or trouble to get involved with the police or were too confused. Of the rest, 34% thought that it was not a police matter or did not want the offender to be harmed, and 2% feared reprisals from the offender's friends or from insurance companies (in cancelling the insurance or increasing its cost).

This nonexperimental research is based on what people say. There has also been some experimental research on the reporting of thefts by observers rather than victims, but I will begin by discussing some experiments on the evaluation of dishonesty. It might be hypothesized that the evaluation of the offence and offender (if known) is a stage which precedes the decision to report. On the basis of research on simulated jurors and moral judgments mentioned in Section II, D, it might be expected that this evaluation would depend, at least, on the intentions and personal characteristics of the offender and on the consequences of the offence. Some of these factors have been studied in experiments. Brickman and Bryan (1975) showed girls a film of a girl stealing 10¢ tokens and found that whether the tokens were stolen to increase or decrease equality had no effect on the evaluation of the thief. Savitsky *et al.* (1976) showed incarcerated juvenile offenders a videotape of someone cheating and found that whether or not the cheating had good consequences (a charity benefitted) did not affect their evaluation of it. However, Savitsky and Babl (1976) found that introductory psychology students delivered more aversive noise in a learning task to someone who had cheated if he had gained by the cheating than if a charity had gained. Maier and Lavrakas (1976) studied evaluations of lying and found that lies with less harmful consequences were rated more acceptable, and that it was considered more reprehensible to lie to a friend than to a stranger. More research on the evaluation of dishonesty is required, preferably using real-life staged thefts, varying such factors as the kinds of offender and victim and the intentions and consequences of the theft.

As mentioned in Section II,C, staged thefts have been used in experiments on crime reporting and bystander intervention in crime. Harari and McDavid (1969) found that schoolchildren who had observed a theft were less likely to name the thief if she was a high-status girl rather than a low-status boy. Steffensmeier and Terry (1973) found that a shoplifter dressed as a hippie was more likely to be reported than one dressed conventionally, but Gelfand et al. (1973) found that hippie dress did not affect the reporting of shoplifting. Both Steffensmeier and Terry (1973) and Dertke et al. (1974) found that the sex of the thief did not affect reporting, but Steffensmeier and Terry found that subjects were more likely to report shoplifters of the opposite sex. Dertke et al. found that black shoplifters were more likely to be reported than whites. Bickman and Green (1975) found an interaction between the cost of the item stolen and the previous contact between the shoplifter and the subject. With a low-cost item, subjects were more likely to report if the shoplifter had previously been rude to them, but with a high-cost item reporting was not related to previous contact.

Shaffer et al. (1975) and Moriarty (1975) found that bystanders were more likely to intervene to prevent a theft if they had previously been asked to do so, and Bickman and Rosenbaum (1977) showed how confederates could encourage bystanders to report. However, Bickman (1975) found that a mass media campaign designed to encourage intervention had little effect. Harari and McDavid (1969) discovered that schoolchildren were more likely to name a thief if they were questioned alone rather than in pairs, and Latane and Darley (1970) also found that witnesses to a theft were more likely to report if they were alone rather than with another person. Similarly, Shaffer et al. (1975) found that bystanders were more likely to intervene to prevent a theft if they were alone than if they were in the presence of a nonreactive confederate.

As with the commission of dishonest acts, several researchers have proposed a cost–benefit model to explain the reporting of theft. For example, Gelfand et al. (1973) pointed out that the rewards of reporting were minimal, since reporters received no money or gratitude and only had the satisfaction of bringing a criminal to justice. These rewards could be contrasted with the potential costs of causing harm to the accused person, being sued by the accused, and the inconvenience of appearing in court. Both of the models outlined in Section III, A could be applied to the reporting of theft. In the general case, it could be suggested that the probability of reporting in any situation depends on a large number of factors, some of which are costs and benefits. In the more specific case, it could be suggested that this probability depends only on the costs and benefits present, and that all factors influence this probability only insofar as they can be treated as costs or benefits.

Up to the present time, no researchers have tried to vary costs and benefits systematically in an experiment and to relate reporting to them. The theory fits in with the nonexperimental results mentioned above. People do seem to be considering costs and benefits when they say that reporting would be a waste of time because the police would not catch the offender, that they do not want to take the time or trouble to get involved with the police, that they do not want the offender to be harmed, or that they fear reprisals from the offender's friends. Furthermore, some of the experimental results could be explained within this theory. It is possible that people are more willing to report low-status thieves, hippies, and blacks because the potential costs are less with these groups, in view of their relative lack of power. Alternatively, it may be that people get more pleasure from reporting these groups than they do from reporting others. Steffensmeier and Terry (1973) found that some of their subjects were enthusiastic about reporting the hippie shoplifter and made statements which reflected their prejudiced feelings toward hippies. People may also get more pleasure from reporting shoplifters who have previously been rude to them than from reporting those who have previously been polite. Within a cost–benefit theory, it is harder to explain the greater reluctance of people to report when in the presence of others than when alone, but in general this theory seems worthy of experimental research designed to investigate it more directly.

IV. Conclusions

Throughout this paper, I have argued that field experimentation with members of the public unwittingly participating as subjects is likely to have the greatest internal and external validity of any research method. Most research on deviance is nonexperimental and hence has low internal validity, while most research by experimental social psychologists has tended to have low external validity, in being far removed from real life. In order to advance our knowledge about deviance, more field experiments with behavioral measures of deviance should be carried out. These need to be backed up by correlational research, to establish the extent to which experimental results can be generalized to real life and to establish which theoretical constructs are being measured. When true experiments involving random allocation cannot be arranged, quasiexperimental analyses should be considered.

One of the major problems in carrying out experiments with deviance as either a dependent or an independent variable or both is to operationalize deviance, and this contribution has reviewed operational definitions used in experiments up to the present time. Of the more serious deviant acts, it seems most possible to study theft and vandalism, and a number of experiments investigating why people steal and why people report or intervene in stealing have been reviewed. Of the less serious acts, further studies of litter dropping and traffic offenses seem feasible and potentially valuable.

Special attention has been given to experiments on dishonesty. These have tended to investigate immediate influences and situational factors, both of which have been neglected in the nonexperimental research. Many of the experiments have been inspired by a cost–benefit theory, in relation to both committing and reporting dishonest acts. This promising theory requires a systematic program of experimental research to investigate the importance of costs and benefits in comparison with other factors and eventually to lead to an explicitly formulated theory with a wide range of applicability. One practical implication which may be drawn from it is that crime prevention efforts which aim to change immediate situational factors may be more successful than the traditional forms of treatment aimed at individuals. It has been argued that experimental social psychologists should undertake practical experiments on the prevention and treatment of deviance.

Real-life experiments on deviance are much harder to arrange than laboratory experiments on less sensitive topics. When it comes to research with ethical difficulties, even on topics perceived to be "relevant," funding agencies are likely to err on the side of caution. Yet our knowledge about the causes, prevention, and treatment of deviance could be advanced greatly by real-life experimentation, and the quality of life of most people would improve if it were possible to reduce deviant behavior prohibited by the criminal law. It is to be hoped that psychologists will have the ingenuity, determination, and social responsibility to meet the challenge of experiments on deviance.

REFERENCES

Adams, S. The PICO project. In N. Johnson, L. Savitz, & M. E. Wolfgang (Eds.), *The sociology of punishment and correction*. New York: Wiley, 1970.

Aronson, E., & Mettee, D. R. Dishonest behavior as a function of differential levels of induced self-esteem. *Journal of Personality and Social Psychology*, 1968, **9**, 121–127.

Baltes, M. M., & Hayward, S. C. Application and evaluation of strategies to reduce pollution: Behavioral control of littering in a football stadium. *Journal of Applied Psychology*, 1976, **61**, 501–506.

Bandura, A., & McDonald, F. J. Influence of social reinforcement and the behavior of models in shaping children's moral judgments. *Journal of Abnormal and Social Psychology*, 1963, **67**, 274–281.

Becker, G. M., & McClintock, C. G. Value: Behavioral decision theory. *Annual Review of Psychology*, 1967, **18**, 239–286.

Becker, H. S. *Outsiders: Studies in the sociology of deviance*. New York: Free Press, 1963.

Beigel, H. G. Experimental production of anti-social acts in hypnosis. *British Journal of Medical Hypnotism*, 1962, **14**, 11–19.

Berg, I., Hullin, R., & McGuire, R. A randomly controlled trial of two court procedures in truancy. In D. P. Farrington, K. Hawkins, & S. Lloyd-Bostock (Eds.), *Psychology, law and legal processes*. London: Macmillan, 1979.

Berkowitz, L., & Walker, N. D. Laws and moral judgments. *Sociometry,* 1967, **30,** 410–422.

Berntsen, K., & Christiansen, K. O. A resocialization experiment with short-term offenders. In K. O. Christiansen (Ed.), *Scandinavian studies in criminology* (Vol 1). London: Tavistock, 1965.

Bickman, L. The effect of social status on the honesty of others. *Journal of Social Psychology,* 1971, **85,** 87–92.

Bickman, L. Bystander intervention in a crime: The effect of a mass-media campaign. *Journal of Applied Social Psychology,* 1975, **5,** 296–302.

Bickman, L. Attitude toward an authority and the reporting of a crime. *Sociometry,* 1976, **39,** 76–82.

Bickman, L., & Green, S. Is revenge sweet? The effect of attitude toward a thief on crime reporting. *Criminal Justice and Behavior,* 1975, **2,** 101–112.

Bickman, L., & Henchy, T. (Eds.), *Beyond the laboratory: Field research in social psychology.* New York: McGraw-Hill, 1972.

Bickman, L., & Rosenbaum, D. P. Crime reporting as a function of bystander encouragement, surveillance and credibility. *Journal of Personality and Social Psychology,* 1977, **35,** 577–586.

Birnbaum, M. P. Anxiety and moral judgment in early adolescence. *Journal of Genetic Psychology,* 1972, **120,** 13–26.

Black, D. J., & Reiss, A. J. Police control of juveniles. *American Sociological Review,* 1970, **35,** 63–77.

Bleda, P. R., Bleda, S. E., Byrne, D., & White, L. A. When a bystander becomes an accomplice: Situational determinants of reactions to dishonesty. *Journal of Experimental Social Psychology,* 1976, **12,** 9–25.

Bord, R. J. Rejection of the mentally ill: Continuities and further developments. *Social Problems,* 1971, **18,** 496–509.

Boshier, R., & Johnson, D. Does conviction affect employment opportunities? *British Journal of Criminology,* 1974, **14,** 264–268.

Bowman, P. H. Effects of a revised school program on potential delinquents. *Annals of the American Academy of Political and Social Sciences,* 1959, **322,** 53–61.

Bramel, D. A dissonance theory approach to defensive projection. *Journal of Abnormal and Social Psychology,* 1962, **64,** 121–129.

Bramel, D. Selection of a target for defensive projection. *Journal of Abnormal and Social Psychology,* 1963, **66,** 318–324.

Brickman, P., & Bryan, J. H. Moral judgment of theft, charity, and third-party transfers that increase or decrease equality. *Journal of Personality and Social Psychology,* 1975, **31,** 156–161.

Brickman, P., & Bryan, J. H. Equity versus equality as factors in children's moral judgments of thefts, charity, and third-party transfers. *Journal of Personality and Social Psychology,* 1976, **34,** 757 761.

Buckhout, R., Alper, A., Chern, S., Silverberg, G., & Slomovits, M. Determinants of eyewitness performance on a lineup. *Bulletin of the Psychonomic Society,* 1974, **4,** 191–192.

Buikhuisen, W. General deterrence: Research and theory. *Abstracts in Criminology and Penology,* 1974, **14,** 285–298.

Buikhuisen, W., & Dijksterhuis, F. P. H. Delinquency and stigmatization. *British Journal of Criminology,* 1971, **11,** 185–187.

Buikhuisen, W., & Jongman, R. W. A legalistic classification of juvenile delinquents. *British Journal of Criminology,* 1970, **10,** 109–123.

Burgess, R. L., Clark, R. N., & Hendee, J. C. An experimental analysis of anti-litter procedures. *Journal of Applied Behavior Analysis,* 1971, **4,** 71–75.

Burns, J. A., & Kintz, B. L. Eye contact while lying during an interview. *Bulletin of the Psychonomic Society,* 1976, **7,** 87–89.

Burton, R. V. Generality of honesty reconsidered. *Psychological Review,* 1963, **70,** 481–499.

Burton, R. V., Allinsmith, W., & Maccoby, E. E. Resistance to temptation in relation to sex of child, sex of experimenter and withdrawal of attention. *Journal of Personality and Social Psychology,* 1966, **3**, 253-258.

Caetano, D. F. Labeling theory and the presumption of mental illness in diagnosis: An experimental design. *Journal of Health and Social Behavior,* 1974, **15**, 253-260.

Campbell, D. T., & Ross, L. The Connecticut crackdown on speeding: Time-series data and quasi-experimental analysis. *Law and Society Review,* 1968, **3**, 33-53.

Campbell, D. T., & Stanley, J. C. *Experimental and quasi-experimental designs for research.* Chicago: Rand-McNally, 1966.

Carlson, R. Where is the person in personality research? *Psychological Bulletin,* 1971, **75**, 203-219.

Chiricos, T. G., & Waldo, G. P. Punishment and crime: An examination of some empirical evidence. *Social Problems,* 1970, **18**, 200-217.

Clarke, R. V. G., & Cornish, D. B. *The controlled trial in institutional research—paradigm or pitfall for penal evaluators?* London: HMSO, 1972.

Coe, W. C., Kobayashi, K., & Howard, M. L. An approach toward isolating factors that influence antisocial conduct in hypnosis. *International Journal of Clinical and Experimental Hypnosis,* 1972, **20**, 118-131.

Coe, W. C., Kobayashi, K., & Howard, M. L. Experimental and ethical problems of evaluating the influence of hypnosis in antisocial conduct. *Journal of Abnormal Psychology,* 1973, **82**, 476-482.

Cornish, D. B., & Clarke, R. V. G. *Residential treatment and its effects on delinquency.* London: HMSO, 1975.

Cowan, P. A., Langer, J., Heavenrich, J., & Nathanson, M. Social learning and Piaget's cognitive theory of moral development. *Journal of Personality and Social Psychology,* 1969, **11**, 261-274.

Cronbach, L. J. *Essentials of psychological testing* (3rd ed.). New York: Harper, 1970.

Deaux, K. Anonymous altruism: Extending the lost letter technique. *Journal of Social Psychology,* 1973, **92**, 61-66.

Denner, B. Did a crime occur? Should I inform anyone? A study of deception. *Journal of Personality,* 1968, **36**, 454-465.

Dertke, M. C., Penner, L. A., & Ulrich, K. Observer's reporting of shoplifting as a function of thief's race and sex. *Journal of Social Psychology,* 1974, **94**, 213-221.

Deutscher, I. *What we say/What we do.* Glenview: Scott Foresman, 1973.

Diener, E., Fraser, S. C., Beaman, A. L., & Kelem, R. T. Effects of deindividuation variables on stealing among Halloween trick-or-treaters. *Journal of Personality and Social Psychology,* 1976, **33**, 178-183.

Diener, E., & Wallbom, M. Effects of self-awareness on antinormative behavior. *Journal of Research in Personality,* 1976, **10**, 107-111.

Dienstbier, R. A. The role of anxiety and arousal attribution in cheating. *Journal of Experimental Social Psychology,* 1972, **8**, 168-179.

Dienstbier, R. A., & Munter, P. O. Cheating as a function of the labeling of natural arousal. *Journal of Personality and Social Psychology,* 1971, **17**, 208-213.

Dmitruk, V. M. Incentive preference and resistance to temptation. *Child Development,* 1971, **42**, 625-628.

Dmitruk, V. M. Intangible motivation and resistance to temptation. *Journal of Genetic Psychology,* 1973, **123**, 47-53.

Dorr, D., & Fey, S. Relative power of symbolic adult and peer models in the modification of children's moral choice behavior. *Journal of Personality and Social Psychology,* 1974, **29**, 335-341.

Ebbesen, E. B., & Konecni, V. J. Decision making and information integration in the courts: The setting of bail. *Journal of Personality and Social Psychology,* 1975, **32**, 805-821.

Edwards, W. Behavioral decision theory. *Annual Review of Psychology*, 1961, **12**, 473–498.

Efran, M. G. The effect of physical appearance on the judgment of guilt, interpersonal attraction, and severity of recommended punishment in a simulated jury task. *Journal of Research in Personality*, 1974, **8**, 45–54.

Ekman, P., & Friesen, W. V. Detecting deception from the body or face. *Journal of Personality and Social Psychology*, 1974, **29**, 288–298.

Empey, L. T., & Erickson, M. L. *The provo experiment: Evaluating community control of delinquency*. Lexington: Heath, 1972.

Empey, L. T., & Lubeck, S. G. *The silverlake experiment: Testing delinquency theory and community intervention*. Chicago: Aldine, 1971.

Ennis, P. H. Crime, victims and the police. In M. Lipsky (Ed.), *Law and order: Police encounters*. Chicago: Aldine, 1970.

Farrington, D. P. Self-reports of deviant behavior: predictive and stable? *Journal of Criminal Law and Criminology*, 1973, **64**, 99–110.

Farrington, D. P. The effects of public labelling. *British Journal of Criminology*, 1977, **17**, 112–125.

Farrington, D. P., & Kidd, R. F. Is financial dishonesty a rational decision? *British Journal of Social and Clinical Psychology*, 1977, **16**, 139–146.

Farrington, D. P., & Knight, B. J. Four studies of stealing as a risky decision. In P. Lipsitt & B. D. Sales (Eds.), *New directions in psycholegal research*. New York: Van Nostrand-Reinhold, 1979, in press. (a)

Farrington, D. P., & Knight, B. J. Two non-reactive field experiments on stealing from a "lost" letter. *British Journal of Social and Clinical Psychology*, 1979, **18**, in press. (b)

Farrington, D. P., Osborn, S. G., & West, D. J. The persistence of labelling effects. *British Journal of Criminology*, 1978, **18**, 277–284.

Feldman, R. E. Response to compatriot and foreigner who seek assistance. *Journal of Personality and Social Psychology*, 1968, **10**, 202–214.

Finnie, W. C. Field experiments in litter control. *Environment and Behavior*, 1973, **5**, 123–144.

Folkard, M. S., Smith, D. E., & Smith, D. D. *Impact. Vol 2: The results of the experiment*. London: HMSO, 1976.

Fowles, A. J. *Prison Welfare*. London: HMSO, 1978.

Franklin, B. J. The effects of status on the honesty and verbal responses of others. *Journal of Social Psychology*, 1973, **91**, 347–348.

Freedman, J. L., Wallington, S. A., & Bless, E. Compliance without pressure: The effect of guilt. *Journal of Personality and Social Psychology*, 1967, **7**, 117–124.

Fromkin, H. I., Goldstein, J. H., & Brock, T. C. The role of "irrelevant" derogation in vicarious aggression catharsis: A field experiment. *Journal of Experimental Social Psychology*, 1977, **13**, 239–252.

Geis, G. Pioneers in criminology: VII. Jeremy Bentham. *Journal of Criminal Law, Criminology and Police Science*, 1955, **46**, 159–171.

Gelfand, D. M., Hartmann, D. P., Walder, P., & Page, P. Who reports shoplifters? A field-experimental study. *Journal of Personality and Social Psychology*, 1973, **25**, 276–285.

Georgoff, D. M., Hersker, B. J., & Murdick, R. G. The lost-letter technique: A scaling experiment. *Public Opinion Quarterly*, 1972, **36**, 114–119.

Grinder, R. E. Parental child-rearing practices, conscience, and resistance to temptation of sixth-grade children. *Child Development*, 1962, **33**, 803–820.

Gross, A. E. Generosity and legitimacy of a model as determinants of helpful behavior. *Representative Research in Social Psychology*, 1975, **6**, 45–50.

Harari, H., & McDavid, J. W. Situational influence on moral justice: A study of 'finking.' *Journal of Personality and Social Psychology*, 1969, **11**, 240–244.

Harris, M. B., & Samerotte, G. C. The effects of actual and attempted theft, need, and a previous favor on altruism. *Journal of Social Psychology*, 1976, **99**, 193-202.

Hartshorne, H., & May, M. A. *Studies in deceit*. New York: Macmillan, 1928.

Heisler, G. Ways to deter law violators: Effects of levels of threat and vicarious punishment on cheating. *Journal of Consulting and Clinical Psychology*, 1974, **42**, 577-582.

Hendrick, C., & Shaffer, D. R. Murder: Effects of number of killers and victim mutilation on simulated jurors' judgments. *Bulletin of the Psychonomic Society*, 1975, **6**, 313-316.

Henshel, A-M. The relationship between values and behavior: A developmental hypothesis. *Child Development*, 1971, **42**, 1997-2007.

Hill, F. A. Attribution of responsibility in a campus stabbing incident. *Social Behavior and Personality*, 1975, **3**, 127-131.

Hill, G. E. Cheating among delinquent boys. *Journal of Juvenile Research*, 1934, **18**, 169-174.

Hill, J. P., & Kochendorfer, R. A. Knowledge of peer success and risk of detection as determinants of cheating. *Developmental Psychology*, 1969, **1**, 231-238.

Himes, S. H., & Mason, J. B. A note on unobtrusive attitude measurement: The lost letter technique. *Journal of the Market Research Society*, 1974, **16**, 42-46.

Hindelang, M. J. Age, sex, and the versatility of delinquent involvements. *Social Problems*, 1971, **18**, 522-535.

Hood, R., & Sparks, R. *Key issues in criminology*. London: Weidenfeld and Nicolson, 1970.

Hornstein, H. A. The influence of social models on helping. In J. Macauley and L. Berkowitz (Eds.), *Altruism and helping behavior*. New York: Academic Press, 1970.

Hornstein, H. A., Fisch, E., & Holmes, M. Influence of a model's feeling about his behavior and his relevance as a comparison other on observer's helping behavior. *Journal of Personality and Social Psychology*, 1968, **10**, 222-226.

Hornstein, H. A., Masor, H. N., Sole, K., & Heilman, M. Effects of sentiment and completion of a helping act on observer helping: A case for socially mediated Zeigarnik effects. *Journal of Personality and Social Psychology*, 1971, **17**, 107-112.

Humphreys, L. *Tearoom trade: A study of homosexual encounters in public places*. London: Duckworth, 1970.

Jacoby, J., & Aranoff, D. Political polling and the lost-letter technique. *Journal of Social Psychology*, 1971, **83**, 209-212.

Jesness, C. F. Comparative effectiveness of two institutional treatment programs for delinquents. *Child Care Quarterly*, 1971, **1**, 119-130.

Jones, C., & Aronson, E. Attribution of fault to a rape victim as a function of respectability of the victim. *Journal of Personality and Social Psychology*, 1973, **26**, 415-419.

Kanfer, F. H., & Duerfeldt, P. H. Age, class standing, and commitment as determinants of cheating in children. *Child Development*, 1968, **39**, 545-557.

Kassebaum, G., Ward, D., & Wilner, D. *Prison treatment and parole survival*. New York: Wiley, 1971.

Kaufmann, H. Legality and harmfulness of a bystander's failure to intervene as determinants of moral judgment. In J. Macauley & L. Berkowitz (Eds.), *Altruism and helping behavior*. New York: Academic Press, 1970.

Keehn, J. D. Unrealistic reporting as a function of extraverted neurosis. *Journal of Clinical Psychology*, 1956, **12**, 61-63.

Kidd, R. F. Manipulation checks: Advantage or disadvantage? *Representative Research in Social Psychology*, 1976, **7**, 160-165.

Kirk, S. A. The impact of labeling on rejection of the mentally ill: An experimental study. *Journal of Health and Social Behavior*, 1974, **15**, 108-117.

Kleinke, C. L. Compliance to requests made by gazing and touching experimenters in field settings. *Journal of Experimental Social Psychology*, 1977, **13**, 218-223.

Kline, M. V. The dynamics of hypnotically induced antisocial behavior. *Journal of Psychology,* 1958, **45**, 239–245.

Kline, M. V. The production of antisocial behavior through hypnosis: New clinical data. *International Journal of Clinical and Experimental Hypnosis,* 1972, **20**, 80–94.

Kohlenberg, R., & Phillips, T. Reinforcement and rate of litter depositing. *Journal of Applied Behavior Analysis,* 1973, **6**, 391–396.

Korte, C., & Kerr, N. Response to altruistic opportunities in urban and nonurban settings. *Journal of Social Psychology,* 1975, **95**, 183–184.

Krauss, H. H., & Blanchard, E. B. Locus of control in ethical risk taking. *Psychological Reports,* 1970, **27**, 142.

Krauss, H. H., Coddington, R. D., & Smeltzer, D. J. Ethical risk sensitivity of adolescents in legal difficulty: First contact and repeat contact groups. *Journal of Social Psychology,* 1971, **83**, 213–217.

Krauss, H. H., Robinson, I., Janzen, W., & Cauthen, N. Predictions of ethical risk taking by psychopathic and non-psychopathic criminals. *Psychological Reports,* 1972, **30**, 83–88.

Krauss, R. M., Freedman, J. L., & Whitcup, M. Field and laboratory studies of littering. *Journal of Experimental Social Psychology,* 1978, **14**, 109–122.

Latane, B., & Darley, J. M. *The unresponsive bystander: Why doesn't he help?* New York: Appleton, 1970.

LaTour, S., Houlden, P., Walker, L., & Thibaut, J. Procedure: Transnational perspectives and preferences. *Yale Law Journal,* 1976, **86**, 258–290.

Lefkowitz, M., Blake, R. R., & Mouton, J. S. Status factors in pedestrian violation of traffic signals. *Journal of Abnormal and Social Psychology,* 1955, **51**, 704–706.

Le Furgy, W. G., & Woloshin, G. W. Immediate and long-term effects of experimentally induced social influence in the modification of adolescents' moral judgments. *Journal of Personality and Social Psychology,* 1969, **12**, 104–110.

Lemert, E. M. *Human deviance, social problems and social control* (2nd ed.). New York: Prentice-Hall, 1972.

Lenga, M. R., & Kleinke, C. L. Modeling, anonymity, and performance of an undesirable act. *Psychological Reports,* 1974, **34**, 501–502.

Lepper, M. R. Dissonance, self-perception, and honesty in children. *Journal of Personality and Social Psychology,* 1973, **25**, 65–74.

Lerman, P. *Community treatment and social control.* Chicago: University of Chicago Press, 1975.

Lerner, M. J., & Agar, E. The consequences of perceived similarity: Attraction and rejection, approach and avoidance. *Journal of Experimental Research in Personality,* 1972, **6**, 69–75.

Lingle, J. H., Brock, T. C., & Cialdini, R. B. Surveillance instigates entrapment when violations are observed, when personal involvement is high, and when sanctions are severe. *Journal of Personality and Social Psychology,* 1977, **35**, 419–429.

Logan, C. H. General deterrent effects of punishment. *Social Forces,* 1972, **51**, 64–73.

Lowe, R., & Ritchey, G. Relation of altruism to age, social class, and ethnic identity. *Psychological Reports,* 1973, **33**, 567–572.

Lykken, D. T. The GSR in the detection of guilt. *Journal of Applied Psychology,* 1959, **43**, 385–388.

Maier, N. R. F., & Thurber, J. A. Accuracy of judgments of deception when an interview is watched, heard and read. *Personnel Psychology,* 1968, **21**, 23–30.

Maier, R. A., & Lavrakas, P. J. Lying behavior and evaluation of lies. *Perceptual and Motor Skills,* 1976, **42**, 575–581.

Mann, J., Sidman, J., & Starr, S. Effects of erotic films on sexual behavior of married couples. In *U.S. President's commission on obscenity and pornography.* Technical Report 8. Washington, D.C.: Government Printing Office, 1970.

Marshall, J. *Law and psychology in conflict*. Indianapolis: Bobbs-Merrill, 1966.

Mathes, E. W., & Guest, T. A. Anonymity and group antisocial behavior. *Journal of Social Psychology*, 1976, **100**, 257–262.

McClintock, F. H. *Crimes of violence*. London: Macmillan, 1963.

McCord, J. A thirty-year follow-up of treatment effects. *American Psychologist*, 1978, **33**, 284–289.

McCord, J., & McCord, W. A follow-up report on the Cambridge-Somerville Youth Study. *Annals of the American Academy of Political and Social Sciences*, 1959, **322**, 89–96.

McGlynn, R. P., Megas, J. C., & Benson, D. H. Sex and race as factors affecting the attribution of insanity in a murder trial. *Journal of Psychology*, 1976, **93**, 93–99.

McManis, D. L. Effects of peer-models vs. adult-models and social reinforcement on intentionality of children's moral judgments. *Journal of Psychology*, 1974, **87**, 159–170.

McMillen, D. L. Transgression, self-image, and compliant behavior. *Journal of Personality and Social Psychology*, 1971, **20**, 176–179.

McNees, M. P., Egli, D. S., Marshall, R. S., Schnelle, J. F., & Risley, T. R. Shoplifting prevention: Providing information through signs. *Journal of Applied Behavior Analysis*, 1976, **9**, 399–405.

Medinnus, G. R. Age and sex differences in conscience development. *Journal of Genetic Psychology*, 1966, **109**, 117–118.

Merritt, C. B., & Fowler, R. G. The pecuniary honesty of the public at large. *Journal of Abnormal and Social Psychology*, 1948, **43**, 90–93.

Milgram, S., Mann, L., & Harter, S. The lost-letter technique: A tool of social research. *Public Opinion Quarterly*, 1965, **29**, 437–438.

Miller, A. G. *The social psychology of psychological research*. New York: Free Press, 1972.

Millham, J. Two components of need for approval score and their relationship to cheating following success and failure. *Journal of Research in Personality*, 1974, **8**, 378–392.

Mills, J. Changes in moral attitudes following temptation. *Journal of Personality*, 1958, **26**, 517–531.

Moriarty, T. Crime, commitment, and the responsive bystander: Two field experiments. *Journal of Personality and Social Psychology*, 1975, **31**, 370–376.

Mudd, S. A. Group sanction severity as a function of degree of behavior deviation and relevance of norm. *Journal of Personality and Social Psychology*, 1968, **8**, 258–260.

Nash, M. M. "Nonreactive methods and the law." Additional comments on legal liability in behavior research. *American Psychologist*, 1975, **30**, 777–780.

Nelson, E. A., Grinder, R. E., & Biaggio, A. M. B. Relationships among behavioral, cognitive-developmental, and self report measures of morality and personality. *Multivariate Behavioral Research*, 1969, **4**, 483–500.

Nelsen, E. A., Grinder, R. E., & Mutterer, M. L. Sources of variance in behavioral measures of honesty in temptation situations: Methodological analyses. *Developmental Psychology*, 1969, **1**, 265–279.

Nisbett, R. E., & Wilson, T. D. Telling more than we can know: Verbal reports on mental processes. *Psychological Review*, 1977, **84**, 231–259.

O'Leary, K. D. The effects of self-instruction on immoral behavior. *Journal of Experimental Child Psychology*, 1968, **6**, 297–301.

O'Neal, E., & Kaufman, L. The influence of attack, arousal and information about one's arousal upon interpersonal aggression. *Psychonomic Science*, 1972, **26**, 211–214.

Palmer, J. W. Punishment—A field for experiment. *British Journal of Criminology*, 1967, **7**, 434–441.

Palmer, T. B. California's Community Treatment Program for delinquent adolescents. *Journal of Research in Crime and Delinquency*, 1971, **8**, 74–92.

Penner, L. A., Summers, L. S., Brookmire, D. A., & Dertke, M. C. The lost dollar: Situational and personality determinants of a pro- and anti-social behavior. *Journal of Personality*, 1976, **44**, 274-293.

Peterson, R. A., Pittman, D. J., & O'Neal, P. Stabilities of deviance: A study of assaultive and non-assaultive offenders. *Journal of Criminal Law, Criminology and Police Science*, 1962, **53**, 44-48.

Phillips, D. L. Rejection: A possible consequence of seeking help for mental disorders. *American Sociological Review*, 1963, **28**, 963-972.

Piliavin, I. M., Rodin, J., & Piliavin, J. A. Good samaritanism: An underground phenomenon? *Journal of Personality and Social Psychology*, 1969, **13**, 289-299.

Prentice, N. M. The influence of live and symbolic modeling on promoting moral judgment of adolescent delinquents. *Journal of Abnormal Psychology*, 1972, **80**, 157-161.

Quigley-Fernandez, B., & Tedeschi, J. T. The bogus pipeline as lie detector: Two validity studies. *Journal of Personality and Social Psychology*, 1978, **36**, 247-256.

Rapoport, A., & Wallsten, T. S. Individual decision behavior. *Annual Review of Psychology*, 1972, **23**, 131-176.

Raymond, B. J., & Unger, R. K. 'The apparel oft proclaims the man': Cooperation with deviant and conventional youths. *Journal of Social Psychology*, 1972, **87**, 75-82.

Reckless, W. C., & Dinitz, S. *The prevention of juvenile delinquency: An experiment*. Columbus: Ohio State University Press, 1972.

Reimer, E., & Warren, M. Special Intensive Parole Unit. *NPPA Journal*, 1957, **3**, 222-229.

Rettig, S. Ethical risk sensitivity in male prisoners. *British Journal of Criminology*, 1964, **4**, 582-590.

Rettig, S. Group discussion and predicted ethical risk-taking. *Journal of Personality and Social Psychology*, 1966, **3**, 629-633.

Rettig, S., & Pasamanick, B. Differential judgment of ethical risk by cheaters and noncheaters. *Journal of Abnormal and Social Psychology*, 1964, **69**, 109-113.

Rettig, S., & Rawson, H. E. The risk hypothesis in predictive judgments of unethical behavior. *Journal of Abnormal and Social Psychology*, 1963, **66**, 243-248.

Rettig, S., & Turoff, S. J. Exposure to group discussion and predicted ethical risk taking. *Journal of Personality and Social Psychology*, 1967, **7**, 177-180.

Rose, G., & Hamilton, R. A. Effects of a juvenile liaison scheme. *British Journal of Criminology*, 1970, **10**, 2-20.

Ross, H. L., Campbell, D. T., & Glass, G. V. Determining the social effects of a legal reform: The British 'Breathalyser' crackdown of 1967. *American Behavioral Scientist*, 1970, **13**, 493-509.

Santrock, J. W. Moral structure: The interrelations of moral behavior, moral judgment and moral affect. *Journal of Genetic Psychology*, 1975, **127**, 201-213.

Savitsky, J. C., & Babl, J. Cheating, intention, and punishment from an equity theory perspective. *Journal of Research in Personality*, 1976, **10**, 128-136.

Savitsky, J. C., Muskin, R., Czyzewski, D., & Eckert, J. The cheating and intention of a partner as determinants of evaluative decisions among juvenile offenders. *Journal of Abnormal Child Psychology*, 1976, **4**, 235-241.

Schachter, S. *Emotion, obesity and crime*. New York: Academic Press, 1971.

Schnelle, J. F., & Lee, J. F. A quasi-experimental retrospective evaluation of a prison policy change. *Journal of Applied Behavior Analysis*, 1974, **7**, 483-496.

Schroder, D., & Ehrlich, D. Rejection by mental health professionals: A possible consequence of not seeking appropriate help for emotional disorders. *Journal of Health and Social Behavior*, 1968, **9**, 222-232.

Schwartz, R. D., & Orleans, S. On legal sanctions. *University of Chicago Law Review*, 1967, **34**, 274-300.

Schwartz, R. D., & Skolnick, J. H. Two studies of legal stigma. *Social Problems*, 1962, **10**, 133–142.

Schwartz, S. H., & Gottlieb, A. Bystander reactions to a violent theft: Crime in Jerusalem. *Journal of Personality and Social Psychology*, 1976, **34**, 1188–1199.

Scroggs, J. R. Penalties for rape as a function of victim provocativeness, damage, and resistance. *Journal of Applied Social Psychology*, 1976, **6**, 360–368.

Sealy, A. P. What can be learned from the analysis of simulated juries? In N. Walker & A. Pearson (Eds.), *The British jury system*. Cambridge: Institute of Criminology, 1975.

Shaffer, D. R., Rogel, M., & Hendrick, C. Intervention in the library: The effect of increased responsibility on bystanders' willingness to prevent a theft. *Journal of Applied Social Psychology*, 1975, **5**, 303–319.

Shaw, M. *Social work in prison*. London: HMSO, 1974.

Shea, M. A. A study of the effect of the prosecutor's choice of charge on magistrates' sentencing behaviour. *British Journal of Criminology*, 1974, **14**, 269–272.

Shelton, J., & Hill, J. P. Effects on cheating of achievement anxiety and knowledge of peer performance. *Developmental Psychology*, 1969, **1**, 449–455.

Shotland, R. L., & Berger, W. G. Behavioral validation of several values from the Rokeach value scale as an index of honesty. *Journal of Applied Psychology*, 1970, **54**, 433–435.

Shotland, R. L., & Straw, M. K. Bystander response to an assault: When a man attacks a woman. *Journal of Personality and Social Psychology*, 1976, **34**, 990–999.

Sigelman, C. K., & Sigelman, L. Authority and conformity: Violation of a traffic regulation. *Journal of Social Psychology*, 1976, **100**, 35–43.

Silverman, I. Nonreactive methods and the law. *American Psychologist*, 1975, **30**, 764–769.

Silverman, I., Shulman, A. D., & Wiesenthal, D. L. Effects of deceiving and debriefing psychological subjects on performance in later experiments. *Journal of Personality and Social Psychology*, 1970, **14**, 203–212.

Simmons, J. L., & Chambers, H. Public stereotypes of deviants. *Social Problems*, 1965, **13**, 223–232.

Slovic, P., Fischhoff, B., & Lichtenstein, S. Behavioral decision theory. *Annual Review of Psychology*, 1977, **28**, 1–39.

Sole, K., Marton, J., & Hornstein, H. A. Opinion similarity and helping: Three field experiments investigating the bases of promotive tension. *Journal of Experimental Social Psychology*, 1975, **11**, 1–13.

Steffensmeier, D. J., & Terry, R. M. Deviance and respectability: an observational study of reactions to shoplifting. *Social Forces*, 1973, **51**, 417–426.

Steffensmeier, D. J., & Terry, R. M. (Eds.). *Examining deviance experimentally*. Chicago: Alfred, 1975.

Steinberg, J., McDonald, P., & O'Neal, E. Petty theft in a naturalistic setting: The effects of bystander presence. *Journal of Social Psychology*, 1977, **101**, 219–221.

Stephan, C. Sex prejudice in jury simulation. *Journal of Psychology*, 1974, **88**, 305–312.

Stephenson, G. M., & Barker, J. Personality and the pursuit of distributive justice: An experimental study of children's moral behaviour. *British Journal of Social and Clinical Psychology*, 1972, **11**, 207–219.

Stephenson, G. M., & White, J. H. An experimental study of some effects of injustice on children's moral behavior. *Journal of Experimental Social Psychology*, 1968, **4**, 460–469.

Stephenson, G. M., & White, J. H. Privilege, deprivation, and children's moral behavior: An experimental clarification of the role of investments. *Journal of Experimental Social Psychology*, 1970, **6**, 167–176.

Sternlieb, J. L., & Youniss, J. Moral judgments one year after intentional or consequence modeling. *Journal of Personality and Social Psychology*, 1975, **31**, 895–897.

Sullivan, D. S., & Deiker, T. E. Subject-experimenter perceptions of ethical issues in human research. *American Psychologist,* 1973, **28**, 587-591.

Switzer, E. B., Deal, T. E., & Bailey, J. S. The reduction of stealing in second graders using a group contingency. *Journal of Applied Behavior Analysis,* 1977, **10**, 267-272.

Sykes, G. M., & Matza, D. Techniques of neutralization: A theory of delinquency. *American Sociological Review,* 1957, **22**, 664-670.

Taylor, I., Walton, P., & Young, J. *The new criminology: For a social theory of deviance.* London: Routledge and Kegan Paul, 1973.

Taylor, S. P., & Lewit, D. W. Social comparison and deception regarding ability. *Journal of Personality,* 1966, **34**, 94-104.

Tickner, A. H., & Poulton, E. C. Watching for people and actions. *Ergonomics,* 1975, **18**, 35-51.

Tittle, C. R. Crime rates and legal sanctions. *Social Problems,* 1969, **16**, 409-423.

Tittle, C. R., & Rowe, A. R. Moral appeal, sanction threat, and deviance: An experimental test. *Social Problems,* 1973, **20**, 488-498.

Törnudd, P. The preventive effects of fines for drunkenness. In N. Christie (Ed.), *Scandinavian studies in criminology* (Vol 2). London: Tavistock, 1968.

Trasler, G. B. Criminal behaviour. In H. J. Eysenck (Ed.), *Handbook of abnormal psychology* (2nd ed.). London: Pitman, 1973.

Tucker, L., Hornstein, H. A., Holloway, S., & Sole, K. The effects of temptation and information about a stranger on helping. *Personality and Social Psychology Bulletin,* 1977, **3**, 416-420.

Valenti, A. C., & Downing, L. L. Differential effects of jury size on verdicts following deliberation as a function of the apparent guilt of a defendant. *Journal of Personality and Social Psychology,* 1975, **32**, 655-663.

Venezia, P. S. Unofficial probation: An evaluation of its effectiveness. *Journal of Research in Crime and Delinquency,* 1972, **9**, 149-170.

Vitro, F. T., & Schoer, L. A. The effects of probability of test success, test importance and risk of detection on the incidence of cheating. *Journal of School Psychology,* 1972, **10**, 86-93.

Walker, L. J., & Richards, B. S. The effects of a narrative model on children's moral judgments. *Canadian Journal of Behavioral Science,* 1976, **8**, 169-177.

Walker, N., & Argyle, M. Does the law affect moral judgments? *British Journal of Criminology,* 1964, **4**, 570-581.

Walker, N., Hammond, W., & Steer, D. Repeated violence. *Criminal Law Review,* 1967, 465-472.

Webb, E. J., Campbell, D. T., Schwartz, R. D., & Sechrest, L. *Unobtrusive measures: Nonreactive research in the social sciences.* Chicago: Rand-McNally, 1966.

Weissbach, T. A., & Zagon, G. The effect of deviant group membership upon impressions of personality. *Journal of Social Psychology,* 1975, **95**, 263-266.

West, D. J., & Farrington, D. P. *Who becomes delinquent?* London: Heinemann, 1973.

West, D. J., & Farrington, D. P. *The delinquent way of life.* London: Heinemann, 1977.

West, S. G., & Gunn, S. P. Some issues of ethics and social psychology. *American Psychologist,* 1978, **33**, 30-38.

West, S. G., Gunn, S. P., & Chernicky, P. Ubiquitous Watergate: An attributional analysis. *Journal of Personality and Social Psychology,* 1975, **32**, 55-65.

White, G. M. Immediate and deferred effects of model observation and guided and unguided rehearsal on donating and stealing. *Journal of Personality and Social Psychology,* 1972, **21**, 139-148.

Wicker, A. W. A failure to validate the lost-letter technique. *Public Opinion Quarterly,* 1969, **33**, 260-262.

Wilkins, L. *Social deviance.* London: Tavistock, 1964.

Williams, M. Aspects of the psychology of imprisonment. In S. McConville (Ed.), *The use of imprisonment.* London: Routledge and Kegan Paul, 1975.

Wilson, D. W., & Donnerstein, E. Legal and ethical aspects of nonreactive social psychological research. *American Psychologist*, 1976, **31**, 765-773.

Wolfgang, M. E., Figlio, R. M., & Selling, T. *Delinquency in a birth cohort*. Chicago: University of Chicago Press, 1972.

Wyer, R. S., Dion, K. L., & Ellsworth, P. C. An editorial. *Journal of Experimental Social Psychology*, 1978, **14**, 141-147.

Zelnio, R. N., & Gagnon, J. P. The viability of the lost letter technique. *Journal of Psychology*, 1977, **95**, 51-53.

Zillman, D. Excitation transfer in communication-mediated aggressive behavior. *Journal of Experimental Social Psychology*, 1971, **7**, 419-434.

Zillman, D., Katcher, A. H., & Milavsky, B. Excitation transfer from physical exercise to subsequent aggressive behavior. *Journal of Experimental Social Psychology*, 1972, **8**, 247-259.

Zimbardo, P. G. The human choice: Individuation, reason, and order versus deindividuation, impulse, and chaos. In W. J. Arnold, & D. Levine (Eds.), *Nebraska symposium on motivation, 1969*. Lincoln, Nebraska: University of Nebraska Press, 1970.

FROM THE EARLY WINDOW TO THE LATE NIGHT SHOW: INTERNATIONAL TRENDS IN THE STUDY OF TELEVISION'S IMPACT ON CHILDREN AND ADULTS[1]

John P. Murray and Susan Kippax

MACQUARIE UNIVERSITY
SYDNEY, AUSTRALIA

I. Introduction 254
II. Television's Culture Context 256
   A. Broadcasting Structures 256
   B. Structure and Content 260
III. Television's Impact on Daily Life 260
   A. Television Use 260
   B. Displacement or Stimulation? 263
   C. Conclusions 267
IV. Impact of Televised Violence 270
   A. Experimental Studies 272
   B. Correlational Studies 276
   C. Causal-Correlational and Field-Experimental Studies 278
   D. Television Violence and Catharsis 285
   E. Conclusions 287
V. Other Aspects of Television's Impact 288
   A. Prosocial Television 288
   B. Understanding Television 290
   C. Advertising and Children 291

[1]Preparation of this chapter and the authors' research were supported by grants from the Macquarie University Research Fund and the Australian Research Grants Committee (Murray & Ahammer, A74/15035 and Murray & Kippax, A74/15190). The ideas presented in this paper greatly benefited from discussions with students and staff during the authors' sabbatical periods at the Center for Children's Television Research, Harvard University (JPM) and the Centre for Mass Communication Research, Leicester University (SK). In addition, our review profited from brief but intensive meetings with researchers at the Centre for Television Research, Leeds University; Programme Research, Organisation Radiodiffusion et Television Francais; Department of Audience and Programme Research, Sveriges Radio; and the Radio and TV Culture Institute, Nippon Hoso Kyokai. Finally, we are indebted to Bill Belson, Jay Blumler, Steve Chaffee, George Comstock, John Cunningham, Cecilia von Feilitzen, Lenni Filipson, Takeo Furu, Henry Mayer, Phil Rushton, Ingegerd Rydin, and Tannis Williams for their comments on an earlier draft.

ADVANCES IN EXPERIMENTAL SOCIAL
PSYCHOLOGY, VOL. 12

VI. Functions of Television 292
    A. A Typology of Needs 292
    B. The Active Audience? 295
VII. Television and the "Real" World 298
    A. Cultivation of Reality 298
    B. Agenda Setting 299
    C. Whose Reality? 300
VIII. Conclusions, Implications, and Research Priorities 301
    A. Effects and Functions 301
    B. Whither Research? 305
    References 307

I. Introduction

This paper is designed to evaluate television's influence within the social context in which the medium is used. The inclusion of contextual variables is important because it emphasizes the notion that television does not affect the individual in isolation, but that its influence must be seen in terms of the audience member's "construal" of the televised message. How the audience will interpret what it views will depend not only upon the content of the programs but also on the nature of the viewer and the context in which the viewing occurs. The mass media are only one source of meanings in the communication of ideas and these meanings coexist with the ideas and meanings inherent in the individual's social situation—both in the narrow sense of the individual's immediate setting and in the broad sense of the individual's cultural context.

Research on the mass media has occupied the talents and time of a large number of researchers in very many countries around the world. However, there have been very few reviews of the literature which compare the results of the efforts of one country with those of another. This paper is an attempt to overcome this deficiency. We not only review the results of studies conducted in a variety of countries, but we attempt to place those results within the cultural contexts of the countries in which the research has been conducted. The nature of television varies from country to country in terms of such factors as the number of broadcast hours available, whether the medium is publicly or commercially owned, and the characteristics of the program content. So, also, there is variation in the characteristics of the audience and the perspectives and orientation of the researchers. It is our aim to reflect this cultural diversity.

The 16 countries from which we have gathered information are Australia, Austria, Canada, Denmark, Finland, France, Germany, Israel, Italy, Japan, Norway, Poland, Sweden, Switzerland, the United Kingdom, and the United States. Each of these countries has a particular view of the nature of television's influence on the lives of its citizens and yet, to some extent, the research results on which this view is based are relatively similar.

The variation in research strategies and theoretical assumptions is quite evident in even the most casual perusal of the cross-national literature. For example, much of the early American research was strongly influenced by learning theory, and particularly social-learning theory. In some of this research there was an overemphasis on the view of the individual as passive rather than active or purposive and the media were seen to affect the individual in a unidirectional rather than in an interactive manner. Later research incorporated societal variables into the framework but often these were reduced to the status of individual variables, such as educational level or socioeconomic status. Similarly, in England and Israel the tendency to emphasize individualistic rather than social perspectives is evident in some aspects of the "uses and gratifications" approach to media research. A basic postulate of this research is that audience members use the media in accordance with the needs that they believe will be satisfied by the media or media content. There is an acceptance of the purposiveness of the individual but the essentially social nature of the media experience is by-passed in as much as these researchers seem to forget that these needs or predispositions of the audience members are socially derived. More recently, in America (Gerbner, 1972; Gerbner & Gross, 1976a, 1976b) and England (McCron, 1976) there has been a move away from the individualistic bias to a social or sociological approach. The mass media are seen to permeate everyday life as major elements in leisure activities. They are also seen as providing information about the wider society as well as establishing a framework of explanations about social and political processes. This framework is not simply a reflection of reality but is, itself, a function of the social, economic, and political contexts within which the media operate. Gerbner and Gross (1976a) nicely summarize this viewpoint: "We begin with the assertion that television is the central arm of American society . . . its function is, in a word, enculturation" (p. 175).

The above view of the media as a definer of social reality, together with the view of the audience as active, is evident in the work of Murdock and McCron (1976) in England and in that of Nordenstreng (1970; 1974) in Finland. Nordenstreng argues that we need both a theory of knowledge and a theory of society in order to understand the role of the media. In other words, first, we need a theory about how an individual's subjective consciousness is formed and how this is related to objective reality (the media constituting part of the input into the formation of this consciousness). Second, we need a theory of society and social relations between members of the society in order to understand how the individual acts on and incorporates the "reality" provided for him or her in part by the media.

With these orientations and perspectives in mind, and with the view that the material conditions and ideologies of the researchers influence the type of research that they do, we turn to the main task of assembling a review of the cross-national evidence concerning television's impact on children and adults. We first look at the manner in which the characteristics of television vary from country to country. Second, we review the ways in which the introduction of television affects the daily lives of children and adults and examine which activities are displaced by television. Third, we examine the effects of televised violence on the viewer's aggressive behavior. Then we summarize other aspects of television's impact, such as the influence of prosocial messages and advertising. Next, we review the area of "uses and gratifications" research and examine the notion that the audience is selective in its use of television. Finally, we shall describe recent research on television as a definer of "reality" and the role that television plays as an agenda setter and purveyor of attitudes and values. In a concluding section, we summarize the main streams of research evidence on television's influence and the likely implications for both further research and the development and implementation of social policy.

II. Television's Culture Context

A. BROADCASTING STRUCTURES

In order to understand the context of the research and research issues, it is necessary to appreciate the extent and nature of the variation in television's characteristics in the countries from which we have drawn the core literature for this review. This description of the nature of television in each country can be summarized in terms of the extent and type of available programming, the mode of ownership and control, and the regulations or proscriptions concerning particular content, such as violence. More detailed descriptions of the structures of television in these countries can be found in the report of the Canadian violence inquiry (Royal Commission on Violence in the Communications Industry, 1976) and a report of an international comparison of children's television which was commissioned by Action for Children's Television (1978). The major aspects of television's structure in 16 countries are outlined in Table I. The emerging picture of the nature of television can be described in terms of geographical and historical similarities.

In the Scandinavian countries, Denmark, Norway, and Sweden, television is controlled by a government monopoly. There is no advertising and television viewing time is generally restricted to about 50 hr/week. There is a strong emphasis on educational and informational programs and a consistently high standard of quality entertainment programs. In Finland a similar picture emerges, although there is a mixed media ownership, both private and government, and limited advertising is allowed.

In the western European countries, Austria, France, Italy, Switzerland, and West Germany, there is a monopolistic control of television by either government-licensed private companies, as in Switzerland, or by government-funded independent broadcast authorities. Viewing time is generally restricted to about 70 hr/week and morning broadcasts are devoted to educational and school programs. In some cases there is very limited advertising, while in other cases more time is devoted to advertising, but none of these broadcasting systems is very dependent on revenue from commercial sources. The programming appears to be slightly "lighter" than that in the Scandinavian countries, but in each country there is special attention given to minority audiences and information and educational programs.

In the only eastern European country examined, Poland, the picture is similar to that of the Scandinavian countries. In Poland, there is a government monopoly and there is very limited advertising. Viewing time is restricted to approximately 50 hr/week on one channel and the second channel, which is devoted to minority interests and cultural and educational programs, is restricted to 22 hr/week.

Israel, the only middle eastern country examined, has a broadcast structure which is modeled on the BBC but is similar to the Scandinavian countries in that there is limited broadcast time (about 30 hr/week) and there is no advertising on television.

In all of the broadcast systems in the countries described above, there are only one or two channels available (there are three exceptions, with three channels) and broadcast time is somewhat restricted. However, when we turn to the Anglo-Saxon countries there is a marked change in the nature of television.

In England, there is no monopolistic ownership of television broadcasting. Of the three channels, two are publicly owned and the third is commercially owned. The average viewing time available is longer in England than in the other countries previously reviewed (broadcasting time is about 90 hr/week). In addition, while the BBC carries educational, information, and quality entertainment programs, the IBA network generally broadcasts "lighter" fare.

In three other Anglo-Saxon countries, Australia, Canada, and the United States, again there is no monopoly ownership of television. Also, in these countries there is a much heavier emphasis on commercial control rather than public broadcasting than is the case in the United Kingdom. All three countries broadcast more hours per week on more channels than any other countries reviewed so far. Furthermore, the commercial networks in these countries carry, or are allowed to carry, much more advertising than any of the other countries above. As both Australia and Canada import many of their programs from the United States (and Canada can receive direct transmissions across the border), there is great similarity in the programming available in all three countries. In general, it would be fair to say that although all three countries have a public television service, the nature of television is dominated by commercial interests which dictate homogeneous programming of a less "heavy" kind than any of the other countries that we have discussed above. There is less attention paid to education,

TABLE I

The Structure of Television Broadcasting in Sixteen Countries

Country	Date of onset	Number of channels or networks and ownership	Broadcast hours	Advertising[a]	Control of violence Formal	Control of violence Informal	Imported content (allowed/actual, %)
Australia	1956	1 public	100 hr/week	None	X		50
		3 commercial	140 hr/week	11 min/hr, P			
				13 min/hr, O			
Austria	1957	1 public	12 hr/day	None			
		1 public	4 hr/day	20 min/day		X	
Canada	1952	1 public	18 hr/day				40
		1 commercial	18 hr/day	12 min/hr		X	
Denmark	1954	1 public	4 hr/day	None		X	52
Finland	1957	2 govt./private	16 hr/day	15%	X		35
France	1945	2 public		Minimal		X	60
		1 public		None			
Germany	1945	1 public	3 hr/day	None		X	40
		2 public	8 hr/day	20 min/day		X	

258

Country	Year	Channels	Broadcast time	Advertising			Percent
Israel	1968	1 public	4 hr/day	None		X	50
Italy	1948	1 public	7 hr/day	5%		X	Minimal
		1 public	4 hr/day	5%			
Japan	1953	1 public	18 hr/day	None	X		10
		1 commercial	18 hr/day	18%		X	
Norway	1960	1 public	50 hr/week	None		X	50
Poland	1954	1 public	9 hr/day	Minimal	X		18
		1 public	22 hr/week				
Sweden	1956	1 public	100 hr/week	None		X	40
		1 public	100 hr/week				
Switzerland		3 govt./private		20 min/day	X		
United Kingdom	1936	1 public	82 hr/week				
		1 public	42 hr/week			X	14
		1 commercial	105 hr/week	6 min/hr			
United States	1939	1 public	16 hr/day	None		X	Minimal
		3 commercial	24 hr/day	9.5 min/hr, P; 13 min/hr, O			

[a]P, prime time, usually 5 to 9 pm; O, other times.

science, and the arts. It is also of interest to note that both Australia and Canada are concerned about the amount of local content shown on their television and are somewhat anxious about the dominance of American programming.

Finally, the last country in our geographical–historical comparison is Japan. It is here that one finds a unique mixture of the European and American broadcast systems. Japan has a very strong and well-regarded public television structure (NHK) as well as an extensive commercial system (NTV). The public system is modeled on the BBC and the commercial system conforms to the American network model. This is not surprising when one considers the history of Japanese broadcasting: an initially British public system which was Americanized following the Second World War.

B.   STRUCTURE AND CONTENT

One might ask, at this point, what is the relationship between these broadcasting structures and program policy and content. It would seem that where there is monopoly control and there is little or no advertising (and these two characteristics of the broadcast structure tend to go together), television policy and programming differ from those instances in which there is private ownership supported by commercial interests. In the former instance, the broadcast day is of a shorter duration, more time is spent on pursuing educational and cultural interests, and the programs, in general, are of a higher quality. Where the broadcasting is primarily supported by commercial interests, as in the United States, Canada, Australia, and Japan, not only are there more hours of television, but less of the programming is devoted to educational and cultural pursuits and more of it is given over to televised violence. There appears to be a relationship between the presence of advertising and the relative predominance of violence on these nation's television screens. This relationship is discussed in more detail in Section IV.

With this summary of the historical and cultural contexts of television in the various countries from which we have drawn the core of the cross-national research, we can now turn to a review of the research findings which are products of these varying milieus.

III.   Television's Impact on Daily Life

A.   TELEVISION USE

1.   Children's Viewing

In the United Kingdom, Greenberg (1976) reports that children spend about 2¾ hr/day watching television. For older children (12–15 years), the average viewing time increases to 3 or 3½ hr/day. These findings for British children accord with the recent results of a survey of the viewing patterns of children and youth (5–18 years) in Australia (Tindall & Reid, 1975; Tindall, Reid, & Goodwin, 1977): (a) children viewed an average of 3 hr/day, with heavier viewing on weekends versus weekdays; and (b) there was a constant rise in the amount of viewing by older children (7–9 years) and preteens (10–12 years). In the United States, various studies (Lyle & Hoffman, 1972; Murray, 1972; Schramm, Lyle, & Parker, 1961) have indicated that children view between 2 and 3 hr/day, and that the amount of viewing increases to a peak in preteen–early teen years and then declines. In Canada, a similar pattern occurs (Canadian Broadcasting Corporation, 1973; 1975) in which young children (2–6 years) watch about 20 hr/week, while older children (7–11 years) watch about 22 hr/week.

In West Germany and Austria, Saxer (in Prix Jeunesse, 1976) reports that the average viewing time for 3- to 13-year-olds is 79 min/day in West Germany and 58 min/day in Austria. An Italian study of the viewing patterns of children aged 0–3 years (Radiotelevisione Italiana, 1974; 1975a) reports considerable contact with television beginning at 4 months. However, these precocious infant viewers were observed to scan the television screen for only brief intervals lasting, at most, only 6 min.

In Switzerland, the picture is very similar to that in Austria and West Germany. A survey of children's viewing, conducted by Schweizerisch Radio- und Fernsehgesellschaft (1974a) indicated that the average amount of viewing was 78 min/day in German Switzerland, 108 min/day in French Switzerland, and almost 2 hr/day in Italian Switzerland. As in other countries, viewing reaches a peak at around 13 years and then declines.

In Sweden, von Feilitzen (1975, 1976) and Filipson (1976) report that the majority of Swedish children start paying serious attention to television at about 3 years. Once they have acquired concentration, preschool children view for about 1½ hr/day. The amount of viewing increases to about 2 hr/day for 10- to 14-year-olds and then, as in other countries, declines rapidly. In Norway, Werner (1971) reports a pattern similar to Sweden, with the average viewing time holding at about 1½ hr/day. In Finland, the average viewing time, according to Haapasalo (1974), is about 2 hr/day.

In Japan, Furu (1971) reports that the average fourth-grade child watches about 2 hr/day, while the tenth-grade child watches about 3 hr/day.

In Israel, where there are only 4 hr of programming per evening, with 3 hr in Hebrew and 1 hr in Arabic, the average amount of viewing is between 2 and 3 hr [despite the fact that there is only a half-hour of children's programming and a half-hour of family programs, such as *Bewitched* (Katz & Gurevitch, 1976; Shinar, Parnes, & Caspi, 1972].

The general pattern that emerges is that countries where there is a large amount of television available (i.e., Australia, Canada, Japan, the United Kingdom, and the United States) are associated with greater viewing on the part of young children, about 2-3 hr/day. In the Scandinavian and European countries for which information was available, the viewing time tended to be lower (i.e., 1-2 hr vs. 2-3 hr). However, in all countries, the age-related pattern of viewing is identical: a gradual rise in viewing time to a peak in early adolescence and then a sharp decline. The differential amount of viewing in these two groups of countries is obviously related to the amount of programming available, both the sheer numbers of hours and the timing of broadcasts (e.g., the first group of countries frequently has programming available in the early morning hours as well as evening-afternoon periods). However, simple magnitude of available television is not the entire explanation because that does not account for the Israeli variation nor the variation in viewing by children living in German, French, and Italian Switzerland.

One further caveat: The figures that we have quoted above are averages and there is a number of variables which are associated with changes in viewing for particular types of children, such as (1) age and intelligence: Among very young children, the bright child tends to spend more time watching than his or her less bright peer, but this pattern reverses in early school years (Lyle & Hoffman, 1972); (2) socioeconomic status: the higher the status the fewer hours spent watching (Dominick & Greenberg, 1970; Bogart, 1972); (3) self-esteem: the higher the self-esteem, the fewer hours spent watching (Edgar, 1977a); (4) sex (Greenberg, 1976); (5) whether the child is a "high media user" or a "high print user" (Furu, 1971); and (6) parental and family viewing patterns (Brown & Linné, 1976). In addition, it is important to note that the amount of time spent viewing television is not normally distributed but is very heavily negatively skewed. For example, Australian data (Murray & Kippax, 1978; Tindall, Reid, & Goodwin, 1977) demonstrate that the majority of children watch, on the average, about 15 hr/week but the overall averages from most studies are inflated because there is a minority (perhaps a substantial minority, e.g., 25%) who view 30-80 hr/week.

2. Adult's Viewing

When we turn to the viewing behavior of adults, a relatively similar general pattern emerges across various countries. In Australia, the mean viewing time for adults is around 17 hr/week, although the majority of adults watch between 9 and 14 hr/week. The heaviest viewers are females, the old, and those from lower socioeconomic groups (Kippax & Murray, 1976, 1977; Murray & Kippax, 1977). Chaffee and Wilson (1975) present a similar picture for the United States. This pattern is echoed by von Feilitzen (1976) for Swedish adult viewers, except it is the men and not the women who are the heaviest viewers—probably because viewing time is limited to the evenings when women are busy with housework. In general, adults, except those over 50 years, spend less time viewing than do children. In Anglo-Saxon countries adults view about 2 hr/day and slightly fewer in the other countries examined, with the exception of Israel, where adults view between 2 and 3 hr/day.

B. DISPLACEMENT OR STIMULATION?

One may ask what changes take place when television is introduced into a community; are some activities displaced and/or does television stimulate other activities? The major studies of the impact of television on children and adults include: Belson (1967), Himmelweit, Oppenheim, and Vince (1958) and Himmelweit and Swift (1976) in England; Coffin (1955) and Schramm, Lyle, and Parker (1961) in North America; and Furu (1962, 1971) in Japan. In addition, smaller scale studies have been conducted in Australia (Murray & Kippax, 1977, 1978), Canada (Williams, 1977), Finland (Nordenstreng, 1969), Italy (Radiotelevisione Italiana, 1975b), Jamaica (Lasker, 1975), Norway (Werner, 1971), Scotland (Brown, Cramond, & Wilde, 1974), Switzerland (Schweizerisch Radio- und Fernsehgesellschaft, 1974a, 1974b), and the United States–Alaska (Corporation for Public Broadcasting, 1975). In general, the results of these studies suggest that there are decreases in radio listening and cinema attendance as well as changes in patterns of daily living, such as sleeping and modifications of social activities, such as visiting friends. However, precise specification of the nature of television's influence is hampered by the difficulty of obtaining sufficiently large, naturally occurring samples of people who do not view television but live in social contexts that are directly comparable to those of the television viewers.

Some of the more recent studies have attempted to gauge television's impact on social life by comparing the daily time budgets of persons living in homes with or without television (e.g., Katz & Gurevitch, 1976; Robinson, 1972a; Edgar, 1977) or in countries with markedly different states of television diffusion (e.g., Szalai, 1972). However, Coffin (1955) and Robinson (1972a) have provided extensive discussion of the methodological problems involved in comparing television owners and nonowners drawn from geographical areas where television is available to both groups as in the case of Edgar's (1977b) study in Australia. Moreover, Belson (1967) has noted that these problems are not resolved by sampling from areas with or without television if the towns are markedly different or are sampled at different historical periods in the diffusion of television. However, with these warnings in mind, we have found that the findings of the various studies, using different approaches in different countries, are remarkably consistent, especially with reference to radio listening, cinema attendance, and reading.

1. Effects on Children

a. *Radio listening.* Schramm, Lyle, and Parker (1961) reported that children from the sixth and tenth grades in Radiotown, a Canadian town without access to television, spent about 3 hr/day listening to radio, while their peers in

Teletown listened to the radio for only 1.3 hr/day. A similar displacement of radio was found in Australia by Murray and Kippax (1978) when they compared the radio listening of 8- to 12-year-old children living in a town without television with the radio listening of their peers who lived in a low-TV town (one channel, for only 1 year) or a high-TV town (two channels, 5-years experience). The children in the no-TV town listened to the radio for more than 4 hr/day, while those in the high-TV and low-TV towns listened for 3 and 2 hr/day, respectively. Himmelweit, Oppenheim, and Vince (1958) reported that their English school children who were the nonviewing controls listened to the radio five times longer than the children who had television. However, they also point out that future viewers were keener radio listeners than the controls before television arrived. In Scotland, Brown, Cramond and Wilde (1974) also noted a marked decrease in radio listening when television was introduced into a small Scottish town. Also, Werner (1971), in Norway, reports decreases in listening to "speech-only" radio programs among younger children while, for adolescents, there was no decline in listening to popular music on radio.

    b. Cinema. A similar pattern of decline in cinema attendance is reported in most countries examined, and many cinemas have been closed. Schramm, Lyle and Parker (1961) in Canada and the United States; Himmelweit, Oppenheim and Vince (1958) in England; Werner (1971) in Norway; and Murray and Kippax 1978) in Australia all report major reductions in cinema attendance. Also, as with radio, the Australian study found a novelty effect in which the largest reductions in cinema attendance occurred among children in the low-TV town, for whom television was newest. In addition, Himmelweit *et al.* (1958) reported that the reduction in cinema was most marked among the 10- to 11-year-olds and the effect was not evident among the 13- to 14-year-olds. The authors suggested that television served the same functions as cinema for the preadolescent, namely, free audiovisual entertainment. However, the function of cinema for the adolescent had little to do with the content that was being shown, serving rather as a reason to leave home and a meeting place for social engagements. Further support for this notion comes from the Australian finding that 1 year after the closure of the only cinema in the high-TV town, parents and youth groups combined to establish an informal weekend cinema in a church hall. We shall return to this topic in the discussion of uses and gratifications research (Section VI).

    c. Reading. The results of various studies of television's impact on reading are somewhat inconsistent. However, it appears that some of this inconsistency can be explained by differentiating between reading comics and reading books. Murray and Kippax (1978) found that reading in general declined when television was available. However, other measures confirmed that the decline was operative only for comics, while book reading actually increased with increasing experience with television. Similarly, Schramm *et al.* (1961), Himmelweit *et al.* (1958), and Brown *et al.* (1974) all report declines in comic reading. With regard to book reading, Schramm reports no difference between viewers and nonviewers, Himmelweit *et al.* report a decrease in book reading followed by a return to pretelevision patterns, and Werner (1971) in Norway reports a drop in the number of books read when television arrived, and this is supported by Furu (1962, 1971) among Japanese children. However, another approach to the question of television's impact on reading is Corteen's (1977) analysis of children's reading skills in three Canadian towns with and without television (Notel, Unitel, and Multitel) as well as before and after the introduction of television in Notel. Corteen found that at time 1 (i.e., before television came to Notel) children in grades 2 and 3 in Notel were superior to their peers in Unitel, and these in turn were superior to the children in Multitel. At time 2 (2 years after television came to Notel) the previous sample was retested and an age–cohort sample was added. The results indicated that the level of reading skills in the Notel children had significantly deteriorated. However, it should be noted that for children in grade 8, there were no differences either across the towns or from time 1 to time 2.

   d. Social life and leisure.   It is more difficult to unravel the effects of television on the social life of the child. This is due, partly, to the different categories used by the various researchers. In general, it is the unstructured outdoor activities that appear to suffer most. Himmelweit *et al.* found a greater decline in walking and being out with friends than in playing or watching sport. Similarly, Murray and Kippax (1978) found linear decreases across the three towns (with increasing television) in general unstructured outdoor activities, but watching sport was also affected. However, the initially large decrement that occurred in the town in which television had just been introduced (low-TV) recovered in the high-TV town.

   Organized social activities, such as dances and clubs, are only very slightly affected by television. Werner (1971), Murray and Kippax (1978), and Himmelweit, Oppenheim and Vince (1958) all report similar results. Once again, moreover, in the Australian study, there was a decline in such activities as clubs, indoor games, and parties with the introduction of television, but the effect was ameliorated with increasing television experience.

   Unlike Himmelweit's *et al.*, the Australian study did not find any decrement in "sitting around doing nothing" nor was there a decrement in playing with friends. This difference between the English and Australian studies may relate to cultural differences in the manner in which these different groups of children conceptualize the dimensions of their daily time budgets. For example, we cannot be sure the "doing nothing" in these two cultures would include the same range of "nonactivities."

    e. Overall effects. The patterns of television's influence on the life styles of children living in America, Australia, Canada, England, and Norway is one of an initial marked decrement in a wide range of activities following the introduction of television, followed by a modest return of interest in these displaced activities. Alternative media (i.e., cinema, radio, and comics) and some unstructured outdoor activities are much more profoundly and persistently affected. However, in the studies in which the design allowed for the measurement of recovery effects, cinema and radio listening manifested some slight return toward the pretelevision levels, although Corteen's (1977) finding of a deterioration in reading skills with increasing experience with television in three Canadian towns raises concern about the qualitative (as opposed to the quantitative) changes in reading that are associated with television viewing. Related to these findings is the continued decrement in reading of comic books which may underscore the functional equivalence of television and comics but not television and books (for comics, the function may be time filling). The decrements in outdoor activities are difficult to explain, but with increasing availability of television, there may be a gain in indoor activity at the expense of outdoor interests. Nevertheless, the overall result is one of a return to pretelevision levels. It is possible that this reemergence of displaced activities is actually stimulated by television viewing. This hypothesis is supported by the increase found for playing with friends (Murray & Kippax, 1978) and the increases in time spent on hobbies (Murray & Kippax, 1978; Werner, 1971). Thus, television, although an initial displacer of social activities, may ultimately foster increased interpersonal contact by serving as a focal point for shared activities, particularly inside the viewer's home.

2. Effects on Adults

    When one turns to studies of television's impact on the life styles of adults, one finds that the results are similar to those described for children but the number of studies is smaller. Murray and Kippax (1977) have studied the patterns of leisure and social activities of adults living in three towns with differing television experiences; Himmelweit (1977) and Himmelweit and Swift (1976) have followed up their sample of children (Himmelweit, Oppenheim, & Vince, 1958) studied during the period of the introduction of television in England; Robinson (1972a) in a UNESCO study (Szalai, 1972), has examined the daily time budgets of television owners and nonowners in 12 countries; Coffin (1955), in the United States, and Belson (1967), in England, have examined alternative media use in competition with the newly arrived television set; Haapsalo (1974), in Finland, has examined the effect of the introduction of television on adult radio listening; and the impact of television on cinema attendance in several countries has been examined by the Royal Commission on Violence in the Communications Industry (1976).

All the above studies found, where examined, decreases in radio listening, cinema attendance, and book reading. However, with the exception of cinema, Murray and Kippax (1977) report a slight recovery effect with increasing experience with television. Thus, as with children, the initial decrements are in part a function of the novelty of television, and with increasing experience with television there is a tendency to return to the abandoned alternative media. The Canadian violence inquiry (Royal Commission on Violence in the Communications Industry, 1976) reported a drop in cinema attendance of about two-thirds of the initial audience during the 10 years following the advent of television in Austria, Denmark, Finland, Germany, and Sweden. In Switzerland there was a 25% drop, while in Norway there was a 50% decrease, but it now seems to be stabilizing and perhaps even increasing. A similar stabilizing effect is now seen in Canada, England, and the United States, where decreases were initially in the range of 50-60%. The younger adults (17-24 years) are the ones who appear to be returning to the cinema. Similarly, in Poland, although 300 cinemas were originally closed down, new cinemas are now being constructed. These results suggest that, although television may serve a function that is similar to cinema, the cinema serves additional functions, particularly for the young.

Robinson's (1972a) analysis of the daily time budgets of television owners and nonowners who were participants in a UNESCO study of life patterns in 12 countries found some interesting increases as well as decreases associated with television ownership. There appear to be decreases in such activities as household care, personal grooming, and some social engagement activities but there are also increases in the time devoted to child care and at-home social contacts. This result mirrors, to some extent, the impact of television on children's activities and, again, there is an increase in home-centered activities. The findings of a recent survey in England (I.P.C., 1975) suggest that television does not eat into leisure time, although it is a large part of it. In general increases were found in some outdoor activities, such as sport, and in the more active pursuits in the home, such as crafts, hobbies, pets, and games. Moreover, Murray and Kippax (1977) found no differences among adults living in the three towns in terms of organized social and club activities and there was an increase in the time devoted to hobbies. However, Williams and Handford (1977), in Canada, have reported that there tends to be a decrease in involvement in community activities in the 2 years following the inception of television, particularly for older adults.

C. CONCLUSIONS

In general, it seems clear that the introduction of television does result in the displacement of some activities for both children and adults. However, it appears that with increasing experience with television, some of this displacement effect dissipates. This rather robust finding can best be illustrated by looking at clusters of activities, such as the use of alternative media or social contacts. In this regard, the data presented in Fig. 1 are drawn from the analysis of the leisure activities and life styles of children and parents living in three Australian towns which have differing levels of experience with television. As described previously, the television experience ranges from none (no-TV) to 1 year and one channel (low-TV) to 5 years and two channels (high-TV). The four clusters of activities that were examined were: alternative media (radio, reading, records, cinema, theater–concerts, and public talks); social engagement (visiting friends, dances–clubs, indoor activities, group activities, outdoor activities, playing sport, and watching live sporting events); individual interests (hobbies and animal care); and time filling (driving around and sitting around doing nothing). It can be seen, in Fig. 1, that as one moves from the no-TV town to the low-TV town, there are marked decrements in all four clusters for children and in three of

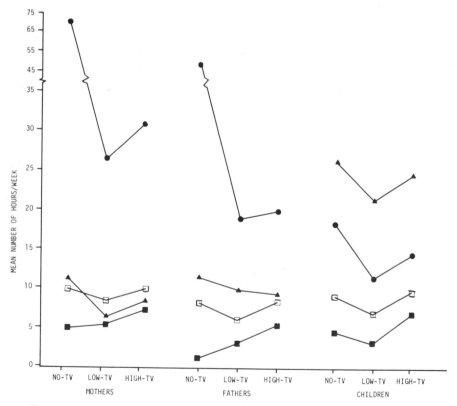

Fig. 1. Parents' and children's leisure activities in three towns. ▲, Social engagement; ■, individual interests; ●, alternative media; □, time filling.

the four clusters for mothers and fathers. Also, the most dramatic decrements were those for mothers' and fathers' involvement in alternative media. However, the other important feature that is evident in Fig. 1 is the fact that many of the activities which were severely depressed in the low-TV town begin to manifest some recovery in the patterns of adults and children's behavior in the high-TV town. Although the recovery effect is most marked for children, there are some modest recovery trends for parents as well. In general, it appears that television does not have a long-lasting displacing effect on adults' and children's life styles. Most of the changes reported in the various studies discussed above were observed when television was establishing itself as a major element in our lives but, as Himmelweit (1977) suggests, when television becomes extensively used, it becomes part of the background of leisure. The foreground, she suggests, is occupied by other things, such as people, music, sport, and hobbies. Those who watch television most are the preadolescent child and the older adult, those from lower socioeconomic background, and the less well educated. Television may be serving a time-filling function for these people; it may fill in time and kill time for those who do not have the education, money, or ability for other outlets. Television is cheap and convenient; it is on tap to be turned to when there is nothing else available.

Another important pattern that emerges from the studies reviewed above is the suggestion that television is, in some ways, functionally similar to radio and cinema. As Himmelweit (1977) points out: "The principle of functional equivalence predicts that an entertainment or activity will be displaced by the newer one provided it serves the same needs as the established activity but does so more cheaply or conveniently" (p. 6). However, it is important to remember that this process of functional equivalence and displacement will vary from individual to individual, or for the same individual at different periods in his or her life. For example, it appears that for adolescents television does not provide the venue for dating that the cinema does, nor does it serve the same function as radio in purveying popular music knowledge which is a coin of exchange for adolescent social contacts (see Chaffee & Tims, 1976).

The notion that television is, at least for adults and younger children, somewhat functionally equivalent to radio and cinema and that the functions served by these media are, to some extent, time filling, is supported by a recent study of families without television in Australia (Edgar, 1977b). These 298 families who answered an advertisement in a Melbourne newspaper had never owned a television set or had got rid of it. Those who participated in this study were middle aged and of higher socioeconomic status and educational attainment than the general population. Ninety-two percent indicated that they belonged to at least one club, and 82% indicated that they had a religious affiliation. They read widely; they were more likely to go to the theater than to the cinema; the majority preferred classical music to other types of music; and over 40% played one or more musical instruments. The chief reason for not having a television set was the fear that it would destroy the quality of their lives. They felt that television "makes people more passive," "it is addictive," and it is a major threat to family relationships and to community life.

Another common feature of viewers' evaluation of television is the feeling that it is a waste of time and, indeed, heavy viewers frequently express feelings of guilt about spending so much time watching television (Bower, 1973; Furu, 1971; Steiner, 1963). Perhaps, television moves into the foreground of the lives of heavy viewers and becomes a habit for those with few other outlets. Thus, although viewing is perceived as a marginal activity, it is one on which a great deal of time is spent. This interpretation may account for the discrepancy in the Himmelweit, Oppenheim, and Vince (1958) result and the Murray and Kippax (1977, 1978) finding that there was no decrement in time-filling activities with the experienced viewers in the high-TV town (although there was an initial decrement in the low-TV town for parents—not children). It may be that, for the experienced heavy viewer, watching television becomes nothing more than filling time by "sitting around doing nothing." We know that for the lighter viewer, television is often turned on for very specific reasons (Kippax & Murray, 1977). Moreover, the lighter viewers are more selective in the programs that they view (Kippax & Murray, 1977). We will return to the issue of the functions of television and the differential "reality" of light and heavy viewers in Section VI and VII.

IV. Impact of Televised Violence

There is probably no other question concerning television's impact that has generated as much public interest and professional study as the question about the influence of televised violence on the viewer's aggressive behavior. During the preceeding decade, there have been numerous reviews and commentaries devoted to this issue (e.g., Bandura, 1973; Berkowitz, 1973; Comstock & Lindsey, 1975; Howitt & Cumberbatch, 1975; Kaplan & R. D. Singer, 1976; Klapper, 1968, 1976; Kniveton, 1976; Liebert, Neale, & Davidson, 1973; Liebert & Schwartzberg, 1977; Murray, 1973, 1976, 1977a; National Broadcasting Company, 1977; Ontario Psychological Association, 1976; Pietila, 1977; J. L. Singer, 1971; Stein & Friedrich, 1975; Weiss, 1969), and not all reviewers are in agreement about the nature and extent of the effects of viewing televised violence. For example, Howitt and Cumberbatch (1975), two British researchers, argued that "the mass media do not have any significant effect on the level of violence in society" (p. vii). However, in that same year, Comstock and Lindsey (1975), two American researchers who reviewed much of the same evidence as Howitt and Cumberbatch, stated: "The widespread belief that the Surgeon General's Scientific Advisory Committee's conclusion that the evidence suggests a causal link between violence viewing and aggression, is correct . . . '' (p. 8; see also Comstock, 1976). Furthermore, the Surgeon General, Dr. Jesse L. Steinfeld, in testimony before the United States Senate Committee which inaugurated the investigation, stated: "While the committee report (Advisory Committee) is carefully phrased and qualified in language acceptable to social scientists, it is clear to me that the causal relationship between televised violence and anti-social behavior is sufficient to warrant appropriate and immediate remedial action. The data on social phenomena such as television and violence and/or aggressive behavior will never be clear enough for all social scientists to agree on the formulation of a succinct statement of causality. But there comes a time when the data are sufficient to justify action. That time has come" (United States Senate, 1972). With this background of controversy we will plunge into the cross-national evidence on the impact of television violence.

The first, and most obvious, fact which emerges from a compilation of the international literature on televised violence is the observation that most of the research in this area has been conducted in the United States. For example, in Andison's (1977) review of 67 studies of television and violence, 54 were carried out in the United States and the remainder in England, Canada, Australia, Japan, and Germany. The only cross-cultural study (i.e., one in which the essential procedures of a study are replicated in another culture) that we have located is a recent study conducted in the United States and Belgium (Parke, Berkowitz, Leyens, West, & Sebastion, 1977). Of course, cross-national comparisons can be made to the extent that researchers have employed either basically similar methods or have based their research on similar theoretical orientations. Nevertheless, in the absence of cross-cultural studies, cross-national comparisons should be tempered by the possibility that the nature of aggression and the factors influencing its expression may vary from culture to culture. For example, Pietila (1976), in Finland, has demonstrated that the nature of violence portrayed on American versus that on Russian television programs differs markedly; in American programs, violence is used for personal gain, while in Russian programs violence is used to further the goals of the state.

A second important feature of the studies that we have assembled is the fact that certain methods are used more frequently with one particular age group rather than others. For example, experimental studies are more likely to be conducted with young children, while correlational studies are more frequent in the adolescent and adult literature on violence. This characteristic of the literature makes it rather difficult to provide direct comparisons across various age groups. However, there are a few studies which allow several points on the age continuum to be mapped. With these caveats in mind, we shall discuss the studies in three methodological clusters: experimental studies, correlational studies, and causal-correlational and field-experimental studies. In each grouping we consider the influence of developmental differences in terms of age and the influence of social and situational factors, where possible. In a fourth section we shall consider the evidence for and against the "catharsis" hypothesis.

A. EXPERIMENTAL STUDIES

The major initial studies of the impact of film and television violence were the experiments conducted in the United States by Bandura and his colleagues (Bandura, 1973; Bandura, Ross, & Ross, 1961, 1963; Bandura & Walters, 1963) with young children, and the studies by Berkowitz and his colleagues (Berkowitz, 1962, 1973; Berkowitz & Geen, 1966; Berkowitz & Rawlings, 1963) with older adolescents–young adults. In a typical study conducted by Bandura (e.g., Bandura, Ross, & Ross, 1963), young children were presented with a film, back-projected onto a television screen, in which an adult model displayed novel aggressive behavior toward an inflated plastic doll. After viewing this material, the child was placed in a playroom setting and the incidence of aggressive behavior was recorded (including, but not limited to, assaults on the plastic doll). The results of several of these studies indicated that the children who had viewed the aggressive film were more aggressive in this setting than those children who had not observed the aggressive model. Similarly, the results of Berkowitz's (e.g., Berkowitz & Rawlings, 1963) studies in which university students viewed violent film clips and then were allowed to express aggression in another setting (e.g., administering electric shocks to a recalcitrant "learner" peer) demonstrated increased aggression among those who had viewed the violent film material. These early studies were criticized because the film material consisted of either segments of a film or a specially produced film sequence and these stimuli were not directly comparable to typical television programs. Also, the studies were criticized because the measures of aggression were not considered to be representative of serious interpersonal aggression. Later studies have attempted to address these criticisms.

1. Children

A more recent example of experimental studies of the impact of televised violence on children's aggressive behavior is an American study conducted for the Surgeon General's research program by Liebert and Baron (1972). In this study, the authors addressed the criticisms of earlier research by studying young children's willingness to hurt another child after viewing videotaped sections of standard typical aggressive or neutral television programs. The aggressive program consisted of segments drawn from *The Untouchables,* while the neutral program featured a track race. Following viewing, the children were placed in a setting in which they could either help or hurt another child by pressing control buttons that would either facilitate or disrupt the game playing performance of the ostensible victim in an adjoining room. The main findings were that the children who viewed the aggressive program demonstrated a greater willingness to hurt another child. The youngest children who had viewed the aggressive program pressed the HURT button earlier and for a longer period of time than did their peers who had viewed an equally stimulating track race. Moreover, when the children were later observed during the free-play period, those who had viewed *The Untouchables* exhibited a greater preference for playing with weapons and aggressive toys than did the children who had watched the neutral programming.

There are, of course, other factors that might moderate the violence-viewing-to-aggressive-behavior equation, such as "selective attention" or "perceptual screening." In order to evaluate these possible contributors to the effects observed in the Liebert and Baron (1972) study, Ekman and his colleagues (Ekman, Liebert, Friesen, Harrison, Zlatchin, Malmstrom, & Baron, 1972), using the children from the study described above, assessed the relationship between children's emotional reactions while they were viewing televised violence and their subsequent aggressive behavior. Children's facial expressions were unobtrusively videotaped while they watched a segment of a violent television program. The researchers could then relate the child's aggressive behavior to facial expressions of emotion while viewing televised violence. They found that children whose facial expressions depicted the positive emotions of happiness, pleasure, interest, or involvement while viewing televised violence were more likely to hurt another child than were children whose facial expressions indicated disinterest or displeasure in such television content.

Further elaborations of more meaningful measures of aggressive behavior can be found in another American study by Drabman and Thomas (1974). These researchers assessed children's willingness to intervene in the ongoing disruptive and assaultive behavior of younger children, following the viewing of aggressive television content. In this instance, children who had viewed the aggressive program were slower to intervene and were more likely to wait until the disruptive behavior had escalated into presumed serious physical assault before they initiated intervention.

Several studies have demonstrated that one exposure to a violent cartoon leads to increased aggression (Ellis & Sekyra, 1972; Lovaas, 1961; Mussen & Rutherford, 1961; Ross, 1972). Hapkiewitz and Roden (1971) found no effects for violent cartoons on children's physical aggression but boys who saw the violent cartoons were less likely to share than their control group peers. In an Australian study (Murray, Hayes, & Smith, 1978a, 1978b), preschool children who had viewed aggressive cartoons, such as *Road Runner,* were more aggressive in a play group than those children who had viewed equally stimulating animated segments of *Sesame Street.* However, these results were mediated by the fact that live peer models of aggression provided by spontaneous play in the postviewing play group were better predictors of aggression than the television programs. The results suggested that viewing aggressive cartoons stimulated aggressive behaviors in some children who, by acting out their aggression, stimulated aggressive behavior in other members of the play group.

Several studies which evaluated children's willingness to use violence to resolve conflict situations following exposure to violent films or television programs (Collins, 1973; Leifer & Roberts, 1972) found somewhat mixed results. In one study conducted by Leifer and Roberts (1972), children who had viewed an aggressive program were clearly more likely to choose violent/aggressive solutions in these conflict situations. However, in another study in the Leifer and Roberts program which employed both violent and nonviolent programs there was no difference in postviewing selection of violent conflict resolution between experimental and control groups. A similar lack of differentiation on this type of measure of aggression was found for children exposed to aggressive or neutral films by Collins (1973).

In an experiment conducted with 5- and 6-year-old children in Sweden, Linné (1971) compared children who had seen 75% or more of the broadcasts of an aggressive American television program, *High Chaparral,* with those who had seen half or less of the series. She found that a higher proportion of the "high-exposure" children chose an aggressive mode of resolving conflict situations. However, she also found that the high-exposure children differed from the low-exposure children in a variety of important dimensions. For example, she found that the high-exposure children watched more television and that their mothers also watch more television. Furthermore, children who chose the aggressive conflict resolutions were more likely to go to bed immediately following viewing of *High Chaparral,* while those high-exposure children who chose nonaggressive solutions were more likely to stay up later and play before going to bed. This study points out a few of the background factors that must be taken into account when pursuing the relationship between television content and social behavior.

2. Preadolescents, Adolescents, and Adults

As mentioned previously, experimental studies of adolescents and adults are considerably less frequent than those conducted with children. However, of the available American studies, those conducted by Berkowitz and his colleagues (e.g., Berkowitz, 1973; Berkowitz, Corwin, & Heironimus, 1963; Berkowitz & Geen, 1966; Berkowitz & Rawlings, 1963), mostly with university students, suggest that exposure to violent films increases the likelihood and magnitude of subsequent aggressive behavior, particularly if the viewer has been previously angered or frustrated prior to viewing the filmed violence. Also, Leifer and Roberts (1972) found that adolescent males and females were more likely to choose aggressive modes of conflict resolution in direct relation to the amount of violence contained in the aggressive program that they had viewed in the experimental setting. Similarly, other studies (e.g., D. P. Hartmann, 1969; Walters & Thomas, 1963) found that male adolescents who had viewed aggressive films were more likely to deliver greater levels of electric shock to a peer in the experimental setting. However, another experimental study with adults conducted by Milgram and Shotland (1973) failed to find any effect on adults antisocial behavior (i.e., breaking into a plastic charity box) during the week following exposure to a television program which repeatedly depicted this act. However, Comstock (1974) provides a detailed review of the Milgram and Shotland study and suggests that the methodology employed was not appropriate to the question of the impact of televised antisocial behavior because the behavior in question (charity box smashing) has such a low environmental base rate that it would be impossible to obtain statistically significant differentials.

In a Swedish experimental study of the impact of televised violence, Linné (1974) examined the effect of both content and context of television/film violence on adult viewer's reactions. She presented adult women with one of three versions of a Swedish "thriller" produced by the professional production training department of Sveriges Radio (SR). Although the three versions contained the same amount of violence and the violent acts were identical in all three versions, the producers had edited the film to produce "low-excitement," "normal-excitement," and "high-excitement" versions. The subjects were told that their main task was to help SR select a new television newsreader but while they were waiting for the videotaped interviews with the five candidates to be arranged, they would be shown some recent films. During the screening of an initial irrelevant film, one of the potential newsreaders entered the room and caused a disruption, insulting the experimenter and the audience. Immediately following this disruption, the women viewed one of the three versions of the violent film. Next, they were asked to evaluate the interviews with the five candidates (including the protagonist). The results indicated that the women who had viewed the high-excitement film were more aggressive toward the newsreader (i.e., evaluated her more harshly) than those in the low-excitement group. In a related additional study, two different sets of films were produced: The first version contained a scene depicting the consequences of aggression in death; the second version did not contain the consequences. In both versions, there was a high-excitement and a low-excitement version. The subjects for this second study were obtained from a random sample of Stockholm adults. The results indicated that, again, those males and females who viewed the high-excitement films were more aggressive than those who viewed the low-excitement versions. However, the second hypothesis, namely, that those who view the full consequences of violence would be more aggressive was not confirmed. Rather, it appeared to be the excitement level which best predicted the extent of aggression following viewing. This arousal hypothesis is a concept that is supported by the results of several studies conducted by Tannenbaum and Zillmann (1975).

B. CORRELATIONAL STUDIES

Most of the studies which have attempted to relate television program preferences or viewing patterns to the viewer's aggressive behavior have tended to concentrate on older children and adolescents. However, a few experimental studies conducted with younger children have also investigated the relationship of home television viewing/preferences to aggressive attitudes and behavior in the experimental setting (e.g., Leifer & Roberts, 1972; Stein & Friedrich, 1972). As was the case with experimental studies of aggression, most of the correlational studies are American, with the exception of a study of television and juvenile delinquency in England (Halloran, Brown, & Chaney, 1970) and two studies in Australia in which an attempt was made to relate film and/or television violence to the viewer's perception/evaluation of violence and aggressive attitudes (Edgar, 1977a; Lovibond, 1967). In addition, the early surveys conducted when television was being introduced into England (Himmelweit, Oppenheim, & Vince, 1958), Australia (Campbell & Keogh, 1962), Japan (Furu, 1962, 1971), and North America (Schramm, Lyle, & Parker, 1961) investigated the relationship between program preferences and aggressive behavior/attitudes.

In general, the correlational studies are fairly consistent in demonstrating that viewing/preference for aggressive television content is related to aggressive behavior and attitudes. Although Himmelweit *et al.* (1958) failed to find a significant relationship between parent's or teachers' ratings of aggressiveness and the presence of a television set in the child's home, all of these early studies in which the researchers related the content viewed or preferred to measures of aggression found positive relationships. For example, Furu (1962, 1971) reported that Japanese children who were rated as high in conflict or high in aggressiveness were significantly more likely to espouse a preference for aggressive hero content. Similarly, Lovibond (1967) found that Australian children whose tastes in several media, such as comics, radio, and television, were aggressive were rated as more aggressive or antisocial. Similarly, Schramm, Lyle, and Parker (1961), reported that Canadian and American children who had high exposure to television and low exposure to print were more aggressive than those with the reverse pattern.

More recent correlational studies continue to support the conclusion that viewing televised violence is significantly related to aggressive behavior but question whether aggressive behavior is necessarily related to preference for violent television content. For example, McLeod, Atkin and Chaffee (1972a;

1972b) have found a strong positive correlation between viewing violence and ratings of aggressive behavior by self, peers, parents, and teachers, but Chaffee (Chaffee, 1972; Chaffee & McLeod, 1972) have reported that, although preference is related to viewing, preference for viewing violence is not strongly related to aggression. Thus, for example, McIntyre and Teevan (1972), who used preference rather than viewing indices, could only report a modest relationship between the violence level of favorite television programs and self-reports of antisocial behavior among older adolescents. However, clear relationships between content and behavior emerge when the studies obtain measures of television viewing. For example, Dominick and Greenberg (1972) found a relationship between extent of violence viewing and willingness to endorse the use of violence by 9- to 11-year-old boys. Also, Robinson and Bachman (1972) found a relationship between the number of hours of television viewing and adolescent self-reports of aggression. In a more extensive analysis of the nature of the content of children's viewing patterns and its relationship to aggressive behavior in 9- to 13-year-old boys and girls, Greenberg and Atkin (1977) found a strong relationship between the extent of violence viewed and aggressive behavior. They report that, on the average, aggressive responses were selected by 45% of the heavy violence viewers compared to 21% of the light violence viewers. Thus, it seems clear that viewing violence is related to aggressive behavior but the relationship between aggressive behavior and preference for televised violence is less clear.

Some of the problems associated with individual differences in children's perception of and reactions to televised violence are illustrated by an Australian study of children's responses to film violence (Edgar, 1977a). In this instance, Edgar found that self-esteem was an important variable in predicting children's reactions in that low-self-esteem children were less likely to understand the screen violence, less able to articulate their concern about disturbing realistic film violence, and less likely to be sufficiently interested in taking action to prevent the occurrence of such realistic violence. However, the picture is further complicated by the fact that these low-self-esteem children were also heavier television viewers, who preferred fantasy rather than realistic programs and tended to use the television set as an electronic companion because they had fewer friends and more disturbed interpersonal relationships.

In summary, it is clear that viewing violence is related to aggressive attitudes and actions. To some lesser extent, moreover, behaving aggressively is related to preference for televised violence. However, whether one is the cause of the other cannot be determined from correlational studies alone. Rather, causal relationships can only be demonstrated by experimental studies and, in some instances, inferred from time-series correlational studies which employ various combinations of partial-correlation or stable-correlate/automatic-interaction detection matching in conjunction with time-lagged correlations between violence preference/viewing and aggressive behavior. Two recent studies which employ some of these techniques are described in the next section.

C. CAUSAL–CORRELATIONAL AND FIELD-EXPERIMENTAL STUDIES

1. Causal–Correlational Analyses

One of the major problems with laboratory-based experimental studies such as those described in Section IV, A, is the fact that the aggressive behavior that can be evaluated in these settings is severely constrained by the obvious ethical concerns. However, this refracted aggression is, of course, criticized on the grounds that it is not identical to the types of aggression or violence that are at the root of the public concern about televised violence. Similarly, the typical correlational study, while dealing with real-life aggression, is usually powerless to elucidate the cause–effect relationship. Therefore, it is necessary to develop alternative strategies which may enhance the causal inference that may be drawn from correlational data. There are two recent studies which address this issue: Lefkowitz, Eron, Walder, and Huesmann (1972, 1977) and Belson (1978).

In the first study, Lefkowitz and his colleagues (Eron, Huesmann, Lefkowitz, & Walder, 1972; Huesmann, Eron, Lefkowitz, & Walder, 1973; Lefkowitz, Eron, Walder, & Huesmann, 1972) confront the issue of ecological validity in studies of televised violence by assessing the relationship between preferences for violent television programs during early childhood and socially significant aggressive behavior in childhood and adolescence. These investigators obtained peer-rated measures of aggressive behavior and preferences for various kinds of television, radio, and comic books when the children were 8 years old. Ten years later, when these young boys had become young men, the investigators again obtained measures of aggressive behavior and television program preferences. Eron (1963) had previously demonstrated a relationship between preference for violent media and aggressive behavior at age 8 but the questions now posed were: Would this relationship hold over a long segment of the child's life span; and, could adolescent aggressive behavior be predicted from knowledge of the person's television viewing habits in early childhood? Using a cross-lagged panel design, it was possible to describe potential causal agents in the televised violence-to-aggressive behavior equation. The simultaneous and time-lagged correlations between preference for violent television and aggressive behavior are presented in Fig. 2. It can be noted that preference for television violence at age 8 years was significantly related to aggression at age 8 years ($r = .21$) but preference for television violence at age 18 was not related to aggression at age 18 ($r = -.05$). When the cross-lagged correlations across the 10-year age span are considered, the important finding is a significant relationship between preference for violent television programs at age 8 years and aggression at

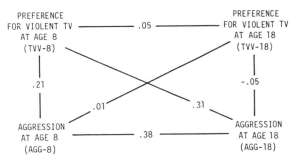

Fig. 2.   Correlations between preference for violent television and aggressive behavior for 8- and 18-year-old boys. (Adapted from Lefkowitz, Eron, Walder & Huesmann, 1972.)

age 18 ($r = .31$). Equally important is the lack of a relationship in the reverse direction (i.e., preference for television violence at age 18 and aggression at age 8 years ($r = .01$). The authors suggest that there is a number of possible interpretations of this pattern of correlations; especially when it is observed that the strongest correlation in the matrix is that between aggression at age 8 years and aggression at 18 ($r = .38$). Therefore, the ultimate interpretation rests upon examining several alternative interpretations and selecting the most plausible. After an examination of some of these alternatives, the authors conclude that: "The single most plausible causal hypothesis is that a preference for watching violent television in the third grade contributes to the development of aggressive habits" (Eron *et al.,* 1972, p. 258). One of the most likely rival candidates is the suggestion that early aggression causes both early preference for violence and later aggression. Figure 3 presents these two interpretations of the data. However, the authors point out that if a partial correlation is computed between preference for violence at age eight and aggression at age 18 while controlling for aggression at age eight, this partial correlation would have to be zero if the

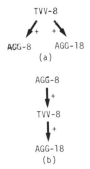

Fig. 3.   Two possible causal hypotheses concerning the relation of preference for televised violence and aggressive behavior. (Adapted from Eron, Huesmann, Lefkowitz & Walder, 1972.)

pattern diagrammed in Fig. 3b is correct. The partial correlation is .25, however, so 3b cannot be the whole explanation. Therefore, Eron and his colleagues favor the causal hypothesis diagrammed in Fig. 3a, namely that preference for televised violence at an early age causes later aggression.

It should be noted that this interpretation is not without controversy and some methodological issues have been raised (e.g., Becker, 1972; Howitt, 1972; Kaplan, 1972; Kay, 1972). Many of these issues have been settled by the reviews of other methodologists (i.e., Kenny, 1972, 1975; Neale, 1972) and the authors have refuted most of the remaining criticisms (Huesmann *et al.*, 1972). However, one criticism that can never be refuted is the claim that both preference for televised violence and aggressive behavior are a product of some third variable. On this issue, however, the authors noted that the correlations between aggression and preference for televised violence were not significantly moderated when they controlled for the child's level of aggression at age eight, socioeconomic status, IQ, parental punishment, parental aggressiveness, parental aspirations for the child, and the number of hours of television watched by the child. However, the multiple regression analyses, for boys, show that preference for televised violence, parental mobility orientation, and identification with the opposite-sex parent are all equally good predictors of aggression at age 18. Also, parental mobility orientation and identification with the opposite-sex parent are good predictors of aggression in 18 year old girls, whereas a girl's preference for televised violence at age eight was negatively related to her aggressive behavior at age 18. It is possible that both preference for televised violence and aggressive behavior are partly related to these two variables, at least for boys.

Another causal–correlational approach to the impact of televised violence can be found in a study commissioned by the American television network, Columbia Broadcasting System, which was conducted in England by an Australian (how delightfully cross-national). Belson (1978) investigated the relationships between long-term exposure to televised violence and the violent behavior of adolescent boys. The results of this study are based upon interviews conducted with a representative sample of 12- to 17-year-old boys residing in London. The total number of persons interviewed in the main study was 1565. The interviews and test procedures conducted on several occasions were focused upon the extent of exposure to a sample of violent television programs broadcast during the period 1959–1971 and upon each boy's involvement in a range of violent acts during the 6 months preceding the interview. The level and types of violence in the television programs were rated by members of the British Broadcasting Corporation's viewing panel. Therefore, it was possible to obtain, for each boy, a measure of both the magnitude and the type of exposure to televised violence (e.g., realistic, fictional, cartoon, etc.). Each boy's level of violent behavior was determined by the frequency of his involvement in any of 53 categories of violent behavior. The degree of violence in the acts reported by the boys ranged from slightly violent aggravation to more serious and very violent behavior such as: ''I tried to force a girl to have sexual intercourse with me; I bashed a boy's head against a wall; I threatened to kill my father; I burned a boy on the chest with a cigarette while my mates held him down.''

The results of Belson's investigation indicated that approximately 50% of the 1565 boys were not involved in any violent acts during the 6-month period. However, of those who were involved in violence, 188 (12%) were involved in 10 or more acts during the 6-month period. When Belson compared the behavior of boys who had higher and those who had lower exposure to televised violence, and who had been matched on a wide variety of variables, he found that the high-violence viewers were more involved in serious violent behavior. Moreover, he found that serious interpersonal violence is increased by long-term exposure to: (a) plays or films in which close personal relationships are a major theme and which feature verbal or physical violence; (b) programs in which violence seems to be thrown in for its own sake or is not necessary to the plot; (c) programs featuring fictional violence of a realistic nature; (d) programs in which the violence is presented as being in a good cause; and (e) violent "westerns." However, Belson also points out that even after a solid and searching matching procedure, it is still possible that the whole or part of this hypothesis is working in reverse. That is, the relationship between televised violence and aggression may be, at least in part, a reflection of the violent boys' tendency to watch the more violent programs just because these boys are violent.

Some additional aspects of Belson's study are, at first glance, rather puzzling, namely, the lack of any significant relationship between the boys' aggressive behavior and attitudes favorable toward the use of violence or callousness concerning aggression. It would seem that the attitudes of these boys were not affected by either viewing televised violence or actual involvement in violence. Certainly, this presents a problem in interpreting this aspect of the study because it is in conflict with the results of many of the correlational studies reviewed in Section IV, B. Belson suggests that this result may have been produced by subtle desensitization effects of viewing televised violence in which behavior change comes about in a gradual sequence in which the viewer adopts an aggressive style of interpersonal interaction but is ''unconscious'' of the reasons for his behavior and, hence, never consciously expresses violent attitudes. Although this rationale presents an intriguing theory, it would require substantially more evidence than is currently available.

2. Field Experiments

Another approach to preserving the ecological validity of both television viewing and response measures is demonstrated in several recent studies of the impact of television or film violence on the social behavior of children and adolescents residing in relatively natural environments, such as the kindergarten classrooms or playgrounds and in the living quarters and grounds of residential institutions.

In one American field experiment conducted with preschool children, Steuer, Applefield, and Smith (1971) attempted to assess the cumulative effects of viewing televised violence. In this small-scale study, 10 preschool children were assigned to five pairs matched on the basis of the amount of home television viewing. Each child was observed in free-play peer interaction for a baseline period of 10 days. Following the baseline period, one child in the matched pair viewed a series of aggressive cartoons and the other child viewed a series of nonaggressive programs. The daily viewing period extended for 11 days. During both the baseline and viewing periods, the frequency of aggressive interaction with peers was recorded for each child. The measures of aggressive behavior were focused on serious aggression, such as physical assaults in the form of hitting, kicking, squeezing, holding down, choking, and throwing an object at another child from a distance of more than 1 ft. The baseline observations indicated that the pairs of children were closely matched on initial level of aggressive behavior. However, by the end of 11 days of viewing, the children who had viewed the aggressive programs were displaying more aggressive behavior in their peer interaction than their matched controls who had viewed the nonaggressive programs. Thus, the significant feature of this study is the demonstrable cumulative effect of exposure to televised violence despite the relatively brief viewing period.

In another, longer term, American study, Stein and Friedrich (1972; Friedrich & Stein, 1973) presented 97 preschool children with a diet of either "antisocial, prosocial, or neutral" television programs. The antisocial diet consisted of 12 half-hour episodes of *Batman* and *Superman* cartoons. The prosocial diet was composed of 12 episodes of *Misteroger's Neighborhood* (a program that stresses such themes as sharing possessions and cooperative play). The neutral diet consisted of children's travelog films. The children were observed through a 9-week period which consisted of 3 weeks of previewing baseline, 4 weeks of television exposure, and 2 weeks of follow-up. All observations were conducted in a naturalistic setting while the children were engaged in daily activities. The observers recorded various forms of behavior that could be regarded as prosocial (i.e., helping, sharing, cooperative play) or antisocial (i.e., arguing, pushing, breaking toys). The overall results indicated that children who were adjudged to be initially somewhat more aggressive became significantly more aggressive as a result of viewing the *Batman* and *Superman* cartoons. Moreover, the children who viewed *Misteroger's Neighborhood* became more cooperative and willing to share toys and to delay gratification.

In a recent Canadian field experiment, the researchers (Joy, Kimball, & Zabrack, 1977) had an opportunity to observe the aggressive behavior of children living in three towns with or without television, Notel, Unitel, and Multitel, and to reassess the children 2 years after television was introduced into Notel. At time 1, the researchers selected a sample of five male and five female children from grades 1, 2, 4, and 5 and at time 2, from grades 1, 2, 3, and 4. In addition, the children who were observed at time 1 were observed again at time 2. Each child was observed for 21 1-min intervals during a 7- to 10-day period. In addition, teacher ratings and peer ratings of aggressive behavior were obtained on all children in the four grades included in the observational study. The results of the longitudinal study of 44 children observed at time 1 and time 2 indicated that there were no differences across the three towns at time 1 but, at time 2, the children in the former Notel were significantly more aggressive, both physically and verbally, than the children in the Unitel or Multitel towns. Moreover, only the children in Notel manifested any significant increase in physical and verbal aggression from time 1 to time 2. The cross-sectional study of 240 children in the three towns at two time periods indicated that children in Notel were significantly more aggressive than their peers in Unitel but not different from their age mates in Multitel. Males were more aggressive than females and children were more aggressive at time 2 than at time 1. For verbal aggression, children in Notel were significantly more aggressive at time 2 than at time 1, but the children in Unitel and Multitel did not increase from time 1 to time 2. The authors suggest that these dramatic increases in Notel at time 2, in contrast to a relatively stable level of aggression in the other towns, might be due to a "disinhibiting" effect rather than to the cumulative effect of viewing, a finding reminiscent of the pattern observed for other social behaviors in the three Australian towns (Murray & Kippax, 1978). The authors suggest that the vehicle by which this disinhibiting effect might operate is through an energizing, activation, or arousal effect, such as that demonstrated by Tannenbaum and Zillman (1975).

In another Canadian field experiment, McCabe and Moriarity (1977) assessed the influence of aggressive or prosocial televised sports programs on the behavior of children and adolescents who were involved in summer training programs in hockey, lacrosse, and baseball. In each of the three programs the children or adolescents were presented with two 30-min edited videotapes of teams playing the relevant sport. In the aggressive condition the tapes were edited to highlight the antisocial verbal or physical accompaniments not infrequently observed in the conduct of that particular sport. Conversely, the prosocial tapes emphasized the cooperative, supportive aspects of team play. The children and adolescents, ranging in age from 6 to 17 (hockey), 7 to 20 (lacrosse), and 6 to 12 (baseball), were observed for evidence of physical, verbal, and nonverbal symbolic aggression and prosocial behavior. The observations were conducted prior to viewing, on the viewing days, and on days following the viewing of the videotaped programs. The only trend in the results was a slight tendency toward an increase in prosocial behavior among the older team members who viewed the prosocial televised sport. It may be that the incidence of antisocial activities on the playing field, particularly for hockey and lacrosse, swamped the television effect, while conversely, the low incidence of naturally occurring prosocial behavior caused the prosocial programs to be something of a novelty for the older, more case-hardened players.

The next field experiment that we shall discuss is the only cross-cultural study of the impact of film or television violence that we have encountered. This series of studies, undertaken in the United States and Belgium, was designed to evaluate the influence of filmed violence on the aggressive behavior of adolescent delinquents (Parke, Berkowitz, Leyens, West, & Sebastian, 1977). All three field studies in this program included the presentation of either aggressive or nonaggressive, unedited, commercial films to groups of adolescent males who were living in small-group cottages in minimum security institutions. Furthermore, the measures of aggressive behavior were based upon naturalistic observations of the boys' behavior in their usual environment. The categories of aggressive behavior observed included physical threats (e.g., fist waving), verbal aggression (e.g., taunting, cursing), and physical attack (e.g., hitting, choking, kicking), as well as a variety of noninterpersonal physical and verbal aggression (e.g., destroying an object, cursing without a social target) and self-directed physical and verbal aggression.

In the first American study, boys in two separate cottages were exposed to a diet of five aggressive or neutral films. These boys had been observed for a 3-week baseline period, followed by a 1-week film-viewing period, followed by a 3-week postviewing observation period. The results of this study indicated that the boys who viewed the aggressive movies were significantly more aggressive in terms of interpersonal verbal and physical aggression ad well as of noninterpersonal verbal and physical aggression against objects and self. In addition, there was a tendency for the greatest increase in aggression to be associated with those boys who were initially somewhat more aggressive.

In the second American study, the duration of observation was increased in the baseline and postviewing periods and the extent of film viewing was varied so that two groups were exposed to five sessions of either aggressive or neutral films and two other groups were exposed to only one neutral or aggressive film. Therefore, the magnitude of effects in relation to the extent of exposure could be analyzed. In general, the results indicated that more dramatic effects of the aggressive movies were obtained in the five-movie diet than in the one-exposure condition. Also, there was an effect for initial level of aggression (those who were initially more aggressive increased most) in the one-film condition but the level of aggression effect was not found in the five-exposure group.

In the third study, the same basic design of the American studies was replicated in a minimum security institution for teenage boys in Belgium. The study included a 1-week baseline observation period, followed by 1 week of film viewing and a 1-week postviewing observation period. There were four cottages involved in which there were two cottages with high aggressive behavior and two with low levels of aggression. One of each pair of cottages was assigned to the aggressive film condition, while the other two viewed the neutral films. The results of this study indicated that only the two initially high-aggressive cottages were affected by the movies; those boys who saw the aggressive movies increased their level of aggression, while those who were exposed to the neutral films reduced their level of aggression. Thus, there is some evidence that predispositional factors related to aggressiveness may be catalysts in producing either increases or decreases in film-mediated behavior.

D. TELEVISION VIOLENCE AND CATHARSIS

Standing in opposition to these accumulated findings on the effects of media violence is a major study by Feshbach and R. D. Singer (1971) which suggests that viewing televised violence reduces the likelihood that the viewer will engage in aggressive behavior. The theory underlying this study stipulates that the child who views violence on television vicariously experiences the violence, identifies with the aggressive actor, and thereby discharges his pent-up anger, hostility, and frustration. In the Feshbach and Singer study, adolescent and preadolescent boys were presented with a "diet" of either aggressive or nonaggressive television programming over a 6-week period while the researchers concurrently measured the day-to-day aggressive behavior of these boys. The results indicated that, in some cases, the children who viewed the nonviolent television programs were more aggressive than the boys who viewed the aggressive programs. However, this research has been seriously questioned on methodological grounds (Liebert, Sobol, & Davidson, 1972; Liebert, Davidson, & Sobol, 1972); the authors have replied to some of these criticisms (Feshbach & Singer, 1972a, 1972b) but serious doubts remain. For example, the reliability of the main measure of aggressive behavior, daily ratings by institutional personnel (e.g., teachers, houseparents) was not clearly established during the study. Furthermore, the raters were untrained and, more serious, were knowledgeable about the treatment condition to which their ratees were assigned. In another instance, the boys who were supposedly restricted to nonaggressive programs were, in fact, allowed to routinely view their favorite program, *Batman* (one of the more violent programs in the aggressive diet).

There are however, more general problems with the catharsis notion when applied to the mass media. The concept of catharsis, as it is formulated in psychoanalytic or dynamic theories of personality development, requires the experiencing of a rather intense emotional involvement which, we know from both common observation and research, appears to be lacking in most television viewing contexts. The only media setting in which the intensity of involvement might possibly be sufficient to postulate the operation of catharsis is the reading

of fairy tales to very young children (Bettelheim, 1976; Murray, 1977a). In this
latter setting, it is possible that the parental mediation of the impact of the fairy
tale by controlling intensity of emotion, sequencing of content, and pacing of
development in response to the child's feedback, could bring about catharsis of
aggressive fantasies; especially when there is an opportunity for a repeated
"working through" of these feelings in subsequent repetition of a fairy tale
selected by the child as one which deals most directly with emotional issues that
are of immediate concern to that particular child.

　　More concretely, in terms of research findings, there is little evidence from
other studies which would support the catharsis notion when applied to televised
violence. For example, a replication of the Feshbach and Singer study by Wells
(1973) failed to demonstrate the existence of a catharsis effect. Furthermore, the
catharsis effect does not square with other, more general research findings to the
extent that, if viewing televised violence leads to a decrease in aggressive behavior, then, in various other correlational studies, preference for and viewing of
violent programs should be inversely related to aggressive behavior (i.e., by
reducing aggressive behavior, aggressive children should ultimately cease viewing and preferring aggressive television programs). Of course, this is not the
case. As Chaffee (1972) points out, children who are more aggressive are also
more likely to view televised violence. For example, in summarizing a range of
recent correlational studies, Chaffee suggests that some of the imprecise findings
in the television violence and aggression literature are due to a failure to differentiate between the effects of preference for televised violence and actual
viewing of violence. When the studies included actual measures of viewing
rather than preference, there was a much stronger relationship of the type diagrammed in Fig. 4. Also, when one includes the findings from laboratory and
field-experimental studies the causal process is clarified. Thus, the weight of the
evidence on the televised violence issue warrants, at the very least, caution and
concern as well as action. The type of action that has been or could be taken will

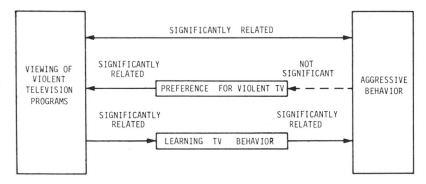

Fig. 4.　Relation of violence viewing to aggressive behavior. (Adapted from Chaffee, 1972.)

vary from culture to culture because we know that television is not the only cause of violence in society.

At this point in the state of the available research on catharsis, the most viable interpretation is the suggestion that, although for some children under some circumstances viewing televised violence may enable the child to discharge some of his or her aggressive feelings, for many children under many circumstances viewing aggression on television leads to an increase in aggressive feelings, attitudes, and behavior. Indeed, one of the principal proponents of the catharsis hypothesis, R. D. Singer, has recently acknowledged (Kaplan & Singer, 1976) that the original formulation of televised catharsis was likely to be erroneous (for a recent review of theory and research on catharsis, see Geen & Quanty, 1977).

E. CONCLUSIONS

Any attempt to provide a concise summary of the state of the research on televised violence and aggressive behavior is fraught with hazards. However, there is one broad conclusion which is quite clear, namely, that there is a relationship between violence on television and violence in society. The relationship is not straightforward and there are many aspects which, in the absence of firm, replicated findings, must be dealt with on the level of reasonable scientific guesstimates. For example, we know that there is a myriad of variables which must be entered into the violence-viewing-to-aggressive-behavior equation. We have outlined some of the major variables such as age, sex, socioeconomic status, preexisting aggressive tendencies, self-esteem, frustration, and other social-situational variables, such as family communication patterns, child-rearing practices, and family structure. Alas, moreover, all of these variables have a nasty tendency to interact, thereby making the task of presenting a succinct causal statement rather risky. However, despite these caveats, there is sufficient cumulative evidence to warrant the view that televised violence is one factor in the production and maintenance of violence in society. Other powerful candidates for the production of violence are such factors as the unequal distribution of income and resources as manifested in ethnic/racial/social class discrimination. Moreover, the questions raised in Section II concerning the intimate relationship between the existence of a commercial television structure and the prevalence of violence on a nation's television screens require further exploration. Thus, there is a need to examine the debate about televised violence within the broader social and cultural contexts in which television has developed in various countries. As Gerbner (1976) has noted, American television is concerned with, among other things, the making of consumers. Perhaps it is, as Halloran (1977) suggests, that the presentation of material goods through advertising "... may increase expectations unrealistically, aggravate existing problems, contribute to frustration, and consequently to the aggression and violence that may stem from this'' (p. 7).

V.   Other Aspects of Television's Impact

Recently, there has been an expansion of research interest in the effects of television on aspects of the viewer's behavior other than aggression. There is an extensive literature on the effects of television on adult voting behavior and the political socialization of children and adolescents, but this material has been discussed at length elsewhere (i.e., Blumler & McQuail, 1969; Comstock, Chaffee, Katzman, McCombs, & Roberts, 1978; Kraus & Davis, 1976; Mendelshon & Crespi, 1970; Tolley, 1973) and is not reviewed in this paper. However, this section includes a brief review of three research topics that have recently received considerable attention, particularly with regard to their effects on children's behavior; namely, prosocial programming, media literacy, and television advertising.

A.   PROSOCIAL TELEVISION

Most of the early research on children and television was focused upon the impact of televised violence to the exclusion of other forms of interpersonal behavior which might be acquired from television (cf. Comstock & Fisher, 1975; Murray, Nayman, & Atkin, 1972). However, it seems reasonable to assume that "prosocial" or "socially valued" behavior, such as sharing, cooperation or helping, could be learned as easily as assaulting. Recently, moreover, there has been an upsurge in research devoted to the impact of prosocial television programs. The review to be presented in this section is condensed because a more comprehensive discussion of prosocial television is provided by Rushton (1979, this volume).

Much of the current research in this area is based upon a social-learning framework which can be seen in some of the attempts to influence children's moral judgment (e.g., Bandura & McDonald, 1963; Cowan, Langer, Heavenrich, & Nathanson, 1969) and cognitive development and conceptual functioning (e.g., Debus, 1970; Murray, 1974; Zimmerman & Rosenthal, 1974). More recent studies have employed standard television programs that are assessed to contain a large number of prosocial messages in an effort to study the impact of more natural television viewing on children's socially valued behavior (see Stein & Friedrich, 1975; Rushton, 1976a, 1976b). For example, the Stein and Friedrich (1972) study which was discussed earlier (Section IV,C,2), found that even a relatively brief exposure to 12 episodes of *Misterogers' Neighborhood,* a program which stressed the themes of sharing and cooperative behavior, was associated with increases in cooperation, nurturance, verbalizing feelings of self and others, and self-regulation. Other studies, all employing various episodes of *Misterogers' Neighborhood* (H. L. Collins, 1974; W. A. Collins, 1975; Cosgrove & McIntyre, 1974; Friedrich & Stein, 1975; and Stein, Friedrich, & Tahsler, 1973), have found increases in the learning of such prosocial concepts as helping, sharing, task persistence, cooperation, and empathy. In addition, two other studies using the same program (Fox, Stein, Friedrich, & Kipnis, 1977; Singer & Singer, 1976) found increases in young children's productive fantasy, imaginativeness of play, and creativity.

Other studies have explored the use of other types of programs, such as *Sesame Street* (Coates, Pusser, & Goodman, 1976) or *Lassie* (Sprafkin, Liebert, & Poulos, 1975), and have reported similar increases in prosocial behavior. In an extension of this line of research, Murray and Ahammer (1977) presented preschool children with a diet of either prosocial or neutral television programs for one-half hour per day, 5 days/week, for 4 weeks. The prosocial diet consisted of standard commercial children's programs, such as *Lassie, I Love Lucy, Gilligan's Island, The Brady Bunch,* etc., which were judged, on the basis of detailed content analyses (Rubinstein, Liebert, Neale, & Poulos, 1974), to be high in prosocial themes. The neutral programs were drawn from many of the same series but were low in both prosocial and aggressive themes. The results indicated significant increases in helping behavior when the children who had viewed the prosocial diet were contrasted with those who had viewed the control, neutral television programs.

The results of these studies which operate within the framework of social-learning theory can be used to develop a wide range of television programs designed to foster specific educational and social skills. Perhaps the most familiar example of this type of programming and applied research is the work of Children's Television Workshop in developing *Sesame Street* (Ball & Bogatz, 1970; Lesser, 1974; Palmer, 1973). A recent addition to this trend in children's television is *Fat Albert,* a series of programs developed by the Columbia Broadcasting System (CBS) in the United States. Each episode in the series is designed around one major theme with a variety of prosocial messages embedded in the program. In assessing the effectiveness of this format for transmission of socially valued information, the researchers (Columbia Broadcasting System, 1974) interviewed children who had viewed an episode of *Fat Albert* under either "captive" or natural (home) viewing conditions. In the captive condition children were presented with a videotape of an episode and interviewed immediately after the viewing period. In the natural viewing condition interviewers contacted the children within 5 hours after the episode had been broadcast on national television. The results indicated that approximately 90% of all children interviewed could recall at least one prosocial message. Furthermore, there was no significant difference between the captive and natural viewing conditions in terms of the number of children receiving one or more prosocial messages. This

American television network has continued this line of research in the production of four additional series for young children (*The Harlem Globetrotters Popcorn Machine* and *The U. S. of Archie*) and adolescents (*SHAZAM* and *ISIS*) and reports similar success in "reaching" these viewers (Columbia Broadcasting System, 1977).

Additional program formats have been designed to encourage American children's awareness of the life styles of children living in other parts of the world (*Big Blue Marble*). In one evaluation of the effectiveness of this program, Roberts and his colleagues (Roberts, Herold, Hornby, King, Sterne, Whitely, & Silverman, 1974) presented young viewers with four episodes of this series and measured pre- and postviewing attitude change in a variety of areas, such as ethnocentrism and perceived similarity. Among the major findings were increases in perceived similarity and wellbeing of children around the world and a decrease in endorsement of ethnocentric beliefs. It should be noted that the range of behavior that could be considered to be "prosocial" is not restricted to simply helping, sharing, and cooperation. Perhaps "socially valued" is a more adequate term to describe these developing programs because the content of these new series addresses such issues as the sex-role stereotyping noted by Sternglanz and Serbin (1974) by presenting competent female heros such as *ISIS* (Columbia Broadcasting System, 1977), or promotes career awareness in programs such as *Countdown to the 70's, Watcha Gonna Do,* and *Bread and Butterflies* (Leifer & Lesser, 1976). Whether prosocial or socially valued, however, it is a format whose time has come.

B. UNDERSTANDING TELEVISION

The literature on children's understanding of television has a fairly short history. Most of the early studies and topics have their origins in research conducted during the development of *Sesame Street* (Lesser, 1974; Palmer, 1973). However, it should be noted that there was an independent growth of interest in studying this topic in several European and Scandinavian countries (e.g., Faith-Ell, von Feilitzen, Filipson, Rydin, & Schyller, 1976; Sturm, 1976). Since a large proportion of the research in this area is of more direct interest to developmental rather than to social psychologists, this material is merely referenced in this section.

The small but growing body of research in understanding television is designed to provide information on how and why children attend to television (e.g., Anderson & Levin, 1976; Anderson, Levin, & Sanders, 1977; Flagg, 1977; Flagg, Allen, Geer, & Scinto, 1976; Levin & Anderson, 1976), the types of cognitive skills that are facilitated or disrupted by television (Corteen, 1977; Furu, 1977; Gadberry, 1977; Harrison & Williams, 1977; Rydin & Hansson, 1970), and the ways in which children develop "media literacy" as a result of their ardent viewing (Rydin, 1972/1976, 1976; Salmon, 1972, 1974a, 1974b, 1976, 1977, Stein & Wright, 1977).

C. ADVERTISING AND CHILDREN

The impact of television advertising on children (and their parents), is a relatively recent research topic in terms of the availability of research findings to the general public. Although there is a long history of research on the impact of various advertisements and advertising strategies conducted for the advertisers by private research firms, this proprietary research is not available for review (and some researchers feel that it would not be of much value because of its parochial nature).

Some of the earliest public research on advertising and children is the American work of Ward and his colleagues for the Surgeon General's research program (Ward, 1972; Ward & Wackman, 1972; Ward, Levinson, & Wackman, 1972). The results of this research indicate that children can remember advertising slogans and jingles, and their knowledge of particular brand-name products results in children's attempts to obtain the advertised goods by influencing their parents in the purchase situation.

Although much of the research on advertising and children has been conducted in the United States, it is a concern in other countries where advertising is permitted on television, such as Australia, England, Italy, and Japan. Recently, researchers at the Servizio Opinioni of Radiotelevisione Italiana conducted a review of the influence of advertising televised on *Carosello* (a half-hour program which follows the evening news and consists solely of advertising). Their report (Instituto DEMOSKOPEA, 1975) suggests that many children watch *Carosello* and most children are influenced by the advertisements. In addition, Italian Television has recently allowed commercials which interrupt the program in a manner similar to that allowed in the United States and Australia, and they report growing concern by parents about this increased advertising. They report that one father described *Carosello* as "an evening initiation ritual for consumers." The researchers conclude that this "ritual" has a broad impact on the consumer socialization of young children. In passing they report on the results of interviews with young children in which a young girl modified Cinderella's story by introducing a Fiat 500 as a gift for the princess, while another 8-year-old longs not for Prince Charming but for "Captain Dash" (p. 280).

Similar concern in the United States led the National Science Foundation to undertake a review of existing research on advertising and children. It has recently issued a summary report and literature review (National Science Foundation, 1977) which concludes that the available research has clearly demonstrated that children attend to and learn from commercials; that advertising is moderately successful in creating positive attitudes toward and a desire to obtain the advertised products; and that the younger viewers are much more vulnerable to the persuasion of advertisers. Further support for these conclusions can be found in a recent report on a program of studies devoted to the child as a consumer by Ward, Wackman, and Wartella (1977). This concern echoes the fears expressed by Gerbner, in the United States, and Halloran, in England, as noted in the concluding remarks to Section IV. Advertising not only may turn children into consumers, but it also supports the very programming—violent programming— which is the cause of grave concern. Once again, it is reasonable to point out that this concern with consumer socialization is closely tied to the social structure of particular countries, such as the United States, Canada, Australia, England, and Japan. Advertising and consumer socialization is not a major issue in the Scandanavian countries except to the extent that they are concerned about the consumer- oriented values implicit in imported programming from England and the United States (von Feilitzen, 1975). Nevertheless, research on consumer socialization can be incorporated within the broad socialization literature and it would appear that children learn consumer values from television in a manner which parallels the learning of aggressive or socially valued behavior.

VI. Functions of Television

Most of the research on the topic of television and children, and a large proportion of the research on adults' involvement with television, has been focused upon the "effects" rather than the "uses" of television. The research question asked most often is: "What does television do to . . . ?" However, one could also pose the question: "What does the viewer do to (or with) television?" It is this second question which provides the focus of research reviewed in this section.

A. A TYPOLOGY OF NEEDS

An audience is composed of a wide variety of individuals who presumably espouse a wide variety of reasons for turning to television, radio, or print for viewing, listening, or reading. The uses and gratifications approach was evolved in an attempt to explore the manner in which the audience member uses specific media or specific content within a medium to gratify particular needs or gratify certain goals or expectations. One of the first attempts was Herzog's (1944) investigation of the gratifications derived from listening to radio soap operas. Herzog found that the American housewives she interviewed expressed three main reasons for listening: (a) to experience emotional release, (b) to engage in fantasy or wishful thinking, and (c) to be informed. Later studies (e.g., Katz & Foulkes, 1962) posited a unifunctional model which suggested that the main function of the media was to provide "escape" from the real world, while Schramm, Lyle and Parker (1961) argued that the media serve two functions: escape and information. However, it was not until the early 1970s that there was a concerted effort to elaborate the empirical bases of the uses and gratifications approach.

In England, McQuail, Blumler, and Brown (1972), studied the pattern of gratifications derived by listeners to a radio serial (*The Dales*) and viewers of television news, adventure, and quiz programs. They hypothesized that: (a) An important part of mass media use is goal directed; (b) these goals can only be discovered from the audience itself, i.e., that the audience is aware of its goals and can verbalize them; and (c) any audience member may be motivated toward any particular medium for a variety of different reasons. The results of this study indicated that audience members can verbalize the reasons they turn to certain media and to certain programs within a medium. A cluster analysis of the various needs identified as being fulfilled by these diverse programs resulted in a fourfold typology of needs relating to: (a) diversion, (b) personal relationships, (c) personal identity, and (d) surveillance. Thus, for example, audience members indicated that they used radio and television to escape the boredom of everyday life, to have something to talk about with others, to compare the people and events in the programs with their own experience, and to keep in touch with the main events of the world. In the United States, Robinson's (1972b) review of a series of related studies of viewing behavior suggests a similar description of the possible functions of television, namely, "utilitarian, ego-defensive, value expressive, and informative." Moreover, this description of the functions of television is very similar to D. Katz's (1960) proposed model of the functions of attitudes.

The studies described so far are in the Herzog tradition. Viewers and listeners were asked to indicate why they selected and used certain media or certain programs. As noted previously, audience members seem quite aware of their needs or reasons for media selection and can express these needs. Katz, Gurevitch, and Haas (1973) provided a further development of this functional theme. They were interested in how the audience evaluated the various media with respect to each medium's role in gratifying needs or fulfilling expectations: They questioned the audience member's perception of the role of the various media in the gratification process. The results of their study in Israel supported the fourfold typology of media-related needs described by McQuail *et al.* (1972), but in addition, Katz and his associates found that the media were perceived as differentially useful in gratifying these needs. In general, these results demonstrated that television was perceived as serving all four clusters of needs. It was perceived as the least specialized of all the media and was seen as useful for "killing time," keeping in touch with world events, and providing vicarious social contact. Radio's functions were similar to television in that it, too, served all clusters of needs. However, books, newspapers, and films were perceived as serving more specific needs. Books served needs related to personal identity; newspapers served information needs; and films satisfied needs for diversion.

A replication of the Katz, Gurevitch and Haas (1973) study in Australia by Kippax and Murray (1976) indicated that the needs of the Australian adults were relatively similar to their Israeli counterparts. A factor analysis of the needs endorsed by these adult respondents could be described as relating to: (a) self and personal identity, (b) social contact, (c) diversion and entertainment, and (d) information and knowledge about the world. Television was perceived as the most gratifying of the media; its functions appeared diverse and it was perceived as satisfying needs contained in all four factors.

The cross-national evidence derived from three studies in England, Israel, and Australia, as well as a review of related studies in the United States, support the basic view of a fourfold typology of media-related needs. Moreover, a review of theory and research in various Scandinavian and European countries provides additional support for a consistent structure of media functions. For example, Kjellmor (1973), in Sweden, indicates that a factor analysis of the functions of broadcast media results in three functions: escape or diversion, self-improvement through information and knowledge, and social utility, which covers both advice and assistance for practical action. In Finland, Nordenstreng (1969, 1970) speaks of the media as providing contact with the world and Pietila (1974) proposes three basic functions: "world view, diversion and social utility." In France, Ripert (Prix Jeunesse, 1975) argues for three similar functions for television, namely, entertainment, information, and utility. In Canada, television's appeal is described in terms of its functions of surveillance and relaxation (Canadian Broadcasting Corporation, 1975). Finally, in one of the few studies to report on the functions of the mass media for children, von Feilitzen (1976) identifies five groups of needs: entertainment, information, social contact, escape, and media preferences. Furthermore, she indicates that after the peak in television viewing at about age 12, escape and entertainment factors gain in importance. Thus, the general picture of the functions of media is constructed from usually four clusters of needs relating to personal identity, personal relationships or social contact, entertainment or diversion, and information or surveillance. (However, when only the broadcast media are included in the study, the personal identity cluster is greatly diminished in value.) Within this framework, use of a particular medium or content within a medium is related to attempts on the part of the audience member to gratify particular types of needs.

The results of the studies described above suggest that the media do satisfy, or are perceived to satisfy, certain needs. However, there are still some major gaps in the empirical validation of the full functional model. This model has been described by Katz and his associates (Katz, Blumler, & Gurevitch, 1974) as concerned with (1) the social and psychological origins of (2) the needs which generate (3) expectations of (4) the mass media or other sources which lead to (5) differential factors of media exposure or engagement in other activities resulting in (6) need gratification and (7) other consequences. Research within the uses and gratifications framework does seem to support the notion that audience members do have expectations of the media which relate to certain needs and that these persons can verbalize their needs. Moreover, the studies by Katz, Gruevitch, and Haas (1973) and Kippax and Murray (1976) demonstrate that the media are perceived as gratifying these felt needs. However, these studies do not show that the audience is active in its selection and use of the media, a strong criticism raised by Elliott (1974) and Chaney (1972).

B. THE ACTIVE AUDIENCE?

The problems associated with the concept of an active audience arise from the circulatity inherent in much of functional analysis. As Chaney (1972) points out, in order to avoid being tautological the researcher must explain why a particular individual has particular needs or expectations, and the researcher must also account for these needs independently of media use. In other words, in order to be able to claim that audience members select certain media to gratify certain needs, a relationship between media use and audience members' needs must be shown to exist over and above the social and situational origins which both variables, needs and media use, have in common. For example, watching soap operas on television can be shown to be related to certain social and situational characteristics of the viewer, such as being a housewife. In addition, these social characteristics can also be shown to be related to the expression of certain needs and media expectations in the viewer, such as "escape." To claim that soap operas function to satisfy escapist needs, however, this relationship must hold over and above the characteristics of being a housewife. If this independent relationship cannot be demonstrated, then the concept of "need" adds nothing to an understanding of media use. Only if these relationships are demonstrated can one claim with certainty, as do McQuail, Blumler, & Brown (1972) that: "The meaning of an example of viewer behaviour is not self-evident from knowledge of content alone, or of the social-demographic parameters of an audience, but can only be explained in terms of a relationship in which the individual takes certain expectations to the interaction and responds with reference to these expectations" (p. 158).

With this in mind, Kippax and Murray (1976, 1977), in Australia, designed two studies to examine whether audience selection and use of the media were goal directed. The first study was focused upon choice among various media, while the second study examined choice within one medium—television. In both studies, it was hypothesized that media/program selection is determined by media/program characteristics and the specific needs of the audience member as mediated by the media user's situational and social role characteristics.

In the first study, Kippax and Murray (1976) found that needs were not clearly related to media use. Selection or use of newspapers, television, or radio could not be predicted by reference to the needs of audience members, although cinema attendance and, to a lesser extent, book reading could be related to the users' needs. It was found that films serve an entertainment function, and books appear to satisfy needs associated with personal identity (although this latter relationship is not clear cut). However, although newspapers were perceived to perform a specific function, that of satisfying information needs, there was no relationship between use of this medium and the need for information and knowledge about the world. The remaining media, television, radio, and magazines, were perceived as serving diffuse needs but, as with newspapers, there was no relationship between the use of any of these media and need gratification. Either the audience is not active in its selection among these media or, as Elliott (1974) noted, the diffuse quality of these media precludes the possibility of identifying the specific functions that these media may serve.

The results of the second Australian study (Kippax & Murray, 1977) do support the arguments that audience members are goal directed in their use of television and that the selection of specific programs is, to some extent, determined by the viewers' needs. These needs are, in turn, related to the situational and social characteristics of the viewer. However, both needs and social characteristics of the viewer contribute to program selection. Television is perceived as best gratifying escape or entertainment and information needs and also, but minimally, social contact and personal identity needs. Moreover, television is not only perceived as gratifying these needs, it is also used as a source of gratification. Individuals who endorse information needs do watch more information programs. Those who endorse social and personal identity needs do watch more of those programs, such as popular drama and movies, which can be seen to serve those needs related to vicarious social contact. However, there are no specific programs that particularly serve those with escapist needs; in this case, any program content suffices.

Program selection is also determined, to some extent, by demographic and situational characteristics. With the exception of age, the demographic characteristics roughly divide the sample into two groups: The males, the better educated, upper socioeconomic groups, and those who go out to work tend to watch more current affairs, information, news, sport, quiz, and variety programs; and the females, the less well educated, the lower socioeconomic groups, and those who do not go out to work watch more popular drama, detective programs, movies, and children's programs. The old in this study tended to watch more of most types of programs while the young watched more comedies, thrillers, and popular drama. The middle aged watch more news, current affairs, information, quiz, and variety programs. These demographic characteristics are, of course, related to one another and they are also related to the amount of viewing. The males, the better educated, those from the upper socioeconomic groups, and the middle aged, watch less television than the females, the old, the less well educated, and those from the lower socioeconomic groups who constitute the heavy and available viewers. Television, it appears, does fill in time and kill time for this latter group. Thus, for those who do not have the education or the money or the time for other outlets, television is the medium of choice. However, television also provides, in a more positive manner, a source of information and relaxation for most, and a source of social contact for some.

Thus is does appear that individuals take certain expectations to the media and that these expectations influence their choice and selection both among the media—at least cinema and books—and within the medium of television. Whether the media also meet these expectations and gratify the audience members' needs is still open to further question. Chaney (1972) argues that the answer to this question must be sought in terms of the normative orientations and symbolic definitions comprising the individual's motivation. There is a need for a much finer and more detailed analysis of the social context and situation of the individual and its meaning for her or him. The demographic and social role variables used in the Kippax and Murray (1976, 1977) studies are too gross and lack the required subjectivity.

There have been a few studies in England, arising out of the work at Leicester and Birmingham universities with subcultural groups, which bear on this problem. One study by Murdock and Phelps (1973) indicates that popular music functions as part of the defining characteristics of certain subcultures. Troyna (1977), in his work on "reggae"—West Indian popular music—and Cohen (1972), in his exploration of "mods' " and "rockers' " use of the media, show how the media may be used in the negotiation of self-identity and definition. As Murdock and Phelps (1973) point out, ". . . the evidence tends to indicate that pupils actively choose both the sort of programs, magazines and records they will look at or listen to . . . the sorts of choices and evaluations which pupils make is not arbitrary or random, rather they appear to be strongly related to their experience of the school system, to their social class background, and to the neighbourhood milieu in which they spend their leisuretime" (p. 125).

Whether these findings can be generalized to all broadcasting media or to television, in particular, remains to be tested. However, the uses and gratifications research of Herzog (1944) has led, after some time, to a large number of studies which have thrown light on the functions served by the media. The studies reviewed in this section support the view that the audience is active in its use of the media and that media use is related to certain expectations and needs that audience members hold. The needs for information and surveillance, entertainment and diversion, and social contact appear consistently across all the studies. Moreover, although the need for self-definition or personal identity appears in only some studies, both Chaney (1972) and Elliott (1974) argue cogently that the media may serve the function of defining the individual or at least supporting his or her definition of self and feelings of personal identity.

There appears to be a growing body of empirical support for the theoretical issues raised in Herzog's (1944) "uses and gratifications" research. Perhaps more important is the fact that advances in functional studies are beginning to make their effects felt in effects research. It appears that one cannot look at what the media do to the audience without also looking at what the audience members do to the media. Further work in the functional approach holds the promise of placing media research in a broader sociological and psychological framework.

VII. Television and the "Real" World

A. CULTIVATION OF REALITY

All television programs, whether news, or documentary, drama, soap opera, or science fiction, present a reality—a televised reality. Television may be seen as a provider of definitions of reality. None of these definitions is necessarily true or false, correct or incorrect, and all of them may be more or less distorted. The viewer, however, is not a passive recipient of televised reality; he or she acts on, interprets, and matches the reality presented on the screen with his or her own view of the world.

Most viewers are prepared to believe that the events portrayed on a news program or in a news format are real (e.g., Feshbach, 1972, 1976). While most viewers have no difficulty in distinguishing entertainment from news programs, moreover, it is likely that entertainment programs also provide the viewer with versions of reality. Noble (1975) in England suggested that children's perceptions of occupational roles and ethnic stereotypes are related to the second-hand or vicarious experiences on television. Other studies conducted with English school children have confirmed the notion that the televised reality is most powerful when the child does not have any first-hand experience. For example, Faulkner (1975) found that Asian adolescent girls, living in Britain in a protected environment which prevented contact with English girls, tended to construe English girls and their families in a manner that resembled the media reality rather than veridical judgments. Similar distortions of reality, resulting from a media-based conception in instances in which the individual lacks first-hand experience, have been demonstrated for children's ethnic stereotypes (P. Hartmann & Husband, 1974).

In a recent study of American children, Greenberg and Reeves (1976) found that the amount of television viewed by 8- to 11-year-olds was related to perceived reality in that heavy viewers were much more likely to perceive television portrayals in entertainment programs as real. These results were strongest for the youngest and the least bright children. One of the surprising findings of this study was that the amount of personal experience with the type of person portrayed in the television programs increased rather than decreased the degree of perceived reality. However, it is difficult to estimate the children's personal experience, when Greenberg's children indicated that they knew policemen or blacks, it may have been a very superficial type of knowing, and such superficial experience would facilitate the acquisition of televised reality constructions.

Similar findings have been demonstrated for adults. In a series of studies in America, Gerbner (1974) and Gerbner and Gross (1976a, 1976b) contrasted the world views of heavy and light viewers of television. They found, in general, that heavy viewing was associated with cultural and social stereotypes, particularly, with regard to sex and occupational roles. They also found that heavy viewers and those adults under 30 (a group that was likely to have grown up with television in its homes) were more likely to exaggerate their estimates of the probability of a violent encounter than were the light viewers. An expanded study, conducted in 1976, confirmed the earlier findings for adults and extended the "cultivation analysis" to children. Thus, Gerbner and his associates (Gerbner, Gross, Eleey, Jackson-Beeck, Jeffries-Fox, & Signorielli, 1977) report: "Heavy viewers in all sex, age, education, income, reading and church attendance groups were more imbued with the television view of a mean world than were light viewers in the same groups" (p. 9). Furthermore, children tended to give more television-world view answers and to learn more of the televised reality.

Hartmann and Husband (1972), in England, demonstrated how the media define or help to define the audience member's view of race relations. Interviewing people both from areas with small and large immigrant populations, they found that those who lived in the more densely populated immigrant areas were more likely to rely on their own experience and less likely to rely on the media. In another study examining adults' conceptions of the role of union and management in industrial relations, Hartmann (1976) nicely captures the potential for media distortion—"who ever heard of a militant employer?"

B. AGENDA SETTING

Another way in which television can influence the viewer's conception of reality is through selective overemphasis on a restricted range of topics or issues. In this instance, the nature of the influence is not a direct imposition of particular content on the viewer in the sense that the viewer is told "what to think," but is told "what to think about." In other words, the media set the agenda and select particular issues that are deemed "important for public debate." It follows that to the extent that there is competition and variation across media, there may, at any one time, be a wide variety of agendas promulgated by newspapers, radio, television, and other media. However, when there is overlap among the various media, the agenda-setting function can be quite powerful. Most of the early research on agenda setting was concerned with political agenda setting during election periods and even very early studies of the impact of media on voting behavior (e.g., Berelson, Lazarsfeld, & McPhee, 1954) have noted that most elections are fought on the "salience" of issues rather than content. Thus, the basic concept of agenda setting has existed in the communications literature for many years, but it has been given new emphasis by the work of McCombs and Shaw (1972).

Following the recent reemergence of agenda setting, there has been considerable research activity in this area. There is a number of excellent reviews of this growing literature (e.g., Becker, McLeod, & McCombs, 1975; Comstock *et al.*, 1978; McLeod, Becker, & Byrnes, 1974) which demonstrate that there is a relationship between media agenda and public agenda in varying contexts. However, as Galloway (1977) points out, the relations between media and public agenda are rather gross and far more needs to be known about the conditions which maximize and minimize the relationship. One of these factors is, of course, the audience and, apart from the relationship of demographic variables, we know very little about which members of the audience are most receptive to the influence of agenda setting.

C. WHOSE REALITY?

In conclusion, it is clear, from the available evidence on agenda setting and cultivation analyses, that televised reality can influence and, in some cases, supplant the individual realities constructed by the viewer. It also has been suggested that the extent of media influence is maximized when the viewer has little personal experience which might provide a countervailing force against the televised reality. Those with relevant personal experience seem better able to negotiate a compromise between the televised and personal reality construction. Support for this explanation comes from a series of studies on the credibility that children and adults ascribe to television (Graves, 1976a, 1976b; Leifer, 1976). In a series of interviews with black and white adults, Graves (1976b) attempted to discover the ways in which viewers evaluated the reality of television portrayals of blacks and whites. Illustrative of some of the difficulties that viewers have in coming to grips with televised reality when they have only limited experience with the issues or characteristics portrayed is an excerpt from an interview with a white woman concerning the portrayal of blacks on American television: "I don't know much about it, but it seems that all the black shows are all the same. It seems that they're showing all the black people in *one way on almost all the shows, so maybe this is true* [emphasis added] ... I think the white people are true-to-life and the black people must be true-to-life. I don't know much about them, but all the shows show them and have them act the same way" (p. 1).

It is clear that television can and does act as a socializing agent. However, whose reality or which version of reality is provided by television? There is a suggestion in the literature (e.g., Gerbner, 1976; Hartmann, 1976) that television is perceived to present a dominant or preferred view of society and the world. All of us may use television as an information source, as Noelle-Neumann (1974) points out. For all questions outside our immediate personal sphere, we are almost totally dependent upon the mass media for the facts and for our evaluation of the climate of opinion, i.e., opinion that can be voiced in public without fear of sanctions and upon which public action can be based. This leads to what Noelle-Neumann (1977) calls a "spiral of silence," whereby the only opinion that a person will voice is one which has come from the media, and the media in turn reiterates this opinion. This process may give rise to a homogeneous, dominant ideology which finds expression in the media and can thereby override or shape the individual's reality construction. Certainly each country presents its own view of the world, and most countries place restrictions on imported programming. However, the socializing process is an interactive one and the audience member will select from among the various definitions of reality provided and match them to his or her own experience.

VIII. Conclusions, Implications, and Research Priorities

A. EFFECTS AND FUNCTIONS

It is not easy to summarize the role that television plays in the lives of children and adults. The use that is made of television and the impact of this use on the attitudes, values, and behavior of the viewer varies, to some extent, across cultures and, to a far greater extent, across age, sex, and social role status within a given culture. The research findings included in this review fall into two broad but differing approaches to media research; namely, effects and functions. Nevertheless, despite this continuing dichotomy in media research, which is reflected in our review, it is possible that the effects and functions approaches can find some common ground in the recent cultivation analysis and agenda-setting studies. Moreover, it would appear that research on the introduction of television, both the early studies (e.g., Furu, 1962; Himmelweit, Oppenheim, & Vince, 1958; Schramm, Lyle, & Parker, 1961) and the more recent additions (e.g., Brown, Cramond, & Wilde, 1974; Murray & Kippax, 1977, 1978;

Werner, 1971; Williams, 1977) have incorporated both effects and functions in their designs and analyses. Moreover, it should be apparent in this review that both effects and functions studies have important roles to play in explicating the puzzle that is television. Such an interpretation, in terms both of effects and of functions, allows for an understanding of the influences of television on its audiences in terms of the audience members' use of the medium, which, in turn, is a function of the particular audience member.

This is not to say that generalizations are not possible. With regard to television's impact on the daily life activities, the evidence suggests that there are extensive and enduring changes, such as a decrease in radio listening, as well as localized and limited changes, such as a change in children's reading habits. The introduction of television has a marked initial effect—a novelty effect. For a time, many activities, such as playing and watching sport, are displaced. However as television becomes more "normal" there is a recovery of many of these leisure activities. In general, the leisure activities that suffer most are those which appear most similar—functionally—to television. Cinema attendance declines, as does radio listening—and unlike nearly all other activities, these do not show a marked recovery. The reading of comic books by children and of some magazines by adults also declines and remains depressed, whereas overall reading by both adults and children, at least in Australia, England, and the United States, appears to be unaffected in the long term.

However, there are marked individual differences. There are some adolescents who do not stop going to the cinema; and there are some children who watch close to 70 hr of television per week and who, presumably, have little time for anything else. There are some families who rid themselves of their television sets, and others who use television to stifle family communication.

Again with regard to the impact of particular television content on the viewers' behavior, attitudes, and values, a general statement can be made. The pattern of results suggests that television content can and does influence the viewer at various levels from changing attitudes to modifying interpersonal behavior. Television does act as a socializing agent. Like the family, the school, and peer groups, television is a source of information and attitudes. It acts in this capacity for both adults and children, although perhaps it has a greater potential for influence on children. As von Feilitzen (1975) points out, it is obvious that children acquire a great deal of knowledge and information from television. "In the first place they learn—both in the short and long term—about what they have experience of and interest in, and which they perceive will be useful to them in their social environment . . . . But at the same time, television provides, both entertaining and informative programs, knowledge of the world outside, a second-hand information which is not based on personal experiences . . . . Television influences children's conceptions of reality—especially about people and places they haven't encountered first-hand" (pp. 72–73).

Similarly, Abruzzini (1974), in Italy, sees television as an instrument of information on extrafamily realities. He notes that its role will be more effective the more easily it is framed within a body of information and values of family derivation. He and De Domenico (1975) stress that the socialization effect of television must be seen within the setting of the family and the school. It is unlikely that television acts in isolation.

The evidence suggests that television is most influential when it is in accord with other sources of influence or when alternative sources are absent. In the latter case, television provides a definition of reality when the audience member has no or only second-hand experience of the phenomenon in question. When the reality provided by television overlaps with that provided by experience, the effect of the television will be mediated by that experience.

For some, especially those who view a great deal of violent television and/or have little knowledge of the crime statistics in our society, the world will be defined as a dangerous and mean place (Gerbner & Gross, 1976). For some, those who watch American and English detective and crime series, violence will be associated with crimes against property, while those who watch Russian programs will perceive violence as associated with crimes against the society or state (Pietila, 1976; Powell, 1975).

There is a plethora of experiments which clearly document that viewing televised violence causes increased aggressive behavior as well as anxiety and fear. Similarly, but to a lesser extent, viewing socially valued behavior results in modest increases in various aspects of altruism. However, controversy rages over the issue of the endurance of these effects and, in the case of violence, the representativeness of the measures of aggression employed in laboratory-based experiments. These latter questions recently have been explored with more panache and some success in field-experimental studies (e.g., Joy, Kimball, & Zabrack, 1977; Parke, Berkowitz, Leyens, West, & Sebastian, 1977; Stein & Friedrich, 1972) and time-series or causal-correlational studies over extended time periods (e.g., Belson, 1978; Lefkowitz, Eron, Walder, & Huesmann, 1972). However, it should be noted that many of these recent studies have also been criticized (e.g., Howitt & Cumberbatch, 1975; Kaplan & R. D. Singer, 1976; Klapper, 1976), although much of the criticism stems from differing philosophies rather than differing findings (Comstock, 1976).

Despite the controversies surrounding the interpretation of the results of specific studies, the pattern of results from this extensive body of literature is sufficiently robust to suggest that television content can and does influence the viewer at various levels from changing attitudes and values to modifying inter-personal behavior. Also, we know that the younger viewer is more likely to be more affected and, within this most susceptible group, there are probably some individuals who, because of previous social experiences, are more readily influenced by particular television content.

In examining the various influences of television, it becomes clear that the audience must be specified before the effects can be properly assessed. There is not an undifferentiated passive audience but a heterogeneous one. Some members of this audience will select from among the available programs, and all members of the audience act on and interpret the content in terms of their expectations concerning the medium and/or programs.

The selection among media, and within a single medium such as television, is complex and not clearly understood. However, we do know that television is seen to satisfy needs associated with information, social contact, entertainment or diversion, and personal identity (e.g., Katz, Gurevitch, & Haas, 1973; Kippax and Murray, 1976, 1977; McQuail, Blumler, & Brown, 1972; Robinson, 1972b). Similarly, cinema attendance and the use of popular music is also seen to fulfill certain needs for self-identity or self-definition as well as entertainment needs.

Evidence of active selection from among the media comes from the work of Cohen (1972), with "mods" and "rockers"; from Murdock and Phelps (1973), with school children; and from Troyna (1977), with adolescent male dropouts. In all three cases, the data suggest that these subgroups or subcultures actively select certain media (in these cases popular music and certain magazines and television programs) in order to identify with the subculture in question and to define themselves.

Other studies have characterized other groups in other ways. For example, Belson (1975) and Howitt and Dembo (1974) have identified delinquent subcultures with greater exposure to and use of the cinema, comic books, and popular music.

As Morley (1974) notes, the accumulated evidence points to a theory or an approach to the study of media which links differential use of the media back to the socioeconomic structure of the society. Such an approach shows how different members of different groups, and different classes, who share different cultural codes, use and interpret the messages provided by the media. This suggestion may be viewed in two ways: (a) that there is a heterogeneous audience reaching out to media which provide heterogeneous content; or (b) that the heterogeneous audience is reaching out to media which, for the most part, provide a preferred or dominant view of reality. Whatever the correct view (and this may vary from culture to culture), it is clear that the audience does select from the given messages. At the same time, it is equally clear that these given messages help us to form a picture of the world as well as help some of us to express ourselves through these messages. At the risk of stating the obvious, the media reflect a reality, or some limited number of realities, which in turn is/are used by the audience members to construct their own view of the world and to define a place for themselves in this constructed world.

The effects that the media may have on our attitudes, beliefs, knowledge, and behavior depends to a large extent on how we decode the given messages;

how we interpret the messages and fit them into our view of the world. In short, the effects may be mediated by the manner in which we use media.

With regard to television, there appear to be two main divisions which account for the bulk of the audience, namely, heavy and light viewers. Various studies in Australia, England, and the United States (e.g., Belson, 1967; Himmelweit & Swift, 1976; Kippax & Murray, 1977; Robinson, 1972b) have suggested that the heavy users of television tend to come from the lower socioeconomic groups in society, have lower educational attainments, and also tend to be those people who spend more time at home (i.e., housewives and elderly)—the "available" viewers. For these available viewers, television is on tap and little effort is needed to gain information, entertainment, or social contact. Himmelweit and Swift (1976) find a similar pattern in the use of the popular media. Heavy use of popular or "on-tap" media is characteristic of those with fewest resources, i.e., those with the poorest education, and those from a working-class background. Himmelweit and Swift (1976) found, as did Edgar (1977a) in Australia, that a good education and a middle-class environment led to a selective use of the popular media. They also found that, within similar ability, education, and socioeconomic groups, personality and outlook influenced both use and "taste." For example, gregariousness and a low need achievement were associated with heavy use of the popular media: "Together they form a dimension at the one end of which is success, adjustment, and a positive outlook, while at the other end is withdrawal, lack of success, and maladjusted passivity" (Himmelweit & Swift, 1976, p. 154).

Therefore, when one turns to a consideration of the effects of the amount of viewing or the content of programs viewed on the behavior of these viewers, it is important to be aware of the other social and situational factors that are associated with viewing. What effect does the content of a particular program have on the behavior of a person who espouses "escape" or diversion reasons for turning to television? Would the effects of televised violence be greater among persons who turn to television for social contact? Perhaps Gerbner's cultivation analyses will offer an opportunity to merge the effects and functions approaches. For example, he finds the greatest cultivation effect among the heavy viewers, and the results of some functional studies (e.g., Kippax & Murray, 1977) indicate the heavy viewers are the ones who are most likely to espouse "escapist" reasons for turning to television where they will watch anything that happens to be on the screen.

B. WHITHER RESEARCH?

In reviewing the history of communications research, Katz (1977) described three main periods in the relatively brief life span of this field of research endeavor. The first period, from 1935 to 1955, was described as the period of the "flowering and withering" of broadcasting research. During the period from 1955 to the early 1960s, the studies of the effects of the introduction of television began; and these studies reawakened the interest in the "uses and gratification" approach.

In the 1960s, several events which occurred outside the field of communications raised anew questions about the power of media. The first event was the upsurge of interest in media effects by a group of researchers who had had relatively little contact with traditional communications research. These new researchers were social or clinical/developmental psychologists whose interest in media effects was more directly related to their investigation of aggressive behavior or child development rather than media, per se. These researchers, unlike the earlier researchers, assumed that the media, particularly the new medium of television, were quite powerful and they set about to demonstrate the power of television.

The effect of these new "effects" studies was to polarize the research literature into effects and functions, and this dichotomy continues to be quite evident in the structure of the present review. It is also quite clear that the "effects" versus "functions" researchers tend to be drawn from differing theoretical/philosophical orientations. Many, but not all, effects studies tend to rely on learning theory, while functional studies employ phenomenological purposive concepts. Further, it should be apparent in this cross-national review that there is a modest geographical division, with most functional researchers residing in Britain/Europe, while effects researchers are to be found in North America, and Australia, which reflects Anglo-American influence, produces a mix of functional and effects studies.

Surveying the field, then, what are the important landmarks in the television research territory which are likely to be mapped in the near future? We feel that one area which has begun to expand, and which will continue to do so over the next few years, is research on cultivation analyses as initiated by Gerbner (Gerbner & Gross, 1976a, 1976b; Gerbner et al., 1977). The reason for predicting growth in this relatively new research topic is the fact that this is the one area in which "functions" and "effects" researchers can find some common ground. Also, cultivation research does not denigrate the power of the medium.

A second research topic, which is closely related to cultivation analyses, "agenda setting," is also a likely area for increased research activity and for largely the same reasons as those outlined for cultivation research (cf. McCombs & Shaw, 1972).

A third area, "formative" research, has evolved from effects studies, but in this instance the interest is in the formal, as opposed to the content, characteristics of television. Research in this area is most clearly demonstrated by the work of Salomon (1977) in Israel and by the work conducted either for or as a result of Sesame Street (e.g., Anderson, 1977; Flagg, 1977; Lesser, 1974).

Other areas which are well established but are also likely to expand are more refined content analyses and a growth in uses and gratification research—to the extent that these become allied to such areas as the cultivation analyses or, further afield, to studies of subcultural groups, in order to clarify functions and effects approaches.

One final area which has received increased attention in recent years is the impact of prosocial or socially valued television programming. Although much of this research is firmly rooted in an effects approach to the impact of television, by virtue of its close association with "formative" research on the production of television programs it is another strong candidate for bridging the gap between functions and effects studies.

One feature that many of these growth areas have in common is a somewhat more "applied" or pragmatic emphasis. It would appear that this change in emphasis has been brought about by the combined influence of the three major groups of "actors" involved in the television world: broadcasters, regulators, and citizen/consumer-action organizations. All three groups have started asking researchers to provide information relevant to their concerns. For example, Katz (1977), in his extensive interviews with BBC production staff, found that many persons, at all levels of creative and administrative responsibility, were concerned to discover whether their programs did in fact convey the message that the producer intended to the audience for which the program was designed. It seems reasonable to suggest that this is an appropriate question for researchers. Indeed, a good example of this type of research is a study conducted at Danmarks Radio (Linné & Marosi, 1976) which evaluated the impact of a British-produced documentary about Vietnam on viewer's attitudes and understanding of issues related to the war. In addition to this example of "evaluative" or "summative" research there are numerous examples of recent developments in "formative" research, which is designed to assist in the production process before the program is broadcast (e.g., Lesser, 1974; Palmer, 1973). In a similar manner, requests for more research directed toward informing social policy and planning are a result of the increased involvement of citizen-action groups in the formulation of the broadcasting policies of regulatory agencies.

The net result of increasing demands for relevant theoretical and research efforts may bring about a closer partnership of researcher and producer, which may also lead to a closer link between the functions and the effects of television.

REFERENCES

Abruzzini, P. *Television and the socialization of children.* Paper presented at the meeting of the International Association for Mass Communication Research, Leicester, August, 1976.
Action for children's television: An international survey of children's television. *Phaedrus,* 1978, **5** (1, whole issue).

Anderson, D. R. *Children's attention to television*. Paper presented at the biennial meeting of the Society for Research in Child Development, New Orleans, March, 1977.

Anderson, D. R., & Levin, S. R. Young children's attention to "Sesame Street." *Child Development*, 1976, **47**, 806–811.

Anderson, D. R., Alwitt, L. F., Pugzles-Lorch, S., & Levin, S. R. *Watching children watch television*. Manuscript, University of Massachusetts, 1978.

Anderson, D. R., Levin, S. R., & Sanders, J. A. *Attentional inertia in television viewing*. Manuscript, University of Massachusetts, 1977.

Andison, F. S. TV violence and viewer aggression: A cumulation of study results 1956–1976. *Public Opinion Quarterly*, 1977, **41**, 314–331.

Australian Broadcasting Tribunal. *Self-regulation for broadcasting?* Canberra: Australian Government Publishing Service, 1977.

Baker, R. K., & Ball, S. J. *Mass media and violence: A staff report to the National Commission on the Causes and Prevention of Violence*. Washington, D. C.: United States Government Printing Office, 1969.

Ball, S., & Bogatz, G. A. *The first year of Sesame Street: An evaluation*. Princeton: Educational Testing Service, 1970.

Bandura, A. *Aggression: A social learning analysis*. New York: Holt, Rinehart & Winston, 1973.

Bandura, A., & McDonald, F. J. The influence of social reinforcement on the behaviour of models in shaping children's moral judgment. *Journal of Personality & Social Psychology*, 1963, **67**, 274–281.

Bandura, A., Ross, D., & Ross, S. Transmission of aggression through imitation of aggressive models. *Journal of Abnormal and Social Psychology*, 1961, **63**, 575–582.

Bandura, A., Ross, D., & Ross, S. Imitation of film-mediated aggressive models. *Journal of Abnormal and Social Psychology*, 1963, **66**, 3–11.

Bandura, A., & Walters, R. H. Aggression. In H. Stevenson (Ed.), *Child psychology*. 62nd Yearbook of the National Society for the Study of Education (Part I). Chicago: University of Chicago Press, 1963.

Becker, G. Causal analysis in R–R studies: Television violence and aggression. *American Psychologist*, 1972, **27**, 967–968.

Becker, L. B., McLeod, J. M., & McCombs, M. E. The development of political cognition. In S. H. Chaffee (Ed.), *Political communication* (Vol. 4). Beverly Hills: Sage, 1975.

Belson, W. A. *The impact of television*. Melbourne: Cheshire, 1967.

Belson, W. A. *Juvenile theft: The causal factors*. London: Harper, 1975.

Belson, W. *Television violence and the adolescent boy*. Westmead, England: Saxon House, Teakfield Limited, 1978.

Berkowitz, L. *Aggression: A social psychological analysis*. New York: McGraw-Hill, 1962.

Berkowitz, L. The control of aggression. In B. Caldwell & H. Ricciuti (Eds.), *Review of child development research* (Vol. 3). Chicago: University of Chicago Press, 1973.

Berkowitz, L., & Geen, R. G. Film violence and the cue properties of available targets. *Journal of Personality and Social Psychology*, 1966, **3**, 525–530.

Berkowitz, L., Corwin, R., & Heironimus, M. Film violence and subsequent aggressive tendencies. *Public Opinion Quarterly*, 1963, **27**, 217–229.

Berkowitz, L, & Rawlings, E. Effects of film violence on inhibitions against subsequent aggression. *Journal of Abnormal and Social Psychology*, 1963, **66**, 405–412.

Berelson, B. R., Lazarsfeld, P. F., & McPhee, W. N. *Voting: A study of opinion formation in a presidential campaign*. Chicago: University of Chicago Press, 1954.

Bettelheim, B. *The uses of enchantment: The meaning and importance of fairy tales.* New York: Knopf, 1976.

Blumler, J. G., & McQuail, D. *Television in politics: Its uses and influences.* Chicago: University of Chicago Press, 1969.

Bogart, L. Warning, the Surgeon General has determined that TV violence is moderately dangerous to your child's mental health. *Public Opinion Quarterly,* 1972, **36,** 491–521.

Bower, R. T. *Television and the public.* New York: Holt, Rinehart & Winston, 1973.

Brown, J. R., & Linné, O. The family as a mediator of television's effects. In R. Brown (Ed.), *Children and television.* London: Collier Macmillan, 1976.

Brown, J. R., Cramond, J. K., & Wilde, R. J. Displacement effects of television and the child's functional orientation to media. In J. G. Blumler & E. Katz (Eds.), *The uses of mass communications.* Beverly Hills: Sage, 1974.

Campbell, W. J., & Keogh, R. *Television and the Australian adolescent.* Sydney: Angus & Robertson, 1962.

Canadian Broadcasting Corporation (CBC). *Patterns of television viewing in Canada.* Toronto: CBC, 1973.

Canadian Broadcasting Corporation (CBC). *Dimensions of audience response to television programs in Canada.* Toronto: CBC, 1975.

Chaffee, S. H. Television and adolescent aggressiveness (overview). In G. A. Comstock & E. A. Rubinstein (Eds.), *Television and social behavior* (Vol. 3); *Television and adolescent aggressiveness.* Washington, D. C.: United States Government Printing Office, 1972.

Chaffee, S. H., & McLeod, J. M. Adolescent television use in the family context. In G. A. Comstock & E. A. Rubinstein (Eds.), *Television and social behavior* (Vol. 3); *Television and adolescent aggressiveness.* Washington, D. C.: United States Government Printing Office, 1972.

Chaffee, S. H., & Tims, A. R. Interpersonal factors in adolescent television use. *Journal of Social Issues,* 1976, **32** (4), 98–115.

Chaffee, S. H., & Wilson, D. *Adult life-cycle changes in mass media use.* Paper presented at the meeting of the Association for Education in Journalism, Ottawa, Canada, 1975.

Chaney, D. H. *The processes of mass communication.* New York: McGraw-Hill, 1972.

Coates, B., Pusser, H. E., & Goodman, I. The influence of "Sesame Street" and "Mister Rogers' Neighborhood" on children's social behavior in the preschool. *Child Development,* 1976, **47,** 138–144.

Coffin, T. E. Television's impact on society. *American Psychologist,* 1955, **10,** 630–641.

Cohen, P. *Subcultural conflict and working-class community.* Working papers in cultural studies, University of Birmingham, 1972.

Collins, H. L. *The influence of prosocial television programs emphasizing the positive value of differences on children's attitudes toward differences and children's behavior in choice situations.* Unpublished doctoral dissertation, Pennsylvania State University, 1974.

Collins, W. A. Learning of media content: A developmental study. *Child Development,* 1970, **41,** 1133–1142.

Collins, W. A. Effect of temporal separation between motivation, aggression, and consequences: A developmental study. *Developmental Psychology,* 1973, **3,** 215–221.

Collins, W. A. The developing child as viewer. *Journal of Communication,* 1975, **25** (4), 35–44.

Collins, W. A., Berndt, T. J., & Hess, V. L. Observational learning of motives and consequences for television aggression: A developmental study. *Child Development,* 1974, **45,** 799–802.

Collins, W. A., & Getz, S. K. Children's social responses following modeled reactions to provocation: Prosocial effects of a television drama. *Journal of Personality,* 1976, **44** (3), 488–500.

Collins, W. A., & Westby, S. *Children's processing of social information from televised dramatic programs.* Paper presented at the biennial meeting of the Society for Research in Child Development, Denver, April, 1975.

Columbia Broadcasting System (CBS). *A study of messages received by children who viewed an episode of Fat Albert and the Cosby Kids.* New York: CBS, 1974.

Columbia Broadcasting System (CBS). *Communicating with children through television.* New York: CBS, 1977.

Comstock, G. Milgram's scotch verdict on TV: A retrial. *Journal of Communication,* 1974, **24** (3), 155-158.

Comstock, G. An attack that misses the target. A review of *"Mass media violence and society"* by D. Howitt, & G. Cumberbatch. *Contemporary Psychology,* 1976, **21,** 269-270.

Comstock, G. A. *Television as a teacher: Television and social values.* Manuscript, Syracuse University, 1978.

Comstock, G., & Fisher, M. *Television and human behavior: A guide to the pertinent scientific literature.* Santa Monica, Calif.: The Rand Corporation, 1975.

Comstock, G., & Lindsey, G. *Television and human behaviour: The research horizon, future and present.* Santa Monica, Calif.: The Rand Corporation, 1975.

Comstock, G., Chaffee, S., Katzman, N., McCombs, M., & Roberts, D. *Television and human behavior.* New York: Columbia University Press, 1978.

Corporation for Public Broadcasting (CPB). *The impact of mini-TV stations in three remote communities in Alaska.* Manuscript, CPB, 1975.

Corteen, R. S. Television and reading skills. In T. M. Williams (Chair) *The impact of television: A natural experiment involving three communities.* A symposium presented at the annual meeting of the Canadian Psychological Association, Vancouver, June, 1977.

Cosgrove, M., & McIntyre, C. W. *The influence of "Mister Rogers' Neighborhood" on nursery school children's prosocial behavior.* Paper presented at the meeting of the Southeastern Regional Society for Research in Child Development, Chapel Hill, March, 1974.

Cowan, P. A., Langer, J., Heavenrich, J., & Nathanson, M. Social learning and Piaget's cognition theory of moral development. *Journal of Personality and Social Psychology,* 1969, **11,** 261-274.

Debus, R. L. Effects of brief observation of model behavior on conceptual tempo of impulsive children. *Developmental Psychology,* 1970, **2,** 22-32.

De Dominico, F. *Programs on television: Family and child socialization.* Rome: Servizio Opinioni, Italian Radio and Television Company (RAI), 1975.

Dominick, J. R., & Greenberg, B. S. Attitudes toward violence: The interaction of television exposure, family attitudes, and social class. In G. A. Comstock & E. A. Rubinstein (Eds.), *Television and social behavior* (Vol. 3); *Television and adolescent aggressiveness.* Washington, D. C.: United States Government Printing Office, 1972.

Drabman, R., & Thomas, M. H. Does media violence increase children's toleration of real-life aggression? *Developmental Psychology,* 1974, **10,** 418-421.

Edgar, P. *Children and screen violence.* St. Lucia: University of Queensland Press, 1977. (a)

Edgar, P. Families without television. *Journal of Communication,* 1977, **27,** 73-77. (b)

Ekman, P., Liebert, R. M., Friesen, W., Harrison, R., Zlatchin, C., Malmstrom, E. V., & Baron, R. A. Facial expressions of emotion as predictors of subsequent aggression. In G. A. Comstock, E. A. Rubinstein, & J. P. Murray (Eds.), *Television and social behavior* (Vol. 5); *Television's effects and further explorations.* Washington, D. C.: United States Government Printing Office, 1972.

Elliott, P. "Uses and gratification" research: A critique and a sociological alternative. In J. G. Blumler & E. Katz (Eds.), *The uses of mass communications.* Beverly Hills, Calif.: Sage Publications, 1974.

Ellis, G. T., & Sekyra, F. The effect of aggressive cartoons on the behavior of first grade children. *Journal of Psychology,* 1972, **81,** 37-43.

Eron, L. Relationship of TV viewing habits and aggressive behavior in children. *Journal of Abnormal and Social Psychology,* 1963, **67,** 193–196.

Eron, L. D., Huesmann, L. R., Lefkowitz, M. M., & Walder, L. O. Does television violence cause aggression? *American Psychologist,* 1972, **27,** 253–263.

Faith-Ell, P., von Feilitzen, C., Filipson, L., Rydin, I., & Schyller, I. Children's research Radio, *Barn och Kultur* [Children and culture], 1976, **4,** 88–91.

Faulkner, G. Media and identity: The Asian adolescent's dilemma. In C. Husband (Ed.), *White media and black Britain.* London: Arrow, 1975.

von Feilitzen, C. *Maternal observations of child behaviours in the course of home televiewing.* Stockholm: Sveriges Radio, 1972.

von Feilitzen, C. *Children and television in the socialization process.* Stockholm: Swedish Broadcasting Corporation (SR), 1975.

von Feilitzen, C. The functions served by the media. In R. Brown (Ed.), *Children and television.* London: Collier Macmillan, 1976.

Feshbach, S. Reality and fantasy in filmed violence. In J. P. Murray, E. A. Rubinstein, & G. A. Comstock (Eds.), *Television and social behavior* (Vol. 2); *Television and social learning.* Washington, D. C.: United States Government Printing Office, 1972.

Feshbach, S. The role of fantasy in the response to television. *Journal of Social Issues,* 1976, **32** (4), 71–85.

Feshbach, S., & Singer, R. D. *Television and aggression: An experimental field study.* San Francisco: Jossey-Bass, 1971.

Feshbach, S., & Singer, R. D. Television and aggression: A reply to Liebert, Sobol, and Davidson. In G. A. Comstock, E. A. Rubinstein, & J. P. Murray (Eds.), *Television and Social behavior* (Vol. 5); *Television's effects: Further explorations.* Washington, D. C.: United States Government Printing Office, 1972. (a)

Feshbach, S., & Singer, R. D. Television and aggression: Some reactions to the Liebert, Davidson, and Sobol review and response. In G. A. Comstock, E. A. Rubinstein, & J. P. Murray (Eds.), *Television and social behavior* (Vol. 5); *Television's effects: Further explorations.* Washington, D. C.: United States Government Printing Office, 1972. (b)

Filipson, L. *The role of radio and TV in the lives of pre-school children: Summary.* Stockholm: Swedish Broadcasting Corporation (SR), 1976.

Firsov, B. *Televideniye glazami sotsiologa.* [Television through the eyes of a sociologist.] Moscow: Progress Publishers, 1971.

Flagg, B. N. *Children and television: Effects of stimulus repetition on eye activity.* Manuscript, Harvard University, 1977.

Flagg, B. N., Allen, B. D., Geer, A. H., & Scinto, L. F. *Children's visual responses to "Sesame Street": A formative research report.* Manuscript, Harvard University, 1976.

Ford Foundation. *Television and children: Priorities for research.* New York: Ford Foundation, 1976.

Fox, S., Stein, A. H., Friedrich, L. C., & Kipnis, D. M. *Prosocial television and children's fantasy.* Paper presented at the biennial meeting of the Society for Research in Child Development, New Orleans, March, 1977.

Friedrich, L. K., & Stein, A. H. Aggressive and prosocial television programs and the natural behavior of preschool children. *Monographs of the Society for Research in Child Development,* 1973, **38** (4, Serial No. 151).

Friedrich, L. K., & Stein, A. H. Prosocial television and young children: The effects of verbal labeling and role playing on learning and behavior. *Child Development,* 1975, **46,** 27–38.

Furu, T. *Television and children's life: A before-after study.* Tokyo: Japan Broadcasting Corporation, (NHK) Corporation (NHK), 1962.

Furu, T. *The function of television for children and adolescents.* Tokyo: Sophia University Press, 1971.

Furu, T. *Cognitive style and television viewing patterns of children*. Research reports, Department of Audio-Visual Education, International Christian University, 1977.

Gadberry, S. *Television viewing and school grades: A cross-lagged longitudinal study*. Paper presented at the biennial meeting of the Society for Research in Child Development, New Orleans, March, 1977.

Galloway, J. The agenda setting function of mass media. In T. Mohen (Ed.), *Proceedings of a conference on interpersonal and mass communication*. Sydney: New South Wales Institute of Technology, 1977.

Geen, R. G., & Quanty, M. B. The catharsis of aggression: An evaluation of a hypothesis. In L. Berkowitz (Ed.), *Advances in experimental social psychology* (Vol. 10). New York: Academic Press, 1977.

Gerbner, G. Violence in television drama: Trends and symbolic functions. In G. A. Comstock & E. A. Rubinstein (Eds.), *Television and social behavior* (Vol. 1); *Media content and control*. Washington, D.C.: United States Government Printing Office, 1972.

Gerbner, G. *Where we are and where we should be going*. Paper presented at the meeting of the International Association for Mass Communication Research, Leicester, 1976.

Gerbner, G., & Gross, L. *Violence profile No. 6: Trends in network television drama and viewer conceptions of social reality 1967-1973*. Manuscript, University of Pennsylvania, 1974.

Gerbner, G., & Gross, L. Living with television: The violence profile. *Journal of Communication*, 1976, **26** (1), 173-199. (a)

Gerbner, G., & Gross, L. The scary world of TV's heavy viewer. *Psychology Today*, April, 1976, 41-45/89. (b)

Gerbner, G., Gross, L., Eleey, M. F., Jackson-Beeck, M., Jeffries-Fox, S., & Signorielli, N. TV violence profile No. 8: The highlights. *Journal of Communication*, 1977, **27** (2), 171-180.

Glushkova, Y. Effects of television viewing. Cited in: Radiotelevisione Italiana. *Televisione e bambini* (Vol. 8) *L'ascoloto della televisione de parte di bamgini da 0 a 3 anni*. (Television and children: Television viewing of preschool children aged between 0-3 years) Rome: RAI Servizio Opinioni, 1975.

Graves, S. B. *Overview of the project Critical evaluation of television*. Paper presented at the annual meeting of the American Psychological Association, Washington, D. C., September, 1976. (a)

Graves, S. B. *Content attended to in evaluating television's credibility*. Paper presented at the annual meeting of the American Psychological Association, Washington, D. C., September, 1976. (b)

Greenberg, B. S. Viewing and listening parameters among British youngsters. In R. Brown (Ed.), *Children and television*. London: Collier Macmillan, 1976.

Greenberg, B. S., & Atkin, C. K. *Current trends in research on children and television: Social behavior content portrayals and effects in the family context*. Paper presented at the annual conference of the International Communication Association, Berlin, May, 1977.

Greenberg, B. S., & Gordon, T. F. Children's perceptions of television violence: A replication. In G. A. Comstock, E. A. Rubinstein, & J. P. Murray (Eds.), *Television and social behavior* (Vol. 5); *Television's effects: Further explorations*. Washington, D. C.: United States Government Printing Office, 1972.

Greenberg, B. S., & Reeves, B. Children and the perceived reality of television. *Journal of Social Issues*, 1976, **32** (4), 86-97.

Haapasalo, J. *The Finns as users of mass media*. Helsinki: *Oy Yleisradio Ab* Finnish Broadcasting Company, 1974.

Halloran, J. D. (Ed.). *Mass media and socialization*. Leeds: International Association for Mass Communication Research, 1976.

Halloran, J. D. *Violence and its causes: Mass communication—symptom or cause of violence*. Manuscript, University of Leicester, 1977.

Halloran, J. D., Brown, R. L., & Chaney, D. C. *Television and delinquency*. Leicester: Leicester University Press, 1970.

Hapkiewicz, W. G., & Roden, A. H. The effect of aggressive cartoons on children's interpersonal play. *Child Development*, 1971, **42**, 1583-1585.

Harrison, L. F., & Williams, T. M. *Television and cognitive development*. Paper presented at the annual meeting of the Canadian Psychological Association, Vancouver, June, 1977.

Hartmann, D. P. Influence of symbolically modeled instrumental aggression and pain cues on aggressive behavior. *Journal of Personality and Social Psychology*, 1969, **11**, 280-288.

Hartmann, P. *The media and industrial relations*. Manuscript, University of Leicester, 1976.

Hartmann, P., & Husband, C. The mass media and racial conflict. In D. McQuail (Ed.), *Sociology of mass communication*. Harmondsworth: Penguin, 1972.

Heller, M. S., & Polsky, S. *Studies in violence and television*. New York: American Broadcasting Company (ABC), 1976.

Herzog, H. What do we really know about daytime serial listening? In P. F. Lazarsfeld & F. N. Stanton (Eds.), *Radio research 1942-1943*. New York: Duell, Sloan, & Pearce, 1944.

Himmelweit, H. T. Yesterday's and tomorrow's television research on children. In D. Lerner & L. Nelson (Eds.), *Essays in honor of Wilber Schramm*. Honolulu: University of Hawaii Press, 1977.

Himmelweit, H. T., & Swift, B. Continuities and discontinuities in media us usage and taste: A longitudinal study. *Journal of Social Issues*, 1976, **32** (4), 133-156.

Himmelweit, H. T., Oppenheim, A. N., & Vince, P. *Television and the child: An empirical study of the effects of television on the young*. London: Oxford University Press, 1958.

Howitt, D. Television and aggression: A counterargument. *American Psychologist*, 1972, **27**, 969-970.

Howitt, D., & Cumberbatch, G. *Mass media, violence and society*. London: Paul Elek, 1975.

Howitt, D., & Dembo, R. A subcultural account of media effects. *Human Relations*, 1974, **27**, 25-42.

Huesmann, L. R., Eron, L. D., Lefkowitz, M. M., & Walder, L. O. Television violence and aggression: The causal effect remains. *American Psychologist*, 1973, **28**, 617-620.

Instituto Demoskopea. *Pubblicita televisiva e comportamento di consumo dei bambini* (Television advertising and the consumer behavior of young children). Rome: RAI, 1975.

International Publishing Corporation (I.P.C.). *Leisure*, Sociological Monographs, No. 12, 1975.

Joy, L. A., Kimball, M., & Zabrack, M. L. Television exposure and children's aggressive behaviour. In T. M. Williams (Chair) *The impact of television: A natural experiment involving three communities*. A symposium presented at the annual meeting of the Canadian Psychological Association, Vancouver, June, 1977.

Kaplan, R. M. On television as a cause of aggression. *American Psychologist*, 1972, **27**, 968-969.

Kaplan, R. M., & Singer, R. D. Television violence and viewer aggression: A reexamination of the evidence. *Journal of Social Issues*, 1976, **32** (4), 35-70.

Katz, D. The functional approach to the study of attitudes. *Public Opinion Quarterly*, 1960, **24**, 163-204.

Katz, E. *Social research on broadcasting: Proposals for further development*. London: British Broadcasting Corporation (BBC), 1977.

Katz, E., Blumler, J. G., & Gurevitch, M. Uses and gratifications research. *Public Opinion Quarterly*, 1974, **37**, 509-523.

Katz, E., & Foulkes, D. On the use of the mass media as "escape": Clarification of a concept. *Public Opinion Quarterly*, 1962, **26**, 377-388.

Katz, E., & Gurevitch, M. *The secularization of leisure: Culture and communication in Israel*. Cambridge, Mass.: Harvard University Press, 1976.

Katz, E., Gurevitch, M., & Haas, H. On the use of the mass media for important things. *American Sociological Review,* 1973, **38,** 164–181.

Kay, H. Weaknesses in the television-causes-aggression analysis by Eron *et al. American Psychologist,* 1972, **27,** 970–973.

Kenny, D. A. Threats to the internal validity of cross-lagged panel inference as related to television violence and child aggression: A followup study. In G. A. Comstock & E. A. Rubinstein (Eds.), *Television and social behavior* (Vol. 3); *Television and adolescent aggressiveness.* Washington, D. C.: United States Government Printing Office, 1972.

Kenny, D. A. Cross-lagged panel correlation: A test for spuriousness. *Psychological Bulletin,* 1975, **82** (6), 887–903.

Kippax, S., & Murray, J. P. *Using the mass media in Australia and Israel: Need gratification and perceived utility.* Manuscript, Macquarie University, 1976.

Kippax, S., & Murray, J. P. Using television: Programme content and need gratification. *Politics,* 1977, **12** (1), 56–69.

Kjellmor, S. *Basic subjective broadcasting media functions.* Paper presented at the Conference on Uses and Gratifications Studies, Stockholm, October, 1973.

Klapper, J. T. *The effects of mass communication.* New York: Free Press, 1960.

Klapper, J. T. The impact of viewing "aggression": Studies and problems of extrapolation. In O. N. Larsen (Ed.), *Violence in the mass media.* New York: Harper, 1968.

Klapper, J. T. Mass communication and social change. In I. Pilowsky (Ed.), *Cultures in collission: Proceedings of the 25th Congress of the World Federation for Mental Health.* Sydney: Australian National Association for Mental Health. Sydney: Australian National Association for Mental Health, 1976.

Kniveton, B. H. Social learning and imitation in relation to TV. In R. Brown (Ed.), *Children and television.* London: Collier Macmillan, 1976.

Kraus, S., & Davis, D. *The effects of mass communication on political behavior.* University Park: Pennsylvania State University, 1976.

Lasker, H. M. *The Jamaican project: Final report to the children's television workshop.* Manuscript, Center for Research in Children's Television, Harvard University, 1975.

Lefkowitz, H., Eron, L., Walder, L., & Huesmann, L. R. Television violence and child aggression: A follow-up study. In G. A. Comstock & E. A. Rubinstein (Eds.), *Television and social behavior* (Vol. 3); *Television and adolescent aggressiveness.* Washington, D. C.: United States Government Printing Office, 1972.

Lefkowitz, M., Eron, L., Walder, L., & Huesmann, L. R. *Growing up to be violent.* New York: Pergamon, 1977.

Leifer, A. D. *Factors which predict the credibility ascribed to television.* Paper presented at the annual meeting of the American Psychological Society, Washington, September, 1976.

Leifer, A. D., & Lesser, G. S. *The development of career awareness in young children.* Manuscript, Harvard University, 1976.

Leifer, A. D., & Roberts, D. F. Children's responses to television violence. In J. P. Murray, E. A. Rubinstein, & G. A. Comstock (Eds.), *Television and social behavior* (Vol. 2); *Television and social learning.* Washington, D. C.: United States Government Printing Office, 1972.

Lesser, G. *Children and television: Lessons from "Sesame Street."* New York: Vintage Books, 1974.

Levin, S. R., & Anderson, D. R. The development of attention. *Journal of Communication,* 1976, **26** (2), 126–135.

Liebert, R. M., & Baron, R. A. Short-term effects of televised aggression on children's aggressive behavior. In J. P. Murray, E. A. Rubinstein, & G. A. Comstock (Eds.), *Television and social behavior* (Vol. 2); *Television and social learning.* Washington, D. C.: United States Government Printing Office, 1972.

Liebert, R. M., & Schwartzberg, N. S. Effects of mass media. In *Annual Review of Psychology* (Vol. 28). Palo Alto: Annual Reviews, 1977.

Liebert, R. M., Davidson, E. S., & Sobol, M. P. Catharsis of aggression among institutionalized boys: Further discussion: In G. A. Comstock, E. A. Rubinstein, & J. P. Murray (Eds.), *Television and social behavior* (Vol. 5); *Television's effects: Further explorations.* Washington, D. C.: United States Government Printing Office, 1972.

Liebert, R. M., Neale, J. M., & Davidson, E. S. *The early window: Effects of television on children and youth.* New York: Pergamon, 1973.

Liebert, R. M., Sobol, M. D., & Davidson, E. S. Catharsis of aggression among institutionalized boys: Fact or artifact? In G. A. Comstock, E. A. Rubinstein, & J. P. Murray (Eds.), *Television and social behavior* (Vol. 5); *Television's effects: Further explorations.* Washington, D. C.: United States Government Printing Office, 1972.

Linné, O. *Reactions of children to violence on TV.* Stockholm: Swedish Broadcasting Corporation (SR), 1971.

Linné, O. *The viewer's aggression as a function of a variously edited TV-film: Two experiments.* Stockholm: Swedish Broadcasting Corporation (SR), 1974.

Linné, O., & Marosi, K. *Understanding television: A study of viewer reactions to a documentary film.* Copenhagen: Danish Radio (DR), 1976.

Lovaas, O. I. Effect of exposure to symbolic aggression on aggressive behavior. *Child Development,* 1961, **32**, 37–44.

Lovibond, S. H. The effect of media stressing crime and violence upon children's attitudes. *Social Problems,* 1967, **15**, 91–100.

Lyle, J., & Hoffman, H. R. Children's use of television and other media. In E. A. Rubinstein, G. A. Comstock & J. P. Murray (Eds.), *Television and social behavior* (Vol. 4); *Television in day-to-day life: Patterns of use.* Washington, D. C.: United States Government Printing Office, 1972.

Madigan, R. J , & Peterson, W. J. Television on the Bering Strait. *Journal of Communication,* 1977, **27** (4), 183–187.

McCabe, A. E., & Moriarity, R. J. *A laboratory/field study of television violence and aggression in children's sport.* Paper presented at the biennial meeting of the Society for Research in Child Development, New Orleans, March, 1977.

McCombs, M. E., & Shaw, D. L. The agenda-setting function of mass media. *Public Opinion Quarterly,* 1972, **36**, 176–187.

McCron, R. Changing perspectives in the study of mass media and socialization. In J. D. Halloran (Ed.), *Mass media and socialization.* Leeds: International Association for Mass Communication Research, 1976.

McIntyre, J. J., & Teevan, J. J. Television violence and deviant behavior. In G. A. Comstock & E. A. Rubinstein (Eds.), *Television and social behavior* (Vol. 3); *Television and adolescent aggressiveness.* Washington, D. C.: United States Government Printing Office, 1972.

McLeod, J. M., Atkin, C. K., & Chaffee, S. H. Adolescents, parents, and television use: Adolescent self-report measures from Maryland and Wisconsin samples. In G. A. Comstock & E. A. Rubinstein (Eds.), *Television and social behavior* (Vol. 3); *Television and adolescent aggressiveness.* Washington, D. C.: United States Government Printing Office, 1972, (a)

McLeod, J. M., Atkin, C. K., & Chaffee, S. H. Adolescents, parents and television use: Self-report and other report measures from the Wisconsin sample. In G. A. Comstock & E. A. Rubinstein (Eds.), *Television and social behavior* (Vol. 3); *Television and adolescent aggressiveness.* Washington, D. C.: United States Government Printing Office, 1972, (b).

McLeod, J. M., Becker, L. B., & Byrnes, J. E. Another look at the agenda-setting function of the press. *Communication Research,* 1974, **1** (2).

McLuhan, M. *Understanding media: The extension of man.* New York: McGraw-Hill, 1964.

McQuail, D. (Ed.). *Sociology of mass communications.* Harmondsworth: Penguin, 1972.

McQuail, D., Blumler, J. G., & Brown, J. R. The television audience: A revised perspective. In D. McQuail (Ed.), *Sociology of mass communications.* Harmondsworth: Penguin, 1972.

Mendelshon, H. A., & Crespi, I. *Polls, television and the new politics.* San Francisco: Chandler, 1970.

Milgram, S., & Shotland, R. L. *Television and antisocial behavior: Field experiments.* New York: Academic Press, 1973.

Morley, D. *Reconceptualizing the media audience: Towards an ethnography of audiences.* Manuscript, Birmingham University, 1974.

Murdock, G., & McCron, R. *Adolescent culture and the mass media.* Manuscript, University of Leicester, 1976.

Murdock, G., & Phelps, G. *Mass media and the secondary school.* London: Macmillan, 1973.

Murray, J. P. Television in inner-city homes: Viewing behavior of young boys. In E. A. Rubinstein, G. A. Comstock, & J. P. Murray (Eds.), *Television and social behavior* (Vol. 4); *Television in day-to-day life: Patterns of use.* Washington, D. C.: United States Government Printing Office, 1972.

Murray, J. P. Television and violence: Implications of the Surgeon-General's research program. *American Psychologist,* 1973, **28,** 472–478.

Murray, J. P. Social learning and cognitive development: Modelling effects on children's understanding of conservation. *British Journal of Psychology,* 1974, **65,** 151–160.

Murray, J. P. Beyond entertainment: Television's effects on children and youth. *Australian Psychologist,* 1976, **11,** (3), 291–302.

Murray, J. P. Of fairies and children. (A review of "The uses of enchantment: The meaning and importance of fairy tales," by B. Bettelheim) *Contemporary Psychology,* 1977, **22** (3), 195–196. (a)

Murray, J. P. Violence in children's television: Continuing research issues. *Media Information-Australia,* 1977, **3,** 1–18. (b)

Murray, J. P., & Ahammer, I. M. *Kindness in the kindergarten: A multidimensional program for facilitating altruism.* Paper presented to the biennial meeting of the Society for Research in Child Development, New Orleans, March, 1977.

Murray, J. P., & Kippax, S. Television diffusion and social behavior in three communities: A field experiment. *Australian Journal of Psychology,* 1977, **29,** (1), 31–43.

Murray, J. P., & Kippax, S. Children's social behavior in three towns with differing television experience. *Journal of Communication,* 1978, **28** (1), 19–29.

Murray, J. P., Hayes, A. J., & Smith, J. E. *When Bobo hits back: Impact of peer and televised models of aggression on behaviour in a preschool playgroup.* Manuscript, Macquarie University, 1978. (a)

Murray, J. P., Hayes, A. J., & Smith, J. E. Sequential analysis: Another Approach to describing the stream of behaviour in children's interactions. *Australian Journal of Psychology,* 1978, **30** (3), 207–215. (b)

Murray, J. P., Nayman, O. B., & Atkin, C. E. Television and the child: A research bibliography. *Journal of Broadcasting,* 1972, **26,** 21–35.

Mussen, P., & Rutherford, E. Effects of aggressive cartoons on children's aggressive play. *Journal of Abnormal and Social Psychology,* 1961, **62,** 461–464.

National Broadcasting Company (NBC). *Public television.* New York: NBC, Department of Social Research, 1976.

National Broadcasting Company (NBC). *Recent developments involving violence on television: A status report.* New York: NBC, Department of Social Research, 1977.

National Science Foundation. *Research on the effects of television advertising on children: A review of the literature and recommendations for future research.* Washington, D. C.: National Science Foundation, 1977.

Neale, J. M. Comment on television violence and child aggression: A follow-up study. In G. A. Comstock & E. A. Rubinstein (Eds.), *Television and social behavior* (Vol. 3); *Television and adolescent aggressiveness.* Washington, D. C.: United States Government Printing Office, 1972.

Noble, G. *Children in front of the small screen.* London: Constable, 1975.

Noelle-Neumann, E. Return to the concept of powerful mass media. *Studies in Broadcasting,* 1973, **9,** 66-112.

Noelle-Neuman, E. The spiral of silence: A theory of public opinion. *Journal of Communication,* 1974, **24** (2), 43-51.

Nordenstreng, K. Consumption of mass media in Finland. *Gazette,* 1969, **25** (4), 249-259.

Nordenstreng, K. Comments on 'gratifications research' in broadcasting. *Public Opinion Quarterly,* 1970, **34,** 130-132.

Nordenstreng, K. (Ed.). *Informational mass communication.* Helsinki: Tammi Publishers, 1974.

Ontario Psychological Association. Submission on violence in the media. In *Report of the Royal Commission on Violence in the Communications Industry* (Vol. 1); *Approaches, conclusions and recommendations.* Toronto: Queen's Printer for Ontario, 1976.

Palmer, E. L. Formative research in the production of television for children. In G. Gerbner, L. P. Gross, & W. H. Melody (Eds.), *Communications technology and social policy.* New York: Wiley, 1973.

Parke, R.D., Berkowitz, L., Leyens, J. P., West, S., & Sebastian, R. J. Some effects of violent and nonviolent movies on the behavior of juvenile delinquents. In L. Berkowitz (Ed.), *Advances in experimental social psychology* (Vol. 10). New York: Academic Press, 1977.

Pietila, V. *Gratifications and content choices in mass media use.* Manuscript, University of Tampere, 1974.

Pietila, V. Some notes about violence in our mass media—especially in fictitious TV programmes. *Instant Research on Peace and Violence,* 1976, **4.**

Pietila, V. On the effects of mass media: Some conceptual viewpoints. In M. Berg (Ed.), *Current theories in Scandinavian mass communication research.* Grenaa, Denmark: GMT, 1977.

Powell, D. E. Television in the USSR. *Public Opinion Quarterly,* 1975, **39** (3), 287-300.

Prix Jeunesse. *Television and socialization processes in the family: A documentation of the Prix Jeunesse Seminar 1975.* Munich: Verlag Dokumentation, 1976.

Radiotelevisione Italiana (RAI). *Televisione e bambini* (Vol. 5); *Televisione e sviluppo della creativita nei regazzi.* [Television and children: Television and the development of creative skills.] Rome: RAI Servizio Opinioni, 1973.

Radiotelevisione Italiana (RAI). *Televisione e bambini* (Vol. 6); *Risonanza di trasmissioni televisive in soggetti di eta scolare.* (Television and children: The impact of television broadcasts on primary school children.) Rome: RAI Servizio Opinioni, 1974.

Radiotelevisione Italiana (RAI). *Televisione e bambini* (Vol. 8); *L'ascolto della televisione da parte di bambini da 0 a 3 anni.* (Television and children: Television viewing of preschool children aged between 0-3 years). Rome: RAI Servizio Opinioni, 1975. (a)

Radiotelevisione Italiana (RAI). *Cambiamento sociale e sistemi di communicasione in un'area in via di sviluppo.* [Social change and mass media in developing areas.] Rome: RAI Servizio Opinioni, 1975. (b)

Reshetov, P., & Skurlatov, V. *Soviet youth: A socio-political outline.* Moscow: Progress Publishers, 1977.

Roberts, D. F., Herold, C., Hornby, M., King, S., Sterne, D., Whiteley, S., & Silverman, T. *Earth's a big blue marble: A report of the impact of a children's television series on children's opinions.* Manuscript, Stanford University, 1974.

Robinson, J. P. Television's impact on everyday life: Some crossnational evidence. In E. A. Rubinstein, G. A. Comstock, & J. P. Murray (Eds.), *Television and social behavior* (Vol. 4); *Television in day-to-day life: Patterns of use*. Washington, D. C.: United States Government Printing Office. 1972. (a)

Robinson, J. P. Toward defining the functions of television. In E. A. Rubinstein, G. A. Comstock, & J. P. Murray (Eds.), *Television and social behavior* (Vol. 4); *Television in day-to-day life: Patterns of use*. Washington, D. C.: United States Government Printing Office, 1972. (b)

Robinson, J. P., & Bachman, J. G. Television viewing habits and aggression. In G. A. Comstock & E. A. Rubinstein (Eds.), *Television and social behavior* (Vol. 3); *Television and adolescent aggressiveness*. Washington, D. C.: United States Government Printing Office, 1972.

Ross, L. B. *The effect of aggressive cartoons on the group play of children*. Doctoral dissertation, Miami University, 1972.

Rota, J., Cojec, J. R., & Kozlowski, O. *Children and television in Mexico: The communication research center of Universidad Anahuac*. Paper presented at a meeting of the International Communication Association, Berlin, May, 1977.

Royal Commission on Violence in the Communications Industry. *Approaches, conclusions and recommendations* (Vol. 1). Toronto: Queen's Printer for Ontario, 1976.

Rubinstein, E. A. Warning: The Surgeon General's research program may be dangerous to preconceived notions. *Journal of Social Issues,* 1976, **32**, (4), 18–34.

Rubinstein, E. A., Liebert, R. M., Neale, J. M., & Poulos, R. W. *Assessing television's influence on childrens' prosocial behavior*. Stony Brook, N. Y.: Brookdale International Institute, 1974.

Rushton, J. P. Socialization and the altruistic behavior of children. *Psychological Bulletin,* 1976, **83**, (5), 898–913. (a)

Rushton, J. P. Television and prosocial behavior. In *Report of the Royal Commission on Violence in the Communications Industry*. Toronto: Queen's Printer for Ontario, 1976. (b)

Rushton, J. P. Effects of television and film material on the pro-social behavior of children. In L. Berkowitz (Ed.), *Advances in experimental social psychology*. New York: Academic Press, 1979.

Rydin, I. *Information processes in pre-school children: I. How relevant and irrelevant verbal supplements affect retention of a factual radio programme*. Stockholm: Swedish Broadcasting Corporation (SR), 1972.

Rydin, I. *The tale of the seed: Facts and irrelevant details in a TV-programme for children*. Stockholm: Swedish Broadcasting Corporation (SR), 1972, 1976.

Rydin, I. *Children's understanding of television: Pre-school children's perception of an informative programme*. Stockholm: Swedish Broadcasting Corporation, (SR), 1976.

Rydin, I., & Hansson, G. *Information processes in preschool children: The Ability of children to comprehend television and radio programmes*. Stockholm: Swedish Broadcasting Corporation (SR), 1970.

Salomon, G. Can we affect cognitive skills through visual media: Explication of an hypothesis and initial findings. *AV Communication Review,* 1972, **20** (4), 401–423.

Salomon, G. Internalization of filmic schematic operations in interaction with learners' aptitudes. *Journal of Educational Psychology,* 1974, **66**, 499–511. (a)

Salomon, G. What is learned and how it is taught: The interaction between media, message, task and learner. In D. R. Olson (Ed.), *Media and symbols: The forms of expression, communications and education*. The Yearbook of the National Society for the Study of Education. Chicago: University of Chicago Press, 1974. (b)

Salomon, G. Cognitive skill learning across cultures. *Journal of Communication,* 1976, **26** (2), 138–144.

Salomon, G. *The language of media and the cultivation of mental skills*. Manuscript, The Hebrew University of Jerusalem, 1977.

Schramm, W., Lyle, V., & Parker, E. B. *Television in the lives of our children*. Stanford: Stanford University Press, 1961.

Schweizerische Radio-und Fernsehgesellschaft. *Kind und Fernsehen: Eine Studie Über das Fernseh-und Freizeitverhalten der Kinder in der Schweiz* [A study of television and leisure-time behavior of Swiss children]. Basel: [Swiss Radio and Television Company]. (SRG), 1974. (a)

Schweizerische Radio- und Fernsehgesellschaft. *Die älteran Hörer und Zuschauer in der Schweiz*. [Older listeners and viewers in Switzerland]. Bern: [Swiss Radio and Television Company]. (SRG), 1974. (b)

Sherkovin, Y. A. Mass information processes and problems of personality socialization. In J. D. Halloran (Ed.), *Mass media and socialization*. Leeds: International Association for Mass Communication Research, 1976.

Shinar, D., Parnes, P., & Caspi, D. Structure and content of television broadcasting in Israel. In G. A. Comstock & E. A. Rubinstein (Eds.), *Television and social behavior* (Vol); *Media content and control*. Washington, D. C.: United States Government Printing Office, 1972.

Singer, J. L. The influence of violence portrayed in television or motion pictures upon overt aggressive behavior. In J. L. Singer (Ed.), *The control of aggression and violence: Cognitive and physiological factors*. New York: Academic Press, 1971.

Singer, J. L., & Singer, D. G. Can TV stimulate imaginative play? *Journal of Communication*, 1976, **26**, (3), 74–80.

Sprafkin, J., Liebert, R., & Poulos, R. Effects of a prosocial televised example on children's helping. *Journal of Experimental Child Psychology*, 1975, **20**, 119–126.

Stein, A. H., & Friedrich, L. K. Television content and young children's behavior. In J. P. Murray, E. A. Rubinstein, & G. A. Comstock (Eds.), *Television and social behavior* (Vol. 2); *Television and social learning*. Washington, D. C.: United States Government Printing Office, 1972.

Stein, A. H., & Friedrich, L. K. Impact of television on children and youth. In E. M. Hetherington (Ed.), *Review of child development research* (Vol. 5). Chicago: University of Chicago Press, 1975.

Stein, A. H., Freidrich, L. K., & Tahsler, S. *The effects of prosocial television and environmental cues on children's task persistence and conceptual tempo*. Manuscript, Pennsylvania State University, 1973.

Stein, A. H., & Wright, J. C. *Modeling the medium: Effects of formal properties of children's television programs*. Paper presented at the biennial meeting of the Society for Research in Child Development, New Orleans, March, 1977.

Steiner, G. A. *The people look at television*. New York: Knopf, 1963.

Sternglanz, S. H., & Serbin, L. Sex role stereotyping in children's television programs. *Developmental Psychology*, 1974, **10**, 710–715.

Steuer, F. B., Applefield, J. M., & Smith, R. Televised aggression and the interpersonal aggression of preschool children. *Journal of Experimental Child Psychology*, 1971, **11**, 442–447.

Sturm, H. The application of Piaget's criteria to television programmes. In P. Werner (Ed.), *Information programmes for children 7 to 12 years old: Fifth EBU [European Broadcast Union] workshop for producers and directors of television programmes for children*. Remscheid, April, 1976.

Surgeon General's Scientific Advisory Committee on Television and Social Behavior. *Television and growing up: The impact of televised violence*. Washington, D. C.: United States Government Printing Office, 1972.

Szalai, A. (Ed.). *The use of time: Daily activities of urban and suburban populations in twelve countries*. The Hague: Mouton, 1972.

Tannenbaum, P. H., & Zillmann, D. Emotional arousal in the facilitation of aggression through communication. In L. Berkowitz (Ed.), *Advances in experimental social psychology* (Vol. 8). New York: Academic Press, 1975.

Tindall, K., & Reid, D. *Television's children*. Sydney: Sydney Teachers College, 1975.

Tindall, K., Reid, D., & Goodwin, N. *Television: 20th century cyclops*. Sydney: Sydney Teachers College, 1977.

Tolley, H. *Children and war: Political socialization to international conflict*. New York: Columbia University Press, 1973.

Troyna, B. The reggae war. *New Society,* 10 March 1977, 481–482.

Tunstall, J. *The media are American: Anglo-American media in the world*. London: Constable, 1977.

United States Senate. *Hearings before the Subcommittee on Communications of the Committee on Interstate Commerce concerning the report of the Surgeon General's Scientific Advisory Committee on Television and Social Behavior, March, 1972*. Washington, D. C.: United States Government Printing Office, 1972.

Walters, R. H., & Thomas, E. L. Enhancement of punitiveness by visual and audio-visual displays. *Canadian Journal of Psychology,* 1963, **17**, 244–255.

Ward, S. Effects of television advertising on children and adolescents. In E. A. Rubinstein, G. A. Comstock, & J. P. Murray (Eds.), *Television and social behavior* (Vol. 4); *Television in day-to-day life: Patterns of use*. Washington, D. C.: United States Government Printing Office, 1972.

Ward, S., & Wackman, D. Television advertising and intrafamily influence: Children's purchase attempts and parental yielding. In E. A. Rubinstein, G. A. Comstock, & J. P. Murray (Eds.), *Television and social behavior* (Vol. 4); *Television in day-to-day life: Patterns of use*. Washington, D. C.: United States Government Printing Office, 1972.

Ward, S., Levinson, D., & Wackman, D. Children's attention to television advertising. In E. A. Rubinstein, G. A. Comstock, & J. P. Murray (Eds.) *Television and social behavior* (Vol. 4); *Television in day-to-day life: Patterns of use*. Washington, D. C.: United States Government Printing Office, 1972.

Ward, S., Wackman, D., & Wartella, E. *How children learn to buy: The development of consumer information-processing skills*. Beverly Hills, Calif.: Sage, 1977.

Weiss, W. Effects of the mass media of communication. In G. Lindzey & E. Aronson (Eds.), *Handbook of social psychology* (Vol. 5). Reading, Mass.: Addison-Wesley, 1969.

Wells, W. D. *Television and aggression: Replication of an experimental field study*. Manuscript, University of Chicago, 1973.

Werner, A. Children and television in Norway. *Gazette,* 1971, **16** (3), 133–151.

Williams, T. M. Introduction. In T. M. Williams (Chair) *The impact of television: A natural experiment involving three communities*. A symposium presented at the annual meeting of the Canadian Psychological Association, Vancouver, June, 1977.

Williams, T. M., & Handford, G. Television and community life. In T. M. Williams (Chair) *The impact of television: A natural experiment involving three communities*. A symposium presented at the annual meeting of the Canadian Psychological Association, Vancouver, June, 1977.

Zimmerman, B. J., & Rosenthal, T. L. Observational learning of rule-governed behavior by children. *Psychological Bulletin,* 1974, **81**, 29–42.

EFFECTS OF PROSOCIAL TELEVISION AND FILM MATERIAL ON THE BEHAVIOR OF VIEWERS[1]

J. Philippe Rushton

UNIVERSITY OF WESTERN ONTARIO
LONDON, ONTARIO, CANADA

I.   Introduction 322
II. Theoretical Constructs for Understanding Television Effects 323
     A. Norms of Appropriate Behavior 323
     B. Direct Emotional Responses 326
III. Television's Effect on Altruistic Behavior 328
     A. Laboratory Studies 328
     B. Naturalistic Studies 330
     C. Discussion of Studies on Altruism 333
IV. Television's Effect on Friendliness 335
     A. Laboratory Studies 335
     B. Naturalistic Studies 336
     C. Discussion of Studies on Friendliness 338
V.   Television's Effect on Behavior Involving Self-Control 339
     A. Laboratory Studies 339
     B. Naturalistic Studies 341
     C. Discussion of Studies on Self-Control 341
VI. Television's Effect on Diminishing Fears 342
     A. Laboratory Studies 342
     B. Naturalistic Studies 343
     C. Discussion of Studies on Diminishing Fears 344
VII. Conclusions 345
     References 346

[1]Much of the material for this review is based on a report by the author to the Province of Ontario (Canada) Royal Commission on Violence in the Communications Industry entitled "Television and Pro-social Behavior." The Royal Commission Report was published in Toronto by the Queen's Printer for Ontario in 1977. I am grateful to the Royal Commission for financial support. I would like to thank Dick Goranson, Joan Grusec, Ken Marchant, and Marsha Stein for reading and commenting on earlier versions of this paper. In addition I would like to thank Lynne Mitchell for typing the manuscript.

ADVANCES IN EXPERIMENTAL SOCIAL
PSYCHOLOGY, VOL. 12

I. Introduction

At present there is a great deal of concern about the effects of television on the social behavior of viewers. This concern, apparent from the earliest studies (e.g., Himmelweit, Oppenheim, & Vince, 1958) has grown to become one of vital importance due in large part to the increasingly voluminous literature demonstrating an apparent causal link between the amount of violence portrayed on television and the amount of violence shown in the social behavior of viewers. It is not the intention of this paper to review again this accumulation of evidence. For this, the reader is referred to reviews and discussions by, among others, Bandura (1973); Bryan and Schwartz (1971); Goranson (1970, 1975); Liebert, Neale, and Davidson (1973); Liebert and Schwartzberg (1977); Murray (1973); Murray and Kippax (1979, this volume); Parke, Berkowitz, Leyens, West, & Sebastian (1977); Rushton (in press); Stein and Friedrich (1975); the five volumes of technical reports to the Surgeon General of the United States (United States, 1972); and the seven volumes of the Report of the Province of Ontario (Canada) Royal Commission on Violence in the Communications Industry (Ontario, 1977). Although there are dissenters (e.g., Kaplan & Singer, 1976; Lesser, 1977), the weight of this evidence points directly to the view that television violence has very definite short-term effects and very probably long-term ones too. This conclusion is made most explicit in the conclusions of the recent Canadian Royal Commission inquiry into this problem:

> The Commission was to determine if there is any connection or a cause-and-effect relationship between this phenomenon [the increasing exhibition of violence in the communications industry] and the incidence of violent crime in society. The short answer is yes. (Ontario, Vol. 1, 1977, p. 50)

and

> If the amount of depicted violence that exists in the North American intellectual environment could be expressed in terms of a potentially dangerous food or drink additive . . . there is little doubt that society long since would have demanded a stop to it . . . . (Ontario, Vol. 1, 1977, p. 51)

The purpose of this review is to consider the growing number of studies that have examined television's power to influence viewers' social behavior in a "positive" direction rather than a "negative" one. To the extent to which it can be demonstrated that television has the power to influence prosocial behavior, then the evidence for a causal link between television and viewers' social behavior generally is strengthened. At this point clarification of the terms "television" and "prosocial" might prove beneficial. The terms are used here in their widest meanings, i.e., "television" will include the specially constructed 5-min videotapes used purely for experimental purposes in addition to commercial television programs. It would seem unnecessarily restrictive to limit this review to the latter, although the nature of the programming is clearly specified throughout the review. The term "prosocial" is used to specify that which is socially desirable and which in some way benefits another person or society at large. This definition will naturally involve a value judgment based on the wider social context. Four categories of prosocial behavior are considered. The first concerns altruistic behaviors, such as generosity, helping, and cooperation. The second concerns friendly behavior. The third category subsumes self-control behaviors, such as delaying gratification and resisting temptation. Finally, the ability of film material to diminish fears is considered.

The studies to be reviewed here have not, in the main, tested mechanisms. Rather, they have involved a "black box" approach with viewers being given a differential diet of television fare, with their behavior subsequently observed without recourse to mediating mechanisms. At the present stage of our knowledge, researchers have been more concerned to demonstrate that prosocial television can have any positive effect than to attempt to partial out the necessary conditions to maximize such effects. I suggest that television's strongest effects result from altering (a) a person's internalized norms of appropriate behavior or (b) a person's direct emotional response to stimuli.

This paper will involve (a) the elaboration of these two concepts and (b) a presentation of the studies reviewed in each of the four prosocial categories (altruism, friendliness, self-control, and diminishing fears), separated into laboratory and naturalistic studies. In concluding each category I attempt to explain the findings in terms of the two explanatory constructs. Although these explanations are inevitably "after the fact" since the studies have not been designed to test mediating mechanisms of prosocial behavior, nonetheless I believe they will allow a more clear ordering of the data. As I have suggested in detail elsewhere, norms and emotional responsivity underlie a great deal of human prosocial behavior (Rushton, in press). We shall now turn to an examination of these theoretical constructs.

II. Theoretical Constructs for Understanding Television Effects

A. NORMS OF APPROPRIATE BEHAVIOR

A *norm* may be defined as a *standard by which events are judged and on that basis approved or disapproved.* An individual might apply such standards to evaluate good from bad, right from wrong, appropriate from inappropriate, beauty from ugliness, or truth from falsehood. Norms vary in the degree to which they are internalized. Norms which are held strongly enough to be considered "oughts" are referred to as "moral principles." Those norms held in a more abstract way are often referred to as "values," while norms which one holds tentatively and finds arbitrary, may be called "social rules." (Certain social philosophers have recently attempted to use this latter notion as the basis for reconstituting the discipline of social psychology. See for example Collett, 1977; Harré, 1977a, 1977b.) For my purposes here the notion of a norm, defined as an internal standard, encompasses all such constructs as rules, values, principles, customs, and folkways.

There are many norms concerned with prosocial behavior. For example there is a norm to provide help to one another. If we asked a stranger in the street for directions, we would expect him or her to provide the information if possible and to apologize if not. If the stranger were instead to turn to us and say "Yes, I do know where that place is but I can't be bothered to tell you," we would be rather surprised. The person would have violated the unspoken expectation as to how he or she ought to have behaved. In fact, people typically do provide this kind of help to strangers (Rushton, 1978). Berkowitz (1972) and Rushton (in press) have reviewed a variety of studies that have examined the norms governing helping behavior. For instance, people tend to be more helpful to a person who is dependent on them, than to someone who is not (Berkowitz & Daniels, 1963, 1964). Berkowitz (1972) explains these studies and a variety of others by invoking the norm of "social responsibility."

It is highly likely that some people have internalized such norms more fully than others. A wide range of studies demonstrates consistency in patterns of "normative altruism" within the individual. Individuals with high scores on verbal measures of "social responsibility," "other-oriented values," or moral reasoning tasks, were more likely to engage in prosocial behavior than those with lower scores on the same tests (Berkowitz & Daniels, 1964; Berkowitz & Lutterman, 1968; Dlugokinski & Firestone, 1973, 1974; Emler & Rushton, 1974; Harris, Mussen & Rutherford, 1976; Krebs & Rosenwald, 1977; Midlarsky & Bryan, 1972; Rubin & Schneider, 1973; Rushton, 1975; Sawyer, 1966; Schwartz, Brown, Feldman & Heingartner, 1969; Schwartz & Clausen, 1970; Staub, 1974; and Willis & Goethals, 1973). In addition, studies have found that peer and teacher ratings predict individual differences in situational altruism (Dlugokinski & Firestone, 1973, 1974; Krebs & Sturrup, 1974; Rutherford & Mussen, 1968).

Postulating the hypothetical construct of a norm (of helping, sharing, etc.) facilitates the organization of numerous data, including individual difference data. A danger of such constructs, however, is that they end up being entirely postdictive rather than predictive, thus providing only pseudoexplanations, i.e., an instance of helping behavior occurs and then we "explain" it by saying that a "norm to help" must have been in operation. In addition, norms often seem to be contradictory, e.g., "help one another" and "mind your own business." However we can break the circularity and solve some of these problems in two ways. First, and perhaps most importantly, we can specify the conditions under which the norms can be acquired and modified. Second, we must recognize that norms are internalized by individuals, and guide behavior only in interaction with other response tendencies elicited by the same situation (Schwartz, 1977).

Given that naturally occurring altruistic behavior can be explained through the construct of internalized personal norms, in what ways are these norms altered by television? A substantial body of evidence indicates that observation of highly salient models is of major importance in the acquisition and transmission of internal standards.

In the prototypic experiment (Bandura & Kupers, 1964), children observed a salient model playing an electronic bowling game, and rewarding himself with tokens which could later be exchanged for a prize. In one condition the model adopted a high standard of performance, rewarding himself for high scores only. When his performance fell short of his standards he denied himself available rewards, and reacted with self-derogation. In another condition the model adopted a low standard of performance, rewarding himself for mediocre scores. Later the children performed the same task, during which they received a predetermined range of scores. The scores for which they chose to reward themselves were recorded. The results revealed that the children's norms for self-reinforcement closely matched those of the model they had observed. Confirmatory studies have been carried out by, among others, Bandura and Whalen (1966) and Mischel and Liebert (1966). Mischel and Liebert (1966) for example, showed (a) that the behaviors were maintained at a 4 week retest period and (b) that the children imposed the same standards on their peers that they had adopted for themselves, thus transmitting their learned self-reward criteria to others. Such studies provide clear evidence that internal standards can be acquired by watching others.

When we turn to the effects of modeling on norms of altruism specifically, we find that there are numerous studies showing clearly that models can affect not only the amount and direction of children's altruistic behavior, but also its durability and generalizability (see Bryan, 1975; and Rushton, 1976, in press, for reviews). In a typical experiment children are allowed to play on a bowling game and win tokens exchangeable for a prize. Prior to the exchange they are given the opportunity to donate some to a poor child depicted on a charity poster. The number given to this poor child constitutes a measure of generosity. Exposing the child to a salient model who subsequently behaves either generously or selfishly can increase or decrease the child's behavior compared to controls. Furthermore the generous or selfish behavior is maintained over a 2-month retest (Rushton, 1975). Results such as these have often been interpreted within a normative framework (e.g., Emler & Rushton, 1974; Grusec, 1972). It is clear that the norms children internalize with regard to helping are powerfully affected by the behavior of the models they observe. Similar findings have been found with adults. In one experiment carried out in a naturalistic setting, modeling significantly increased the number of observers who donated blood, even when the opportunity to donate blood occurred an average of 6 weeks after observation of the model (Rushton & Campbell, 1977).

In all of the above studies, the observed models were directly in front of the observer. We shall examine in this review the extent to which such norms can be acquired from the observation of behavior on a television screen.

B. DIRECT EMOTIONAL RESPONSES

It seems unnecessary to experience a stimulus directly in order to acquire an emotional response to it. Rather, it is suggested, emotional responses can be acquired vicariously, as when we witness models exhibiting strong emotional reactions in the presence of particular stimuli. This phenomenon was illustrated in a series of experiments in which watching another person supposedly receiving electric shock in the presence of a particular stimulus caused subsequent galvanic skin responses in the observers, though they themselves had not been shocked (Bandura & Rosenthal, 1966; Berger, 1962). Such "vicarious classical conditioning" may partially explain the development of intense positive and negative emotional attitudes toward various objects, minority groups, nationalities, or even abstract "life-styles," in the absence of personal contact.

Such phenomena are not uncommon within clinical contexts. For instance, one frequently finds persons who exhibit intense fears of animals (e.g., snakes) though they have had no harmful experience with them. It is likely that young children acquire such responses by observing significant others such as parents exhibiting fear responses to these same stimuli. Support for this hypothesis is provided by correlational studies which show correspondence between children's fear reactions and those of their parents (Bandura, Blanchard, & Ritter, 1969; Bandura & Menlove, 1968). In Section VI we will examine studies demonstrating "vicarious extinction" of such fear responses.

One "direct emotional response" highly implicated in prosocial behaviors, such as altruism and helping, is empathy. The workings of empathy have been demonstrated in a series of experiments reviewed by Stotland (1969). Essentially, a confederate of the experimenter pretends to undergo some pain while taking part in an experiment. Observers who watch the "volunteer" have a variety of physiological measures taken from them. When the volunteer showed signs of pain, the observers reacted physiologically. Their heart rates, blood pressures, and galvanic skin response scores went up. These physiological indices were also correlated with the observers' statements of empathy for the subject he observed. Stotland's findings also showed that empathy could be increased or decreased by the type of information presented to the observer. For example, the more it was suggested that he attend to the volunteer's pain, the more empathic he felt. Furthermore, the more similar to himself the observer believed the volunteer to be, the more empathically he responded.

Aderman and Berkowitz (1970) added to these findings by demonstrating a relationship between empathic responding and helping behavior. They presented college students with tape recorded conversations between two people; one who needed help and another who was in a position to give it. The students were divided into two groups, one group being told to pay special attention to the needer of help and the other group to the potential giver of help. In some conversations the potential benefactor gave his help and received great thanks for it; in others he gave his help and was not thanked, and in still other conversations, he refused to help. After they had listened to these conversations, the students in the experiment were offered a chance to help somebody themselves. Those who gave most help had either (a) attended to the person needing help when he hadn't received it or (b) attended to the helper who had been thanked. Thus the empathic experience of either the victim's distress or the pleasure of the profusely thanked helper had heightened the listener's motivation to aid others.

A study carried out by Krebs (1975) also demonstrated the workings of empathy on altruism. The psychophysiological responses (skin conductance, blood pulse, heart rate) of observers were measured while they observed either a similar or dissimilar other win money, and experience pain while playing a game. Subjects who believed they were similar to the performer tended to react more strongly than subjects who thought they were different. Similar subjects reported identifying with the performer most, and feeling the worst while he waited to be shocked. When subsequently required to choose between helping themselves at cost to the performer or helping the performer at cost to themselves, the subjects who had previously empathized the most now behaved the most altruistically.

How is empathy acquired? Aronfreed (1970) has argued for a classical conditioning paradigm and Hoffman (1977) has implicated the use of "other-oriented induction." There is strong reason to believe, however, that empathy can be acquired through the observation of models (and hence from television). Empathy can, after all, be viewed as a specific case of vicarious classical conditioning (Bandura, 1977). Specific experiments have not as yet been carried out, but it is likely that seeing a salient model expressing deep concern and distress at the distress cues of another, would lead the viewers to feel similar empathic responses. One could certainly reinterpret Aronfreed and Paskal's (1965, 1966) studies on the "classical conditioning" of empathy and sympathy in this way, as Krebs (1970) did. By the same token, we would also expect that the sight of prestigious models who express unconcern and callousness in the face of another's obvious distress would inhibit natural tendencies for empathy and helping. Support for this latter notion has been well documented in Milgram's obedience studies (Milgram, 1963, 1965). We shall examine in this review a number of studies of television effects which can be interpreted within the framework of direct modification of emotional responses.

III.   Television's Effect on Altruistic Behavior

A. LABORATORY STUDIES

In a series of studies, Bryan (Bryan, 1971; Bryan & Walbek, 1970a, 1970b) showed several hundred 6- to 9-year-old children, of both sexes, a specially constructed 5-min videotape film of a model who played on a bowling game, won gift certificates, and donated or did not donate some of these gift certificates to a charity. In addition, sometimes the TV model preached either that one should or should not donate to the charity. The child was then allowed to play on a similar game and win gift certificates. At the same time, the child was watched through a one-way mirror to see how much of his or her winnings he or she donated to a similar charity. The results showed that children were strongly influenced by what they had seen the models doing on TV. Those children who had watched the videotape model behave generously gave more of their certificates to the charity than did those children who had watched the model behave selfishly. Of additional interest in Bryan's studies was the fact that whereas the way the model behaved significantly affected the children's subsequent behavior, what the model preached had no effect whatsoever, i.e., actions seemed to speak considerably louder than words.

Two other studies using similar procedures have replicated Bryan's findings on the effectiveness of a TV model's behavior in influencing viewing children's generosity. These studies also tested for generalization and duration effects. In regard to this, however, they were less successful. Thus, while Elliot and Vasta (1970) were able to show that 5- to 7-year-old children were influenced both in how much candy and money they shared, the researchers were not able to demonstrate generalization to a third measure of altruism (that of letting another child play with the more attractive of two toys). Although Rushton and Owen (1975) found that 8- to 10-year-old British children were also influenced to donate tokens to a charity by watching TV models do so, the effects had worn off by the time the children were retested 2 weeks later. Rushton and Owen (1975) also replicated Bryan's finding that what the TV model said failed to influence the children's donations, despite attempts to substantially increase the manipulation of the preaching variable in this later study.

The studies discussed above demonstrated that children's generosity in laboratory situations could be modified after watching generosity portrayed by others on television. One limitation, however, is that the film material used in the above studies was not like that produced for commercial purposes. It lasted for only 5 min and showed one model acting a number of times in just one way (e.g., being generous) in one highly specific situation. A second limitation is that the child who watched was then tested in exactly the same situation in which he or she had seen the model act. Furthermore, the test for the program's effects was administered immediately.

Responding to the criticism that previous laboratory research had used highly contrived film material, Sprafkin, Liebert, and Poulos (1975) carried out an investigation with a highly successful commercial television program, *Lassie*. They divided 30 5-year-old, white, middle-class children into three groups and showed each group one of three half-hour television films, complete with commercials. A prosocial *Lassie* program involved Jeff, Lassie's master, risking his life by hanging over the edge of a mine shaft to rescue Lassie's pup. A neutral *Lassie* film and a neutral non-*Lassie* film made up two control groups. After watching the programs the children were taken to another room where they could earn points toward a prize by playing on a game. During the course of playing the game they had an opportunity to aid puppies in distress by calling for help by pressing a "help" button. Pressing the "help" button, however, would interfere with earning points toward the prize. The average time spent pressing the "help" button for children who had watched the prosocial Lassie was 93 sec, whereas in the two netural conditions it was 52 and 38 sec, respectively. Thus, the study supported the previous laboratory studies using a program from a highly successful commercial series.

Collins and Getz (1976) also carried out a laboratory investigation using a regular commercial program complete with commercials. They edited a commercial television action–adventure drama made for adults so that in one version a model responded constructively to an interpersonal conflict, while in another he responded aggressively. Fourth, seventh, and tenth graders ($N = 54$) saw either one of these versions or a wildlife documentary control. They were then given an opportunity either to help or to hurt a fictitious peer who was apparently completing a task by either pressing a "help" button which shut off a distracting noise or a "hurt" button which increased it. Children who had seen models of constructive coping behavior showed greater prosocial responding than subjects in the other two conditions, i.e., they gave more help responses than children who viewed either the aggression or the control programs.

Finally, Murray and Ahammer (1977) provided kindergarter-children in Australia with a series of half-hour standard television programs (edited to remove the commercials), including such material as *Lassie, I Love Lucy, The Brady Bunch,* and *Father Knows Best.* On the basis of a detailed content analysis some of these programs were designated as high in prosocial content while others were designated as neutral. The prosocial programs had a high frequency of display of prosocial themes, such as expressing concern for others' feelings, sympathy, task persistence, and explaining feelings of self or others. The children were either assigned as a class to a "prosocial" viewing condition or to a "neutral" viewing condition. The viewing took place ½ hr/day, 5 days/week, for 4 weeks. The children were pretested on a variety of measures 1 week prior to the onset of television viewing and were posttested on these same measures one week after the conclusion of training. The results indicated that the prosocial television condition was associated with increases in a situational test of helping (for boys only) and increases in a test of cooperation (for both boys and girls). Helping had been measured by the child's willingness to forego playing with some attractive toys in order to help another absent child complete a task which consisted of placing marbles in a box one at a time. Cooperation was indexed by the number of candies that the child won, in contrast to his or her partner, while playing on a Madsen cooperation/competition table. Thus, observation of standard television programs in which the main characters displayed concern for others, was effective in facilitating altruism in specific situational tests quite dissimilar from the situations seen on the programs.

B. NATURALISTIC STUDIES

The first study to be referred to in this section could be included in both the laboratory and the naturalistic studies sections because it used both "laboratory" situational tests and naturalistic measures. Paulson (1974) divided 78 male and female 4-year-olds into a "view" and "non-view" condition in their regular day care centers. The "view" children watched several hours of *Sesame Street* over a number of days for 1 hr/day. The "nonview" children were not shown this special diet of television. The *Sesame Street* programs had nine special "inserts," all concerned with children cooperating with one-another to achieve goals (e.g., "Gordon and Bob discover that it is possible to put toys into a box only when one holds the lid while the other inserts the toys"). The program impact was measured in three tests, including first, a picture recognition test to see whether or not the children were familiar with the content of the experimental inserts (e.g., "pick the picture in which the children are cooperating"). The second tests were situational (e.g., one child was given paint, another brushes; instruction: Paint a picture). Scored were both specific cooperation, as modeled directly from the solution presented on *Sesame Street,* and general cooperation, based on any cooperation whatsoever during the test. Further, these tests were of two kinds: those based on situations previously presented as inserts, and generalization tests not based on inserts. The third test was free play behavior. All measures of cooperation were scored using a "blind" procedure. The results showed that on tests of knowledge, and of both directly modeled and general cooperation on those tests based on TV inserts, the "view" group scored significantly higher than the "nonview" group in cooperation. There were no differences between the "view" group and "nonview" group, however, either on the generalized situational tests or in the children's free play behavior. Thus, it was only when tested in situations similar to those presented on the program that children's cooperative behavior had altered.

A pioneering study of prosocial media effects was carried out by Stein and Friedrich (1972) (see also Friedrich & Stein, 1973). They studied 97 children 3–5 years old attending a 9-week summer nursery school program at Pennsylvania State University. For the first 3 weeks all the children's naturally occurring free play behavior in the classroom was coded into categories, such as "aggressive," "prosocial" and "self-control," and baselines for each child were established. "Aggressive" included verbal aggression, such as teasing, vigorously commanding, and tattling as well as physical aggression. "Prosocial" included such subcategories as cooperating, being nurturant, and verbalizing positive feelings. "Self-control" consisted of adhering to rules, tolerating delay, and persisting at tasks.

Over a 3-week period the baselines were reliably established for each child in each of the categories (75% agreement between raters for subcategories; 79% for general categories). The children were then randomly assigned to one of three groups and exposed to 4 weeks of specially selected television. The first group watched aggressive television films, such as *Batman* and *Superman* cartoons. A second group watched "neutral" films, such as children working on a farm, and a third group watched a prosocial educational program called *Mister Rogers' Neighborhood,* which stresses social and emotional development. The program includes the following themes: cooperation, sharing, sympathy, affection and friendship, understanding the feelings of others, verbalizing one's own feelings, delay of gratification, persistence and competence at a task, learning to accept rules, controlling aggression, and adaptive coping with frustration. During the 4 weeks a total of 12 1-hr television programs was shown to each group, approximately one session every other day.

During this 4-week period the children's free play behavior was recorded by observers who were "blind" as to experimental condition. In addition, during the last 5 days of the following (and final) 2 weeks, the children's behavior was likewise recorded in order to evaluate the extended effects of TV viewing.

The results of this experiment demonstrated that the programs the children watched affected their subsequent aggressive or prosocial behavior only marginally. Exposure to the aggressive television content led to increased interpersonal aggression only for those children who were above average in such aggression at baseline. Furthermore, the effects did not generalize to the 2-week retest. Exposure to the prosocial television content led to increased prosocial behavior only in the children from the lower half of the socioeconomic status distribution. Here too, the results failed to extend to the 2-week retest. Somewhat stronger effects of both the aggressive and the prosocial films were found on the measures of self-control. These findings are discussed in Section V.

Friedrich and Stein (1975) carried out a second study examining further the effects of *Mister Rogers' Neighborhood*. Seventy-three kindergarten children were randomly assigned to one of five conditions. One group of children watched four "neutral" programs about nature and other topics unrelated to interpersonal behavior. The other four groups saw four programs from *Mister Rogers' Neighborhood* which were chosen to form a dramatic sequence. In this sequence, a crisis arose in which one of the characters feared that she would be replaced by a fancy new visitor. Action centered on the attempts of friends to understand her feelings, reassure her of her uniqueness, and help her. Children watched the television programs in groups of three or four over 4 days. Three sets of tests were given to the children shortly after they had viewed each of the films.

A test of knowledge of content indicated not surprisingly, that children who had watched prosocial television verbalized this content better than children who had watched neutral films. Of more importance, they also verbally generalized the content of the programs to new situations more closely related to everyday life. On a second test, a puppet-playing game in which the experimenter manipulated one puppet and the child a second, situations were enacted either parallel to the television program *Mister Rogers' Neighborhood* or somewhat different from it. The child's spontaneous verbal and nonverbal prosocial behavior was observed within this puppet-playing context. In addition, the experimenter asked the child specific questions, e.g., "How do friends show they like you?" Children who had watched the prosocial television films gave more prosocial responses than children who had watched neutral films. This was true both in situations that were similar to those in the *Mister Rogers' Neighborhood* program and also to those that involved new situations. On the third test, a behavioral measure of helping another child in a quite different context, there were no overall differences between those children who had watched prosocial television programs and those who had watched the neutral television programs. However, when watching the prosocial television was paired with direct training to be helpful through "role-playing" techniques, then children in this condition were more helpful compared to children who had been given the training but no diet of prosocial television. This suggests the possibility of using prosocial television as an adjunct to other training procedures when attempting to teach or enhance prosocial tendencies in children—as nursery school teachers and parents might well wish to do.

In an experimental field study with 183 married couple volunteers, Loye, Gorney, and Steele (1977) used the method of participant observation to assess the cumulative effects over 5 days of one of five "diets" of television programming. These were (1) high in prosocial or "helpful" content; (2) high in violent or "hurtful" content; (3) neutral or light entertainment content; (4) mixed, i.e., both prosocial and violent content; and (5) natural, i.e., unedited content. Viewing took place between 7:00 p.m. and 11:00 p.m. on seven consecutive evenings, Monday through Sunday. Programs were chosen from the schedules of 28 channels available via the local cable television network. In all groups, each husband watched the television programs selected and each wife worked as an observer reporting on his daily behavior. Examples, respectively, were "Husband took five-year-old son for a walk on the beach while I rested" versus "Husband lost temper while driving car." Wives kept confidential daily reports of all instances of husbands' "helpful" and "hurtful" behavior. Results showed no significant differences among viewing groups in helpful behavior. For hurtful behavior, however, differences among the groups were found. The prosocial group showed the least hurtful behavior; next lowest was the neutral group. The two highest levels of hurtful behavior were found in the natural and violence viewing groups. Effects of television content were also found on ratings of mood. With baseline scores covaried out, viewers in the violence group showed an increase in aggressiveness, whereas viewers in the prosocial group showed a decrease.

Finally, a particularly ambitious and realistic study was conducted by Moriarty and McCabe (1977) using 259 children and youth engaged in organized team sports. Participants in Little League baseball, lacrosse, and ice hockey were included. Before, during, and after experimental treatment, measures were obtained as to the at-home viewing habits and preferences of the players and the antisocial and prosocial behavior of the players on the field. The treatment consisted of providing antisocial, prosocial, or control video presentations of the sport relevant to the team. The prosocial material consisted of (a) altruism—helping, encouraging, and team work; (b) sympathy—compassion, pity, and caring for another's plight; (c) courtesy—displays of respect; (d) reparation—correcting a wrong or apologizing; and (e) affection—any overt expression of positive feelings toward another. The results indicated that exposure to such prosocial media increased the level of prosocial behavior for the hockey and lacrosse players, but not for baseball players. In addition, the survey data indicated a tendency for those who played in the most prosocial manner (averaged over the experimental conditions) to prefer watching prosocial television at home.

C. DISCUSSION OF STUDIES ON ALTRUISM

Thirteen different studies were reviewed in this section. The strongest effects of prosocial television content were found in the seven laboratory studies. Most of these studies presented 5-min television films in which highly salient models engaged in very specific behavior, followed by assessment of their effects on children who were placed in highly similar situations. Two exceptions were the studies by Sprafkin, Liebert, and Poulos (1975) and Collins and Getz

(1976), which used 30-min commercial television programs and assessed the effects in laboratory settings. Five studies used naturalistic settings in order to assess the effects of prosocial television content. Statistically speaking, these effects were much weaker than those of the laboratory studies and seemed to depend on interaction with other variables to reach significance (e.g., high baseline rate of the behavior, socioeconomic status, other training procedures). However, the results were clearly in the same direction as the laboratory experiments.

The above findings suggest that television programming can exert an influence on viewers' prosocial behavior. The clearest explanation is that the television or videotape material altered or introduced new normative expectations of which behaviors are appropriate in given settings. It is probably in part for this reason that the effects were found to be strongest in the laboratory studies. Here no previous norms had been acquired by the children for they had never been in the situation before. It would be natural therefore for them to use as the standard of behavior that which they had seen others doing in the same situation. This applies in particular to the studies by Bryan and Walbek, (1970a, b), Bryan, (1971), Elliot and Vasta, (1970), and Rushton and Owen (1975), where the topography of both the child's situation and the appropriate behavior were more or less identical to that of the model. These studies can be explained as direct "behavior matching" with no recourse necessary to the concept of internalized norm. However it is clear from the laboratory studies by Collins and Getz (1976), Murray and Ahammer (1977), and Sprafkin, Liebert, and Poulos (1975) that television effects can also occur when the situation and topography differ. It appears that a generalizable "rule" is abstracted by the child from the television content and then applied to the new situation. For example, in the Collins and Getz (1976) study, when the children saw a model respond constructively despite the potential for an alternative aggressive response, they seemed to internalize the principle that "conflict situation should lead to constructive and not aggressive response." In a later dissimilar situation in which both aggressive and constructive responses were possible, this same norm was activated and the appropriate behavior was displayed.

The notion of norm activation can also be used to explain the somewhat weaker effects in the natural settings (Friedrich & Stein, 1973, 1975; Loye et al., 1977; Moriarty & McCabe, 1977; Paulson, 1974). Here it is suggested, although television or videotape presentations do shift the children's norms of expected behavior in the prosocial direction, when it comes to these norms guiding their behavior, that the effects will be weaker given (a) often competing elicitors of behavior in the situation and (b) the competition from previously acquired norms within those situations.

The data become far less certain when we turn to our second explanatory construct of direct emotional responding. Nonetheless, it seems possible that at least two of the studies reviewed above have had their effects by increasing empathic responding. The youngsters in the Sprafkin, Liebert, and Poulos (1975) study who watched Lassie's master risking his life to rescue Lassie's pup may have experienced considerable emotional arousal. First, there was the distress experienced by Lassie at the loss of her pup down the mine shaft. Second, there was the danger involved in the young boy risking his own life. It seems highly likely in that situation that empathic distress would be experienced by the 5-year-old viewers. When the children were later able to press a button to help other puppies in distress, part of their motivation to act in this situation might have been due to empathic emotional arousal.

The normative and emotional arousal processes might also interact in increasing prosocial behavior. This interaction might have produced the Moriarty and McCabe (1977) findings that prosocial programming increases prosocial behavior in ice hockey and lacrosse players. Their subcategories of "courtesy—displays of respect" and "reparation—correcting a wrong or apologizing" would be particularly amenable to normative explanations of behavior change, their subcategory of "affection—any overt expression of positive feelings toward another" would seem appropriately explained by both normative and empathic considerations. Undoubtedly, norms do exist in sporting events regarding expression of affection and joy or compassion. (Even if not genuinely felt, a player might be expected to look pleased when a teammate does well.) However, when norms are operating that allow expressions of affection, it would also seem reasonable to expect that the genuine feelings of empathically experienced joy and affection would also grow in intensity as there was now no "normative check" on their expression (as there may well be in regard to, say, the expression of anger).

IV.   Television's Effect on Friendliness

A.   LABORATORY STUDIES

Fryrear and Thelen (1969) assigned 30 boys and 30 girls of nursery school age to one of three television viewing groups: a group which observed an adult male demonstrating "affectionate" behavior toward a small stuffed clown; a group which observed an adult female demonstrating the same behavior; and a control group. Children were subsequently given an opportunity to play with a group of toys which included the small clown. An observer sat in the back of the room and watched to see whether the child imitated the affectionate behavior toward the toy. Children who watched television films of affectionate behavior were subsequently more likely to express similar affection than children who had not seen such behavior on television. An important and interesting qualification to the Fryrear and Thelen (1969) findings were that boys were likely to become more affectionate only if they had seen an adult male behave that way. If the same behavior had been demonstrated by an adult female, the boys were not so influenced. Thus, television seems similar to real life in this. Children select those who are appropriate models for them and perceived similarity of these models can be important.

B. NATURALISTIC STUDIES

O'Connor (1969) conducted a dramatic and potentially important study to see if television programs could be used to enhance social interaction among those nursery school children who tended to isolate themselves from their peers. Thirteen severely solitary children were chosen for the study. These children interacted with others on fewer than five of 32 possible occasions reliably observed over 8 days. One group of these isolated children was then shown a specially prepared sound–color film shown on a television console. This film portrayed a graduated sequence of 11 scenes in which children interacted in a nursery school setting with reinforcing consequences, accompanied by a female narrator describing the actions of the model and the responses of the other children. For comparison purposes a second group of the isolated children was shown a film of dolphins engaging in acrobatic feats. The results were quite dramatic. Children who had watched the film portraying youngsters engaging in social interaction increased from their baseline score to an average of nearly two interactions to nearly 12 interactions out of the possible 32. The control group had no increase over their baseline scores. Furthermore, a follow-up at the end of the school year indicated that the changes endured over time.

In a subsequent study, O'Connor (1972) selected 33 social isolates from four nursery school populations using both teacher ratings and behavioral samples obtained by trained observers. In a 2 × 2 factorial design, half of the children viewed a specially constructed 23-min modeling film depicting appropriate social behavior, while the other half viewed a control film. Half of the subjects in each film condition then received social reinforcement contingent upon the performance of peer interaction behaviors. Modeling was shown to be a more rapid modification procedure than was shaping and resulted in more stable social interaction patterns over time, with or without the attendant social reinforcement. In the follow-up asessments, modeling subjects remained at the original baseline level of nonisolates, while social reinforcement and control subjects returned to the isolate baseline level.

In another study of a similar nature, Keller and Carlson (1974) showed 19 socially isolated preschoolers either four 5-min videotapes in which social skills (e.g., how to socially reinforce peers) were modeled (treatment) or four sequences of a nature film (control). The frequency with which subjects dispensed and received social reinforcement and the frequency of social interaction were rated by observers pre- and posttreatment and at follow-up. Results indicated that the treatment produced increases in all three dependent measures.

Fechter (1971) carried out a study with mental retardates (mean age, 11 years; mean IQ, 36). One group watched a 5-min film of a 12-year-old child beating up a large inflatable Donald Duck doll. Another group viewed a 5-min film of the 12-year-old child playing in a friendly manner with the same doll. The behavior of the retardates was then observed for 5 min in the experimental room and for 30 min on the ward and coded either as friendly (e.g., talking) or aggressive (e.g., fighting) by observers who were not aware of which films the patients had seen. In the ward the number of aggressive responses increased slightly (but significantly) after the aggressive film and decreased following the friendly film. The change in the number of friendly responses in the ward was not significant, however.

Coates, Pusser, and Goodman (1976) carried out an experiment to assess the effects of both *Sesame Street* and *Mister Rogers' Neighborhood* on children's social behavior in the preschool. First of all, 32 children of both sexes aged between 3 and 5 years were observed over several days and the frequency of their different behaviors were recorded into one of the following three main categories which the authors described as follows: (1) *positive reinforcement:* giving positive attention, such as praise and approval, sympathy, reassurance, and smiling and laughing; giving affectionate physical contact, such as hugging, kissing, and holding hands; giving tangible reinforcement, such as tokens, prizes, and other objects; (2) *punishment:* giving verbal criticism and rejection, such as criticism, negative greetings, obvious ignorings, and sarcasm; giving negative physical contact, such as hitting, biting, and kicking; withdrawing or refusing tangible reinforcement, such as taking away a toy; and (3) *social contact:* any physical or verbal contact between a child and another child or adult.

Following these baseline measures children watched either 15 min of *Sesame Street* or 15 min of *Mister Rogers' Neighborhood* for each of 4 days. These programs had originally been shown on the United States Public Broadcasting System in March 1973 and had been scored on the basis of a content analysis (Coates and Pusser, 1975) for the frequency of occurrence of positive reinforcement and punishment that took place within the program. After the children had seen these programs in a group, each child was observed for a 3-min period and the frequency with which he or she emitted one of the behaviors mentioned above was recorded. In addition, for 4 days following, during which time no television programs were shown, each child was again observed for 3 min/day for the frequency of giving of positive reinforcement and punishment to other children and to adults in the nursery school.

The results indicated that exposure to the 15-min television programs did affect the children's social behavior in a significant manner, and particularly on the immediate postviewing tests. For all children, *Mister Rogers' Neighborhood* significantly increased the giving of positive reinforcement to, and social contacts with, both other children and adults. In the case of *Sesame Street* the effects were only found for children who had low baseline scores. For these children, watching *Sesame Street* significantly increased the giving of both positive reinforcement and punishment to, and social contacts with, other children and adults in the preschool. *Sesame Street* had no significant effect on behavior for children whose baseline scores were high. Furthermore, the authors felt that the pattern of results were generally consistent with the content analysis of the two programs they had carried out earlier.

C. DISCUSSION OF STUDIES ON FRIENDLINESS

The results of one laboratory and five naturalistic experiments have demonstrated that the type of interpersonal interaction engaged in can be affected by the content of the television programs that are seen. Friendly behavior increases among people who have seen friendly behavior portrayed on television. Although the friendliness had been directed to inanimate objects in two of the studies, the remaining three studies clearly showed an effect on friendliness directed toward people.

The expression of friendliness and affection is particularly explainable in terms of both norms and emotional arousal, and the interaction of same. Norms undoubtedly exist in regard to how much friendliness or affection is appropriate in given situations. Too much or too little of either is likely to elicit control procedures by others. Indeed, the studies by O'Connor (1969, 1972) and by Keller and Carlson (1974) were carried out directly because normative expectations were being violated.

The remarkably effective behavior modification procedures instituted by O'Connor may first be interpreted in terms of vicarious extinction of fear responses, and then later in terms of normative behavior change. It is quite likely that many of the isolated children in these studies were excessively shy and afraid of interacting with peers socially. The graded nature of the experimental films, and the vicarious reinforcements being received by the model could have facilitated extinction of the inappropriate emotional reactions. Subsequently, the children might have learned what was appropriately friendly behavior from the model's behavior. This possibility was made explicit in the study by Keller and Carlson (1974) which was designed to teach the children how to socially reinforce other children appropriately.

Normative explanations can be used to account for the initial changes in friendliness over baseline in the Fryrear and Thelen (1969) and the Coates, Pusser, and Goodman (1976) studies. These investigations employed children who were already normal in terms of friendliness. Here the amount of friendliness or affection was simply altered in a direction that paralleled the content of the programs watched. It is possible that normative effects interacted with emotional arousal to disinhibit emotional responsiveness. That is, if the children had acquired norms that checked their natural exuberance somewhat, the sight of other youngsters behaving in a very friendly manner might disinhibit their emotional responsivity. A new norm would have been adopted, resulting in greater emotional responsivity.

V. Television's Effect on Behavior Involving Self-Control

A. LABORATORY STUDIES

In an early study Walters, Leat, and Mezei (1963) first forbade 5-year-old male kindergarten children from playing with some rather attractive toys. The children were then divided into three groups. Two groups of youngsters observed a film in which a child model, a boy of the same age as themselves, played with the toys which the subjects had previously been forbidden to touch. One group observed a film in which the boy model was "rewarded" by his mother for playing with the toys; one group observed the model "punished" for playing with the toys. The remaining group constituted a control group, who saw no film. All the children were subsequently left alone in the experimental room with the forbidden toys for 15 min and their behavior observed. Both in terms of the length of time before children gave in to the temptation to touch the forbidden toys and in terms of the total number of times the child touched the toys, there was a clear effect of the experimental treatment: Observation of the model-rewarded film made it harder for the children to resist the temptation and observation of the model-punished film made it easier for them to resist.

Stein and Bryan (1972), in a laboratory experiment, explained to 80 8- and 9-year-old girls the rules by which they could win money by playing an electronic bowling game. Before playing the game the children watched a television program in which they saw a same-sex peer model playing the same game. This peer model behaved either in violation of these rules or in accordance with them. Half of the children within each of these groups also heard the model verbally encourage either violation of the rules or conformity to them. Children who watched the television program that both modeled and preached keeping to the rules cheated to the extent of rewarding themselves incorrectly an additional 12.5¢. However, children who had watched a TV model both violate the rule and preach the rightness of such violations rewarded themselves incorrectly an additional 28.2¢. Thus, keeping or breaking rules and, in effect, stealing, could be affected by brief television programs. Interestingly, in the Stein and Bryan (1972) study there was an interaction between the model's practices and his preachings such that both what the model *said* would be good behavior and what he actually *did*, were a source of behavioral influence on the viewer. This, it may be remembered, did not occur in the case of altruism. Bryan and Walbek (1970a) had found that a television model's behavior was a potent influence while preachings were not.

Other studies, too, have been carried out to see whether television programming could influence children's self-control in "resistance to temptation" situations. In an experiment carried out by Wolf and Cheyne (1972), 7- to 8-year-old boys were taken to a games room and allowed to play with some toys. They were forbidden, however, to touch or play with one particularly attractive toy. The investigators reported that an average of 4 min and 40 sec would go by before an average boy in this situation would touch the toy. However, if the boy had watched a TV program of another same-age boy playing with similar toys, who had not touched the toy, the average boy would wait nearly 8 min before transgressing. If, on the other hand, the TV program had depicted another boy touching the forbidden toy, the average subject was apt to touch the toy within less than 3 min. Very similar results were found when the measure of the child's resistance to temptation was based on the length of time he played with the toy. The average boy played with the forbidden toy for about 1 min out of the 10 min that he was observed. If he saw the TV program portraying violation of the rules, he played with the forbidden toy for nearly 4 min out of the 10 min. However, he touched the forbidden toy for only about 7 sec if he had watched a TV program showing adherence to the rules. Wolf and Cheyne (1972) brought the boys back 1 month later and put them into the same situation. The results still showed an effect of the television program. Whereas the children who had seen no television film 1 month earlier managed to resist the temptation for nearly 6 min, the boys who had seen a model giving in to the temptation only resisted for 4 min. However, no effect was found for the "self-controlled" model in this 4-week retest; i.e., although the deviant model had an effect on increasing deviancy, the self-controlled model did not manage to increase self-control in observers. In a subsequent study, Wolf (1973) again showed that televised models who obeyed rules had an influence on teaching children to obey, whereas televised models who deviated from rules influence children to deviate. Interestingly enough once again, however, television had more effect as a bad example than as a good one.

Another form of self-control is the ability to delay gratification to a later point in time. Yates (1974) carried out a study with 72 8-year-old New Zealand children. Baselines were established by asking children if they would prefer a smaller reward immediately, or a larger one requiring them to wait 7 days. Some time later some of the children watched television programs in which an adult female model exhibited high-delay behavior and/or verbalized reasons for delaying gratification. Other children did not watch such programs. Compared to the controls, the children who had seen the television programs showing delay of gratification were subsequently more likely to choose to delay their own gratification for a larger reward later. The greatest magnitude of change occurred when modeling and persuasive cues were combined. Furthermore, when the children were retested 4 weeks later, their behavior still showed the effects of the exposure to the television film.

B. NATURALISTIC STUDIES

In research described previously in the section on altruistic behavior (Friedrich & Stein, 1973; Stein & Friedrich, 1972), either the prosocial television program *Mister Rogers' Neighborhood,* the aggressive television programs of *Superman* and *Batman,* or neutral fare was shown to 93 4-year-old nursery school children for a 4 week period. During this time their naturally occurring free-play behavior was observed. In addition to the "prosocial" and "aggressive" categories already described, three categories of self-control behavior were recorded. These were obedience to rules, tolerance of delay, and persistence at tasks. In regard to the obedience to rules category, aggressive films decreased this behavior relative to neutral films, while the prosocial films increased it, producing an overall marginally significant difference ($p < .10$). No condition differences existed in the retest 2 weeks later. In regard to tolerating delay, the aggressive films significantly decreased such behaviors compared to both the neutral and the prosocial conditions which did not differ from one another. Furthermore, these effects maintained their statistical significance in the 2-week retest. Finally, the prosocial television content marginally ($p < .10$) increased persistence at tasks over the neutral and aggressive films on both the immediate and later observations.

C. DISCUSSION OF STUDIES ON SELF-CONTROL

Five laboratory experiments and one naturalistic study have demonstrated that self-control can be affected by what children watch on television. Cheating on games, touching forbidden toys, and delaying gratification have all been influenced by TV in laboratory settings. In two of the studies the effects lasted to a 4-week retest. The results of the naturalistic study, while statistically weaker than the laboratory ones, dovetailed rather nicely with them. Of additional interest is the finding that these behaviors could be influenced in either a positive or a negative direction depending on what kind of film models the children were exposed to.

Normative explanations of self-control behavior seem particularly useful here. Not cheating on a game, for example, seems analogous to resisting temptation in many real-life situations. A person's resistance depends largely on how much they have internalized standards of right and wrong. These standards in turn will inevitably be subject to modification by the normative behavior of significant others. The studies by Stein and Bryan (1972), Walters *et al.* (1963), Wolf and Cheyne (1972), and Wolf (1973) have all demonstrated that norms about cheating can be strengthened or weakened depending on how salient models acted. Furthermore, Wolf and Cheyne (1972) noted that these new standards can endure over a 4-week retest, at least for the model who lowered the standards. Yates (1974) extended these conclusions by showing that norms affecting the delay of gratification could also be altered depending on exposure to television programming, and that these norms also endured over a 4-week retest.

The results of the naturalistic study by Stein and Friedrich (1972), although statistically weaker than the laboratory studies, also serve to illustrate the value of the normative approach. For example, in this research, the prosocial film content of *Mister Rogers' Neighborhood* increased the children's persistence at tasks in both the immediate and the later observational periods. It is extremely unlikely that there was any direct behavior matching going on; the "persistence" observed in the television program was quite different from that displayed in the free-play period at the school. It would seem that the children's own internal standards for themselves in relation to a whole class of activities had been changed. It would have been instructive in these studies if the children had been given the opportunity to verbalize to another child what appropriate behaviors were expected of them in the situation. That would have given us converging validation that norms were indeed in operation.

VI.   Television's Effect on Diminishing Fears

A. LABORATORY STUDIES

The first study to be reported here concerns young children who were inappropriately afraid of dogs (a common fear in young children). Bandura and Menlove (1968) measured 3- to 5-year-old children's willingness to approach and play with a cocker spaniel, on a number of occasions, to determine which children were afraid of dogs. Some children were then shown eight specially prepared 3-min film programs over an 8-day period in which the youngsters saw other children playing with dogs. Another group of fearful children were shown movies of Disneyland instead. After watching these films the children were again given opportunities to approach live dogs. Those children who previously had been fearful but had watched other children showing courage were now much more likely to approach and play with the dogs than the children in the control group. Moreover, this reduction in fear generalized to dogs quite different from those seen in the film, and was maintained over a 4-week retest period. A similar study by Hill, Liebert, and Mott (1968) obtained similar results with similar age children using a large German shepherd as the film stimulus. Eight of nine boys in a film group were subsequently willing to approach ~~~t, and feed the live German shepherd, while only three of nine boys in tʰ ⁱⁿtrol group did so, despite high levels of fear in each group prior to testi

A study by Bandura, Blanchard, and Ritter (1971) ı ᵢstigated whether film programming could help adolescents and adults reduce their fear of snakes. Only those who reported having a severe fear of snakes were used. Their dread of snakes had actually to be so severe as to interᶠ re with their ability to do gardening or go camping. These people were tʰ ᵢ shown films of young children, adolescents, and adults engaging in progressively threatening interactions with a large king snake for 35 minutes. Behavioral measures were then taken in the presence of live snakes. The findings were clear. Those who had watched the film significantly reduced their fears. It should be mentioned that the behavioral measures were quite stringent and included actually holding the snake in the hands. The ultimate test (which 33% passed) included allowing the snake ʻo lie in their laps while they held their hands passively at their sides. Bandura and Barab (1973) subsequently replicated these findings.

Weissbrod and Bryan (1973) attempted to see whether similar techniques would succeed with 8- to 9-year-old children who had indicated an extreme fear of snakes on a fear inventory, and also refused to pet a snake during a pretest. These children watched a 2½-min videotaped sequence involving a model either approaching a live 4-ft boa constrictor (the experimental group) or a stuffed 5-ft toy snake (the comparison condition). All children watched their respective films twice through and then, 2 days later, watched them twice through again. Following this second showing of the movie the children were taken to an aquarium which housed a 4-ft boa constrictor and asked to touch, pet, and then hold the snake. The experimental group were able to go further into the sequence than the control comparison group, and furthermore, maintained their superiority on another test taken 2 weeks later. For example, while none of the 10 children in the control condition was able to actually handle the snake 2 weeks after watching a "neutral" film, 11 of the 40 children in the experimental condition were able to handle the snake.

B. NATURALISTIC STUDIES

To 60 children aged 4–12 years who were about to undergo elective surgery for hernias, tonsillectomies, or urinary–genital tract difficulties, Melamed and Siegel (1975) showed either a relevant peer modeling film of a child being hospitalized and receiving surgery or an unrelated control film. The experimental film was 16 min in length and consisted of 15 scenes showing various events that most children hospitalized for elective surgery encounter. Both groups received extensive preparation by the hospital staff. State measures of anxiety, including

self-report, behavioral observation, and palmar sweat index, revealed a significant reduction of preoperative (night before) and postoperative (3-4 week post-
surgery examination) fear arousal in the experimental as compared to the control
film group. In addition, the parents reported a significant posthospital increment
in the frequency of behavior problems in the children who had not seen the
modeling film.

Effects for the therapeutic value of film modeling have been demonstrated
in a number of other studies. O'Connor (1969, 1972) used film models to
decrease children's fear of social interaction. Jaffe and Carlson (1972) and Mann
(1972) treated test-anxious university and high school students with videotaped
modeling procedures and found significant improvement on performance measures. Shaw and Thoresen (1974) demonstrated that specially constructed films
can effectively reduce adults' fears of dental treatment. These authors used actual
visits to the dentist for treatment as their measure of success. Melamed and her
colleagues showed that films can be used to overcome similar fears in children
(Melamed, Hawes, Heiby & Glick, 1975; Melamed, Weinstein, Hawes &
Katin-Borland, 1975). Video desensitization has been successfully applied to the
treatment of sexual dysfunction among women (Wincze & Caird, 1976). It
would seem, as Rosenthal and Bandura's (1978) review of the literature
suggests, that modeling films have vast therapeutic potential.

C.   DISCUSSION OF STUDIES ON DIMINISHING FEARS

Fourteen separate studies have dramatically illustrated the power of television to modify people's fears. The potential for television programs to be used
effectively in the therapeutic context have thus been demonstrated. The investigations reviewed in this section used specially constructed film material. Furthermore, the movies were shown in what might be called a therapeutic context.
These factors mean, of course, that we need further evidence before we can
generalize directly to commercially produced programs watched by viewers sitting in their living rooms. Nevertheless, it seems right to include this material in
this survey. If such powerful emotional reactions as fear of snakes and surgery
can be modified by brief (albeit specifically constructed) films, it does support
the possibility of television for reducing many other fears through normal programming.

Perhaps the best way to explain these findings is to invoke the notion of
vicarious extinction. Seeing a somewhat similar model gradually going through
the feared sequences and emerging none the worse for it allows the observers'
own fear responses to be extinguished. In addition to these direct modifications
of emotional expression, however, there may also be an alteration of norms.
Particularly in the fear of dogs and snakes studies by Bandura and Menlove
(1968); Bandura, Blanchard, and Ritter (1971); Hill *et al.* (1968); and Weissbrod

and Bryan (1973), the viewers' standards as to what is appropriate behavior for themselves (cowardly versus brave) have been changed as well as the levels of fear they directly experienced.

VII.   Conclusions

Thirty-five different experimental studies have been reviewed from both laboratory and naturalistic settings, demonstrating that television and film programs can modify viewers' social behavior in a prosocial direction. Generosity, helping, cooperation, friendliness, adhering to rules, delaying gratification, and a lack of fear can all be increased by television material. This general statement accords with the partial reviews of this same literature that have been carried out previously (Bryan & Schwartz, 1971; Liebert *et al.*, 1973; Rushton, 1977; Stein & Friedrich, 1975). The studies reviewed here, therefore, indicate that television does have the power to effect the social behavior of viewers in a positive, prosocial direction. This conclusion supplements that even larger body of research suggesting a relationship between television and antisocial behavior.

To the extent to which it has been demonstrated that television has the power to influence prosocial behavior, the evidence for a causal link between television and the viewer's social behavior generally is strengthened. Although there have been criticisms of many of the particular studies carried out to demonstrate a link between television and antisocial behavior (e.g., Kaplan & Singer, 1976; Lesser, 1977), the current conclusions lend "construct validation" to the literature on television and violence.

It appears that television has the power to influence the social behavior of viewers in the direction of the content of the programs. If, on the one hand, prosocial helping and kindness make up the content of television programming, the audience will come to regard this conduct as appropriate, normative behavior. On the other hand, if antisocial behaviors and uncontrolled aggression are shown frequently, the viewers will think of this kind of action as the norm. This statement should not be surprising. Advertisers spend billions of dollars a year on United States television. They believe, correctly, that brief, 30-sec exposures of their product, repeated over and over, will significantly modify the viewing public's behavior in regard to those products. It is interesting to note that while television companies contend that their commercials can influence their audiences, they are not so eager to agree that their drama sequences can also affect their viewers' conduct. The television companies cannot have it both ways. The message therefore is quite clear: Viewers learn from watching television and what they learn depends on what they watch.

This conclusion also implies that we ought to alter our conceptualization of the nature of television. As has also been suggested elsewhere (e.g., Liebert,

Neale, & Davidson, 1973; Ontario, 1977; Rushton, in press); television is much more than mere entertainment. It is also a source of observational learning experiences, a setter of norms. It helps to determine what viewers will judge to be appropriate behavior in a variety of situations. Indeed, television may well have become one of the major agencies of socialization that our society possesses. There seems to have been some reluctance to adopt this view of television—and probably for the very good reason that television was never intended to have such a role. However, once we recognize that TV is an agency of socialization (however unintentionally), issues of power and control become more apparent. It might conceivably be asked, for example, whether a greater degree of public control ought to be exerted over the content of television drama than currently exists. While there is some evidence that adults' evaluative comments about the behavior being portrayed on a television screen effect the scene's impact on young viewers (Grusec, 1973), we might wonder whether adults can possibly continually monitor their children's TV viewing. Perhaps control must be exerted over the content of television before it comes on the air! The content of programs today are not, of course, uncontrolled. In the main they are controlled by commercial considerations. For example, television violence is shown for two main reasons: it spices up very dull scripts, and it is inexpensive to produce. However, the question of whether the larger purposes of society ought to be considered can at least be asked: "Can we afford to have the content of television programs controlled primarily by these commercial considerations?"

REFERENCES

Aderman, D., & Berkowitz, L. Observational set, empathy, and helping. *Journal of Personality and Social Psychology*, 1970, **14**, 141–148.

Aronfreed, J. The socialization of altruistic and sympathetic behavior: Some theoretical and experimental analyses. In J. Macaulay & L. Berkowitz (Eds.), *Altruism and helping behavior*. New York: Academic Press, 1970. .

Aronfreed, J., & Paskal, V. *Altruism, empathy, and the conditioning of positive affect*. Unpublished manuscript, University of Pennsylvania, 1965. Reported in Aronfreed, J. The socialization of altruistic and sympathetic behavior: Some theoretical and experimental analyses. In J. Macaulay & L. Berkowitz (Eds.), *Altruism and helping behavior*. New York: Academic Press, 1970.

Aronfreed, J., & Paskal, V. *The development of sympathetic behavior in children; An experimental test of a two phase hypothesis*. Unpublished manuscript, University of Pennsylvania, 1966. Reported in Aronfreed, J. The socialization of altruistic and sympathetic behavior: Some theoretical and experimental analyses. In J. Macaulay & L. Berkowitz (Eds.), *Altruism and helping behavior*. New York: Academic Press, 1970.

Bandura, A. *Aggression: A social learning analysis*. New York: Prentice-Hall, 1973.

Bandura, A. *Social learning theory*. New York: Prentice-Hall, 1977.

Bandura, A., & Barab, P. G. Processes governing disinhibitory effects through symbolic modeling. *Journal of Abnormal Psychology*, 1973, **82**, 1–9.

Bandura, A., Blanchard, E. B., & Ritter, B. The relative efficacy of desensitization and modeling approaches for inducing behavioral, affective and attitudinal changes. *Journal of Personality and Social Psychology*, 1969, **13**, 173–199.

Bandura, A., & Kupers, C. J. Transmission of patterns of self-reinforcement through modeling. *Journal of Abnormal and Social Psychology*, 1964, **69**, 1–9.

Bandura, A., & Menlove, F. L. Factors determining vicarious extinction of avoidance behavior through symbolic modeling. *Journal of Personality and Social Psychology*, 1968, **8**, 99–108.

Bandura, A., & Rosenthal, T. L. Vicarious classical conditioning as a function of arousal level. *Journal of Personality and Social Psychology*, 1966, **3**, 54–62.

Bandura, A., & Whalen, C. K. The influence of antecedent reinforcement and divergent modeling cues on patterns of self-reward. *Journal of Personality and Social Psychology*, 1966, **3**, 373–382.

Berger, S. M. Conditioning through vicarious instigation. *Psychological Review*, 1962, **69**, 450–466.

Berkowitz, L. Social norms, feelings, and other factors affecting helping and altruism. In L. Berkowitz (Ed.), *Advances in experimental social psychology* (Vol. 6). New York: Academic Press, 1972. Pp. 63–108.

Berkowitz, L., & Daniels, L. R. Responsibility and dependency. *Journal of Abnormal and Social Psychology*, 1963, **66**, 429–436.

Berkowitz, L., & Daniels, L. R. Affecting the salience of the social responsibility norm: Effects of past help on the response to dependency relaionships. *Journal of Abnormal and Social Psychology*, 1964, **68**, 275–281.

Berkowitz, L., & Lutterman, K. G. The traditionally socially responsible personality. *The Public Opinion Quarterly*, 1968, **32**, 169–187.

Bryan, J. H. Model affect and children's imitative behavior. *Child Development*, 1971, **42**, 2061–2065.

Bryan, J. H. Children's cooperation and helping behavior. In E. M. Hetherington (Ed.), *Review of child development research* (Vol 5). Chicago: University of Chicago Press, 1975.

Bryan, J. H., & Schwartz, T. Effects of film material upon children's behavior. *Psychological Bulletin*, 1971, **75**, 50–59.

Bryan, J. H., & Walbek, N. H. Preaching and practicing self-sacrifice: Children's actions and reactions. *Child Development*, 1970, **41**, 329–353. (a)

Bryan, J. H., & Walbek, N. H. The impact of words and deeds concerning altruism upon children. *Child Development*, 1970, **41**, 747–757. (b)

Coates, B., & Pusser, H. E. Positive reinforcement and punishment in "Sesame Street" and "Mister Rogers' Neighborhood." *Journal of Broadcasting*, 1975, **19**, 143–151.

Coates, B., Pusser, H. E., & Goodman, I. The influence of "Sesame Street" and "Mister Rogers' Neighborhood" on children's social behavior in the preschool. *Child Development*, 1976, **47**, 138–144.

Collett, P. The rules of conduct. In P. Collett (Ed.), *Social rules and social behavior*. Oxford: Basil Blackwell, 1977. Pp. 1–27.

Collins, W. A., & Getz, S. K. Children's social responses following modeled reactions to provocation: Pro-social effects of a television drama. *Journal of Personality*, 1976, **44**, 488–500.

Dlugokinski, E. L., & Firestone, I. J. Congruence among four methods of measuring other-centeredness. *Child Development*, 1973, **44**, 304–308.

Dlugokinski, E. L., & Firestone, I. J. Other centeredness and susceptibility to charitable appeals: Effects of perceived discipline. *Developmental Psychology*, 1974, **10**, 21–28.

Elliot, R., & Vasta, R. The modeling of sharing: Effects associated with vicarious reinforcement, symbolization, age, and generalization. *Journal of Experimental Child Psychology*, 1970, **10**, 8–15.

Emler, N. P., & Rushton, J. P. Cognitive-developmental factors in children's generosity. *British Journal of Social and Clinical Psychology*, 1974, **13**, 277–281.

Fechter, J. V. Modeling and environmental generalization by mentally retarded subjects of televised aggressive or friendly behavior. *American Journal of Mental Deficiency,* 1971, **76,** 266-267.

Friedrich, L. K., & Stein, A. H. Aggressive and pro-social television programs and the natural behavior of preschool children. *Monographs of the Society for Research in Child Development,* 1973, **38** (4, Serial No. 151).

Friedrich, L. K., & Stein, A. H. Pro-social television and young children: The effects of verbal labelling and role playing on learning and behavior. *Child Development,* 1975, **46,** 27-38.

Fryrear, J. L., & Thelen, M. H. Effect of sex of model and sex of observer on the imitation of affectionate behavior. *Developmental Psychology,* 1969, **1,** 298.

Goranson, R. E. Media violence and aggressive behavior: A review of experimental research. In L. Berkowitz (Ed.), *Advances in experimental social psychology.* (Vol. 5). New York: Academic Press, 1970. Pp. 1-31.

Goranson, R. E. The impact of TV violence. *Contemporary Psychology,* 1975, **20,** 291-292.

Grusec, J. E. Demand characteristics of the modeling experiment. Altruism as a function of age and aggression. *Journal of Personality and Social Psychology,* 1972, **22,** 139-148.

Grusec, J. E. The effects of co-observer evaluation on imitation: A developmental study. *Developmental Psychology,* 1973, **8,** 141.

Harré, R. Rules in the explanation of social behavior. In P. Collett (Ed.), *Social rules and social behavior.* Oxford: Basil Blackwell, 1977. Pp. 28-41. (a)

Harré, R. The ethogenic approach: Theory and practice. In L. Berkowitz (Ed.), *Advances in Experimental Social Psychology.* (Vol. 10). New York: Academic Press, 1977. Pp. 283-314. (b)

Harris, S., Mussen, P., & Rutherford, E. Some cognitive, behavioral and personality correlates of maturity of moral judgment. *Journal of Genetic Psychology,* 1976, **128** 123-135.

Hill, J. A., Liebert, R. M., & Mott, D. E. W. Vicarious extinction of avoidance behavior through films: An initial test. *Psychological Reports,* 1968, **22,** 192.

Himmelweit, H., Oppenheim, A. N., & Vince, P. *Television and the child: An empirical study of the effects of television on the young.* London: Oxford University Press, 1958.

Hoffman, M. L. Moral internalization: Current theory and research. In L. Berkowitz (Ed.), *Advances in experimental social psychology* (Vol. 10). New York: Academic Press, 1977.

Jaffe, P. G., & Carlson, P. M. Modeling therapy for test anxiety: The role of model affect and consequences. *Behaviour Research and Therapy,* 1972, **10,** 329-339.

Kaplan, R. M., & Singer, R. D. Television violence and viewer aggression: A re-examination of the evidence. *Journal of Social Issues,* 1976, **32**(4), 35-70.

Keller, M. F., & Carlson, P. M. Social skills in preschool children with low levels of social responsiveness. *Child Development,* 1974, **45,** 912-919.

Krebs, D. L. Altruism—An examination of the concept and a review of the literature. *Psychological Bulletin,* 1970, **73,** 258-302.

Krebs, D. L. Empathy and altruism. *Journal of Personality and Social Psychology,* 1975, **32,** 1134-1146.

Krebs, D. L., & Rosenwald, A. Moral reasoning and moral behavior in conventional adults. *Merrill-Palmer Quarterly,* 1977, **23,** 77-87.

Krebs, D. L., & Sturrup, B. Role-taking ability and altruistic behavior in elementary school children. *Personality and Social Psychology Bulletin,* 1974, **1,** 407-409.

Lesser, H. *Television and the preschool child.* New York: Academic Press, 1977.

Liebert, R. M., Neale, J., & Davidson, E. S. *The early window: Effects of television on children and youth.* New York: Pergamon, 1973.

Liebert, R. M., & Schwartzberg, N. S. Effects of mass media. *Annual Review of Psychology,* 1977, **28,** 141-173.

Loye, D., Gorney, R., & Steele, G. Effects of television: An experimental field study. *Journal of Communication,* 1977, **27**(3), 206-216.

Mann, J. Vicarious desensitization of test anxiety through observation of videotaped treatment. *Journal of Counseling Psychology,* 1972, **19**, 1–7.

Melamed, B. G., Hawes, R. R., Heiby, E., & Glick, J. The use of filmed modeling to reduce uncooperative behavior of children during dental treatment. *Journal of Dental Research,* 1975, **54**, 797–801.

Melamed, B. G., & Siegel, L. J. Reduction of anxiety in children facing hospitalization and surgery by use of filmed modeling. *Journal of Consulting and Clinical Psychology,* 1975, **43**, 511–521.

Melamed, B. G., Weinstein, D., Hawes, R., & Kallin-Borland, M. Reduction of fear-related dental management problems using filmed modeling. *Journal of the American Dental Association,* 1975, **90**, 822–826.

Midlarsky, E., & Bryan, J. H. Affect expressions and children's imitative altruism. *Journal of Experimental Research in Personality,* 1972, **6**, 195–203.

Milgram, S. Behavioral study of obedience. *Journal of Abnormal and Social Psychology,* 1963, **67**, 371–378.

Milgram, S. Some conditions of obedience and disobedience to authority. *Human Relations,* 1965, **18**, 57–75.

Mischel, W., & Liebert, R. M. Effects of discrepancies between observed and imposed reward criteria on their acquisition and transmission. *Journal of Personality and Social Psychology,* 1966, **3**, 45–53.

Moriarty, D., & McCabe, A. E. Studies of television and youth sport. In *Ontario. Royal Commission on Violence in the Communications Industry. Report* (Vol. 5). Toronto: Queen's Printer for Ontario, 1977.

Murray, J. P. Television and violence: Implications of the Surgeon-General's research program. *American Psychologist,* 1973, **28**, 472–478.

Murray, J. P., & Ahammer, I. M. *Kindness in the kindergarten: A multidimensional program for facilitating altruism.* Paper presented to the biennial meeting of the Society for Research in Child Development, New Orleans, March 1977.

Murray, J. P., & Kippax, S. From the early window to the late night show: A cross-national review of television's impact on children and adults. In L. Berkowitz (Ed.), *Advances in experimental social psychology.* (Vol. 12). New York: Academic Press, 1979.

O'Connor, R. D. Modification of social withdrawal through symbolic modeling. *Journal of Applied Behavior Analysis,* 1969, **2**, 15–22.

O'Connor, R. D. Relative efficacy of modeling, shaping, and the combined procedures for modification of social withdrawal. *Journal of Abnormal Psychology,* 1972, **79**, 327–334.

Ontario. Royal Commission on Violence in the Communications Industry. Report. Vol. 1, *Approaches, conclusions and recommendations;* Vol. 2, *Violence and the media: A bibliography;* Vol. 3, *Violence in television, films and news;* Vol. 4, *Violence in print and music;* Vol. 5, *Learning from the media;* Vol. 6, *Vulnerability to media effects;* Vol. 7, *The media industries: From here to where?* Toronto: Queen's Printer for Ontario, 1977.

Parke, R. D., Berkowitz, L., Leyens, J. P., West, S., & Sebastian, R. J. Some effects of violent and nonviolent movies on the behavior of juvenile delinquents. In L. Berkowitz (Ed.), *Advances in experimental social psychology.* (Vol. 10). New York: Academic Press, 1977.

Paulson, F. L. Teaching cooperation on television: An evaluation of *Sesame Street* social goals programs. *Audio-visual Communication Review,* 1974, **22**, 229–246.

Rosenthal, T. L., & Bandura, A. Psychological modeling: Theory and practice. In S. L. Garfield and A. E. Bergin (Eds.), *Handbook of Psychotherapy and Behavior Change.* New York: John Wiley, 1978.

Rubin, K. H., & Schneider, F. W. The relationship between moral judgment, egocentrism and altruistic behavior. *Child Development,* 1973, **44**, 661–665.

Rushton, J. P. Generosity in children: Immediate and long-term effects of modeling, preaching, and moral judgment. *Journal of Personality and Social Psychology*, 1975, **31**, 459–466.

Rushton, J. P. Socialization and the altruistic behavior of children. *Psychological Bulletin*, 1976, **83**, 898–913.

Rushton, J. P. Television and prosocial behavior. In *Ontario. Royal Commission on Violence in the Communications Industry. Report* (Vol. 5). Toronto: Queen's Printer for Ontario, 1977.

Rushton, J. P. Urban density and altruism: Helping strangers in a Canadian city, suburb, and small town. *Psychological Reports*, 1978, **43**, 987–990.

Rushton, J. P. *Altruism and society*. Englewood Cliffs, New Jersey: Prentice-Hall, in press.

Rushton, J. P., & Campbell, A. C. Modeling, vicarious reinforcement and extraversion on blood donating in adults: Immediate and long-term effects. *European Journal of Social Psychology*, 1977, **7**, 297–306.

Rushton, J. P., & Owen, D. Immediate and delayed effects of TV modeling and preaching on children's generosity. *British Journal of Social and Clinical Psychology*, 1975, **14**, 309–310.

Rutherford, E., & Mussen, P. Generosity in nursery school boys. *Child Development*, 1968, **39**, 755–765.

Sawyer, J. The altruism scale: A measure of cooperative, indivdualistic, and competitive interpersonal orientation. *American Journal of Sociology*, 1966, **71**, 407–416.

Schwartz, S. H. Normative influences on altruism. In L. Berkowitz (Ed.), *Advances in experimental social psychology*. (Vol. 10). New York: Academic Press, 1977. Pp. 221–279.

Schwartz, S. H., Brown, M., Feldman, K., & Heingartner, A. Some personality correlates of conduct in two situations of moral conflict. *Journal of Personality*, 1969, **37**, 41–57.

Schwartz, S. H., & Clausen, G. T. Responsibility, norms, and helping in an emergency. *Journal of Personality and Social Psychology*, 1970, **16**, 229–310.

Shaw, D. W., & Thoresen, C. E. Effects of modeling and desensitization in reducing dental phobia. *Journal of Counseling Psychology*, 1974, **21**, 415–420.

Sprafkin, J. M., Liebert, R. M., & Poulos, R. W. Effects of a pro-social example on children's helping. *Journal of Experimental Child Psychology*, 1975, **20**, 119–126.

Staub, E. Helping a distressed person: Social, personality and stimulus determinants. In L. Berkowitz (Ed.), *Advances in experimental social psychology*. (Vol. 7). New York: Academic Press, 1974. Pp. 294–341.

Stein, A. H., & Friedrich, L. K. Television content and young children's behavior. In J. P. Murray, E. A. Rubinstein, & G. A. Comstock (Eds.) *Television and social behavior* (Vol. 2). *Television and social learning*. Washington, D. C.: U. S. Government Printing Office, 1972.

Stein, A. H., & Friedrich, L. K. Impact of television on children and youth. In E. M. Hetherington (Ed.), *Review of Child Development Research* (Vol. 5). Chicago: University of Chicago Press, 1975.

Stein, G. M., & Bryan, J. H. The effect of a televised model upon rule adoption behavior of children. *Child Development*, 1972, **43**, 268–273.

Stotland, E. Exploratory studies of empathy. In L. Berkowitz (Ed.), *Advances in experimental social psychology* (Vol. 4). New York: Academic Press, 1969. Pp. 271–314.

United States. Surgeon General's Scientific Advisory Committee on Television and Social Behavior. Television and Social Behavior: Technical Reports to the Committee. Vol. 1, *Media content and control;* Vol. 2, *Television and social learning;* Vol. 3, *Television and adolescent aggressiveness;* Vol. 4, *Television in day-to-day life;* Vol. 5, *Television's effects: Further explorations*. Washington, D. C.: United States Government Printing Office, 1972.

Walters, R. H., Leat, M., & Mezei, L. Inhibition and disinhibition of responses through empathetic learning. *Canadian Journal of Psychology*, 1963, **17**, 235–243.

Weissbrod, C. S., & Bryan, J. H. Filmed treatment as an effective fear-reduction technique. *Journal of Abnormal Child Psychology*, 1973, **1**, 196–201.

Willis, J. A., & Goethals, G. R. Social responsibility and threat to behavioral freedom as determinants of altruistic behavior. *Journal of Personality,* 1973, **41,** 376-384.

Wincze, J. P., & Caird, W. K. The effects of systematic desensitization and video desensitization in the treatment of essential sexual dysfunction in women. *Behavior Therapy,* 1976, **7,** 335-342.

Wolf, T. M., Effects of televised modeled verbalizations and behavior on resistance to deviation. *Developmental Psychology,* 1973, **8,** 51-56.

Wolf, T. M., & Cheyne, J. A. Persistence of effects of live behavioral, televised behavioral, and live verbal models on resistance to deviation. *Child Development,* 1972, **43,** 1429-1436.

Yates, G. C. R. Influence of televised modeling and verbalization on children's delay of gratification. *Journal of Experimental Child Psychology,* 1974, **18,** 333-339.

SUBJECT INDEX

A

Altruistic behavior,
television effects on
discussion, 333–335
laboratory studies, 328–330
naturalistic studies, 330–333
Architecture, social behavior and, 132–136

C

Categories, nature at different levels of abstraction
exercise in construction of person taxonomies, 15–19
gains and losses at different levels, 19–25
summary and future directions, 25–28
taxonomies for objects and people, 13–15
Cognitive biases
resulting from stereotypic conceptions, 64–65
conclusions, 75–76
influence on causal attributions, 65–68
influence on processing information about groups, 72–75
influence on processing information about persons, 68–72
resulting in stereotypic conceptions
conclusion, 64
consequences of categorization process, 55–59
power of stimulus salience, 59–64
Crowding, study of, 136–138
Crowding stress, arousal, density and, 139–149

D

Density
arousal of crowding stress and
crowding and control, 141–143
group size and excessive stimulation, 139–141
response to anticipated crowding, 143–149
study of, 136–138
Deviance
experimentation and
alternative methodology, 212–214

definition of deviance, 208–210
definition of experiment, 210–212
operationally defining and measuring
dishonesty as dependent variable, 214–219
dishonesty as independent variable, 224–227
ethical issues, 229
other dependent measures of deviance, 219–224
other independent measures of deviance, 227–229
Dishonesty, experiments on
evaluating and reacting to dishonesty, 238–241
factors influencing dishonest behavior, 230–238

F

Fears, television effect on
discussion, 344–345
laboratory studies, 342–343
naturalistic studies, 343–344
Friendliness, television effect on
discussion, 338–339
laboratory studies, 335–336
naturalistic studies, 336–338

I

Individual, in social psychology
reciprocal influence of individual and situations, 188–123
in search of behavioral consistency, 111–115
self-monitoring and the self, 123–124
situation and, 115–118

P

Person categorization, orientation
empirical implications of fuzzy categories, 12–13
goals and functions of person categorization, 5–8
overview, 13
person categories and object categories, 8–12
purpose, 4–5

Prototypicality, determining, 28–29
  approach, 29–31
  from prototypes to social behavior, 42–43
  rules: full view, 31–36
  rules: restricted view, 36–42

R

Residential density, architectural mediation of, 149–150
  density, crowding and pathology, 170–172
  group development and stress modification, 169–170
  persistent stress and social withdrawal, 160–165
  reactance and helplessness, 165–169
  residential experience, 155–157
  social density in residential settings, 150–155
  social use of space, 157–160

S

Self-control, television and
  discussion, 341–342
  laboratory studies, 339–341
  naturalistic studies, 341
Self-monitoring
  conceptual ancestry of, 87–88
  consequences of
    creation of consistencies in expressive behavior, 96–97
    dynamics of social relationships, 98–100
    links between attitudes and behavior, 97–98
    situational specificity of self-presentation, 93–95
    situational variability of social behavior, 95–96
  construct of, 88–89
  identification of
    construct validity, 90–92
    discriminant validity, 92–93
    self-monitoring scale, 89–90
  processes of, 100–101
    behavioral enactment of person-in-situation scenarios, 106–109
    building blocks of person-in-situation scenarios, 104–106
    cognitive construction of person-in-situation scenarios, 106

conceptions of the self, 101
  strategies of self-monitoring; 109–111
  from thought to action, 101–104
Social behavior
  applications
    housing needs, 201–202
    telecommunication needs, 200–201
  architecture and, 132–136
  cross-cultural perspective, 177–179
  ecological-cultural-behavioral model, 179–185
  studies
    implications of the model, 185–190
    independence, 190–200
Social psychology, individual in
  reciprocal influence of individual and situations, 118–123
  in search of behavioral consistency, 111–115
  self-monitoring and the self, 123–124
  situation and, 115–118
Stereotypes, behavioral consequences of, 76–79
Stereotypic conceptions
  cognitive biases resulting from, 64–65
    conclusion, 75–76
    influence on causal attributions, 65–68
    influence on processing information about groups, 72–75
    influence on processing information about persons, 68–72
  cognitive biases resulting in
    conclusion, 64
    consequences of categorization process, 55–59
    power of stimulus salience, 59–64
Structure, in the head or in the world, 43–44
  object domain, 44–45
  person domain, 45–47

T

Television
  conclusions, implications and research priorities
    effects and functions, 301–305
    whither research?, 305–307
  culture context of
    broadcasting structures, 256–260
    structure and content, 260
  effect on altruistic behavior
    discussion of studies on altruism, 333–335

laboratory studies, 328–330
naturalistic studies, 330–333
effect on behavior involving self-control
    discussion, 341–342
    laboratory studies, 339–341
    naturalistic studies, 341
effect on diminished fears
    discussion, 344–345
    laboratory studies, 342–343
    naturalistic studies, 343–344
effect on friendliness
    discussion, 338–339
    laboratory studies, 335–336
    naturalistic studies, 336–338
functions of,
    active audience, 295–298
    typology of needs, 292–295
impact of violence shown, 270–272
    catharsis and, 285–287
    causal-correlational and field-experimental
        studies, 278–285
    conclusions, 287–288
    correlational studies, 276–278
    experimental studies, 272–276
impact on daily life
    conclusion, 267–270

displacement or stimulation, 263–267
    use, 260–263
other aspects of impact
    advertising and children, 291–292
    prosocial television, 288–290
    understanding television, 290–291
real world and
    agenda setting, 299–300
    cultivation of reality, 298–299
    whose reality?, 300–301
Television effects, theoretical constructs for
        understanding
    direct emotional responses, 326–327
    norms of appropriate behavior, 323–326

V

Violence, televised, 270–272
    causal-correlational and field-experimental
        studies, 278–285
    conclusions, 287–288
    correlational studies, 276–278
    experimental studies, 272–276
    violence and catharsis, 285–287

CONTENTS OF OTHER VOLUMES

Volume 1

Cultural Influences upon Cognitive Processes
  Harry C. Triandis
The Interaction of Cognitive and Physiological
Determinants of Emotional State
  Stanley Schacter
Experimental Studies of Coalition Formation
  William A. Gamson
Communication Networks
  Marvin E. Shaw
A Contingency Model of Leadership
Effectiveness
  Fred E. Fiedler
Inducing Resistance to Persuasion: Some
Contemporary Approaches
  William J. McGuire
Social Motivation, Dependency, and
Susceptibility to Social Influence
  Richard H. Walters and Ross D. Parke
Sociability and Social Organization in Monkeys
and Apes
  William A. Mason
Author Index-Subject Index

Volume 2

Vicarious Processes: A Case of No-Trial
Learning
  Albert Bandura
Selective Exposure
  Jonathan L. Freedman and David O. Sears
Group Problem Solving
  L. Richard Hoffman
Situational Factors in Conformity
  Vernon L. Allen
Social Power
  John Schopler
From Acts to Dispositions: The Attribution
Process in Person Perception
  Edward E. Jones and Keith E. Davis

Inequity in Social Exchange
  J. Stacy Adams
The Concept of Aggressive Drive: Some
Additional Considerations
  Leonard Berkowitz
Author Index-Subject Index

Volume 3

Mathematical Models in Social Psychology
  Robert P. Abelson
The Experimental Analysis of Social
Performance
  Michael Argyle and Adam Kendon
A Structural Balance Approach to the Analysis
of Communication Effects
  N. T. Feather
Effects of Fear Arousal on Attitude Change:
Recent Developments in Theory and
Experimental Research
  Irving L. Janis
Communication Processes and the Properties of
Language
  Serge Moscovici
The Congruity Principle Revisited: Studies in the
Reduction, Induction, and Generalization of
Persuasion
  Percy H. Tannenbaum
Author Index-Subject Index

Volume 4

The Theory of Cognitive Dissonance: A Current
Perspective
  Elliot Aronson
Attitudes and Attraction
  Donn Byrne
Sociolinguistics
  Susan M. Ervin-Tripp
Recognition of Emotion
  Nico H. Frijda

Studies of Status Congruence
  Edward E. Sampson
Exploratory Investigations of Empathy
  Ezra Stotland
The Personal Reference Scale: An Approach to
Social Judgment
  Harry S. Upshaw
Author Index–Subject Index

Volume 5

Media Violence and Aggressive Behavior: A
Review of Experimental Research
  Richard E. Goranson
Studies in Leader Legitimacy, Influence, and
Innovation
  Edwin P. Hollander and James W. Julian
Experimental Studies of Negro-White
Relationships
  Irwin Katz
Findings and Theory in the Study of Fear
Communications
  Howard Leventhal
Perceived Freedom
  Ivan D. Steiner
Experimental Studies of Families
  Nancy E. Waxler and Elliot G. Mishler
Why Do Groups Make Riskier Decisions than
Individuals?
  *Kenneth L. Dion, Robert S. Baron, and
  Norman Miller*
Author Index–Subject Index

Volume 6

Self-Perception Theory
  Daryl J. Bem
Social Norms, Feelings, and Other Factors
Affecting Helping and Altruism
  Leonard Berkowitz
The Power of Liking: Consequences of
Interpersonal Attitudes Derived from a
Liberalized View of Secondary Reinforcement
  Albert J. Lott and Bernice E. Lott
Social Influence, Conformity Bias, and the
Study of Active Minorities
  Serge Moscovici and Claude Faucheux
A Critical Analysis of Research Utilizing the

Prisoner's Dilemma Paradigm for the Study of
Bargaining
  Charlan Nemeth
Structural Representations of Implicit
Personality Theory
  Seymour Rosenberg and Andrea Sedlak
Author Index–Subject Index

Volume 7

Cognitive Algebra: Integration Theory Applied
to Social Attribution
  Norman H. Anderson
On Conflicts and Bargaining
  Erika Apfelbaum
Physical Attractiveness
  Ellen Bersheid and Elaine Walster
Compliance, Justification, and Cognitive
Change
  *Harold B. Gerard, Edward S. Connolley, and
  Roland A. Wilhelmy*
Processes in Delay of Gratification
  Walter Mischel
Helping a Distressed Person: Social,
Personality, and Stimulus Determinants
  Ervin Staub
Author Index–Subject Index

Volume 8

Social Support for Nonconformity
  Vernon L. Allen
Group Tasks, Group Interaction Process, and
Group Performance Effectiveness: A Review
and Proposed Integration
  J. Richard Hackman and Charles G. Morris
The Human Subject in the Psychology
Experiment: Fact and Artifact
  Arie W. Kruglanski
Emotional Arousal in the Facilitation of
Aggression through Communication
  Percy H. Tannenbaum and Dolf Zillmann
The Reluctance to Transmit Bad News
  Abraham Tesser and Sidney Rosen
Objective Self-Awareness
  Robert A. Wicklund

Responses to Uncontrollable Outcomes: An
Integration of Reactance Theory and the Learned
Helplessness Model
    Camille B. Wortman and Jack W. Brehm
Subject Index

Volume 9

New Directions in Equity Research
    *Elaine Walster, Ellen Berscheid, and G.
    William Walster*
Equity Theory Revisited: Comments and
Annotated Bibliography
    J. Stacy Adams and Sara Freedman
The Distribution of Rewards and Resources in
Groups and Organizations
    Gerald S. Leventhal
Deserving and the Emergence of Forms of
Justice
    *Melvin J. Lerner, Dale T. Miller, and John
    G. Holmes*
Equity and the Law: The Effect of a Harmdoer's
"Suffering in the Act" on Liking and Assigned
Punishment
    *William Austin, Elaine Walster, and Mary
    Kristine Utne*
Incremental Exchange Theory: A Formal Model
for Progression in Dyadic Social Interaction
    L. Rowell Huesmann and George Levinger
Commentary
    George C. Homans
Subject Index

Volume 10

The Catharsis of Aggression: An Evaluation of a
Hypothesis
    Russell G. Geen and Michael B. Quanty
Mere Exposure
    Albert A. Harrison
Moral Internalization: Current Theory and
Research
    Martin L. Hoffman

Some Effects of Violent and Nonviolent Movies
on the Behavior of Juvenile Delinquents
    *Ross D. Parke, Leonard Berkowitz, Jacques
    P. Leyens, Stephen G. West, and Richard J.
    Sebastian*
The Intuitive Psychologist and His
Shortcomings: Distortions in the Attribution
Process
    Lee Ross
Normative Influences on Altruism
    Shalom H. Schwartz
A Discussion of the Domain and Methods of
Social Psychology: Two Papers by Rom Harre
and Barry R. Schlenker
    Leonard Berkowitz
The Ethogenic Approach: Theory and Practice
    R. Harre
On the Ethogenic Approach: Etiquette and
Revolution
    Barry R. Schlenker
Automatisms and Autonomies: In Reply to
Professor Schlenker
    R. Harre
Subject Index

Volume 11

The Persistence of Experimentally Induced
Attitude Change
    Thomas D. Cook and Brian R. Flay
The Contingency Model and the Dynamics of
the Leadership Process
    Fred E. Fiedler
An Attributional Theory of Choice
    Andy Kukla
Group-Induced Polarization of Attitudes and
Behavior
    Helmut Lamm and David G. Myers
Crowding: Determinants and Effects
    Janet E. Stockdale
Salience, Attention, and Attribution: Top of the
Head Phenomena
    Shelley E. Taylor and Susan T. Fiske
Self-Generated Attitude Change
    Abraham Tesser
Subject Index